The King's Plunder, The King's Bodies

Prize Laws, the British Empire and the Modern Legal Order

The King's Plunder, The King's Bodies

Prize Laws, the British Empire and the Modern Legal Order

RAHUL GOVIND

Tulika Books

Published by
Tulika Books
44 (first floor), Shahpur Jat, New Delhi 110 049, India
www.tulikabooks.in

First edition (hardback) 2023

ISBN: 978-81-958394-1-4

Printed at Chaman Offset, Delhi 110 002

for Sanghamitra
driftwood from the tide of words

Contents

Preface

This writing was precipitated by the pandemic. It exists because of the asymmetry between the wanton leisure of the few and the horrific suffering of the many, from which the governing powers and the political economy of the day cannot escape blame. In a specific – not general – sense, it was therefore written under circumstances vastly different from the stratospherically nestled environs of my previous book, *Infinite Double*, to which it may be taken as a companion. The royal rights to plunder and empire, the subject of the present work, are starkly evident to even the most cursory of archival investigations. While much more needs to be done in terms of writing a rigorous, exacting history, it is no accident that little has been done so far even towards its thematization.

B-4 Reids Line, University of Delhi RAHUL GOVIND
March 2023

Acknowledgements

Though written at a rather feverish pace on some seemingly obscure figures and laws, in its orientation this work owes something to the protracted accretion of years of teaching my students, and my students teaching me, at the University of Delhi. For the M.A. the stampede was always outwards, but fourteen years has meant that even so there are one too many to mention. I nonetheless name my research students with whom I have had detailed discussions on their M.Phil and doctoral dissertations, and thanks to whom my horizons have widened considerably: Sikandar Kumar, Bharathan Chandrashekaran, Arighna Gupta, Abdul Najeeb, Sabujkoli Mukherjee, Vishal Singh and Vishal Singh Deo. The History Department and the University of Delhi as a public university have enabled, so far, independent and conference-free research, and I can only hope that amidst the noise such institutions have a bright future.

I am thankful to Arighna Gupta and Sarath Pillai who kindly sent me archival records/texts from online collections/libraries hosted in American institutions. I also wish to record my debt to archival texts and academic work that have been made freely available online through Google books and archives.org, as well as websites such as sci-hub and libgen, those hold-outs in the cybernetic seas of sovereign regulation.

Sections of Part II draw on my paper, 'The King's Plunder, the King's Justice: Sovereignty in British India, 1756–76', which was published in *Studies in History*, Vol. 33 (2).

I am thankful to Peter Robb, Elizabeth Robb and Harriet Horne for being generous hosts on more than one occasion during trips made to London to work at the archives on grants. I express my gratitude to Peter Robb and Peter Fitzpatrick who had kindly and perspicaciously commented on my published paper on Plunder and Prize, which has been developed into book-length form here. And to Lawrence Liang who kindly read the concluding section at insanely short notice, giving me the benefit of his comments. James Whitman, Prasanta Chakravarty, Faisal Devji and Upendra Baxi generously read versions of the present manuscript, and I am deeply grateful for their insightful engagement. Professor Baxi's chapter-wise comments, while by no means adequately addressed, will help orient the task from here. The referee report was detailed and perceptive, which I wish to acknowledge and thank here. As convention demands, it must be said that I alone am responsible for this work, for in truth no one else will take the blame.

I couldn't have asked for a more understanding editor than Indira Chandrasekhar. I thank her, Basanta and the team at Tulika Books.

Nikhil and the meandering quality of our conversations in and out of academics inhabit this effort in ways difficult to define. Gayathri has always been wonderfully encouraging, and the resonance between this work and an earlier novel of hers is serendipitous. If Ani reads this book she might consider revising her views on the charms of British royalty, expressed firmly when all of five. Ma and Deta have shared with us their affection, as much as the anguish of current times in whose shadow academic work struggles for meaning. The loving encouragement and freedom that Papa and Mummy had given me to pursue what I thought to be of value forms an inseparable part of an endeavour such as this. Down the corridor Sanghamitra was writing a book of her own, and but for her this work would have neither begun nor been.

Introduction

Conceptual Outwork

While it may be held that sovereignty requires some form of territorial expression, the question as to whether it is possible to formulate a rationale between the two, remains. If the principles of sovereignty and their spatial coordinates cannot be rationally explained or expressed in universally acceptable formulae, such loci would have to be considered historically contingent. Boundaries thereby remain open to contestation, and it becomes difficult if not impossible to conceive of a lasting peace. And yet it appears unassailable today that the recognition of sovereignty involves the recognition of territorial integrity. If contemporary sovereign states claim a delimited territory as central to their exercise of sovereignty, this principle is embedded in a consensus that took shape in the charter of the United Nations against the use of force by sovereign states against each other with the object of territorial acquisition. If the world wars of the twentieth century resulted in such a normative grammar which anchored sovereignty in the nexus that bound a spatial locus to a sovereign people (nation) in mutual recognition, this was clearly not the case previously.[1] It is in the search for the principles, mechanisms and effects of sovereignty prior to this moment that the present study situates itself. That some insight into the current situation may thereby also be gained is not impossible, even if merely the negative one of warning against the anachronistic projection of the abstract values and institutions of the day.

In more concrete terms, if prior to the twentieth century, no localized people-entity such as the nation-state can be assumed sovereign, this inquiry stages and deciphers the sovereign figure in terms of its ratio, which, apart from its direct claim of allegiance, involved the will to – legally enshrined claims over – plunder as much as its realization in practice. The ratio of King and empire[2] from the seventeenth to the nineteenth centuries, including East India Company jurisdictions which derived their legitimacy, in part, directly from Royal charters including those of Prize, are put to work as the subject of this present study. The (British) empire from the seventeenth to the nineteenth centuries has to be understood as an imperial formation that was in fact dynastic monarchy partaking in an arrangement with other European powers, so as to constitute an 'international' law aimed at consolidating and furthering its interests. In order to understand the subterfuge involved in the figure and configuration of royal sovereignty[3] as much as the emerging discourse of 'international relations', a story of the longer history of Prize and plunder, property and life, their laws, norms as well as practices, needs to be told. Rather than begin with the assumption of a nominal identity like 'British' as a predicate to 'empire', it discerns in the doctrine of the King's acts and the King's bodies, as fully established in the case of *Postnati* (1608),[4] the formation of the sovereign's claim over allegiance (rather than any notion of citizenship), and the motor and rationale of sovereign territorialization (unimpeded by any grammar of international law). In other words, it will be established that the King's acts refer to the principal formation and actualization of jurisdiction(s), whereas the King's bodies embodies the correlative multiplicity of jurisdictions developing in empire, a legal framing that lasts until the nineteenth century and beyond. Through King and conquest are traced the governing norms of 'international' relations which attentively pored over the rights to and distribution of plunder, giving a miss to the treatment of the vanquished. Such once-flourishing Prize jurisprudence, particularly around maritime militarization in commerce and war, circled around the distribution of property rights to all that the defeated owned. Life or what to do with the vanquished was but incidental, not thought worthy of inquiry or process, a matter of indifference or conventions, never theorized as 'right' amongst the empires of the day.[5] Not until late nineteenth-century Europe, arguably in the Hague Convention of 1899, did there even emerge attempts at an 'international' consensus over the formalization of rules of combat during war and the treatment of prisoners, which however applied largely to land wars and not sea battles.[6] Of course such fragile and indeterminate conventions merely sealed the centuries which had marked the radiating conquest of the planet by European kingdoms, and seemed utterly inadequate to contain what turned out to be the genocides of the next century.[7]

The present work will have little to say directly to this important question of the wars of the twentieth century except by way of indicating the political-imperial forms which constituted its historical and institutional context. While the focus of this study is the ('British') empire, its doctrinal grammar as much as the diction of its practices, the parties to the international conventions of the late nineteenth century were not 'nation-states' or even states as is conventionally understood today, but rather imperial formations which did not recognize either universal rights, principles of national self-determination or territorial integrity.[8] In such a world it was not self-evident that a (colonial-imperial) subject of empire had more rights than the subject of an alien but friendly empire, since among much else, franchise was limited and subjects were not as such guaranteed political participation or representation. Therefore, the starting point of any analysis cannot afford to be either the state or the subject as conceived by normative grammars of a later period when universal rights, democratic representation and territorial integrity might have been acknowledged.

What follows is a brief schematic overview of the parts that form the present book.

Part I undertakes an investigation of the constitutional significance of royal authority and its practices in the seventeenth century: an authority which had the unique powers of forming corporations such as the East India Company as well as jurisdictions distinct from (English/British) statute. *Postnati* (1608), in its discussion of sovereignty and allegiance, outlined both the war- and peace-making authority of the King, of which a branch was Prize jurisdiction; such authority remained untouched in the eighteenth and nineteenth centuries.[9] While taking *Postnati* as a point of departure, this part of the book analyses the laws of war and conquest in the writings of Mathew Hale, Thomas Hobbes, John Locke, William Molyneux, Prize jurisdiction and the case of *East India Company v. Sandys*, as well as the trading, warring and governing practices of the East India Company and the jurisprudence and legislation around it. Sovereignty is thereby established as a set of acts tested against as well as manifesting doctrines and practices in which the role of the King is central, whether acting through his (Privy) Council, through his Courts, or jointly with 'representative' and legislative assemblies such as parliament.

The major sections of this part involve the delineation of the King's powers in conquests and settlement, distinguished from King-in-Parliament, through the study of common law and natural law, while the last section outlines the nature of Prize jurisdiction and its implementation in the case of the Company. As will be shown, notwithstanding the great civil wars and the 'glorious' revolution, the powers of the King, in relationship to the problem that is being investigated, are reaffirmed by the settlement of 1688–89. The centrality of the King lay in the fact that the rights and liberties of the subject relied on allegiance to him, and this enabled the subject to appeal to the courts. These rights were given more shape and substance if he was propertied enough to qualify to sit in representative–legislative assemblies such as parliament where he might participate in the laws, including those related to taxation. His position therefore depended on his ownership of property and the specific jurisdiction which he inhabited, whether for instance in England, Ireland, other jurisdictions such as the Isle of Man, or in one of the American colonies. The concluding sections of this part analyse the King in its authorization of the powers of the East India Company, including powers to trade, war, govern and plunder. The Company functions as a measure of royal sovereignty, since it derives its authority from prerogative. All these issues of place in terms of the kinds of jurisdiction, as well as subject in terms of its 'degrees' (natural-born or denizen), are analysed in terms of the texts and archives named above. Amidst this diversity, the relationship between conquered subjects and law, on which much was written, will form an important thread.

In this sense, the very logic and formation of empire is discerned as involving specific channels of jurisdiction and distinctive modes of subject-formation, including acts of conquest. Part II of the book establishes that the East India Company's conquests in the subcontinent can only be comprehended in terms of long-standing royal authority in relationship to the Company – more precisely through royally sanctioned Prize charters. That the Company's conquests and powers of treaty making in the mid-eighteenth century were specifically derived from royal charters of Prize is not acknowledged by contemporary historiography, even while this was well recognized by justices and jurists in the eighteenth and nineteenth centuries, as will be shown. Prize laws formed an aspect of the King's rights of conquest, historically traced in Part I, though statutes emerged on the matter from the very end of the seventeenth century, particularly in the contexts of war. Part II establishes the fact that royally sanctioned Prize charters form a crucial aspect of the constitutional and jurisprudential bases of the English East India

Company's fabled conquests of the Indian subcontinent from the middle of the eighteenth century onwards.[10] More specifically, the royal letters-patent granted to the Company at their request in 1756–57 enabled the Company not merely to appropriate Prize and plunder, but simultaneously both treaty with as well as conquer native polities.[11] These letters-patent were part of a specific channel of jurisdiction whose source was royal authority, notwithstanding the existence of statutes on the subject. In this context it is important to note, as is discussed in Part II, that when the East India Company applied to be given the rights to Prize under an existing statute, they were advised to directly apply to get such a grant from the King. Therefore the letter-patent of 1757–58 granting rights to Prize, war and treaty was of enormous importance to the rights of the East India Company, emerging as they did from royal authority, not parliamentary statute. The Prize cases of the eighteenth century and even nineteenth century therefore were adjudicated by royal channels reaching up to the Privy Council, not parliament. On the other hand, the Company's very corporate identity, apart from specific powers of governance and adjudication, depended on forms of royal jurisdiction notwithstanding the existence of statutes to legitimate them broadly.

To understand and elucidate this set of issues, Part II begins with a discussion of Martial and Military law as they took shape in the early eighteenth century, moving on to an analysis of Prize jurisdiction and *Campbell v. Hall*. All of these form crucial sites for the elaboration of the categories and practices of war, conquest and nationality, articulated as they are in their inter-relations. The question of the legal basis of the Company in its conquests is analysed through the celebrated trial of Warren Hastings where the ambiguities regarding the accountability of the Company are affirmed. Apart from archival material on the East India Company, legal cases (*Campbell v. Hall*, *Le Caux v. Eden*, the Impeachment Trial of Hastings) and specific writings of Bentham are analysed in this part as the inauguration of an obfuscating discourse on law and 'international' relations, that all the same lay the groundwork for an epistemic structure of long-lasting significance.

If royally sanctioned Prize charters enabled the acquisition of property through war, the question naturally arises about the rights of native individuals, populations and rulers who were thereby being dispossessed in the course of conquest. Here, key judicial cases such as *Postnati* (1608) and *Campbell v. Hall* (1774), as well as *Mayor (of Lyons) v. East India Company* (1836), with reference to India outline a theory of the formation of the subject and his rights in the course of conquest which necessarily take the form of his ability to participate in the making of laws through (representative) assemblies. However, in the case of the East India Company's conquests, natives are disabled from the possibility of any such rights because there is no firm legal indication of the cessation of war and the emergence of rights including property rights of the native subjects. Prize cases of the nineteenth century, as analysed in Part III, show in effect this legally sanctioned perpetual state of war in India. Such a confirmation only complements the great revenue settlements framed by the East India Company from the eighteenth century onwards, which, in refusing to involve the participation of those from whom revenue was demanded, voided property right in its own ways. Property right as defined by the right to participate in formulation of laws with regard to taxation – the very essence of representative assemblies – was clearly announced as far back as *Postnati* but was not to be found in India well into the twentieth century. The formation of jurisdiction in India was thus one with the receding of all law and property.

Part III makes the argument that while the Company's unabated conquests and the dispossession of sovereigns and subjects in the subcontinent continue, such conditions are obfuscated by the emerging jurisprudential discourse from John Austin to Henry Maine and John Stuart Mill, thereby building upon Jeremy Bentham. To illuminate such concrete conditions and their veiling, two sites are chosen, one in India and the other in Britain, sites that are themselves divided into two parts. The first part of the Indian site is the legal dispute between the Company and the Mughal ruler Akbar Shah II, over the interpretation of a treaty/agreement between them. This dispute is analysed in part through the figure of Rammohan Roy, who recognizes the centrality of the (British) King in empire and therefore demands accountability from London. The second part of this site consists of two interlocking judicial cases in relation to what are called the Anglo-Maratha wars of the early nineteenth century. One regarding Prize money, heard by the Lords of the Treasury and the Privy Council, hailed as the most important case on land war since Richard II; and the second, which also reaches the Privy Council from the Supreme Court in Bombay, linking Prize money to martial law. In both cases the systematic dispossession of sovereigns and subjects in India are illustrated.

The second site involves an analysis of the writings of John Austin and Henry Maine. Following from this, the discourse of late eighteenth-century British international lawyers on the questions of sovereignty, conquest, and the incorporation of peoples and territories is examined. In the writings of John Austin, John Stuart Mill, Henry Maine and F.W. Maitland,[12] the role of the King is obscured and repressed even while the international lawyers, such as Travers Twiss and John Westlake, actively manoeuvred the jurisprudential arguments derived from royal sovereignty in defending and articulating the burgeoning of conquest of the late nineteenth century. This is particularly evident in the complex articulations of territory, jurisdiction and sovereignty as they take shape in the relationship between the Queen, 'British territory' and the 'princely states'. Direct 'Crown' rule enunciates a modus operandi that in fact merely continues and consolidates the strategies adopted by the East India Company regime, itself authorized by the King's specific authority, as is argued in Part III.[13] It is not accidental that some of these international lawyers and jurists articulating this discourse were actively involved as lawyers in the adjudication of Prize. This role in 'foreign' affairs no doubt has a trace in land law too, where technically all land in England was held of the King even as forms of taxation – and therein proprietary right – were necessarily linked to representative-legislative assemblies such as King-in-Parliament. Both sites, in India and in Britain, therefore confirm the role of the King and the royal apparatus in distinctly illuminative ways, often without necessarily intending to do so, as is shown in the interpretation of Austin and Maine. Apart from legal cases (The Deccan Prize Money Case, *Elphinstone v. Bedreechand*), jurisprudential and philosophical literature (Austin, Maine, Mill, Philimore, Westlake, Hall and Twiss) and colonial writings on the princely states are analysed in Part III.

Having completed this brief overview of the contents and trajectory of this work, the broader implications of such an approach for the validity of concepts such as 'rule of law' and 'parliamentary sovereignty' associated with a British tradition is sketched in what remains of this section. The constitutional and jurisprudential bases of the authority of the East India Company make it clear that no simple argument about the (British) parliamentary limitation of the King, or general argument about growing liberties and democratization, can be made for the period – particularly in the face of the forms of territorialization, 'the King's bodies', that were rampant in the eighteenth and nineteenth centuries. Such an analysis of sovereignty in terms of the legality that justified and dictated modes of sovereign acquisition, which involved the laws of conquest and plunder, gives lie to a normative order that claims territorial integrity as a basis – an order that is slowly coming into being towards the end of the nineteenth century. But such territorial integrity referred only to imperial territories in relationship to one another, and not those territories and populations denied the qualification of statehood and civilization.

If war-booty provides a clue to the constitution of international relations, this will only strike the practitioners of international law today[14] as odd or embarrassing. Eminent jurists of the nineteenth century were well aware of the originary function of Prize jurisdiction, focused on the seas, maritime commerce as much as war.[15] Little more than the fact that the so-called founder of international law, Hugo Grotius, had cut his teeth in crafting a mammoth work of advocacy, *Commentary on the Laws of Prize and Booty*, to the cause of plunder is necessary to whet the appetite.[16] Such was the jurisprudential matrix of an evolving 'common' – civil but not always so[17] – law between European empires, whether monarchical or republican.[18] Here germinated the precise procedures and principals involved in the rights to appropriate the properties of enemies and neutrals during conditions of war and hostility. There was no discourse with regard to continental warfare or the inter-polity conventions on the treatment or rights of prisoners, equivalent to the conqueror's right to property, between the seventeenth and nineteenth centuries[19] – the chronological framework of this thesis. It is through war and its principles – seen as constitutive of sovereign activity – as much as its effects on populations and countries, that the present thesis argues for in the construction of the sovereign state as much as the global order therein spawned. Focusing merely on the ideological self-representation of sovereignty in philosophical treatises of the period between the seventeenth and the nineteenth century lets the most important slip by. It also enables a 'vanishing act' on imperial territorialization that is legible in the academic common sense which sees the development of a sovereign state, rather than empire, as that through which the practices and procedures of democracy and nationalism are said to have come into their own in the nineteenth century.[20]

Prize jurisdiction certainly had an ancient history going back to Greek and Roman writers, as much as Biblical scripture,[21] which the seventeenth-century writers were well aware of and scrupulously built upon.[22] From this early modern period, it was largely an affair of the seas, jurisprudentially and militarily nourishing the growing commercial trades across the oceans of the globe. Such a history of Prize will turn out to be a double of a history of trade and commerce, that 'cunning civility' of Europe.[23] Modern international conventions regarding the rules of warfare, commerce, neutrality and nationality, it will be argued, cannot be grasped outside their historical and institutional emergence from the framework of royal authority, military warfare and Prize jurisdiction. In other words, beginning with the laws and conventions of war, such a story of sovereignty will disabuse any theory which attributes the latter to nation or population as *sui generis* constitutive principles. These do not have any constitutive role in institutional terms until, arguably, the late nineteenth century,[24] where the present inquiry ends, and will in fact have to wait really until well into the twentieth century, as the conclusion argues. The rationale for taking the early seventeenth century as a point of departure for this work lies in the argument that this moment articulates a paradigm of sovereignty that remains resilient for centuries to come.

If citizenship is what defines political identity in terms of rights and obligations as norms today in democratic nation-states, allegiance would have to be considered the equivalent of this concept for the period between the seventeenth and nineteenth centuries. Allegiance to the natural person of the King (and heirs) in a spatial order of diverse and diversifying jurisdiction, as much as temporally changing authorities, was unmistakable, and constitutionally as much as jurisprudentially enshrined. That allegiance was owed to the natural person of the King (and heirs) was established in *Postnati* (1608), and had as its converse the fact that treason was attracted by the very imagining of the death of the King (his natural person and his heirs).[25] This irrefutable legal fact characterizing the multiplying jurisdictions of empire, all of whose subjects were bound in their allegiance to the natural person of the King, is comprehensible solely through the seemingly obscure jurisprudential doctrine of the King's bodies. The doctrinal ratio of the King's bodies was lucidly outlined in *Postnati*, but ignored or wilfully obscured by the jurists and political commentators of the late nineteenth century, as argued in Part III that in many senses sets the basis for current historiography on the figure of the King, the eminence of parliament and the chaos of empire.[26] This was no accident, for these late nineteenth-century thinkers building on the jurisprudence of Jeremy Bentham, analysed in Part II, attempted to enunciate a whole new epistemic programme to occlude both the doctrinal ratio of empire as much as and the imperial practices of conquest and control which formed its precipitates. Therefore, the present work argues, it is in the denial of the one doctrine which effectively accounted for, and legally formed, imperial conquest in its exuberance, that can be found the poisoned seeds of the modern disciplines of political philosophy and jurisprudence.[27]

One sees this, for instance, in Walter Bagehot's stunning argument in 1867, that in England royalty worked as a 'disguise' to enable the real rulers – what he theorizes, perhaps for the first time, as the cabinet – to change 'without heedless people knowing it'.[28] Elsewhere he speaks of a 'double government' of the prerogative and 'Downing Street', to which he traces several of the 'superficial peculiarities' that mark the constitution.[29] And even while the text speaks of the 'real power' of the cabinet, his introduction to the second edition of the text outlines both the undefined nature of the prerogative as much as all that could be done by it in law, which could bring all government and life itself to a standstill.[30] And yet Bagehot can do no more than note the overwhelming powers of prerogative rather than search its origins and logic, because to do so would have led to the unearthing of an unseemly mix of despotic royalty and militaristic imperialism which the late nineteenth century did not wish to confront in its civilizational ardour. It is towards such an end of unearthing the origins and logic of the King's bodies that the present work is directed.

This work will thus inevitably involve an analysis and discussion of the doctrine of the King's bodies as a blade of conquest hidden in the shadows of discourse. It will refuse to enter into the question of whether and why particular individual Kings of England did or did not employ a particular juridical doctrine at a particular moment in time, or why several of the powers of prerogative thought formally in existence were not used by English monarchs. A.V. Dicey's argument that the prerogatives of the Crown reflected in fact the privileges of the people,[31] is refuted not merely by the fact that a large proportion of the adult male population, even in the United Kingdom at this time, did not get the vote, but equally importantly, the fact that the vast proportion of the subjects of the King, in places like India, had no such privilege. So whether the undeniable legal powers of royal prerogative were in fact being manoeuvred by the cabinet or not in the late nineteenth century, the point is not merely to take cognizance of the undeniable existence of such powers,[32] but equally to trace in such powers the history and jurisdictional hierarchies[33] which composed empire and enabled as well as structured exploitation and violence. When Dicey emphasizes the allegedly unique features of English common law, claiming that unlike in France, martial law is 'unknown to the law of England', he has to immediately bury an important qualification in the footnote, where it is stated, 'this statement has no reference to the law of any country other than England, even though such a country may form part of the British Empire'.[34] The royal person as much as royal prerogative will be shown as manifesting forms of imperial territorialization that are central to the nineteenth-century definition and hierarchical calibration of the jurisdictions that made up the British Empire. Those asserting the increasingly sovereign powers of parliament have to merely read the histories of the fourteenth and seventeenth centuries and witness the bloodied corpses of Kings to see what equally elite parliamentary groupings[35] were capable of in relationship to royal power, and ask why indeed was the royal person maintained at all as a political principle well after? For the restricted debate about the relative powers of parliament and King turn out in fact to be a decoy to avoid their orchestration of the planetary violence of empire.

Only on an illegitimately narrow view that takes the spatial boundary of England or the United Kingdom as the analytic compass can the argument be made – as Dicey makes it, as well as the great reams of scholarship in his wake until the present – that royal power had historically been inversely related to parliament.[36] Empire is the only ratio within which can be interpreted the 'development' of the United Kingdom, and not so much who or what in reality operated the strings of prerogative but its logic and its effects, which formed the grammar of conquest and rule in multiple jurisdictions, that will frame the following studies. Pointing to a less visible cabinet, elected by a miniscule proportion of those in actual political subjection, as the force behind the prerogative does little to advance the notion of democracy of nation, and in fact returns us to the lap of the oldest myth of the oriental despot, who was not to be feared in himself but feared because of the 'vizir' and vested interests operating the strings from behind. In the present context, the importance of royal prerogative, as formally distinct from parliament, is more than in evidence in situations as diverse as the normative importance of the King for the American colonists in the 1760s, the royal authority involved in the militaristic-territorial expansion of the East India Company, or the importance of the Queen for international lawyers in the late nineteenth century.

Political identity was defined in terms of allegiance, and Fitzjames Stephen's historical and legal discussion of treason establishes that the figure of the King/Queen is central to the establishment of the 'state', for he says, complementing Maitland, that unlike in the continent, in England there was no distinction between sovereign and state,[37] and therefore legal provisions with regard to treason in the continent 'differs from English law in the recognition of the state as being the object of the crime as distinguished from the King'.[38] The 1848 Act on treason meant the 'imagination' and 'compassment' of the death or deposition of the King/Queen, as well as 'levying war' against the King which would include 'conspiracy' or 'riots for political objects';[39] no separation between the natural body (and/as heirs) of the King/Queen and the state could be contemplated. The nineteenth century clarified and established in statutory form 'constructive treason' which was shaped through the King, the widening of what was called the state and its powers over subjects, and though Stephen does not invoke the doctrine of the King's bodies, no other rationale explains his juristic reasoning about the jurisprudence of treason.[40] The King could create peerages and not until the twentieth century did the House of Lords, in some sense, lose its legislative power. Not from the lives and predilections of particular kings or queens or by searching the ultimate motives of powerful cliques, but only from the doctrinal grammar of the King's bodies and its institutionalized expression and effects, can one find the ratio and language of allegiance and conquest, as much as the multiplying jurisdictions of empire – embedding the logic of both Prize jurisprudence in general and its singularly cynical application in the subcontinent.

There is no other way that the realities of empire will be salvaged from the obfuscations of the giant epistemic structures – from nation-states to democratization in this period – that have been hoisted as decoys for centuries. No theory of 'social contract' or 'rights' has any explanatory value in understanding the formation of this empire and the violence of its conquests as recorded in histories from the seventeenth to the nineteenth centuries. In their abstraction, such theories have enabled a dubious epistemological distinction between theory and locus, action and identity. Only through such obfuscation is one blindsided into believing that a specific interpretation of a theory can be affixed to a particular time, place or cultural identity, and explain historical movement. And yet miraculously, in such abstraction, all the so-called modern values, whether they be that of the nation-state or freedom, right or self-representation, are to have constituted the very essence of a place and time, in the conjunction of which one is to find the autotelic identity of the 'modern west'. While a theoretical critique and articulation of method involved in the present thesis can be found in the 'note' at the conclusion of this introductory chapter, the next sections discuss some of the lineaments of the thesis to better situate it within the broader historiography.

The Royal Sole/Soul, Many Bodies

To approach such a figure as that of the English sovereign, an Aristotelian idiom requires an introduction, howsoever elliptically, since such was the atmosphere soaked in by the then extant jurisprudence. In Aristotle, a principle is an account and therein the individuation of phenomenon. As form and actuality, a principle is distinct – not separable – from matter, which itself in being inherently diverse is a potentiality.[41] The soul of a natural body accounts for its life, in the very being of its identity, in the accomplishment of its purpose by living. The rational being thus has a soul that accounts not merely in its living, but in its living-well. In Aristotle's striking imagery, if the eye was an animal, the soul would be its sight.[42] In another illustration repeated several times, if the house had brick and mortar for its matter, it had as its form (soul), the purpose of protection. In no other way could the house be distinctively individualized as home, or distinguished from a three-dimensional image or a fictitious replica on stage or elsewhere.[43] The form-principle as purpose as much as account described and accounted for the individuation, while matter is understood as that in which lay the possibility of being an indefinite number of things that could (potentially) build the house – whether brick and mortar(or possibly something else) that might serve as ingredients. Potentially there could be an indefinite number of ingredients, but in definition the purpose had to be one. If a house was being used as a prison, that is what it would be in fact. Therefore, the purpose of 'being protected' is the individuation that necessarily takes form in matter. Material ingredients are necessary to the constitution of a house, as of anything, but the house is not therein defined. It is defined by the purpose of protection rather than an enumeration of the materials which could (potentially) make a house.

That this set of issues is not merely a matter of abstract meditation but vital for our current propositions is evident when we try to read and understand Francis Bacon's argument,[44] in his advocacy of *Postnati* (1608), that only the individual natural-bodied King had a soul whereas a corporation did not, and therein lay the crucial distinction between the monarchical form of England and that of republics such as Venice.[45] While this is discussed in detail in Part I, some of its main threads are gathered here for the purpose of situating the present thesis within the larger literature.

In the arguments around *Postnati*, the royal soul (and heirs) formed a (sovereign-political) identity by accounting for and remaining the same, notwithstanding alterations of matter (biological bodies and political body-politics). The soul is discernible in the King and his heirs, while a corporation as an artificial construction could not be said to possess any inherent unity. It had no soul, and without it was incapable of individuation and inherently plural. This monarchical feature of the soul was absolutely central for Francis Bacon as much as Lord Coke. Only therein could the primary fact of political obligation and allegiance even be formulated. Having no soul or an inherently unifying principle, ever-changing in terms of time-history (once elected, once not) as well as its space-constituents (once this member, another time that), corporations and republics could never inspire allegiance. Such was certainly not – and could not be – the condition of monarchy in England, Scotland, Ireland and other jurisdictions, which, notwithstanding the undeniable diversity of laws, all the same consisted of subjects who owed allegiance to the natural person of the King, as forcefully held by *Postnati*. No doubt, this ideological elaboration of monarchy against republics might have well been provoked by the rebellious wars undertaken by Dutch republican provinces against the Spanish monarch.[46] And yet, whatsoever the weight of the specific historical context, for the purpose of this thesis it is important to underline that this doctrine of allegiance to the natural person of the King, apart from the civil wars and interregnum of the seventeenth century, provided the soul of law and political obligation in the empire called 'British', well into the twentieth century.

In Baconian–common law terms,[47] the King accomplishes his sovereign objective in the formation of the body-politic in the growth, differentiation and multiplication of jurisdictions. This 'natural-biological' identity of King (and heirs), which unifies and sustains the political formations of diverse jurisdictions in space as well as in time, is precisely that which 'makes' or gives life to distinct corporations; therein the basis of a corporation like the English East India Company. Corporations by their very nature require incorporation, since they are inherently multiple and without an individuating principle. Hence one sees the common law doctrine of the King as the unique source of corporations – as forms of body-politics and jurisdictions. This growth of the political formation and spatial order in its differentiations takes the form of sovereign 'titles'. The King may be said to inherit jurisdictions (such as Scotland and England) or conquer (such as Ireland) them – and therein lay the rationality, the very vitality, of empire. As this thesis will establish, such is the ratio of the multiplication ('growth') of the empire from the settlements in America to the territories in India, from the seventeenth century into the nineteenth century.

This expanded notion of movement is not unrelated to inherited Aristotelian arguments about the soul. First, if the Aristotelian idea proposes that the soul as principle accounts for (the) body, it does so to account for change and alteration, 'growth' and 'expansion'. If nothing remained the same and everything was inherently multiple, one could not describe or intelligibly speak of, let alone account for, change and alteration. It is therefore not surprising that in Aristotle, 'nature' does not refer to either an abstract definition or classification, nor an empirical description derived from observation, but rather is interchangeable with motion, process and alteration, of that which is individuated. A rational motion or alteration is characterized as having a purpose, in terms of which the ratio of change is discernable, the purpose being impossible to divide into the binary of 'native/inherent' or 'foreign/external'. Action 'for the sake of' refers to both the object-objective as well as the subject which realizes its nature by accomplishing its purpose. It is in this sense that the King as political principle is formed.

Secondly, this argument about the soul as the principle of movement is not unrelated to the critique of void-space. Aristotle established that the very notion of the void lead to impossibilities and was therefore irrational. Hence there was neither a void-space in politics (*res nullius* referred not to empty place but to the fact of there being no one recognized authority[48]) nor could a void in time or succession be conceived, and therefore the King was conceivable as corporation sole or conquest conceived of as a title. It is revealing that the Greeks defined 'nothing' as no-one-thing, and therefore the indefinite many rather than the simple void which would have been held unintelligible. It is this no-one-thing that one can discern in the Roman '*res nullius*' or common law doctrines on conquest. That these were not mere abstract theories is clear from the fact that the Dutchman William's claim was construed as 'conquest' by many, since a break had occurred in time with James's 'abdication', as discussed in Part I. It is therefore not surprising that Bacon and Coke, in the discussions of *Postnati*, recognized only inheritance and conquest when it came to sovereign title, even while this distinction was not necessarily held to be a categorical or lasting one. Since there was no concept of an empty place, this meant that it was always assumed that jurisdiction of some sort existed in a place. If a place was uninhabited, the individuals who occupied it did so not as abstract human beings but as subjects of a sovereign. If inhabited, conquest of the place always involved the question of sovereignty, since the rights of conquest pertained to the sovereign and not the subject.

In such a context, the pertinent, much-discussed jurisprudential question revolved around whether the prior laws of the vanquished were to be retained or whether the laws of the conqueror's jurisdiction came to apply – questions that will be seen to be germane to the set of issues involving the East India Company and conquest, as discussed in Part II. *Postnati* and subsequent jurisprudence through text and case law affirmed that when it came to conquest, the conqueror was the King; and therefore it was through him that laws would be formed, beginning with the 'law of conquest' that might include Prize. In other words, place was always a jurisdiction, and the 'growth' of a body-politic always required a living sovereign principle, i.e. a soul. The idea of the void begins to get established in scientific circles later in the seventeenth century, and even while it remains impossible in common law, it finds refuge in the political fables of a 'state of nature'. These ideas acquire their sharpest salience in the context of war and civil war, whether in the works of Thomas Hobbes or John Locke, as will be argued in Part I. The very wording of 'state of nature' portends a radical shift in the basic conceptualization of law because nature was no longer now seen as a principled process or alteration, but rather envisioned as 'state'. A void-space lacking in jurisdiction was conceived as something constituted by individuals each of whom was formed by a reason inherent and natural to themselves as particular beings. This provided the epistemic origin as well as the explanatory framework for politics. Such an argument of the radical constructability of the body-politic – one with no natural basis in human experience or conceptualization – was precisely what Bacon sought to critique (and anticipate) when he envisioned natural laws and the sovereign soul as the origin of jurisdiction.

Analogously, the political theory of the void as the surround-individuating boundary of the object – in no other way could the individual be so resolutely bound – is traceable to the 'inertial' framework.[49] The abstract object moving through empty space becomes the prototype of the abstract individual in a state of nature emptied of jurisdiction, and therein the relations and ratio by which individuals enter into larger wholes. From such an initial postulate the laws of political motion are deduced, and taking the individuals as primary leads to the idea of the artificial state, Hobbes's 'mortal god'. The emerging political norms manifested the irresolvable antinomies between 'natural right' and 'positive constitutions', because no heuristic remains to offer a rationale to decide between one or the other, the natural or the political (state). Such a paradigm, while providing a global normative grammar, does not confront the more precise problems of jurisdiction – the King's bodies – which emerge persistently in the common law jurisprudence in-mixed with the practices of imperial conquest and rule.

Debates about global norms, such as the natural and the positive, lack the granular attention required to check the sovereign pulse of imperial conquest as it colours the spatial coagulations of jurisdiction from the American continent to the Indian subcontinent. A jurisdiction which was driven by a marine – and militarized – ecology, which was reflected in common law as much as the imperial institutions of rule, was wilfully repressed in the idiom of politics as it developed late in the nineteenth century. Part III of the book, building on the analysis and descriptions of such a marine ecology in Parts I and II, establishes that whether one turns to the 'liberal' philosophy of John Stuart Mill or the historical jurisprudence of Maine and Maitland, they all had as a common intention the postulate of a historico-civilizational logic of cultural-racial difference. This postulate performed a vanishing trick on empire by taking form in the strained denial of the actual history which had produced their comfortable condition, i.e. empire as formulated by the King and his jurisdictions from the seventeenth to the nineteenth centuries.[50] While a historico-civilizational logic, its grand formulations were undertaken so as to screen modes of conquest – the legal framing of which was well known and even better practised – through which empire pervaded the planet. Such baseless historicizing had as its task the simultaneous negation of both the natural right tradition (which in its argumentation could always lead to an appeal to war and rebellion, and could not but be seen as radically subversive) and the concrete historical forms of conquest (the specific juridical framing of which is analysed in the following parts of the book).[51] In other words, there can be no conflation between British political-legal thought with its arguments about laws, subjects and jurisdiction, and the idea of a fundamental universal individual right that surfaces in moments of revolutionary fervour, whether in 1640s England, 1790s England, or Marxist inspired and other 'revolutionary' pockets in Europe, Russia or India, as argued in the conclusion.

The analysis of Austin, Maine and Mill undertaken in Part III is therefore an analysis of a forgetting, of a silence. Such a silence and forgetting lays the foundation of an orientation that is unable to perceive the central role of the King in nineteenth-century Britain as well as the historical formation of the British Empire – even if such a pall could not completely succeed with the exertions and articulations of Rammohan Roy, the imperial subject, as argued in Part III. The jurisdictional dismemberment and carving of the world and its populations into subjugation is disguised as a historical-civilizational logic that equally propels the emerging discourse of international law in the late nineteenth century that wilfully obscures the doctrinal, juridical, military and economically extractive features of imperial conquest. The categorical identities, whether 'British' or 'French', are staged as surrogates of value – civilized and uncivilized – remaining untouched by historical developments or geographic expansion. On the other hand, the monarchical imperialism is harnessed as a medium of differentiated territorialization by international lawyers to emerging imperial consensuses in the late nineteenth century, as argued in Part III. The basis of modern humanitarian international law will thus have to be analysed as it emerges from the grill of such imperialisms.

While Aristotle might have anticipated the *aporias* of classical mechanics, he was also responding to Eleatics such as Zeno. Zeno denied the possibility of motion by remarking that at every moment the flying arrow was at rest and therefore no such series of restful positions could count as movement. Aristotle's attempts at the denial of a void-space, or absolute position, were undertaken with the intent to enable a characterization of an object in motion – form and individuation.[52] Some modern epigones of Zeno have unknowingly deployed such arguments to resist the possibility of seeing in motion the formation of objects – articulated as acting and acted-upon – and thereby the internal logic of the development of an identity. This is manifested as much in the uncritical use of categories like 'English' and 'British' across centuries as in the repudiation of empire by claiming that one cannot know or prove the formation of an object over time.

In other words, the familiar arguments against teleology refuse the possibility of knowing how the political formation called England in the seventeenth century was indeed the same as that which it would become, or became, in the nineteenth century. This denial takes the pseudo-epistemic form of negating the possibility of explaining how something at one time (seventeenth century) becomes something in a subsequent period (nineteenth century). And yet this very dismissal in turn renders any kind of analysis – and even the simplest of experiences – unintelligible, senseless and impossible because space or time as a series of points will in fact, in the ultimate Zenoian conclusion, enable motion. Not such a conclusion but the ideological determination of certain categories and their existence, without offering an account of their existence, is what imbues much of the scholarship that constitutes the study of empire.[53] This form of strategic sceptical-suicidal argumentation, if taken seriously, in fact renders any action unintelligible in dividing up the action into a series of indefinite or infinite points in time, space and identity. Hence the characterization, sceptical-suicidal.[54]

The Historiographical Context

The difficulties involved in the developing and exhibiting of a ratio of territorialization, or the acquisition of territories and conquests, exhibits itself in the influential work of Lauren Benton. A central organizing framework of her important study, *A Search for Sovereignty*, claims that between 1400 and 1900 CE,'territory' was not central to sovereignty in the way it was to develop thereafter.[55] In describing the rationale of the period of study between the fifteenth and the twentieth centuries, Benton states that 'territorial control was a contingent element of imperial rule, not a property firmly associated with sovereign jurisdiction'.[56] However, it might well be the case that such an under-evaluation of formal territorial claim is itself a deceptive form of control, and the present work documents this in myriad ways, most spectacularly in the East India Company's strategy and practice of staging and disavowing the territorial authority of native sovereigns in the course of conquest, as are described in Parts II and III.[57] Not investigating the rationale of imperial expansion and the Company's transformative interventions in the vast domains of land, revenue, law and trade, is to accept at face-value the ideological subterfuges of empire.[58] The refusal to identify sovereignty in terms of a specific territory cannot amount to the proposition that the exercise of sovereignty does not manifest territorially. Moreover, Benton does not offer a conceptual account of the relationship between sovereignty and territory or the distinct kinds of subject formation in the course of imperial conquest – a key guiding thread of the analysis undertaken in the present work. As is contended, while (English-British) monarchical forms of sovereignty are not characterizable in terms of specifiable territories, the jurisprudential doctrine of the King's bodies is meant to precisely explain and describe conquest and territorialization.

This lack of a conceptual account of sovereignty results in indiscriminate use of categories like 'English', 'Spanish' and 'French', which might at most have a heuristic-descriptive content and not a legal or juridical intelligibility, let alone force, in the period under study. No one did, or could, claim a right based on such a category, except as it conjugated, certainly in the English-British case under investigation, with subjection to the sovereign.[59] The use of contemporary political-national distinctions – in a time when nationality has a legal force – can hardly be projected into times when they would have not crossed the threshold of intelligibility. This is so particularly because there is little explanation of the relationship between such national-cultural terms, and political and juridical right, in much of the scholarly work on the subject. The uncritical use of such categories, such as that of a 'British political community' as an explanatory framework for the 'British Empire', is what needs to be questioned in David Armitage's *Ideological Origins of the British Empire*. While Armitage takes it as his task to explore the ideological origins of *empire* from the seventeenth to the nineteenth centuries, it is perplexing that there is no discussion let alone sustained analysis of kingship, which was persistently recognized in this period as central to conceptualizing the unity of the diverse jurisdictions that constituted the ('British') empire.

Armitage begins his intellectual quest very succinctly by stating that 'the "concept" of the British Empire means the idea that an identifiable political community existed to which the term empire could be fittingly applied, and which was recognizably British, rather than for example, Roman, French or English'.[60] This, he argues, was achieved at the very earliest in the late seventeenth century, but was to really come into its own only in the eighteenth century. The chief features of this imperial identity Armitage describes as 'Protestant, Commercial, Maritime and Free', features that were to have characterized this imperial identity as developed in the complex negotiation between maritime trade and liberty.[61] While this may indeed be a defensible description of the writings of the individuals that Armitage studies, such an interpretation risks being merely nugatory if it does not relate itself to either the legal conceptions or political practices – and their inter-relations – which defined the empire: a context in which the question of kingship and jurisdiction become unavoidable. For it is impossible to navigate around the relationship between 'community' and 'political membership', to use Armitage's words, because the only feature that bound individuals across the jurisdictions of empire was allegiance to the natural person of the King. It was this undeniable fact that formed the normative framework for the conflict over distinct jurisdictions, both ideological and practical, whether that of Ireland or the colonies in America. It is not accidental, therefore, that Armitage ends his narrative in the early to mid-eighteenth century, since to consider the discourse of the American colonists in the 1770s would be to face the awkward fact that (even) at this time the figure of the King as the allegiance-demanding sovereign, and the questions pertaining to British statutory jurisdiction, remained central – issues of burning concern in relation to the Company's conquests in the east.

By ignoring the doctrinal basis and legal channels of empire, Armitage appears to anachronistically project a notion of 'British identity' that scarce helps capture the nature and life of the empire purportedly under study. Equally damagingly, the ideological distinction between (British) maritime trade with its associations of peace and liberty, and (European) continental war with its associations of war and conquest, appear to have been taken rather uncritically. Not only did many figures of the seventeenth and eighteenth centuries see in 'overseas trade' forms of political subjugation and maritime violence of a degree that were not to be found in land wars.[62] More tellingly, as is detailed below in Parts I and II, maritime-militarized trade regulations such as the Navigation Acts were at the heart of jurisdictional disputes and grievances, whether it be the Irish or the American-colonial case. The brazen cruelties of the British East India Company's conquests in the Indian subcontinent consisted in no small part of transposing the militarized regulations of maritime warfare, including Prize laws, into territorial wars, as argued in Part II.

Not taking into cognizance the function and powers of the King means to miss the complex ways in which the jurisdictional contestations within the British Empire were but intensified in expression in (further) imperial expansion.[63] The King's role during conquest was undisputed, whether in the seventeenth century or thereafter, and this reflected both the history of the empire (Ireland, for instance) and novel modes of its expansion in conquest (such as the East India Company). It is this subtle rationale between empire itself and its expansion that has been left out of account in several recent historical studies of 'international relations', whether it be Armitage's subsequent book, *The Foundations of Modern International Thought*,[64] or Jennifer Pitts's *Boundaries of the International*.[65] These works have no place for analysis of the legal doctrines of the conquests or jurisdiction, and therefore the jurisprudence of sovereignty or the rationalizations of imperial territorialization and their institutional-effective practices. While Armitage devotes a whole chapter to 'Parliament and International Relations' in the eighteenth century, even when judicial doctrine and judicial practice had made it clear that this was the domain of the King,[66] Pitts's discussion of the impeachment of Warren Hastings neither analyses the juridical basis of Company power nor investigates precisely what counts as 'indigenous' in Hastings's institutionalization of Hindu and Muslim law.[67] Here too, much like in Benton, the lack of an interest in a sustained investigation into the modalities of rule, doctrinal and institutional, and the effects of empire on subject-populations,[68] renders any comprehension of the impeachment trial and its basis nugatory.

There has been relatively less effort, as the above scholarship indicates, expended in exploring imperial expansion so as to analyse the accepted rationale of state-empire formation in the British Isles. Such epistemically and historically unwarranted bracketing of territorial conquest as emerging from the logic of empire enables the image of a growing parliamentary authority at the expense of the King.[69] While this perhaps has been the dominant paradigm that nests the trumpeted and trumped-up claims of liberty and freedom as being distinctively English and European, there are exceptions to the trend. A critical line of scholarship has deepened one's understanding of contemporary configurations of powers – their force and basis – by arguing for the crucial role of empire and imperialism in the formulation of modern categories such as that of the state and international law, and it is to this set of works that one needs to turn.

Edward Keene's *Beyond the Anarchical Society* takes up this set of issues by making three crucially interlinked arguments.[70] First, late nineteenth- and twentieth-century international law which works with a normative framework of a 'society of states'cannot be traced to the seventeenth century, as conventional scholarship of international law would have it. Rather, it has to be traced to a specific counter-revolutionary early nineteenth-century conjuncture where states were to be understood as specific dynastic monarchies. Second, this normative picture, particularly before the mid-twentieth century, was confined to relations within a specific consortium of European powers, and did not apply to the mechanisms of imperialism by which European powers conquered and dominated non-European powers from the seventeenth to the twentieth century. And finally, seventeenth-century thinkers like Hugo Grotius, conventionally treated as a founder of modern international law, did not in fact provide the framework for the normative picture of a 'society of states' which conditions contemporary images of international law.[71] Rather, almost paradoxically, Keene argues that one can find specific concepts in Grotius's writings that succeed in capturing and anticipating the actual practices of imperial conquest from the seventeenth to the nineteenth centuries.

The arguments about the divisibility of sovereignty and the rights of private entities to wage public wars in defence of property articulate two such concepts.[72] Keene traces these concepts in their functioning to imperial practice, such as when the Dutch used force and coercion to treaty with local rulers resulting in sovereign powers which were (ostensively) divided between themselves and local rulers, articulating thereby the notion of 'divisible sovereignty'. However, such division, as Keene argues, was contingent on particular imperial interests, and often led to, or laid the basis for, a more complete conquest or annexation of the native polity. Divisible sovereignty cannot therefore be seen as referring to an actual division of sovereignty, but must be integrated into its function in the narrative of imperial conquest. The second crucial concept from Grotius regarding the justification of private wars based on property was initially drafted with the aim of defending the actions of the Dutch VOC in the early 1600s. It later served almost as a template for the Dutch in the course of their imperial expansion in the seventeenth and eighteenth centuries, as argued by Keene.[73] However, his argument that individual property right was central for 'international law' from Grotius to the nineteenth century will be questioned, particularly with regard to Prize law and empire.[74] Notwithstanding which, Keene's work provides a critique of the dominant paradigm of international relations by emphasizing the need to distinguish between developing intra-European norms from the nineteenth century onwards, on the one hand, and the longer history of imperialist practices within which such norms developed, on the other.

Keene does not overtly theorize how one is to understand this distinction as a way of characterizing the development of modern state-empires; a task which is explicitly taken up by Nasser Hussain's important study, *The Jurisprudence of Emergency*.[75] Hussain too takes a similarly long view of history, arguing that seventeenth-century ('English') constitutional conflicts on the nature of law and prerogative, while resolved in one sense in England-Britain, in fact continued to evolve in (English) colonial practices from the eighteenth to the twentieth century. Thus, he argues that while Coke's distinction in *Postnati* between titles of descent and of conquest was intended to put a restraint on royal prerogative in the kingdoms of descent (such as Scotland and England), such a distinction in fact enabled the less retrained use of prerogative in the colonies, particularly in India from the eighteenth century onwards.[76] Hussain insightfully interprets the mechanisms of prerogative and unrestrained despotism in the colonies as a 'shadowy' despotism marking English constitutionalism in the Isles, which flashes out clearly in certain contexts, such as the exercise of martial law in the event of riots.[77] He is thus implicitly critical of a position which sees in colonial law merely the different standards of rule adopted for metropolis and colony, because such a position does not see the violence of colonialism's features as embedded in that which claimed to be the rule of law in the 'metropolis'.

By complicating and conjoining the trajectories of English and imperial history Hussain enables a closer and harder look at the nature of European state formation, which was marked by the polarity of prerogative and law, emergency and normality. James Whitman's *The Verdict of Battle*,[78] while consciously confining its attention to an intra-European non-colonial site, contributes to an understanding of this problematic by linking European state formation and (non-colonial, non-maritime) war during this very period of the eighteenth and nineteenth centuries. His argument is that the eighteenth century did indeed witness a more limited war in the form of the pitched battle when it came to intra-European land conflicts, and this, according to him, was to be attributed to two primary reasons: the monarchical monopolization of power (not an aristocratic culture as much historiography has argued), and the clear formulation of the (law of) battle as a civil legal procedure (which had its roots in the Christian 'just war' theory). War, according to such a paradigm, was conceived of as a legitimate means to acquire property and rooted itself in a 'just war' theory aiming at the acquisition and defence of property rather than the punishment of criminal infraction.[79]

Whitman traces the decline of such a law of battle – and its corresponding practice – to the later nineteenth century, particularly as expressed in the American civil war and the Franco–Prussian conflict. This transformation in war is attributed to the decreasing legitimacy of monarchies, the rising importance of 'honour' in international relations, and the involvement of irregulars and non-military populations in a war that was increasingly difficult to contain.[80] Whitman thus insightfully raises questions on conventional, and critical, accounts of the relationship between what Nasser Hussain might have called prerogative and law, the modern state and its justifications for conflict. The book's larger, more provocative argument concerns the claim that eighteenth-century elaborations of the law of war with its explicit recognition of war as a means of property acquisition might have been more successful in containing war, than modern humanitarian attempts to restrict war to mere necessity. This argument cannot be engaged with here, except to say that a consideration of colonial war and sea battles, as undertaken by the present work, might require a certain amount of reconsideration of what precisely is meant by that which is termed the 'limited war' of the eighteenth century. For the purposes of the present set of investigations, however, it is important to underline Whitman's centring of dynastic monarchy as much as the legal rationalization of property-territory acquisition in war as germane to discerning the relations between sovereignty, jurisdiction and territory.

In such a narrative Whitman contests the more conventional account of the law of war, as given by Sharon Korman's *Right of Conquest*,[81] which had argued for a more clearly linear development in the abandoning of 'just war' theories for the slowly developing principles of national self-determination, originally attributed to the French Revolution, from the seventeenth to the twentieth century. Apart from the specific questions raised by Whitman regarding the resilience and rationality of just war theories,[82] three issues of broader import may be raised with respect to Korman's argument. First,

Korman often takes specific treaty clauses in intra-European conflicts allowing for the outmigration of subjugated peoples from the acquired territory as evidence for the principle of national self-determination.[83] This is hardly satisfying, since self-determination would have to require some form of self-government, and such treaty-clauses regarding options of outmigration were available even in the context of the dynastic monarchies of the eighteenth century, as is clear from *Campbell v. Hall*, as discussed in Part II. Secondly, these clauses were not necessarily applied and did not remain as a central feature of even intra-European conflict, let alone imperial wars, as Korman herself shows us.[84] And finally, Korman does not analyse the discrepancy between the discourses against the use of conquest as a title and the practices of conquest, and their juridical rationalization, that continued well into the twentieth century. This makes any kind of argument for a global movement from the legal principles of conquests to national self-determination difficult to sustain.

While studies of colonialism as a form of 'British' state-empire formation in the eighteenth century are not common, Sudipta Sen's *Distant Sovereignty*[85] and Mithi Mukherjee's *India in the Shadows of Empire* prove to be among the exceptions.[86] Mukherjee's broader contention is that while a central characteristic of the Indian polity is the notion of justice as equity, this notion ought to be traced to a specific configuration of imperial justice in the colonial period. The first steps – historical and conceptual – towards such a configuration are traced to Edmund Burke's speeches indicting Warren Hastings in the course of impeachment proceedings at the House of Lords. This discourse was to have provided the first template for the idea of a deterritorialized natural law standard of justice-as-equity, which is contrasted to a 'colonial' absolutist conception of law having as its embodiment the arguments and defence of Hastings's conquering actions.[87] Mukherjee argues that the Burkean idea of justice acquires a more robust shape after 1857 with the advent of Crown rule, where the monarch appears as the highest court of appeal. This image of justice in the figure of the monarch is consistently contrasted with competing ideals, whether the ruthless 'colonial' idea of *raison d'état* or self-representation in the form of independent legislatures that characterized the 'nation-states' of Europe.

Mukherjee does not take sufficient cognizance of the precise royal institutional bases of her argument about imperial justice, and such a focus would have forced a complication to the nation-state cum legislative trajectory that she takes for granted, much like standard conventional accounts of European modernity.[88] That is to say, as is argued in the present work, precisely because the institutional bases of sovereignty, as the nexus or relations between royal sovereignty and jurisdiction, were so riven with complexities from the seventeenth century onwards, it would not be possible to discern any category or narrative of the 'nation-state' in Europe during this period that was unmistakably imperial in form. This difficulty in characterizing the 'British' political form is recognized in Sudipta Sen's *Distant Sovereignty*, when he suggests *both* that the frontiers between empire and nation are obscure in the eighteenth century, and also that the Company's treatment of despotism in India ought not to be disentangled from the renewed symbolic reinvigoration of the English monarchy at the end of the eighteenth century.[89] Yet, more concerned with the establishment of the East India Company's rule as much as 'distance' at the colonial frontier, Sen is less interested in tracing the precise channels of royal jurisdiction through which the Company operated, and their implications for theorizing the relationship between sovereignty and jurisdiction. This also means that there is less attention to the institutional bases or doctrinal grammar through which imperial territorialization was accomplished.

In their study of the colonial period, Sen and Mukherjee depart from the dominant tendencies of the scholarship on the East India Company from the seventeenth to the nineteenth centuries and its relationship to 'Crown rule' post 1857. From David Washbrook and Christopher Bayly to Robert Travers and John Wilson, the trend has been to treat Company rule as a distinctive phase or regime, without investigating the channels of jurisdictions – or their rationale – on which such rule operated. Elided thereby are a whole host of jurisprudential questions, including those pertaining to subjecthood. Attributing the nature and rationale of the Company to 'local' forces within the subcontinent then becomes a way of refusing to inscribe the logic of the Company to that of an imperial logic emerging and emanating from the metropolis.[90] British institutional and ideological development are thereby steered clear of the murky waters of empire. Philip Stern's *The Company State* has been the exception in taking as its object the juridical basis of the Company in the seventeenth century as a 'body-politic' to better understand its eighteenth-century incarnations. He outlines his historiographic intention as one that 'take[s] the early Company as a body politic in its own terms'.[91] Stern then moves on to argue that his book explores a 'vision of an early modern "empire" that was constituted by a variety of competing and overlapping political and constitutional forms in both alliance and tension with the national-state and its claims to coherent and central power'.[92] The problem here is that he does not explicate one crucial feature of English corporations, which is the fact that they were seen to be 'made' by the creative power of the King.[93] This is discussed and explained in *Postnati*, and remains un-contradicted in Blackstone's *Commentaries*. Such a feature of the King's 'creative' act is, not surprisingly, germane to the Company's existence as much as to its governing and commercial capacities, as is argued from Parts I to III in this book. It is only by omitting these constitutive features that one can speak of the Company 'in its own terms'. For precisely the same reason, it would be deeply anachronistic to project on to the seventeenth century a 'national-state',[94] a category inapplicable to the form of empire that we now variously call as English or British. As mentioned earlier, political identity could not be captured by anything but allegiance to the natural person of the King well into the nineteenth century and beyond.

Stern's argument for the sovereign independence of the East India Company remains complicit with the ideological labours of the nineteenth century, and takes shelter under John Seeley's grandiose two-fold proposition: that the Company's conquests were not an 'Act of State', and that such conquests became British only when parliament asserted its rights to them.[95] Seeley's obfuscation of the detailed and long-standing bases of the Company, from the King's and subsequently the King's and King-in-Parliament's legitimation through charters and statute, constituted part of an ideology in Britain in the late nineteenth century which sought to diminish the role of the King in the British constitutional set-up, while happy to preserve it for purposes of empire. Such manipulation also enabled the screening of the development of the 'British' body-politic of the seventeenth and eighteenth centuries – the King's many bodies – and therein the violent imperialism which formed its generative grammar. Such an ideological programme amplified the masking strategies of the East India Company regime and worked to deny the plundering ways of the British Empire so as to take the moral high ground when it came to the imperialism of other European powers in the late nineteenth century. This attempted obscuring of the King, and the serious conceptual and historical difficulties it entailed, can be clearly discerned in the legal scholarship of Seeley's contemporary, F.W. Maitland.

Unlike Seeley, Maitland demonstrated an acute grasp of the contemporary late nineteenth-century constitutional position, and he did recognize that the accurate description of the situation would be that of the 'King as head of which government and parliament were organs'.[96] Maitland thereby recognized that neither 'state' nor 'nation' nor 'commonwealth' were apt as accurate legal descriptions of the state of affairs, even as some unease at the growing powers of the King/Queen is more than evident in his work.[97] While seeing in the doctrine of the 'Crown as corporation' an existing legal doctrine with effects, he at the same time finds it of little real use, arguing that, in any case, most legal work was being accomplished by statute. In fact, Maitland's essay is undertaken with the explicit purpose to demonstrate the utter inconsistencies and even absurdities of the then existing legal doctrines regarding the King/Queen and his/her bodies. It must be stated at the outset that unlike Stern, Maitland demonstrates a clear knowledge of the fact that according to English law and practice, Kings 'made' corporations.[98] While this constitutes an undeniable legal fact, what Maitland rails against is the jurisprudential doctrine that is meant to lie at its base. In his historical investigation, he traces the idea of the corporation to Roman law doctrines of corporations, and their subsequent ecclesiastical appropriations finally reaching the humble figure of the parson who is meant to form the theoretical basis of the 'Crown as corporation'. In Maitland's quip, English history told the story not of the personification of the King but his/her parsonification. And yet, notwithstanding the scholarship summoned in his essay, Maitland does not, shockingly, take into account the explicit rejection of this King–parson analogy in the explication of the King as corporation, in the discussions around the seminal case of *Postnati*, as argued in Part I. Therefore, Maitland's analogy with the parson cannot stand, resulting in the inadequacy of his theoretical critique cum construal of the 'Crown as corporation' and the King's bodies.

Considering Maitland's scholarship, it is difficult to believe that these arguments of *Postnati* were unknown to him; it might well be easier to believe that he was merely complicit in the late nineteenth-century programme of chipping away at the figure of the King, to thereby conceal the imperial logic that lay at its heart. Ernst Kantorowicz's deeply scholarly work takes Maitland as a point of departure in providing an immensely rich and intricate theoretical account of the doctrine in its genealogical and juridical dimensions.[99] Contrary to Maitland, Kantorowicz establishes the various ways in which the doctrine did in fact work in the constitutional order of England, though confining himself largely to the period before the eighteenth century. Yet, in this study of the conceptual configurations he is less concerned with the nexus of its relations that provided a generative grammar for territory and jurisdiction from the seventeenth to the nineteenth centuries, which could go a long way in explaining the rationale of imperial practice. This is a serious lacuna for such a fine study on sovereignty.

For a clue to this nexus between sovereignty and territorial jurisdiction one would need to return to Maitland, and particularly his examination of the (American) colonies as corporations and their unification in terms of the figure of the King.[100] This argumentative line, for it is little more, is amplified much more powerfully in Charles McIlwain's thesis on the constitutionality of claims made by the American colonists in the 1760s and 1770s in asserting their allegiance to the King while resisting the statutory reach of the British parliament.[101] The emerging and contested distinction between the realm and the dominions is articulated as a theoretical grid to analyse problems of jurisdiction and allegiance, particularly as they erupt in the late eighteenth century. In McIlwain's argument the problem of jurisdiction is taken with the seriousness it deserves, since his is an argument for taking the constitutionality of the American argument in the 1760s and 1770s that British parliamentary statute and particularly the powers of taxation were not applicable to the colonies, whose status in the empire was solely as subjects to the King (and assemblies) not parliament.

However, there is a tension in McIlwain's thesis. On the one hand, there is his argument about the constitutionality of the American argument which is derived from the seventeenth-century Irish critique of (English-British) parliamentary domination while affirmative of royal sovereignty. On the other hand, he appears to accept that the affirmation of parliamentary sovereignty from the period of the interregnum is in fact confirmed by the settlement of 1688–89, a perspective from which it would be difficult to take seriously enough the constitutional claims of the American colonists about kingly prerogative and sovereignty in the 1760s and 1770s. The present thesis veers towards taking the former position on the question of jurisdiction interpreting the settlement of 1688–89 as less conclusive of (English-British) parliamentary sovereignty. A position that is amplified by an investigation into the East India Company, where too the problematic of the King's jurisdiction is taken as primary, even while the vitality of royal jurisdiction is given a much more ample 'after-life' in the form of the long and arduous trajectory that the Company and ultimately direct 'Crown' rule takes. While McIlwain's thesis has received renewed attention in recent times, the sensitivity to the essential question of the King and jurisdiction is jettisoned for a more abstractly conceived 'prerogative', and is therefore less relevant for the present study.[102]

Notwithstanding McIlwain's thesis, it is his nineteenth-century predecessors who appear to have set the terms in laying the ground to conceptualize empire and its history. Henry Maine and John Stuart Mill are complicit with Seeley and Maitland in screening the specific rationale of conquest and its doctrinal bases. This, as argued through in Part III of this book, is accomplished through larger philosophico-historical theories of custom and liberty. The logic of these categories is inscribed in civilizational terms so grand as to conceal the granular details of conquest that in fact formed the lineaments of empire. Mill's philosophical work has often been falsely inducted to construct a coherent body called liberalism, from which any critique of empire aims to be no more than a critique of his double standards, rather than take aim at the moving acquisitive ratio inherent to empire.[103] I have previously argued for the irreconcilable differences between the seventeenth-century natural law tradition and Mill's liberalism which could never have a place for as radical a theory as 'natural right' – a theory which would have been able to contest empire and therefore unthinkable for Mill.[104] In fact, from Bentham to Mill and beyond, the very concept of fundamental right – often associated with the excesses of the French Revolution – was rendered suspect and exiled from any serious theorization. Even in the twentieth century, the English could not understand the demands of nationalist leaders who wished to emulate the revolutionary tradition in their conception of fundamental rights when envisioning an independent constitution.[105]

In other words, while Mill's liberalism could be construed as an attempt to guarantee specific liberties in the metropolis, it could never entertain a theory of fundamental individual right that would have challenged monarchy at home and empire abroad. In one sense, therefore, Mill's argument is entirely compatible with English thought and practice in which right is only legible through specific legal channels and a jurisdictional idiom. In this context, his defence of both the East India Company and imperialism in general, exhibiting a hierarchical differentiated set of orders, is completely consistent, as is elaborated upon in the present work. Such a defence is only strengthened by his adoption of a historical-civilizational logic having as its providential agent, Britain. An abstract focus on merely his philosophical postulates on liberties for society or the harm principle, without the English legal infrastructures that he leaves unchallenged, does little more than help create the myth of Mill as an advocate for individual fundamental rights and (genuine) self-representation.

Notwithstanding the above, among intellectual histories, Uday Singh

Mehta's *Liberalism and Empire* is most sensitive to the question of empire in the broadest sense in seeing imperial differentiation as a central nervure of liberal thought. This same philosophical argumentation revolving around sovereignty and exceptions, while on a very different register, has been acutely attended to in the works of Giorgio Agamben and Carl Schmitt. Yet such an orientation has several epistemic and political costs that can only be indicated here, since I have dealt with them elsewhere.[106] The present work analyses at its core a specific doctrinal form of sovereignty and its territorial-jurisdictional expression, along with their entailing implications. Schmitt's *Nomos of the Earth* pitches its argument at the broader conceptual level of sovereignty and territoriality, plotting a narrative about the ways in which a particular international order – itself based on a global exclusion of the non-European world – is compromised in the twentieth-century criminalization of state entities as a result of the world wars. It is the victor's justice in Nuremberg against which Schmitt poses his romance of the pre-twentieth-century international order: a romance according to which the golden age of the eighteenth century had overcome the medieval 'just cause' theory of war by formulating a doctrine of state equality among European powers.[107] While Schmitt recognizes that this form of state equality applied to European state systems and was oriented by the fact that no such rules existed for the domination of the extra-European world, he does not analyse the implications of these distinctions for a theory of the European state form. Moreover, he supplies the logic of this state form in terms of both specific seventeenth-century theories of natural right and longer-term trajectories, beginning in Renaissance reinterpretations of Roman dictatorship.[108]

Such an understanding of a state form that traverses such a long period without being attentive to either the distinctions in discourses (natural law and nineteenth-century positivism, Hobbes, Rousseau and Bentham) or their expressions in practice (English imperialism and German imperialism) is what lies at the basis of Agamben's unimpeded tracing of twentieth-century fascism to elements of the French Revolution.[109] This means that the specific configuration of norms and practices as much as their differentia, whether Mill's discourse and English imperialism or the Corporation sole and royal territorialization, is abandoned for a general theory of the state that reduces all normative vocabularies of natural right to that of state sovereignty. The theoretical possibility and empirical instance of such conversion do not account for the spatial and temporal leaps of natural right from, for instance, 1640s England to 1790s France and 1920s India, each case articulating and envisioning a polity constituted by the rational actions of natural rights-bearing individuals through (self)-representation – an issue that is taken up in the conclusion. A thesis such as that of Agamben does grave injustice to the revolutionary norms, whether based on 'natural' right or not, as much as the historically differentiated engines of power, by reducing all political concepts to a night of exception where all norms are grey. An attempt at a greater sensitivity to the more specific formulations of power – and their jurisdictional expression – is therein attempted in this study of the empire.

In the course of analysing the role of the King and the constitution of empire from the seventeenth to the nineteenth century, this work brings into relief the fact that questions of nationality arise in legal-historical terms only within the interstices of statute, Prize jurisdiction, the laws of war and the specific regulations of a long-standing militarized commerce. Thus, unlike extant broader theories of nationalism, such a history recovers in the granular contestations of law, the doctrinal as well as operational aspects of nationality from the seventeenth to the nineteenth century in the (British) empire.[110] Such a narrative helps reflect on conceptualizing sovereignty and modern statehood, as well as the nation, as generated from a historical logic of territorialization itself emerging from the manoeuvres of maritime trade as much as and maritime war. Perhaps the boundary-faking of contemporary global finance that manoeuvres through legal and strategically staged national territories owes something to this. Notwithstanding the fact that nation-states appear to have acquired an ideological root today,[111] the emergence of this norm must be traced only to the first wave of decolonization after the Second World War. This, even while the older empires, such as the French in South East Asia, merging into the newer rhetoric of American imperialism, national self-determination and territorial integrity as its correlate, appeared to have been acceptable as a norm in the wake of the world wars. For such a correlation would have been impossible in the earlier age of empires, even as newer forms of control outside the channel of juridical and political accountability emerged in both the military and economic spheres. In one sense, imperialism in the age of nation-states renewed the older East India Company policies of setting up fictive sovereignty – 'puppet regimes' – in the furtherance of class and national interests. These iterations, it is argued, are best analysed by recognizing the emergence of the nation-state era from the age of empires in the mid-twentieth century. And commerce remains the double of war – a doubling whose history is sought here, once more.

The present calls to a 'civilizational state' in global politics, while attempting to counter 'the west', only seem insecure offshoots of the civilizational imperium of the Euro-American order that constituted the late nineteenth- and early twentieth-century political order. This discourse of 'civilization' in several states does little less than conceal, pre-empt and attack communities and contestations in the name of an autochthonous and civilizational identity, while borrowing and appropriating the methods and techniques of the very imperial 'western' state-forms which they decry. The haunting presence of the earlier imperial moment in its precise mechanisms and principle is engaged with in the conclusion, in the context of the will to hope and justice that a universalist revolutionary tradition provides one with.

Note on Method

This thesis, in its conceptualization and history of empire, finds inspiration in an Aristotelian–Marxist epistemology that focuses on praxis, which is both a measure for intelligibility and the unit of narrative. Such an approach may be contrasted with the dominant model of human sciences that are rooted in the concepts of position and velocity of classical mechanics. In the latter, kinematics is taken to be independent of, and the basis for, dynamics. Space, time and motion form the (mathematical) basis for understanding and calculating the movement of (physical) objects independently of any 'inherent properties' that such objects possess (mass, for instance).[112] These physical objects are therefore construed in the image of mathematical objects, defined by their motion or rest independent of having any ratio with their medium or other objects – the inertial framework. It was the difficulty of reconciling kinematics with dynamics in the form of gravity, the distinguishing of inertia and force, that led to the conceptual and observational anomalies in Newton.[113] Whatsoever the material properties of objects, they are all the same conceived as mathematical objects in an absolute space–time. If Aristotle saw the relationship between the object and its medium in terms of an active ratio, Galileo converted this into an arithmetical difference enabling the movement of the mathematical object in a void, establishing the still dominant epistemic framework.[114]

For the social sciences, more often than not, the function of such posited, imaged *sui generis* mathematical objects takes the form of categorical identities such as 'British' and 'Indian'. These categories in themselves cannot be interpreted in terms of their ratio with other objects being the ideal inertial objects in a void-space. Even when they are said to emerge at a point in time, this does not negate their essential epistemic character of emerging whole, fully formed. Their properties, once formed, are rendered independent of their movement through space and time. No conceptual account is given of the categorical identities that are assumed to be independent of, and equivalent to, the inferential law-like generalizations that may be made about them. The old theological question of why did God not create the world one moment before he actually did applies unassailably to such an epistemology in the form of, why not begin the story from an earlier moment.[115] Neither question is answerable within the classical mechanical framework presupposing that time, space and motion are absolute and independent of the order of things. Just like Leibniz had argued, that such a conception of absolute space and time would mean that any change in the order of time and space, even hypothesized, would not affect the epistemic-mathematical object, is something that one finds exhibited in the arguments of historians who hold that neither Britain nor India was in any sense affected by empire, whether as agent or subject.[116]

But both questions, theological and historical, can be responded to if time and space are interpreted to in fact lack any absolute independence from the formation and identity of the object. That is to say, an adequate response involves the breaking down of the basic conceptions of classical mechanics such as void-space. The specific Aristotelian argument against the space-void is well known: if space was a void and therein defined as lacking in parts, impossibilities – such as motion being instantaneous and in all directions – would follow.[117] Therefore space had to be conceptualized as the 'inner' border bordering the container and the contained, action and being-acted-upon. The ratio of the acted and being-acted-upon has no *a priori* empirical correlates in terms of identities; rather, the latter are only intelligibly formed and de-formed therein. Space is not that which envelops contact but is indeed contact, and is best captured by the sensory perception of 'touch'. Unlike sight, no medium can be abstracted between what is all the same the undeniable difference of touching and touched.[118] A non-sublimable difference may disguise the actuality of force under the guise of the distinct natures of self-identity, that *a posteriori*, historically, take the form of castes, races, nations and other such identities. The touching–touch difference cannot be mediated in the way that light is held to mediate between the eye and the object. Politics as action does not proceed in space in the form of a political or national identity, but in fact forms space in the sense of jurisdiction, place being the spatial articulation of a specific authority rather than an absolute position. Thus the (British) empire did not simply expand in space, leaving both the 'British' and the 'Indian' untouched, but rather formed spaces in the multiplying regulation of jurisdictions through differentiation.

This identity-fixation also implies a grounding relativity – the relativity of motion – that Leibniz critiqued Descartes for. If More could jibe Descartes by stating, 'When I am quietly seated, and another, going [as one who is in the act of running] a thousand paces away, is flushed with fatigue, it is certainly he who moves and I am at rest',[119] imperial historians too have the last laugh saying that while imperialism might have been deeply violent, one cannot really say whether it was the 'British' or the 'Indians' who were indeed acting. Any relationship between the two leaves, once again, each identity unperturbed, since motion is but a relative change in position and not a force. It was such a theory that Leibniz questioned by arguing that causality and force were required to explain motion and change, just as the present thesis argues for the attribution of causality to empire, in the course of which identities get formed and formulated. The essential argument is that categorical identity or [the] individual is not an *a priori* but necessarily a ratio, and is only to be understood in terms of the process of individuation that has to be epistemically discerned and narratively plotted. Just as the intentionality of an action cannot be judged by mere reference with the information about the identity of the actor or the victim independent of the individual individuating in actuality, comprehending the movement of history is scarcely to be accounted for by ultimately arbitrary descriptions of particular identities assumed to be frozen in timelessness. Here the line of force or intentionality is a concept-norm, which in the present study is 'empire', in terms of which the narrative and argument in terms of sovereignty, violence and state, among other categories-in-action, are formulated.

Notwithstanding the power of Aristotelian arguments regarding force and nature, they might lend themselves to more static hierarchical formations such as the 'great chain of being' argument so favoured at one time. Though 'nature' is conceptualized as 'process' or 'actuality',[120] to cite only the most forceful example, Aristotelian arguments might also be found, in a contrary vein, to be justifying slavery as 'natural' and drive some of the most horrendous conquests of human history.[121] This tendency is detonated in Marx, as inheritor and transformer of the French Revolution's theory of universal human rights and freedom, on the basis of which is re-engineered the Aristotelian emphasis on activity. Hence Marx's description of labour as 'purposive activity' as a feature of human beings is critical for an understanding of the essentially social forms through which one is able to conceptualize the fundamental motor-categories of alienation and revolution. If labour is defined as 'purposive activity', capitalist expansion is itself based on the prior 'logic' or discernable ratio between capital and labour.[122] It is labour as 'purposive activity' that accomplishes its will to revolution in terms of recognizing the universal demand for justice, rather than rely on any faith in the so-called laws of the social and economic sciences, which do no more than reify and amplify the historical and geographic asymmetries of individual and collective right as though they were *sui generis* objects.[123]

When Marx argues that 'capital by its nature drives beyond every spatial barrier',[124] or that 'the circulation of capital is at the same time its becoming, its growth, its vital process',[125] this is because he has already abandoned the classical concepts of space and time, and rooted movement in a relationship of force between capital and labour. In his words,

> When the worker's objectified labour is, in this process, at the same time posited as the worker's non-objectivity, as the objectivity of a subjectivity antithetical to the worker, as property of a will alien to him, then capital is necessarily at the same time the capitalist, and the idea held by some socialists that we need capital but not the capitalists is altogether wrong. It is posited within the concept of capital that the objective conditions of labour – and these are its own product – take on a personality towards it, or, what is the same, that they are posited as the property of a personality alien to the worker.[126]

This relationship of force, itself formed by the process of primitive accumulation, which had violently separated the worker from his means of production, is what conditions the 'expansion' of capital, which necessarily bursts through every conceivable spatial barrier. This 'logic' is exactly that of the political right and 'free labour', and unleashing the historical impetus and dynamic force of this uniquely modern moment is essential to its revolutionary negation.[127] For it was the free labour of 'right' that was to have formed the uniquely capitalist forms of alienation, none of which were reducible to the elements of national identity or territory; it is the uniquely human feature of labour as 'purposive activity' in its socialization that can aim for and achieve a revolutionary transformation. While these questions have been dealt with in my previous works, it suffices at present to state that in its attempt to focus on concepts in their praxis as much as the refusal to take national identity, territorial loci or temporal bracket as an epistemic *a priori*, this work takes inspiration from Marx. The elemental force involved in expropriation as described in Marx in the property relation is worked outwards in tracing the constitution of territory, jurisdiction and sovereignty.

From here empire is construed as a root-norm from which emerges the dissembling of forms, whether in the false identification of territory and nation, the true distinguishing of property and person, or the perfection of conquering violence in law.

Notes

1 It could no doubt be open to question as to whether, and in what sense, political forms like the United States of America or the erstwhile Union of Soviet Socialist Republics could be called 'nation'-states, but the more limited point being made here is the clear correlation between specified territory and sovereignty in an order where sovereign entities mutually recognize principles of territorial integrity. On the other hand, even as the most cursory look at global politics shows that the United Nations Charter was hardly effective in putting an end to war or truly building a consensus on crucial issues, its normative underpinnings on territorial integrity and state sovereignty cannot be denied. Only from such a standpoint can the manipulation, perversion, reinterpretation or development as forms of practice be understood.

2 While this work in the main is a study of what is now called the English and then the British Empire from the seventeenth to the nineteenth century, the argument militates against such characterizations. For instance, the common style followed in statutes and charters describing the body-politic would be something like, 'William the Third, by the Grace of God, King of England, Scotland, France and Ireland, Defender of the Faith & c' – this is how the charter granted to the East India Company in 1698 begins. See *A Collection of Statutes and Charters with Reference to the East India Company* (1817): vii. What today is understood as political identity was defined in terms of being the King's subject throughout this period. Moreover, I continue to use the term 'King' even when at times 'Crown' was used, because this movement to the use of the word Crown is itself traced as an ideological manoeuvre to conceal the undeniable importance of the King in this period. While this will be the substance of the entire work, to suggest that this is not entirely an improbable endeavour, I cite the impeccable scholarship of Fredric William Maitland, who writes towards the end of the nineteenth century: 'I believe, however, that an habitually and perfectly ambiguous personification of the Crown – in particular, the attribution of acts to the Crown – is much more modern than most people would believe. It seems to me that in fully half the cases in which Sir William Anson writes "Crown", Blackstone would have written "King". In strictness however, "the Crown" is not, I take it, among the persons known to our law, unless it is merely another name for the King. The Crown by that name, never sues, never prosecutes, never issues writs or letter patent. On the face of formal records the King or Queen does it all.' See Maitland, 'The Crown as Corporation', in Runciman and Ryan, eds (2003): 40. Moreover, citing the Statute of 1887, he clarifies that 'her majesty, state and crown have the same meaning' (ibid.: 41). On the other hand, Fitzjames Stephen too states clearly in his discussion of treason that in England, unlike in the continent, no distinction was

made between 'state' and 'sovereign', and for the 'public', one would have to substitute 'King'; see *A History of Criminal Law of England* (1993), Vol. II: 285–87.

3 This has been well established in the scholarship cited above, particularly that of Keene and Anghie. For a philosophically sustained argument regarding the centrality of the colonial-imperial in the making of modern law, see Peter Fitzpatrick's *The Mythology of Modern Law* (1992). For an important recent argument about the crucial importance of empire in a history of modernity from a very different perspective, see Utsa Patnaik and Prabhat Patnaik, *Capital and Imperialism* (2021).

4 *Postnati*, alternatively called *Calvin's Case*, concerned the legal question as to whether Robert Calvin as a child who was born in Scotland after the Union of Crowns under King James VI and I (1603) could be considered by common law to be an English subject. The legal decision, involving luminaries such as Francis Bacon and Edward Coke, went against the resolutions of the English House of Commons and ruled that Robert Calvin was to be considered an English subject and entitled to the benefits of English law. In making this ruling the case enunciated principles of sovereignty, subjecthood and allegiance that became a central reference point for common law jurisdictions on these matters.

5 It is therefore hardly surprising that when debating the one critical issue germane to the very foundation of international law, i.e. John Austin's critique that international law could not be even considered law because there was no recognized court or institution for its adjudication, the eminent jurist Fredrick Pollock pointed to Prize law. Pollock's *The Expansion of the Common Law* (1904: 120) argued that 'It is said that a system of rules cannot be law when it lacks the sanction of a tribunal and regular decisions: and the view that international law depends merely on convention (which Lord Stowell declared to be fit only for Barbary pirates) may be found not only in text books, but reported judgments given in cases of great importance. I do not admit the validity of the argument, if the fact were as alleged; but the supposed fact is in truth subject to large exceptions. Not only international questions of allegiance and territorial jurisdiction, of the existence and consequences of war between foreign powers (whether officially recognized as sovereign states or not), of blockades and its incidents, and the like, may be and have been frequently subjects of decisions of municipal courts; but a material part of the law of war, namely the law of Prize, have been administered and still may be, by courts of admiralty, as expressly international and not local law. Prize courts administer the law of nations and have never purported to administer anything else.' Only 'Prize jurisdiction' could be enlisted as recognizable 'international law' (law of nations).

6 Norman Bentwich, in *The Law of Private Property in War* (1907), argues for the need to apply such convention to sea battles. Such was not the case and though the present investigation ends in the late nineteenth century, in fact Prize jurisdiction continued well into the world wars; its end took place only in 1949 with the English forfeiting such rights. Bentwich also notes that British law did not recognize the binding rights of international conventions, and recognized no right to property when it came to conquests or 'acts of state'. This was accomplished through rendering immune the acts of a state to the judicial review of municipal law, and early twentieth-century judicial cases in this regard referred to eighteenth-century and earlier conquest theory. Here, Bentwich notes the ways in which the British lagged behind their European counterparts, and particularly the Rousseauist principle that war was a relation between states and therefore should to the extent possible

protect the non-combatant individual and his property (see ibid.: 19–25). These issues are taken up in Part III. The consensus on only the late nineteenth century being the moment when conventions regarding prisoners were being formalized is accepted by more recent scholarship too. For very different approaches though embodying such a consensus, see Koskenniemi (2001): 87 and Whitman (2012): 223–24.

7 'Race', more than nationality or statehood, might better capture what the extant scholarship consents to be an intra-imperialist consensus on how to treat the non-western world as much as the importance of race-based ideology for its articulation, using civilization as a standard for statehood – the historical exception being the recognition of the Japanese on the imperial table. This consensus on the nature of law being an agreement amongst such imperial powers may be found in works as diverse as Carl Schmitt's *Nomos of the Earth* (2003), Edward Keene's *Beyond the Anarchical Society* (2002) and Antony Anghie's *Imperialism, Sovereignty and the Making of International Law* (2005). James Whitman, in *The Verdict of Battle* (2012), provocatively raises the question, on the basis of insightful study, as to whether the non-humanitarian principles of war prior to the late nineteenth century might indeed have been more successful in containing war than the humanitarian principles, the articulation of which witnessed the bloodiest and most bloodless (with gassing) of genocides. This is a question that unfortunately cannot be addressed here except to suggest that, certainly from the perspective of this inquiry, the pre-humanitarian period does little really to contain war. While it must be said in fairness to Whitman that he explicitly excludes maritime and colonial warfare, the question remains as to whether and how such exclusions can be made and interpreted.

8 The 'right of conquest' was well established and never refuted at least until the aftermath of the Second World War. An entry point into this literature would be the dissentient judgment of Justice Radhabinod Pal at the International Military Tribunal for the Far East, where, in his close examination of the law, he concludes that until the Second World War, war was not recognized as a crime in international life; his remark that only a lost war was a crime in its pithiness is nothing less than a deeply insightful commentary on the nature of international law and the historical developments of the period. Pertinent reference is also made by Pal to the use of the atomic bomb. For the historiography one may consult Sharon Korman, *Right of Conquest* (1996); Korman does not discuss Pal's dissentient judgment or his insights, but in her discussion of the Covenant of the League of Nations and the Kellogg-Briand Pact, does recognize that there was no consensus that aggressive war or the title of conquest were considered illegal or a crime during the inter-war years. Apart from all of this, empires were composed of diverse jurisdictions, often placed in a hierarchy of relations with one another, leading to a classification of subject populations that had different grades of rights. It was this set of features, the position of jurisdiction and subject populations and the refusal to accept territorial integrity as a principle, that constituted these entities as 'empires', which could of course take either monarchical or republican form. No doubt, contemporary developments might cause one to question the effectiveness of the United Nations charter against the use of force, and to spot continuities with the earlier period. However, it is the hope that such a discussion will gain from a clearer understanding of this earlier period, that is attempted in this book. These issues are also returned to in the conclusion of this work.

9 As R.G. Marsden, an early twentieth-century authority on Prize law put it in 1915,

emphasizing the powers of the 'Crown', 'The almost complete absence from the Statute Book of any other legislation upon the subject indicates the extent the prerogative in matters of Prize.' As he argues, statutory intervention in the sense of Prize Acts from earlier periods to the nineteenth and early twentieth centuries did not negate the powers of the Crown, and the latter's power to make and amend Prize law was grounded in its right to Prize. See Marsden (1915): 90–94.

[10] While the several legal cases of 'Prize' are examined in Parts II and III pertaining to the conquest of the subcontinent, this treatment is by no means meant to be exhaustive; for instance, the most notorious Kohinoor case, which forms part of this history, has not been undertaken here. The archive of Prize would be voluminous, and no doubt merits much further inquiry.

[11] This will be discussed and defended in Part II, and it must be remembered that the Prize charters of 1757–58 merely renewed rights of plunder, treaty-making, war and peace with non-Christian polities.

[12] A.V. Dicey's work, *Introduction to the Study of the Law of the Constitution* (1889), and the implications of his deduction of royalty – and the rise of the so-called doctrine of parliamentary sovereignty along with its implications for India – are analysed in the conclusion. Suffice it to note that in his discussion of Bagehot, Dicey does not take into account the 'paradox' of a disguised constitution or the 'double government'.

[13] Karuna Mantena's argument in *Alibis of Empire* (2010), therefore, about the 'origins' of 'indirect rule' as emerging in a particular context of the mid-nineteenth century, may well be critiqued from a much longer genealogy of empire with its logic of territorialization. The specific interpretation of Maine provided in this text too will be subject to critique in Part III.

[14] None of the growing volume of works engaging with the history of international law today sufficiently recognizes the importance of Prize jurisdiction in this regard, as is detailed in this work.

[15] The nineteenth-century international lawyers like Philimore, Westlake, Hall and Twiss, some of them even fighting cases of Prize jurisdiction; all of this is discussed in Part III. For a detailed study of Prize jurisdiction and the procedures involved in both America and England, see Francis Upton (1861).

[16] The scholarship well recognizes the relationship between Grotius and Prize money; see, for instance, Edward Keene's *Beyond the Anarchical Society* (2002) and Lauren Benton's *A Search for Sovereignty* (2009).There is little, all the same, by way of a systematic study of its history, reach and implications in terms of understanding the institutional-legal logic of modern empires. For an intellectual history of 'international relations' in Europe, see Richard Tuck, *The Rights of War and Peace: Political Thought and the International Order from Grotius to Kant* (2001).

[17] This is simply because, as discussed below in the book, civil law, as opposed to common law, was practised by the Admiralty Courts in their exercise of Prize jurisdiction, since such law was seen as most apt for the law of nations.

[18] It must of course be remembered that 'republics' such as the Dutch went on to become great empires.

[19] This point, as discussed in Part II, was declaimed by no less an authority than Lord Mansfield in the late eighteenth century. It was also noted by eighteenth-century commentators like Matens.

[20] While this is discussed in greater detail in the section on historiography in this introduction as well as in the conclusion of this book, one might mention here Hobsbawm's arguments regarding nationalism and democraticization as nineteenth-century phenomena – arguments which take no account of either the precise state forms of empire or their institutional logic. This lack of attention to the longer history of the royal person and the institutional logic of empire as discussed in the present work is also missing in what are seen to be the pioneering works of British history, such as John Brewer's *The Sinews of Power* (1989) and Linda Colley's *Britons: Forging the Nation* (1992). The important work that has been called the 'new imperial history', such as Kathleen Wilson's *The Island Race* (2003), does much to correct the singular focus on Britain by bringing in the concepts of race and empire, but does not attend to the royal and institutional logic that informs the present work. These issues are revisited in the conclusion of this book.

[21] For recent treatments of the sanctioned rights to plunder in Biblical scripture, see Robert Yelle, *Sovereignty and the Sacred* (2019): 126–56 and James Whitman, *The Verdict of Battle* (2012): 106–09, where critical historical interventions and reinterpretations of scripture, including those of Augustine, in relation to war are outlined. The acquisition of property during war or war-booty as a legal claim also existed and was elaborated upon in Islamic juristic discourse: J.T. Johnson, *The Holy War Idea in Western and Islamic Traditions* (2001): 148, as well as the texts of the *Dharmasastras*; Richard H. Davis, *The Lives of Indian Images* (1997): 60–62. It must be stated here that the present study is not directed at the conceptual vocabulary or practices of war- and peace-making 'native' to the subcontinent, important as it is and towards which C.H. Alexandrowicz's pioneering work, *An Introduction to the History of the Law of Nations in the East Indies* (1967) gestured, notwithstanding the effective critique by Keene (2002): 28. However I hope, in an ironic turn, the present book's critique of 'British' forms of war- and peace-making is not in turn accused of eurocentrism, an accusation possible only through a form of nominalism that is critiqued in this work.

[22] Hugo Grotius, in his *Laws/The Rights of War and Peace* (1625), gives a most detailed discussion of Greek and Roman practices, as well as the Biblical precedents.

[23] As is pointed out, a range of writers from John Pocock to Albert O. Hirschman, Donald Winch to David Armitage, have pointed to the new ways in which eighteenth-century Europe imagined and articulated commerce, civility and sociality as intertwined values. However, these writers do not account for the explicit militarization of commerce that was aggressively enforced through legislation such as the Navigations Laws, in their theorization of 'commerce'. This is one channel that joins the present work with my previous book, *The Infinite Double* (2015).

[24] While the revolutionary ideas of self-representation were no doubt powerful forces in the nineteenth century, they did not stabilize into an institutional set-up. Newly emerging states, whether Belgium or Germany, were not democratic polities with universal franchise, but kingdoms with limited representation and very soon empires in search of colonies; much like in Britain, one cannot afford to leave undiagnosed the artificial separation between a growing franchise in the colony with undeniable colonial and imperial belligerence. On the other hand, many of these states, particularly in Eastern Europe cannot be delinked from the wars with the Ottoman Empire.

[25] The jurisprudential basis for this doctrine is best elaborated in *Postnati*, and is discussed

in Part I. It is one that continues well into the nineteenth century, the end point of the thesis, and as argued in Part III, a conventional account that the *Stepney Election Petition* of 1886 ended *Postnati*'s doctrine of allegiance is challenged. On the centrality of the King in conceptualizing the 'public', see the above references to Fitzjames Stephen.

26 In the eighteenth century, Blackstone's commentaries well recognized the political capacities of the King, though it might be argued that attempts at juridical containing royal prerogative can certainly be marked here. It is thus no wonder that A.V. Dicey begins his *Introduction to the Study of the Law of the Constitution* (1889) with a critique of Blackstone, in whom he sees both the seemingly incompatible doctrines of royal prerogative and parliamentary sovereignty, even while both he and his predecessor recognize parliament to be 'King-in-Parliament'.

27 In a specific sense, this builds and accompanies arguments made in Govind (2015).

28 Bagehot (1867): 80.

29 Ibid.: 317. It is perhaps a matter of irony, but not entirely so, that 'double government' was the appellation used by Clive to describe the East India Company, and this is discussed in terms of John Stuart Mill's 'divided government' in his defence of the East India Company, in Part III.

30 This demands an expansive citation. Bagehot (1973) writes, 'I said in this book that it would very much surprise people if they were only told how many things the Queen could do without consulting Parliament, and it certainly has so proved, for when the Queen abolished Purchase in the Army by act of prerogative (after the Lords had rejected the bill for doing so), there was a great and general astonishment. But this is nothing to what the Queen can by law do without consulting parliament. Not to mention other things she could disband the army (by law she cannot engage more than a certain number of men but she is not obliged to engage any men); she could dismiss all the officers, from the General Commanding-in-Chief downwards; she could dismiss all the sailors too; she could sell off all our ships of war and all our naval stores; she could make a peace by the sacrifice of Cornwall, and begin a war for the conquest of Brittany. She could make every citizen in the United Kingdom, male or female, a peer; she could make every parish in the United Kingdom a "university"; she could dismiss most of the civil servants; she could pardon all offenders. In a word, the Queen could by prerogative upset all the action of civil government within the government, could disgrace the nation by a bad war or peace, and could, by disbanding our forces, whether land or sea, leave us defenceless against foreign nations'(ibid.: 31–32). Bagehot goes on to discuss what he calls 'checks' to these possibilities in terms of the impeachment of ministers, but himself recognizes these to be all too ineffective. If Bagehot did extend his purview a little, he would have seen astonishing actions – such as distributing and alienating territory – being performed in the subcontinent. See Part III for the same.

31 Dicey (1982): 390. This argument is undertaken with reference to Bagehot's views of the prerogative, cited just above.

32 Dicey cannot but recognize that the non-use of royal prerogative powers such as the 'legislative veto' cannot be taken to mean that they might not in the future in fact be used. But he does not analyse this fact. See ibid.: 107–08, note 2.

33 Therefore, Dicey does admit that while the royal veto was 'obsolete' with reference to the English parliament, with reference to the colonial assemblies it stood on 'a different footing' (ibid.: 108). If he paid a little more attention to India, even more of the

prerogative powers would be witnessed. But these facts cannot be analysed as they would threaten the neat equation Dicey wishes to posit between a parliamentary representation and the people (or the 'nation').

34 Ibid.: 182. In his critique of prerogative as a source of 'martial law' (ibid.: 409–10), it is thus not surprising that Dicey confines his attention to 'England', ignoring the imperial expansion in which the later was inextricably enveloped on historical and jurisdictional registers, as the present work tries to establish. The taking into cognizance of empire undermines what Dicey sees as many of the unique features of English law, such as the independence of the courts as contrasted with French administrative law. More recent works such as Jeffrey Goldsworthy's *The Sovereignty of Parliament* (1999) are also susceptible to such critiques from the perspective of King and empire.

35 As should be made clear, the 'elitism' of the British parliament must be measured not against the population of Britain, but against the territories and populations over whom it governed. This would prove to be an adequate measure to compare it with the parliaments of the fourteenth and seventeenth centuries.

36 Ibid.: 392, note 2.

37 Fitzjames Stephen (1993) Vol. II: 285.

38 Ibid.: 287.

39 Ibid.: 281. In fact Stephen argues that the 1848 Act clarified in statutory form the existing judicial reasoning that was found in Coke, Hale and Forster.

40 Stephen cites late eighteenth-century case law (ibid.: 278–79) to establish that 'imagining the King's death' could not be confined to proving a threat to the King's natural body. And hence conspiracies in Ireland and America which might not pose a direct threat to the King's natural body since he did not reside there could still be treated as 'treasonous' in their imagining the King's death. This once again establishes that the state was inconceivable outside the King and was never abstracted from him even if a distinction was necessarily recognized.

41 See H.G. Apostle, *Aristotle's Metaphysics* (1966): VII–IX, and Lawson-Tancred, trans., *Aristotle: De Anima* (1986), Bk II: 11.

42 Ibid.

43 The example is repeated in both texts cited above.

44 The relation posited here between Aristotelian notions and Bacon's argument is limited to the understanding of the royal soul; there is no intention to enter into the larger debate of Baconian 'New Science'.

45 These arguments are discussed in detail in Part I.

46 It must be remembered that the Dutch VOC attack on Portugal was simultaneously an attack on the Spanish Crown, both in the sense that Portugal was part of the Spanish Empire and that the Dutch were rebelling and warring against the Spanish Empire.

47 This is discussed in Part I.

48 The issues involved are discussed in Parts I and III (in relation to Henry Maine), but it might be noted here that Lauren Benton and Benjamin Strauman frame their argument on Law, Empire and '*res nullius*' by a critique of what they argue to be the false understanding of colonialism and conquest by the use of *res nullius* in scholars such as Anthony Pagden and David Armitage; see Benton and Strauman (2010). However, there is surprisingly no reference to the detailed work of M.F. Lindley, *The Acquisition and Government of Backward Territory in International Law: A Treatise on the Law and Practice*

Relating to Colonial Expansion (1926), close to a century ago that had clearly argued for the use of cession and conquest rather than *res nullius* in conquest and colonization.

49 For a more detailed discussion, see the concluding methodological 'note' in this introductory part.

50 This is discussed in detail in Part III.

51 See Rahul Govind, *Infinite Double* (2015) and 'The Fade-Out of the Political Subject: From Locke to Mill' (2013a), for the establishment of this thesis on natural law and 'liberalism'.

52 This in turn led to the discussion of forces as 'violent' and 'natural'. For a scholarly entry point into the ways in which the more general Aristotelian concept of 'motion' led to the specific one of classical mechanics, see the work of Anneliese Maier, particularly 'The Nature of Motion', in Sargent, ed. and trans. (1982).

53 For a recent instance of the attempted rendering of a study of imperialism impossible, see Jon Wilson's argument in *India Conquered* (2016) with reference to the wars between the Company and native polities in the late seventeenth century: 'As with later conquests its purpose was not to capture large areas of territory. The history of empire was a history of action in the heat of the moment, not of coherent plans and ideas. The British dominance of India grew from the cumulative response of passionate and often angry men to the situation they had put themselves in India. What marked British actions from 1686 onwards was their effort to create invulnerable pockets of British power, followed by the reluctance of the Company's administrators and soldiers to negotiate. That reluctance allowed violence to grow over the next two and a half centuries; without negotiation it was hard for the British to end wars. The result by the 1850s was that British armies had spread through every part of the Indian subcontinent.' In attributing the history of British rule to personal predilections of individuals, trivialization has achieved an acme that will be difficult to match. Therein is also protected the entire history of metropolitan Britain from the actions of these 'passionate' and 'angry' Englishmen, that are elsewhere described as 'isolated' 'lonely' and 'prickly'. Such is the reason for the devastation that is the record of empire.

54 This argument has been developed in Govind (2015).

55 'It is tempting to interpret such patters [changing and locally differentiated qualities of rule within geographic zones] as merely temporary formations on the way toward more evenly expansive territorial rule and settled sovereignties'; Benton (2009): 3.

56 Ibid.: 288.

57 While these strategies of dissimulation will be analysed in this book, for analogous arguments regarding 'fictive sovereignty', and inter-imperial arrangements of 'international law' for the conquest and exploitation in Africa, see Martti Koskenniemi (2001): 116–27.

58 After pointing to the fact that Indians had an ambiguous subject-status in English courts, Benton writes (in *Law and Colonial Cultures*, 2004: 133), 'resolving the ambiguity of such questions gained a new urgency when, continuing the British strategy of inserting themselves in the Mughal governance and revenue system, the BEIC assumed the official Mughal post of *Diwani* for the regions of Bengal, Bihar and Orissa in the region'. This is quite a stunning abridgement of an entire policy of militarized trading, war and revenue demand that has engaged the attention of an entire historiography, and which is returned to in Part II of this book. Phrases like 'inserting themselves in the Mughal governance

and revenue system' do scarce justice to either the havoc created by the British or their political subterfuges of 'double government' in the course of these events. For detailed studies which establish that the conflict between the English East India Company and the Nawabs of Bengal were deep-rooted and involved notions of legality and power, and betrayed the sustained desire for aggrandizement on the part of the Company, as well as the transformations wrought on the interconnected registers of the legal and the economic, see Chaudhury (1995); A.K. Bagchi, 'Land Tax, Property Rights and Peasant Insecurity in Colonial India' (1992); Iliopoulou (2001); Bhattacharya-Panda (2008).

59 Benton insightfully recognizes the importance of allegiance and what she calls the 'portability of subjecthood' in *A Search for Sovereignty* (2009: 3, 286). However, she doesn't investigate the doctrinal grammar or concomitant laws and practices which manifest as a strategy of sovereign territorialization, confining herself to discerning 'territorial variations' and 'uneven geographies'.

60 See David Armitage, *Ideological Origins of the British Empire* (2000): 7.

61 Ibid.: 100–46 in particular.

62 This issue is discussed and analysed in Parts II and III.

63 One notices this in Armitage's discussion of 'international law' which he sometimes takes to mean 'the law of nations', without noticing the changing historical and conceptual specificities. For instance, he argues, in *Foundations of Modern International Thought* (2013), that it is to Blackstone's *Commentaries* that one can trace the doctrine that the 'law of nations was part of the law of England'. This evinces a complete misunderstanding of 'the law of nations' which could mean something specific like Prize law, which was recognized as admiralty law in the 'British' context in relation to the Crown. It could also relate to 'natural law', and as shown in Part I, there is a detailed discussion on the law of nature, the law of nations and common law in *Postnati.* This is also taken up in the context of Maine in Part III.

64 Armitage (2013).

65 Pitts (2018): 92–108.

66 Even while recognizing the importance of the King when he states in *Foundations of Modern International Thought* that 'The royal prerogative included – indeed, still includes – sending and receiving ambassadors; entering into treaties, leagues and alliances; and making war and peace' (Armitage 2013: 140), it is indeed perplexing that Armitage spends so little on the nature of such prerogative.

67 For instance, when Pitts casts Hastings as an 'admirer of Indian civilization', or one who believed 'a cultural chasm' (ibid.: 103) to have existed between Britain and Indian legal systems, in *Boundaries of the International* (Pitts 2018: 101, 103), it is unclear how one is to understand such statements without a detailed investigation into both the nature of the system that emerged from Hastings's legal framework, and the precise contexts and reasons for Hastings to make an argument for the preservation of the indigenous. These issues are taken up in Part II, but it may be indicated here that Hastings's argument for the preservation for the 'indigenous' and for radical cultural difference was in fact to preserve the despotic authority of the Company state against channels of accountability that might otherwise have been created between Britain and India.

68 For a measure of the sovereign engineering of territory and populations and their devastating effects, as much as a critique of legal histories that elide the effects of law, see Sanghamitra Misra (2021).

[69] This relationship is engaged with in all the parts that follow.

[70] See Edward Keene's *Beyond the Anarchical Society* (2002).

[71] Ibid.: 14–40.

[72] Ibid.: 40–60.

[73] Ibid.: 76–96.

[74] Ibid.:104–05. Interestingly, Keene cites the work on Katzarov's *The Theory of Nationalism* (1964) to establish the centrality of individual property right for international law from Grotius to the nineteenth century. Katzarov indeed speaks of individual property right in this context but states that studies of the subject in international law are 'inadequate' or 'lacking', and refers to the literature on Prize law. But an investigation of Prize law and its implications for a theory of individual property is not undertaken, and this work will suggest that such an endeavour puts into question such a general framing of 'individual property right'. See Katzarov (1964): 284.

[75] See Nasser Hussain, *The Jurisprudence of Emergency* (2003).

[76] Ibid.: 22–24, 44–47.

[77] Ibid.: 102–18.

[78] J.Q. Whitman, *The Verdict of Battle* (2012).

[79] Ibid.: 95–132.

[80] Ibid.: 215–44.

[81] Sharon Korman, *Right of Conquest* (1996).

[82] Whitman (2012): 67–69.

[83] Korman (1996): 37–40.

[84] Ibid.; see in particular note 90 on p. 39 on 'natives'.

[85] Sudipta Sen's *Distant Sovereignty* (2002).

[86] Mithi Mukherjee's *India in the Shadows of Empire* (2010).

[87] Ibid.: 14–19.

[88] There are arguments in *India in the Shadows of Empire* about the 'nation-state' and 'national interest' with respect to Britain (ibid.:5), as well as 'popular sovereignty and the real representation of the people grounded in their freedom to make law', which is contrasted to the 'colonial' (ibid.: 62).

[89] Sudipta Sen (2002): xxiv, 1–27. Sen very pertinently writes, 'One of the tasks of this book is to return some of the burden of authenticity to the agents of empire, rather than lay it once more on those who were subjected in various capacities as a rejoinder in part to the ever-increasing volume of scholarship on the construction of national identity as indigenous responses to colonial rule' (ibid.: xxxi). The effort in this work has been to not limit the task to question the 'authenticity' of nationalism in the metropolis by showing the crossovers, intimacies and distantiations at its points of enunciation, as Sen demonstrates well, but to interpret empire as central to rethinking both the periodization and substantive grounds of nationalism.

[90] Partha Chatterjee in *Nation and Its Fragments* (1993: 26–34) and Nicholas Dirks in *Castes of Mind* (2001: 303–13) have persuasively critiqued Washbrook and Bayly, among others, for occluding the workings of colonial power through making an argument about (ostensive) 'Indian agency'. The effort here has been more towards diagnosing the staging of 'Indian agency' as part of a long imperial heritage going back to East India Company officials such as Hastings who argued for the setting up of 'local laws' to avoid accountability. What is thereby accomplished is the refusal to treat the Company as a

function of the imperializing metropolis. The present works builds on a previous critique of the historiography – including the work of C. Bayly, D. Washbrook, R. Travers and J. Wilson – undertaken in Rahul Govind, 'The King's Plunder, The Kings' Justice: Sovereignty in British India' (2017a). Bayly's strategy of protecting metropolitan empire from the Company is indicated even in his works on global history, where one might have expected a greater sensitivity to global empire. In *Making of the Modern World*, he states, 'The decline of the Saffavids and the Mughals let loose a great wave of turbulence which stretched from Mesopotamia in the West to Thailand in the East. The main beneficiaries were the European powers, perched hungrily on the periphery. Between 1757 and 1765 the English East India Company seized the rich weaving and rice growing territory in Bengal. Local conditions and local conflicts made this possible' (Bayly 2004: 90). While his earlier work, *Imperial Meridian*, had 'argued' that, 'For instance, the critical events of the conquest of Bengal between 1757 and 1765 were driven by the conflicts between Indian rulers jealous of their trade and revenue privileges and Company personnel terrified at the prospect of their loss of investment' (Bayly 1989: 58).

[91] Philip Stern, *The Company State* (2011): 6.

[92] Ibid.

[93] Ibid.: 7–8. This lack of attention to the royal basis of the Company's corporate capacity and specific charters leads Stern to argue, with regard to the famous *East India Company v. Thomas Sandys* (1684), that 'The judges' arguments, particularly those made by Jeffreys, need to be seen not as a confirmation of the Company's position but as introducing a third side, the Crown, into the debate' (ibid.: 57). As all three parts show, including Part I which specifically analyses the Sandys case, right from the beginning the King was an irreducible component of the juridical and constitutional basis of the Company. See note 98 below.

[94] Ibid.: 6.

[95] The line from J. Seeley, cited by Stern as authority, reads as follows: 'The sum of what I have urged is that the conquest of India is not in the ordinary sense a conquest at all because it was not the act of a state and was not accomplished by the army or money of a state.' See Seeley, *Expansion of England* (1902): 214. This book will work towards establishing the obfuscation spawned by such a sentence on the nature of the state, the army and empire. One might begin by pointing to the fact that a court case roughly contemporancous with Seeley confirms the delegated sovereignty of the Company and the fact that its acts could be cognized as 'acts of state'. See *The Secretary of State in Council of India v. Kamachee Boye Sahaba*. The Lords of the Committee of the Privy Council conclude their judgment on the appeal in *The East India Company v. Kamachee Boye Sahaba* as follows: 'The result, in their Lordship's opinion, is, that the property now claimed by the Respondent has been seized by the British Government, acting as a Sovereign power, through its delegate, the East India Company; and that the act so done, with its consequences, is an act of State over which the Supreme Court of Madras has no jurisdiction.' This followed a long series of court judgments on the delegated sovereignty of the East India Company and its immunities from a municipal court, beginning from the *Nawab of Arcot v. East India Company* in the 1790s; see https://swarb.co.uk/nabob-of-the-carnatic-v-east-india-company-28-jan-1793/.

[96] See Maitland, 'The Crown as Corporation', in Runciman and Ryan, eds (2003): 40.

[97] One has already drawn attention to the fact that Maitland notes that the deployment of

the term Crown cannot obfuscate the fact that it is the King/Queen being referred to.

[98] Maitland argues, in *Township and Burrough*, that with regard to charters, 'the King makes something. He constitutes and erects a body-corporate and politic in deed, fact and name (in er, facto, et nominee)' (Maitland 1898: 18). The classic juristic doctrine of corporations often refers to Coke, who had 'reported' that 'none but the King alone can create or make a corporation' in the case of the Sutton Hospital in 1612; this juristic contention remains in Hale, Blackstone, Smith and beyond. See the chapter on corporations, chapter eighteen in Book one from Blackstone's *Commentaries on the Laws of England* (1765) and Adam Smith, *Wealth of Nations* (1999 [1776]): 142. The King 'made' the corporation independently or in parliament and even 'prescription' was interpreted by Blackstone, as in the case of London, as presuming the King's consent which could no longer be remembered. The King was seen as involved in all the four ways mentioned by Coke in the Sutton Hospital case, i.e. common law, as by the King himself, the King's charter, (King-in-)Parliament, and prescription (as 'lost grant'). More recently, Paul Halliday, examining Coke and Hale, among others, writes: 'In his report on the case of Sutton's Hospital, Coke recognized that Parliament had passed an act for the creation of the hospital. But he explained that the act did not create the corporation, it simply permitted the establishment of one, which the King then made.' A little later, with clear reference to the King, he goes on to say that 'Throughout the seventeenth and eighteenth centuries, all commentators recognized the sole power of the sovereign to make corporations.' See Halliday, *Dismembering the Body Politic* (1998): 32–33. It is only in the mid nineteenth century that one sees *general* statutes enabling the incorporation of joint-stock companies, such as the critical one of 1844. However even here, the King in the form of the Privy Council is given central importance in the registration of companies. B.C. Hunt argues that the 1720 'Bubble Act' reiterated the centrality of the Crown, but also notes the increase in incorporation by Special Acts beginning with canal and water companies in the late eighteenth century. See B.C. Hunt, *Development of the Business Corporation* (1936). In general, the fact that a parliamentary act involves the King's act and cannot be considered antithetical to the King is a theme and problematic that this book constantly returns to.

[99] See E. Kantorowicz, *The King's Two Bodies* (1957).

[100] See Maitland, 'The Crown as Corporation', in Runciman and Ryan, eds (2003): 41–45. In a separate chapter of this volume Maitland also has a brief ten-page discussion of the 'unincorporated body' whose historical development is less clearly sketched out except for its connection with the trust and 'uses'; one feature appears to be its limited time-period as illustrated by a sixteenth century statute. Ibid.: 60.

[101] See Charles McIlwain, *The American Revolution: A Constitutionalist Interpretation* (1923).

[102] Eric Nelson, *The Royalist Revolution: Monarchy and the American Founding* (2014): 6–7. Nelson explicitly traces his broader argument to McIlwain's thesis on the importance of prerogative but sees its distinctive contribution as lying in the retention of the 'royal' prerogative in the 'republican' form of the American president. Here Nelson doesn't engage directly with the relationship between *dynastic* monarchy and prerogative, and neither is there a larger reflection on such a modern institutionalization of prerogative and its relationship between republicanism and democracy as for instance undertaken in G. Agamben's *State of Exception* (2005), where the function of the American president is specifically analysed.

[103] This might well be true of even the sharpest critiques of J.S. Mill from the ground of empire, such as that of Bhikhu Parekh, 'Decolonizing Liberalism: A Critique of Locke and Mill', in Alexander Shtromas, ed. (1994): 85–103, and Uday Singh Mehta, *Liberalism and Empire* (1999).

[104] See note 40 above.

[105] This issue is taken up in the conclusion of this work.

[106] See Rahul Govind, 'Criminalizing unto Death' (2021a).

[107] Carl Schmitt, *Nomos of the Earth* (2003 [1950]).

[108] See Carl Schmitt's *Political Theology* (1985) and *Dictatorship* (2014).

[109] See Giorgio Agamben, *State of Exception* (2005).

[110] This is the case for the major studies of nationalism, whether they be those of Ernst Gellner, Benedict Anderson or Eric Hobsbawm. The present work builds on an earlier critique of these perspectives undertaken in Rahul Govind, 'Nation-State in the Age of Imperialism' (2013): 48–58.

[111] I have elsewhere argued that the root of the paradigm of nationalism, that is to say, the origins of the idea of a community that is in itself sovereign, requires to be traced to the Christian perception of Judaism, a perception that haunts the development of the modern nation-state, rather than familiar notions such as liberalism and democracy. The intelligibility of sovereign community is otherwise difficult in the institutional–ideological contexts of empire which this work tries to establish as central until the twentieth century. See R. Govind, 'The Haunting Image of the Frozen Jew (in Christian Self-Understanding), the Self-Determining Universality of Human Reason and Anticipating the Secular Nation-State: From Hobbes to Kant and Beyond' (2023), and 'Equality, Right and Identity: Rethinking the Contract through Hobbes and Marx' (2011b).

[112] See Louis De Broglie, *The Revolution in Physics* (1953): 'One of these hypotheses was that the framework of space and time in which we seek almost instinctively to localize all of our sensations is a perfectly rigid and fixed framework where each physical event can, in principle, be rigorously localized independently of all the dynamic processes which are going around it. Thereupon, all the evolutions of the physical world are necessarily represented by modifications of local states of space in the course of time, and that is why in classical science dynamic quantities such as energy and momentum appeared as derived quantities constructed with the aid of the concept of velocity, kinematics thus serving as the basis for dynamics' (ibid.: 14–15).

[113] In the words of the mathematician Hermann Weyl, '[Newton] accomplishes only the dynamic separation of uniform translation as the pure inertial motion of a body uninfluenced by external forces, from the other states of motion; but he does not succeed in isolating the state of rest among these translations.' In fact, according to Weyl, Newtonian gravity is a 'dialectical dodge', and the assumption is that the universe has a centre and the centre is at rest, even if the common centre of the solar system moves uniformly along a straight line. Therefore, 'no attempt, whatever [is] being made to give a reason for this identification of the centre of gravity the planetary system with the hypothetical stationary centre of the world. Weyl (2009):100–01.

[114] See E.A. Moody's detailed study, 'Galileo and Avempace', in *Studies in Medieval Philosophy, Science and Logic* (1975): 203–86. Moody argues, 'This ambiguity and paradox, implicit in Galileo's conception of space, has haunted classical physics ever since his time – to

fulfil the needs of physics, space must be both full and empty, corporeal and incorporeal, real and ideal, at the same time. Why did this paradox not bother Galileo? How was he able to entertain the assumption that ponderable bodies can be compared, precisely with respect to weight with the weightless void? He could do so, because he conceived of relative weight and relative density to be determined by arithmetical difference, and not by ratio or proportion. For though we cannot divide a finite quantity by zero and get a finite quotient, we can subtract zero from a finite quantity and get a finite reminder. But velocity of a natural motion, for Galileo, was determined by the density of the mobile body, less the density of the medium; hence if the latter is zero, the speed will be of a finite degree, uniquely determined by the density of the mobile body. For Aristotle, by contrast speed is determined by the ratio of the densities of mobile body and medium; consequently, if the medium is of zero density, the velocity must be infinite' (ibid.: 215). See also the work of Anneliese Maier referred to in note 52 above.

[115] Leibniz's Fourth Letter to Clarke, in R. Ariew, ed. *G.W. Leibniz and S. Clarke Correspondence* (2000): 15, 24. Towards the end of the letter Leibniz explains his critique of the void, on Aristotelian terms.

[116] In note 53 above, attention has already been drawn to Jon Wilson's retention of the passionate, prickly, lonely, angry Britisher as the analytic anchor for centuries of imperial conquest, while note 90 refers to C. Bayly and D. Washbrook's strategy of attributing imperialism to Indian contexts, to 'mind the gap' between Britain and India. On the other hand, critics of such views, such as Partha Chatterjee, in *Lineages of Political Society* (2012a): 13–14, presuppose a 'gap' by hypothesis of a core of autonomous Indic alterity that is recoverable, with the right effort, notwithstanding centuries of empire. He thus is able to argue, building on Sudipta Kaviraj's work, that the 'West' and India were to be characterized by 'alternate sequences', where the relationship between rational bureaucracy, the welfare state, universal franchise and industrialization, in their sequence, was to have differed in the 'West' compared to that in 'India'. Thus none of these terms, whether franchise or industrialization, is seen to be analysable in terms of the logic of empire, but rather they are meant to be abstract self-sustaining categories that might be differently sequenced in different places, like 'India' and the 'West'– identities that are meant to pre-exist such phenomena. This formulation supplements that of an autonomous peasant community which is understood to have remained 'autonomous' in relation to the entire apparatus of the colonial economy from land and property to trade and law, and is a feature that is traceable to Chatterjee's early work. In *Bengal 1920–1947: The Land Question* (1984), Chatterjee had argued that to understand anti-state and anti-authority mass upsurges such as were witnessed in twentieth-century colonial Bengal, one would have to posit a distinction between two domains: the first one 'organized according to legal political principles laid down by the state', including 'the legal-political requirements of colonial appropriation', and the other domain to exist outside this (ibid.: xxxviii–xlviii and 105–06). Even while such is the theoretical model, in the course of the text, drawing on the extant literature, Chatterjee himself documents the impossibility of maintaining this distinction, whether between the colonial state/economy and the peasantry or between organized (anti-colonial) politics and the peasantry. In fact, as he states at the end of ten chapters: 'We have not, of course, produced any evidence here on the basis of which we could hazard a hypothesis about the mechanics of this autonomous domain of politics. To do this we would need to know much more about

the social ideology of the peasantry in eastern Bengal, about the activities of the so-called "itinerant maulavis" who emerged in this period as a sort of organic leadership of the Muslim peasantry, about the channels and modes of communication through which information about developments in provincial politics filtered down to the village and those through which news was passed from village to village. We would then know if what we have called unorganized politics also has an identifiable structure and how far politics unorganized is really "unorganized". But unfortunately, we do not have data of this level and range for any of the eastern or north Bengal districts.' Notwithstanding this acknowledgement on p. 125 of the work, and the evidence for the linkages between peasant movements and organized parties like the Congress and the KPP that Chatterjee provides by drawing on the extant work of historians such as H. Sanyal and B.B. Chaudhuri, the preface adopts this very same model of 'organized' and 'unorganized' as the work's distinctive methodological orientation (ibid.: xxxviii–xlviii). Fighting free of the need for any evidentiary substantiation, and rather than following the dicta of the need to 'do much more', this very methodological assumption reappears towards the end of *Nationalist Thought and the Colonial World* in 1986, in *The Nation and its Fragments* in 1993 (p. 171), and yet again in 'Democracy and Economic Transformation' in 2008. The resultant schema of a peasant community as a category, aspects of which could have remained 'autonomous' in the colonial period as well as the several decades of the post-colonial period, has however been overwhelmingly refuted by economic historians as much as those historians studying the interlocking aspects of a colonial agrarian structure and peasant politics even as this very same under-theorized 'autonomy' is replicated in the analysis of 'nationalism'. Marxist scholars such as Sumit Sarkar and Tom Brass have effectively critiqued such a line of argument, from which the present critique draws.

117 See R. Waterfield, trans., *Aristotle's Physics*, Bk. IV, 6–9 (1999).

118 See H. Lawson-Tancred, trans., *Aristotle: De Anima*, Bk. II, 11 (1986).

119 Cited by Bergson in *Matter and Memory* (1912): 105. Many of these arguments are indebted to Bergson's work on the nature of motion, with reference to the Greeks as much as classical mechanics.

120 For a forceful argument on the importance of action to conceptualize the problem of knowledge and individuation, see Edward Halper's detailed commentary on the central books of Aristotle's *Metaphysics* in *One and the Many in Aristotle's Metaphysic: The Central Books* (1989).

121 See Anthony Pagden's *The Fall of Natural Man: The American Indian and the Origins of Comparative Ethnology* (1987).

122 These propositions build upon previous work, such as that undertaken in *The Infinite Double* (Govind 2015).

123 This dimension has specifically been explored in 'Method Object Praxis: Marx and the Historians of Science', in Renny Thomas and Gita Chadha, eds, *Mapping Scientific Method: Disciplinary Narrations* (2022).

124 Karl Marx, *Grundrisse* (1993): 524.

125 Ibid.: 517.

126 Ibid.: 512.

127 I have argued for the conjugation of primitive and capitalist accumulation in Marx, in 'Capitalism and Imperialism: A Vanishing Point?' (Govind 2022b: 29–46).

PART I

Sovereign Kingship

Multiplying Jurisdictions and Degrees of Allegiance in the Seventeenth Century

Introduction: The King's Bodies

This part outlines the jurisprudential and conceptual basis for understanding the ratio of the various jurisdictions that composed what is retrospectively known as the 'British' empire in the seventeenth century.[1] It argues that the celebrated case of *Postnati* (1608) affirmed kingship as a principle of diverse jurisdictions, which enabled a framing of empire that remained at the end of the century and was to continue well beyond. It was only such jurisprudence of kingship that rendered intelligible the composition, expansion and multiplication of various types of jurisdictions that constituted the empire, whether in the Americas or in the Indian subcontinent. A particular manifestation of this jurisprudence was the unique powers attributed to kingship, which enabled it to constitute corporations (whether a municipal/city corporation or those such as the East India Company) as well as decide on matters of war, peace and foreign affairs – the latter including the powers to grant commissions of Prize (as were granted to the East India Company). To grasp such an imperially differentiated formation, it has been found necessary to enter into the jurisprudential understanding of kingship, jurisdiction and territory (the initial sections of this part) so as to discern the legal bases on which the East India Company operated in its military, commercial and legislative capacities, on land and sea (later sections of this part[2]). Case law, jurisprudential and philosophical writings, statutes and royal charters, and historical records form the basis of such an interpretation.

But for the civil wars and the interregnum, it might be contended that kingship gave unity, and therein identity, to the ('English') empire in its diverse jurisdictions during the long seventeenth century. The clearly articulated constitutional position of *Postnati* (1608) defined kingship to have the following three essential features: the King in his natural person was the object of allegiance; he was essential for the enactment of law (statutory or common law); and he was the source of jurisdictions distinct from both common law and parliamentary statute. None of these features was denied by the settlement of 1689–90, a denial that certainly characterized the period of the civil wars and the interregnum. Such features marked an empire which involved and included the distinct kingdoms and jurisdictions of England, Scotland, Ireland, Wales, the county palatines, Gascoigne, the Isle of Man, and territories-colonies in the Americas and settlements of the East India Company in the Indian subcontinent. The 1533 Henrican Act of Restraint of Appeals had defined England as empire and the King as the supreme head of a body-politic composed of various jurisdictions; the King was Pope of the realm.[3] In 1603, James VI had by inheritance become the King of both England and Scotland. And just a few years later, the precise nature of kingship in relationship to the body-politic in its diverse jurisdictions was clarified in the celebrated case of *Postnati.*

The judges of *Postnati* (1608) articulated the position of the King as the supreme head of the body-politic and specifically affirmed it as the fulcrum of various forms of law-jurisdictions that were differentiated in space, from the kingdoms of Scotland and Ireland to 'outposts' in the Americas. It is important to recognize that the judges articulated their position in refutation of the resolution of the House of Commons and the juridical positions which had held that allegiance was due to the laws and *not* to the King.[4] In their own formulation of the constitutional position, the judges of *Postnati* not only emphasized the allegiance due to the *natural person* of the King, they also thereby outlined a theory of the relationship between the King and his jurisdictions, as is closely analysed in the next section. Such a conception of kingship drew upon certain strands of Elizabethan jurisprudence on the King's bodies,[5] where natural and political capacities were ineluctably conjoined into a unity – a unity that in turn was capable of unifying and multiplying jurisdictions. It was in such a capacity, where the King conjoined *both* the natural body and political jurisdictions, that kingship founded and formed the body-politic. Such an understanding of the King as the autonomous origin – unity and source – of the body-politic was disrupted by the civil wars and the interregnum, but re-emerged thereafter throughout the century, notwithstanding the settlement of 1688–89. *Postnati* retained its judicial force,[6] whether in jurisprudential writings, or case law, or in the legal practices involved in the American colonies or East India Company settlements.

This emphasis on the conjoining of the natural and political bodies should be taken as a distinctive formulation of hereditary monarchy because, at the time, there were various kinds of elective monarchies embodying different partitions of power between individuals and assemblies. It has been argued that the early modern absolutism was distinctive in the emerging dominance of the hereditary form rather than characterizations of royal power.[7] In England, the importance of kingship can be measured by common law in the paradigmatic form of *Postnati*, as well as by the 'natural law tradition' associated with Thomas Hobbes and John Locke. Among the several crucial differences, which are analysed below, one may signal right away the absence of a theory of the King's bodies in the latter, which reflected deeper differences on the conceptualization of 'nature' and 'law'.[8] In a broad sense, notwithstanding the debates surrounding the constitutional implications of the settlement of 1688–89, it will be argued that the jurisprudential basis of the King's unique prerogative powers in forming corporations and acting as a source of jurisdiction distinct from that of (English) parliamentary statute was confirmed – the conceptual account of which was the theory of the King's bodies. The latter in the form of the unique royal prerogative at times became the basis for the assertion of various kinds of such jurisdictions from Ireland to the American colonies, from the 1640s to the 1760s. For instance, William Molyneux in the 1690s affirmed a systematic and long-standing discourse, though not necessarily one affirmed by the emerging case law, when he insisted on the King's prerogative powers so as argue for the autonomy of Ireland in relationship to the English parliament – a constitutional issue that would come to a boil in the next century with the arguments of the American colonialists that drew on the Irish discourse.[9] This set of arguments resisted what they perceived to be English parliamentary interference in their legislative autonomy, which they upheld as subjects of the King who were to be governed through a channel of kingly jurisdiction (and their colonial assemblies) distinct from that of the English parliament.

While the constitutionality of the colonial 'case' and the derivation of powers from the King's grants have been much discussed and debated in the extant literature,[10] this part will supplement its discussion of the constitutional arrangement by analysing the less-examined channel of the King's specific governmental and jurisdictional authority that formed the basis of the East India Company – its military and commercial rights, as well as the authority of and over its settlements in the Indian subcontinent. On the whole, it will be shown that the Company and its settlements need to be understood and analysed in the light of the general ground of kingship and its particular role in jurisprudence of conquest, allegiance and subjecthood in the jurisdictionally differentiated body-politic(s) of the seventeenth century. The Company and its bases thus have to be interpreted as a specific form of imperial expansion that is enabled by the kingship and its unique powers, apart from that of parliamentary statute.

Any narrative about understanding the seventeenth century solely in terms of the increasing powers of the English parliament in relation to the King fails to attend to the juridically and spatially differentiated nature of the body-politic composed of various settlements, from Scotland and Ireland to the American colonies and the East Indian outposts. Moreover, the King was constitutionally considered germane even to parliamentary legislation since all parliamentary bills required his assent to become law; hence King-in-Parliament. Apart from the civil wars and the interregnum, this power of the King in relationship to statute – including the implied power to veto – remained intact in the 1690s and was left undisturbed by the 'bill of rights'. In addition, the King retained prerogative powers unique to his person, from which flowed his ability to constitute corporations, grant patents for establishing colonies, call and dissolve parliament, grant commissions for reprisals, and declare war and peace. Allegiance, or what we might understand as a mixture of subjecthood and citizenship, was owed to the King's natural person, while even 'imagining' his death, or that of his heirs, constituted high treason.[11] None of this was to change even in the nineteenth century.

When the judges of *Postnati* held kingship to be the foundation of laws as much as the diverse jurisdictions, they were emphatically affirming that the identity of the body-politic lay in laws, and that laws were themselves rooted in the King. The King in a sense founded laws, and wielded his prerogative powers even in a context when no laws could be seen in operation, such as in conditions of conquest, war or foreign jurisdiction. The ephemeral contingency of 'nation' – or community as an ethno-linguistic group – is well illustrated by key juridical texts and cases repeatedly invoking John Fortescue's words about the unity and continuity of the kingdom lying in its laws and not in any particular nation. In the oft-repeated words of Fortescue, the kingdom had historically been possessed by diverse nations, from the Romans to the Danes to the Normans to the English, with the kingdom finding its identity and continuity in its specific laws.[12]

Postnati explicitly repudiated quasi-republic arguments which held that sovereignty was artificial and the result of a collective contract by a people or nation. In the context of England, legally speaking, a community with political and legal powers was considered a corporation, a body-politic. But a corporation had to be incorporated by the King. This was so because a corporation as an artificial construction did not have a soul and therefore required grounding in the authority of the King in his natural person, who had the power to form corporations and body-politics.[13] This was the reason why allegiance was owed to the natural person of the King, and such an understanding reverberated as much in jurisprudential thought as in legal practice well beyond the seventeenth century.

The importance of the King thus lay in its being a 'principle' of the body-politic. Only through the acts of the King could the body-politic exist, remain the same in time and swell in space, whether through territorial conquest, 'colonization' (where subjects settled in foreign lands on the basis of the King's grants), or the delegation of sovereign powers to corporations such as the East India Company to war, trade and govern settlements. While each of these instances takes shape in this long seventeenth century, only a systematic analysis of the role of the King enables this history of the changing morphology of empire to become legally legible, or even intelligible. The principle of imperial expansion therein can only be derived from the specific prerogative powers of the King, including his war- and peace-making authority.

The nature of empire, sovereign rule and laws lies in the various ways by which diverse jurisdictions were either inherited or incorporated into the body-politic by *actions* of the King. Jurisdictions therefore depended on a historical understanding of their status, a status that was embodied in what were called the 'titles' of the King, and which included inheritance as well as conquest. While these titles may mark the origin of a jurisdiction, with time the nature of the jurisdiction could change: a dukedom could become a kingdom. And so, characterizing the precise nature of jurisdictions was jurisprudentially delicate as well as politically volatile. Moments of crisis threw up questions on the nature of jurisdictions that did not find easy or clear-cut answers – the nub of which was the jurisprudence around the King's conquests, and such modes of power and incorporation that constituted the shifting body-politic and a differentiated subject-status.

For instance, if Ireland was initially considered conquered territory, it was soon enough 'settled' with and by English law. Yet, as was indeed asked, how was the 'conquest' of Ireland to be distinguished from the Norman 'conquest'?

In response to such delicate questions, common lawyers like Mathew Hale differentiated the category of conquest from within, while philosophers like Molyneux openly challenged distinctions such as those made between the Norman conquest and the Irish conquest. It was thus no surprise that it was also asked whether the Dutchman William's 'accession' in 1688–89 was indeed a 'conquest', something affirmed by many contemporaries, which raised difficult constitutional questions on the relationship between sovereignty and jurisdiction. Analogously, legal principles authorizing the incorporation of Ireland appeared to parallel the incorporation of the 'regency' of Bombay, just as the prerogative powers of the King that enabled his chartering a Company for foreign trade were legally held by some to be indistinguishable from his powers to set up a mart in England or give exclusive rights to the export of butter and cheese.[14]

If *Postnati* had established that the subject in Scotland could inherit in England as the King's subject, the relationship between property, laws and kingship was clearly reaffirmed. Yet the nature of subjecthood was also dependent on jurisdiction, itself traced to the King's titles, whether of inheritance or conquest. The writings of Thomas Hobbes and John Locke are interpreted and reinterpreted within this specific historical-cum-jurisprudential topos as much as the historical contexts of the specific and varied articulations between King, conquest and property. The general lack of this specific contextualization in much of current historiography has meant that insufficient attention has been paid to Hobbes and Locke and their specific contentions on conquest and property, resulting in the far too general and familiar trope of the 'social contract'. Hence this part interprets Hobbes and Locke in the impinging historical and jurisprudential context of the King's many bodies and his multiple jurisdictions – a context that is challenged but which therefore remains crucial to consider.

This emphasis on kingship is not meant to undercut the role of parliaments or the courts; the former too, it might be recalled, was conceived of as a King's Court.[15] Court judgments were themselves interpretations of the statutes and declarative of the laws. In the words of the all-important Act for the Restraint of appeals, the King was incorporated with the people just as the people were incorporated with him; he was the head, they the body-politic.[16] While individuals and communities did indeed have rights, they did not have sovereign rights in the common law tradition. The importance of analysing court judgments in such a common law tradition is that these cases in their reiterated 'logic' come close to a framing of constitutional principles. They reflect not merely the contemporary understanding of the subject at a point in time but serve as critical nodal reference points for successive judgments across time. *Postnati* was a central reference point to the eighteenth-century case, *Campbell v. Hall*, and continued to be a crucial reference point for defining citizenship into the late nineteenth century. *Stepney Election* (1886) upheld the legal force of the principles enunciated in *Postnati*,[17] even though there might be controversy over the way it might also have parted ways with it.

As distinct from political and philosophical treatises, legal cases emerged from, as well as oriented, specific forms of political action. In this sense, they touched and were touched by historical events, in a manner different from other forms of discourse such as philosophical texts. Historical events acquired a theoretical status and resting point in a continually cross-referencing jurisprudential tradition. Closely linked to concrete historical developments, they are therefore unlike the postulates of a philosophy that one might encounter in theoretical treatises. It is in the light of this case law, its jurisprudence as much as the militarized practices of its politico-discursive context, that the classical theories of state as advanced by Thomas Hobbes and John Locke are analysed.

Notions of sovereignty, consent and conquest are measured against the common law tradition, institutional self-understanding, and historical acts such as the trades and wars of the King and his chartered East India Company. The concluding sections on the East India Company underline the ways in which the problem of political territorialization is not identical with the extensions of English statutory legislation, and it is this difference that is occupied by the powers unique to the King. With time, such a difference may be historically bridged or reconfigured (as in Ireland) as well as bridged, but simultaneously destroyed (as in the Americas, where the fight for independence was initially against English parliamentary interference). The larger story of this book, beginning with this first part, is the narration of the complex ways in which these particular powers of the King enabled the East India Company and its jurisdictions. The emergence, form and growth as it related to parliament, and was reconfigured in the aftermath of 1857 when the Crown was declared sovereign, forms the theoretical marrow of this study.

Beginning with a critical discussion of common law principles on kingship, allegiance and conquest through a study of *Postnati*, this part then analyses these themes in the writings of the eminent jurist Mathew Hale. Hale is seen to rearticulate important principles on the nature of kingship, the body-politic, and the laws of war and peace, in the aftermath of the interregnum. In the light of this discussion, the arguments of Hobbes and Locke, as pertaining to the themes at hand, are investigated and analysed. All of this foregrounds the contestations and formulations of fundamental categories like sovereignty, prerogative, allegiance and conquest, as a constellation crucial to understand the nature of the empire and its metastasis.

As a particular illustrative channelling of this constellation, this part then turns to the operations of the East India Company by beginning with a discussion of what was called the Great Monopoly case (*East India Company v. Thomas Sandys*, 1684), to establish the fact that the Company's actions operated as a branch of royal prerogative, which included letters of marche, Prize and the Admiralty Courts. The latter was construed to issue from the domain of the King's exclusive war- and peace-making authority, the domain of foreign affairs. This issue was clarified in the King's Bench judgment on the case. While in the 1690s, parliamentary statute intervened to ground the corporate trade to the east, the King's powers of incorporation remained untouched. Hence, his specific charters were required to give a legal basis to the governing powers of the Company in its settlements in the east. An examination of the close interlinkage of King and Company rounds off the discussion of the importance of royal authority in determining the specific modes and nodes through which sovereignty crystallizes on land and sea. Sustaining this argument requires interweaving the historical basis of royal Prize jurisdiction and its relevance for the larger jurisdictional bases of Company rule, as is undertaken. The traditional philosophical focus on Hobbesian and Lockean 'social contract' would prove to be unhelpful as a theoretical lens in understanding either the jurisprudence or history of the empire and its jurisprudential-jurisdictional expressions.

Sovereign Kingship, the Degrees of Allegiance and the Ends of Conquest: *Postnati* and Common Law

Postnati is a succinct articulation of a specific legal resolution of complex philosophical, jurisprudential and institutional questions. Its importance cannot be overestimated, and it was singled out as the definitive legal resolution on issues of allegiance and subjecthood by the next most critical statement on the subject, i.e. Mansfield in *Campbell v. Hall* (1774). The issue to be adjudicated was whether a Scotsman born after the union of Crowns in 1603 had rights to inheritance in England. The case, and its final resolution, reflected deeply, systematically and acutely on the relationship between sovereignty, allegiance and the laws, and in effect rejected the position of the Houses of Parliament on the crucial matter of allegiance. Sovereignty was clearly established as monarchical sovereignty and the conceptualization of the King in his/her various capacities was therein definitively clarified.

One has to initially understand that the very question of the subject's rights to inheritance is posed in terms of the relationship between the laws and the King. Citing Fortescue, lawyers appear to agree on the fact that 'nations' do not constitute sovereignty. Rather, the laws of the kingdom of England ensured that despite being ruled by several nations – the Romans, Britons, Danes, Saxons, Normans and English – it was the laws that provided the element of continuity.[18] Successive nations each violently establishing itself in turn was not considered disruptive, because monarchical sovereignty and its laws provided the crucial element of continuity and identity. However, the question of the nature of the laws of the kingdom and the King was posed more acutely when it came to the diversity of laws in diverse spaces that were nevertheless held to be unified at any given moment in time, i.e. the nations of the English, Scots, Irish, Welsh, Gascoigne, among others, were jurisdictions of the same King. While the unifying nature of the royal Crown was not in dispute, questions arose regarding the relationship between the laws which pertained to a particular place and a particular people, and the King who, in establishing law, was sovereign over several people and jurisdictions.

In resolving this situation, an analogy with the parson was sought, since a parson too was a single person, yet in charge of several churches. Notwithstanding the suggestions of the learned scholarship of Maitland, this analogy between the parson and king was however systematically repudiated.[19] The thorny issue was not merely of integrating a diversity of jurisdictional bodies, as might be the case with the parson, but equally of establishing continuity in time. Here, critically, the parson's line in time was seen as artificial and not natural. That is to say, succession did not emerge from his natural body.[20] On the other hand, it was ultimately resolved by the Lord Chancellor and twelve judges including the two Chief Justices, that the King's natural body was crucial to his several political capacities which underpinned the King's founding and unification of diverse jurisdictions as continuous, in time and space, and through which allegiance and subjecthood took shape. Allegiance therefore flowed from the 'law of nature'. This attachment to the King's natural person – which was always conjoined with his political capacities – and not any specific law of any kingdom, characterized allegiance.[21]

Those who argued against the right of a Scotsman to inherit in England did not question the King's sovereignty over both Scotland and England.[22] The argument was that one who held allegiance of the King as King of Scotland was an alien born in relation to the same yet distinct King, as King of England.[23] The King having several titles and several allegiances had several distinct 'politic capacitates' where the 'legiance of each nation is several and divided'.[24] In arguing against naturalization, where one person of one nation with its own laws would be allowed to inherit in another place which was occupied by another nation with its own laws while under the same King, these jurists emphasized the role of the laws as concerning a specific place and community as a source of allegiance. This was an attempt to safeguard particular nations and their jurisdictional identities as norms.[25] However, these judges were clear that they did not intend to undermine royal sovereignty since they were more than ready to recognize the King's powers in being able to specifically grant such rights inherent to individuals in a place where they were not originally from. That is to say, they recognized the specific powers of the King to grant a specific Scotsman such rights in England as a matter of particular favour. However, they otherwise saw allegiance as something that pertained to law, to a specific jurisdiction, which they argued pertained to a particular place or kingdom in the normal course of affairs, and not the King as such.

It was in arguing against such a position that jurists at *Postnati* elaborated on the relationship between kingship, sovereignty and the laws of place. One forceful line adopted in this jurisprudential thicket, emphasizing the sovereignty of the King over that of the laws, was the proposition that allegiance operated before, after and beyond the laws.[26] Allegiance to the King was 'natural', not 'politic', and was neither to be contained in time nor space. This was evidenced by the fact that if one was conquered and the laws were no longer in operation, one still owed allegiance to the King, who might return in a re-conquest.[27] Analogously, in a conquest the vanquished population owed allegiance to the victorious King, only after which (municipal) laws were established. Allegiance to the King was thus prior, both conceptually and in real time, to the establishment of laws.

If these examples pertained to the milieu of time, in terms of space–place–jurisdiction, the subject owed allegiance to the King even when he was beyond the realm, whether beyond the seas or in a foreign country. The Fleta case is cited more than once, where Edward's silver cutlery was stolen while he was on a visit in France, and after much discussion the French parliament recognized Edward's jurisdiction over his subject, even though both were otherwise in the territorial jurisdiction of France. The accused was thereafter promptly tried by Edward's marshall, and hanged.[28] This was a concrete case, repeatedly cited, where martial law worked and allegiance held even when (municipal) laws did not. That people of diverse nations, such as the Scots and the English, could be summoned in war was also dictated not by specific territorial laws in Scotland and England, but the natural one of being subject of and owing allegiance to the King.[29]

The nature of the jurisdiction – laws particular to people and place – might change, and that which remained and supported such change was royal sovereignty; dukedoms could become kingdoms, and kingdoms could become dukedoms.[30] Those born outside the realm to parents who owed allegiance (and were subjects) themselves were held to owe allegiance, while those born within the realm even to foreigners owed allegiance by virtue of their birth in the realm.[31] Allegiance was formed by virtue of blood and territory, the only common element being subjecthood to the King and not to any particular kingdom (place or territorial jurisdiction). An alien could be 'disabled' only if it could be established not merely that he was outside of the allegiance of the King, but also that he was born in allegiance to another king.[32] The King remained a King and one to whom allegiance was owed wherever he reigned, and his writs ran – writs such as Habeas Corpus radiated across the various jurisdictions and territories.[33] All of this shows that one could not assume a self-same territorially bounded set of laws, since these were themselves only upheld and regulated by royal sovereignty. However, none of these contentions was to detract from the importance of place and territory when it pertained to certain important matters. For instance, it is made clear that one could not be taxed in the usual course from a place in which one was not earning a livelihood, because taxes and other such impositions had to emerge from the particular place (jurisdiction) where one lived and worked;[34] these were arguments that would rage in the context of Ireland as much as in the American colonies half a century and more later.

A more detailed argument regarding the nature of royal sovereignty as independent of the laws and specific jurisdictions was provided by Francis Bacon in parliament. Early on, Bacon distinguishes the English monarchy from forms of the commonwealth which were not monarchies.[35] He does so by pointing to the fact that non-monarchical commonwealths were always divided into various offices and never perpetual, since authority was elected.[36] The constant change in offices due to constant elections could not constitute continuity and thereby establish an actual body-politic. These commonwealths were necessarily guided by prior laws and precedents that were written or unwritten, each of which caused further differences and disagreements. On the other hand, in the case of monarchies, 'submission is natural and simple', which are afterwards perfected by laws.[37]

The grounds are laid in nature, and the three 'patterns and platforms' – 'works of nature' – forming monarchies were specified: Patriarchal, Sephardic (from scripture) and Divine (from scripture, in the sense of the 'monarchical' rule of the world by God).[38] Bacon argued that while there were indeed laws regulating the powers of parents, no one could seriously affirm that the obedience of the son is due by law. Such obedience was always to be considered 'natural'. While Greek and Biblical sources referred to the Sephardic mode to indicate that shepherds govern but do not own their sheep,[39] this analogy with divine power was used to distinguish monarchies from commonwealths.[40] Traditionally, Kings had been endowed with something of divine power, but never had senates or cantons been so endowed.

The natural origins of the submission to Kings were derived from patriarchal power, from some virtue of the King, his leadership in war, or through subjection in conquest.[41] For Bacon, all these were situations in which laws did not exist, but they all provided the fundamental contexts and grammar for the development of laws.[42] Situations of paternal authority and war were the primary 'natural' context from which laws were established and settled. Once such a settlement came to be, then its regular functioning might involve debate, dispute and consent. But the natural person of the King could not ever be subject to the law since his authority was the 'work of the law of nature'.[43] History too provided many examples and records where laws were established after Kings, and the time previous to such establishment involved a form of governance regulated by the 'natural equity' of the King in person, 'without law'.[44] The King was not a creature or fiction of law, as was the case clearly with the non-monarchical commonwealth.

From here, the categories of allegiance are seen to be determined directly by the actions of the King, rather than having anything to do with (municipal) law. An alien enemy – one who owed allegiance to a hostile sovereign – was categorized as one who had no allegiance to, and protection from, the King.[45] However, if an alien enemy was given safe passage by the King, he could appeal for justice to the King or the Privy Council whose decree may be aided by the Chancery. He had to appeal to natural equity and not 'the rules of law'.[46] An alien friend was defined as one whose sovereign had a confederacy with the King or was one with whom there was no hostility. A denizen was one who was made so by the King's charter, the King's 'grace and gift'; it could never be acquired by mere residence in a place.[47] However, this status allowed him to inherit land and initiate an action in law, and his progeny, if they were born after his acquisition of denizenship, were to be understood as natural-born subjects. Finally, when it came to the natural-born subject, this was a status acquired by birth or by act of parliament.

However, just as the first three degrees of status – alien enemy, alien friend and denizen – depended wholly on the King's act and not law or parliament, so too the last status of the natural-born subject, while emerging from birth and law, in operation 'respecteth only the King's person without respect of subjection to law or parliament'.[48] All these arguments were mobilized to establish the fact that allegiance was owed to the King in his natural person and not to laws or kingdoms, and the status of individuals, from alien enemies to natural-born subjects, were in turn conditioned by allegiance to the King and not laws *per se*.

In underlining the importance of the King, Bacon was actively repudiating the argument that a Scotsman could not be naturalized because naturalization was effected by the law of England, thereby implying that English law did not operate in Scotland. Against this, Bacon brings in conquest, and states that naturalization operated through conquest and it was therefore unreasonable, in such a legal context, to suppose that naturalization would not be applicable in the case of a Scotsman who was from a kingdom that had been acquired by descent. The very distinction between conquest and descent turns out to be moot because the Irish were considered naturalized even though Ireland was originally conquered, and so in the fitness of things, it would only be reasonable and just that the Scotsman too be naturalized as a subject of the King who had inherited the Scottish Crown.[49] Moreover, Ireland was seen to be subject to the laws of England by virtue of the King's charter, and not by conquest. It would anyway be absurd to argue, Bacon held, that the laws of England were introduced into a conquered populace by conquest, but were not be applicable to a Scotsman. In other words, the Scotsman was naturalized because he was a subject of the King's natural person, and not because he was the subject of the King as King of England.[50]

In arguing for the distinction between the King and the laws, Bacon dilates on the legal contexts of conquest where subjects were naturalized. In such cases, he emphasizes the fact that the laws of England were not 'superinduced' into peoples and countries conquered and naturalized. Rather, the old laws of the conquered place and people remained 'until the King by his proclamation or letters patent declared other laws; and then he may declare laws repugnant to the laws of England'.[51] Bacon is once again explicitly repudiating the idea that the subjects of conquest are naturally and immediately subject to the laws of England. Such an argument had as its basis the fact that since English treasure was used for conquest, English laws would therein operate on the conquered people. Countering this, Bacon avers that war involved not merely the English but other nations such as the Scottish, and therefore, in such contexts, no distinctions could be made in terms of nations' jurisdictions.[52]

Drawing out the implications of not regarding the King as central to allegiance, Bacon points out that if one defined allegiance in terms of the laws of England, there was no way to explain the naturalization of a man born in Jersey or Berwick.[53] The birth of a Jerseyman or an Irish person or the children of English outside the country owed allegiance from birth. The statutes made it clear that allegiance emerged from either birth in the King's domains, or because of birth from parents who were subjects even if the birth took place in foreign jurisdictions.[54] Naturalization was a 'branch of the law of nature', and what made England fit for empire was that it was open to the naturalization of all kinds of peoples,[55] not only those of a different *soli* (earth) but of a different *caeli* (air).[56] Allegiance remained even at the 'cessation' of laws such as in times of war. 'He may proceed by his supreme authority and martial law without observing formalities of the laws of his kingdom';[57] the same with peregrination.[58] Finally, Bacon reiterates the distinction between the King and the laws by stating that the King was not to be characterized as (merely) 'rightful' or 'lawful', but rather, a 'natural liege sovereign'.[59] It was allegiance to the natural person of the King that marked the subject from birth as a natural-born subject.

After pointing to the various ways in which allegiance to the King extended beyond the realms of the King and specific jurisdictions, such as the possibility of treason and allegiance in foreign lands and beyond the seas, Bacon moves on to clarify the way in which the Crown had to be distinguished from other familiar figures of civil and ecclesiastical law. He argues forcefully against the applicability of the civil law principle, that two rights concurrently in one person retain the distinction without causing confusion to King or Crown. Bacon strongly held that the civil law and ecclesiastical principle operated in the case of the parson (as rector in two churches) or bishop (in two sees), but could not by any stretch apply to the King because in such a civil principle the 'vigour or operation' of the 'natural person', so essential to kingship, is denied. Such a denial of the natural person was indeed applicable in the structure and functioning of corporations, where the natural body was nothing but 'stock to uphold and bear out the corporate body'.[60] On the other hand, for the King, the political capacity and the natural capacity worked in turn upon each other.[61] Drawing on previous juridical pronouncements, Bacon argues that 'mutual and reciprocal intercourse' as much of the communication of qualities between each other meant that the Crown induced perfections in the King that included the impossibility of being within age or corrupt, resulting in the immortality of the body in law. The natural person too affected the body-politic, by making it move through descent. Unlike a corporation which had successors, the King had heirs.[62] This crucial characteristic of kingship was certainly not repudiated for centuries to come.

This importance of the natural person of the King was also testified by the fact that it was considered treason to encompass the death of the Queen and the Prince, even though corporations did not have kin and there was nothing of the body-politic (political capacity) in either son or queen. It was the natural person of the King that operated, not only on his wife and son but also on his subjects, which therein had a direct bearing upon the case at hand. It was through his natural person that the subject of one kingdom had a legal relation with the subject of another kingdom, all within the realm of the King.[63]

Crown and King could not be treated as separable, even if they could be recognized as distinct. To treat them as separate would constitute treason as exemplified in previous infamous attempts, such as the Spencers in the fourteenth century, where the King was fought against in the name of the Crown.[64] It is another matter that this idea was successfully executed in the 1640s, and therefore the importance of the repudiation of this separability by Restoration and post-Restoration jurisprudence. Bacon's arguments, which withstood the test of time, emphatically distinguished kingship from other corporations by pointing to the fact that one could not be faithful – hold allegiance – in sincerity to a 'fiction'. A corporation as an aggregate did not have a soul, and being a fiction of the law, a construction of policy, it could not be the object of allegiance. Linked to this was not merely the powerful and paradoxical idea of the Crown as corporation sole, but also the inverse notion of the corporation being ensouled in the natural person of the King. The corporation sole was a corporation soul, and therefore the King could neither be compared with the parson nor 'parsonified'.[65]

Parliament in the Act of Recognition spoke of the two realms of England under one 'imperial crown'.[66] However, allegiance was necessarily owed to the

King even by those born outside the King's realm, and such allegiance could not refer to a specific territory of jurisdiction or the laws of a place, such as the 'laws of England'.[67] Territories were incorporated and ruled differently[68] with their different laws; for instance, the duchies were governed by their own laws, and were guided by civil law and had no juries operating with testamentary laws in relation to land.[69] They were not subject to England and had their own distinctive laws (ordinary justice), although the King's writ of Habeas Corpus ran there.[70] Parliaments could not meddle with these laws in a separate jurisdiction, and English parliaments were only applicable to English subjects in non-English jurisdictions such as Gascoigne, which were subject to the (same) King.[71] Charters governed the Gascoigne subjects, and in matters of trade and mercantile activities between the two jurisdictions, only violation of laws there by Englishmen, not local Gascoigne subjects, needed to be controlled by English laws. While arrests would be made by local law officers, punishments would be meted out in England in such cases. The King appointed

> committees in the upper house to receive petitions from Normandy and the rest, not for the ordering of governments there but for the liberties and good usage of the subject of those parts when they came hither; or vice versa for the restraining of the abuses and misdemeanours of English subjects when they went hither.[72]

Such powers of the King – and the limits of laws to their jurisdictions – enabled the naturalization of subjects across vast arenas including the West Indies.[73] And this is a situation which Bacon reads as having no legal difference from the naturalization of subject populations that resulted from conquest. The implication was the 'overthrow' of the distinction between descent and conquest. Countries conquered were not made a 'parcel' of a particular kingdom or jurisdiction such as England;[74] if such were not the case, absurd inconsistencies were bound to follow. If it were argued that conquest meant the transfer of laws to the conquered, in cases where conquests were made by the Scots and English, by their arms and treasures, would the conquered country and its inhabitants be a 'parcel' of both, having both their laws extended – even while denying the same 'communication' of laws between one and the other, i.e. England and Scotland?[75]

Such would be the contradictory consequences of attaching conquest to a particular place rather than being linked to the King's natural authority. Moreover, the argument that conquest was attributed to place and kingdom because conquest led to the vanquished being subject to the laws of England also held no water by either reason or precedent. For, upon conquest, the old laws remained until the King ordained by his letters patent and proclamation of new laws (in altering the old), and these laws, Bacon held, may well be utterly different, even 'repugnant' to the laws of England.[76] Ireland was not subject to English laws immediately upon conquest but rather due to the specific charters of Kings. The same could be said of several other jurisdictions.[77]

It was therein the natural person of the King that maintained both titles of descent (as in Scotland) and conquest (as in Ireland), and therefore there was no substantive distinction between the two. Bacon emphasizes the various forms of naturalization including dedition (surrender), donation, conquest and descent, all of which flowed from the natural person of the King. This was grounded in the fact that since human beings were originally naturalized to one another and mankind descended from the same being, it was more foundational than the law of nations. It is in such a context that one is to understand *naturalization* in the laws of England as a 'branch' of the law of nature, always to be deemed as more fundamental than the laws of *a* kingdom. Hence, born in England from Spaniards, a subject was naturalized, and born in Spain from English parents, he was naturalized. It was in these terms that empire was envisioned, for in Bacon's words, 'this magnanimity [is what] made a war like people fit for empire'.[78]

Postnati similarly affirmed that allegiance was due to the King 'by the law of nature',[79] by which it meant that allegiance was not to be considered a fiction; something treated as a result of an intended action of any sort, whether personal or collective. Allegiance was natural, marking one's birth and drawn from the 'power and protection' of the prevailing King.[80] Since one's birth and flourishing were possible only by the guarantee of such power and protection, one could not choose one's sovereign. Conversely, sovereignty too was natural as it descended from King to King without interval, and this accomplishment of sovereignty could well take various forms – also called titles – including heredity and conquest. However, the descent or royal blood was deemed sovereign, and it was to the 'natural' living body of the King that the subject owed allegiance. Subjection and sovereignty formed an indissoluble bond that was to be clearly distinguished from place and territory.

The judges in 1608 clearly affirmed that the diverse laws which existed in distinct domains and kingdoms such as Ireland and Scotland were all the same unified in the person of the King, to whom the subject in each of these domains and kingdoms owed allegiance,[81] and each of whom was in the power and protection of the King. One might speculate that the correlate of allegiance designated by the doublet 'power and protection'– with no place for 'lawful' or 'rightful' – indicated the natural status of such a bond as much as a frightful realism. Allegiance and sovereignty were the ground of law, and the fundamental importance of allegiance to the *de facto* sovereign was not incommensurate with important discourses on the subject, such as the prayer book.[82] Elizabethan jurists had justified allegiance to Henry VII by his victory over Richard II, despite him having been tainted as attainder. By the title of conquest he became King, and once King, his political capacity erased any taint that he might ever have had; such was the elaboration of the theory of the King's bodies.[83] This 'realism' with regard to conquest and possession is also concretely expressed by the fact that the judges in *Postnati* held that even though the King of England claimed lands in France, in fact, the subjects of those regions did not and need not have held allegiance to the King of England because he did not actually possess the region.[84] Thus, sovereignty was expressed in actual possession and only there from required allegiance in turn.

The sovereign–allegiance doublet upheld various jurisdictions in the forms of domains and kingdoms, and itself varied in nature.[85] The judges named these various jurisdictions as the various political capacities of the King. The jurisdictions were also called 'mystical bodies', and though distinct, they were unified in and through the natural person of the King.[86] Notwithstanding this, the judges underlined the fact that allegiance is owed to the natural person. It was the natural person and the concrete descent of blood which ensured that there was no interval in rule; coronation and other such ceremonies were to be construed as but outward forms of an already pulsating sovereignty. This becomes clear when it is held that the crime of treason, which involved the encompassment of the death of the King, was a crime of the encompassment of the death of the King as a natural person, since there could not be encompassment of the death of an immortal being (the political capacity).[87] Just as treason was a violation of a natural law, it was from such a law that the powers of pardon and mercy which characterized a royal sovereign were to be understood.[88] Pardoning power enabled the King to reach into the law of nature and pluck the convicted person out from the jaws of the municipal laws where he might have been condemned to death. Once again, natural law subtended municipal laws through the natural person of the King.[89]

The differentiated nature of jurisdictions or political capacities of the

King could be characterized in tracing it to the King's actions. From the distinctiveness of domains, different kinds of subjects were formulated depending on the precise form of their subjection.[90] The judges outlined four kinds: the natural-born subject was one who was born into the protection and power of the King; the denizen was one who acquired subjecthood; the 'local' subject was one who in temporary measure was a subject (such as a foreign merchant); and finally, taking the oath of allegiance was the fourth form of subjecthood.[91] However, the distinction between 'natural born' and 'acquired subjecthood' (denizen) turns out to be merely one that is about origins and not substance. In effect, mirroring Bacon, the judges maintained that there was little to distinguish one from the other.[92] The progeny of subjects retained protection and therein owed allegiance.

Further elaborating on the typology, the judges held that acquired allegiance might be the settling of an alien within the domain of the King in peace, such as merchants did.[93] Or it might be the (protracted) coming-into-being of the subject in the course of the conquest of a territory-people. Conquest, well-recognized as a title to sovereignty, could therein also be conversely a title of subjecthood. In delineating this issue, the judges make further distinctions. They delineate a distinction between the conquest of a Christian kingdom and the conquest of an infidel kingdom. In the case of a Christian kingdom gained by title of conquest, the victorious King may alter and change the laws, until which time the older laws were to be considered valid; whereas in the case of a kingdom gained from the title of descent, the King could not alter or change the laws but with the consent of parliament.[94] Yet, as in the case of Ireland which was acquired by conquest, once the laws of England were given to Ireland, the King could not change or alter the laws except with the consent of parliament.[95] On the other hand, in the case of the conquest of an infidel country, the existing laws *ipso facto* were dissolved as being against Christianity. Until the King established municipal laws, he ruled by 'equity'. Thus, until the establishment of 'municipal laws', pure discretion – of the King's and anyone empowered by him – was rule of law. Equity is another name for nature and so, in a sense, it is the law of nature that rules a conquered populace, not a settled system of laws.[96]

The judges do not explicate or dwell on the conditions of the conquest of an 'infidel' country. Neither time nor norm is given as a concrete measure of the distance between the end of conquest and the beginning of subjecthood. However, the latter condition of subjecthood is recognized as a possibility, even demanded as one. Even if only equity, discretion or 'nature' is initially given, the horizon, the possibility of a municipal law coming into being, is recognized, if not elaborated upon. This seems to lie in tension with the taxonomy of subjecthood that was undertaken elsewhere. For the judges also spelt out that one could only be either a subject born or an alien born. An alien was held to be either a friend (with whom one was in public league) or an enemy (with whom one shared nothing and with whom one was at open war). While a friend might have certain kinds of rights in the country, the alien enemy could have no such rights because he could not cause or initiate an action in law. An enemy may be temporary or permanent. Non-Christians were subsumed under the latter as a 'subject of the devil', since their conversion was but a 'remote possibility'.[97]

This classification does not seem to encompass the political-legal consequences for the infidel in the conquest of an infidel country, which is sketched out, in howsoever brief and tenuous a manner – something that we touched on above. However, this conceptualization of an enemy as he with whom one did not have a public league and who therefore did not have any rights in law, was to have been taken very seriously by many, including the trader–pirate–corporates in the eastern seas. Just about a decade or so after the *Postnati*, Grotius in his *History of the Late Wars* writes that the English indulged in rapines and slaughters in the eastern seas and justified the same; 'it was so directed by the Customs and Laws of their Ancestors, because whatever was committed against Foreigners, with whom no publike League was made, was justified so far in *Britain,* as there could be no compensation got for any injury done'.[98] Of course, read the other way, the revered judges might well have been codifying or confirming the violence of a long-existing seafaring tradition. The open enemy was put to death by martial law and not common law, before the constable and marshall whose authority derived directly from the King, as happened with the cutlery thieves in France. The emergence of municipal law was the emergence of a 'system' of law – which was the essential mark of property and heritability – and could not take place at the mildewed time of conquering. Laws required courts, including the highest courts such as parliament, none of which could be construed as present in the time of war. For only in peace could one initiate an action in law, unlike in the condition of open war where martial law or the law of nature prevailed.

Clarifying a range of issues on sovereignty, subjecthood and the laws, the final decision of *Postnati* stated that notwithstanding Scotland and England being two distinct kingdoms (jurisdictions with their own laws) in so far as subjects were concerned, because both owed allegiance to the same natural

King and not two distinct kingships in their political capacity, Calvin as a Scotsman could inherit land in England after the union of Crowns.

The King's Conquests: Strands of *Postnati* Elaborated in Mathew Hale in the Late Seventeenth Century

In the late seventeenth century, the writings of Mathew Hale – whose status as a jurist remained unblemished, notwithstanding the course of the bloody civil wars and the commonwealth – renewed the exploration of the infinitely brittle distinctions between the titles of inheritance and conquest, distinctions that otherwise differentiate and peg the various political capacities of the King.[99] The distinctions of *Postnati* acquire legal sinew in Hale's work, after the very notion of legality and sovereignty were shaken to the core during the civil wars and interregnum. The sovereignty of the King is proclaimed once more as 'emperor', subject to no earthly power, and sovereign not merely over the people distributively but over the estates collectively, and all the people represented therein.[100] Allegiance was due, as in *Postnati*, to the natural person of the King.[101]

Rather than focusing on the Christian–infidel distinction in *Postnati*'s consideration of conquest, Hale divides the title of conquest into either a victory *in populum* (of the population) or a victory *in regem* (in the King).[102] While William in 1066 CE was to have acquired his title to England through a victory *in regem*, Henry's victory over Ireland was defined as a victory *in populum* too; both having acquired territory through the title of conquest.[103] That is to say, according to Hale, when the crown passed on to William after his victory in battle in 1066, he did not therein acquire proprietary title over the people's estates and properties. Rather, he accepted and acknowledged the ancient existing rules of property, tenure and law while rightfully claiming the Crown through the law of victory. Whatever redistribution of lands and titles had taken place after the defeat of Harold, was done in the immediate wake of war, and was therefore in no sense to be taken as a right over the properties, the people or their laws in their entirety.[104] Other actions were to be derived from William's sovereign status and not as a conqueror. Thus, the victory in battle through conquest did not result in an alteration of the fundamental laws of the kingdom, and notwithstanding the immediate aftermath of violence and plunder, surrender resulted in the maintenance of the constitutional order even as the Crown changed hands.[105] The acceptance of William as much as William's acceptance of the existing legal order signified that there was a 'mixture' of conquest and consent. This meant that though undeniably a conquest, this was a conquest of the King (*in regem*) and not of the people (*in populum*).[106]

In Hale's writings, this form of conquest is distinguished from the subsequent conquest of Ireland where there was a conquest of the population too. Here, unlike in the previous instance, conquest signalled a destruction of the old order, with Ireland being 'annexed' to the Crown of England. While in the case of England in 1066, victory was perfected in the acceptance of existing laws, in the case of Ireland a full conquest happened, with the perfection of laws accruing only in a slow progressive manner with time. This meant that the free Englishmen in their plantations in Ireland enjoyed liberties as Englishmen, in victory over a country which assured not merely supervisory rights but full-scale proprietary rights.[107] Notwithstanding which, Hale conjoins this statement with the seemingly contrasting claim that it was the slow burning of time that had ensured an implied consent by the Irish. According to this latter logic, things had come to such a pass that there could no longer be a fundamental distinction between Irishmen and Englishmen as subjects of the King.[108]

Much as in *Postnati,* for Hale too, the slow settling of English laws in Ireland took place through the actions of the King, independent of parliament. It was the legal feature of being a conquered people/territory that made Ireland subordinate to England, even though it had its own parliament and laws and was therein considered a distinct kingdom. Subordination nonetheless was expressed not only in concrete legal terms where the King's Bench in Ireland could be corrected by the King's Bench in England, but also in terms of the Navigation Laws which bound Ireland to England's benefit. The principles of *Postnati* were somewhat ambiguous about whether Ireland was subordinate to the English parliament,[109] and explicitly argued for the subordination of kingdoms to the King and not each other. As we will see below, William Molyneux explicitly challenged Hale's characterization of Ireland as subordinate to England without naming him, notwithstanding which the ambiguities in Hale regarding Ireland's status seem to derive from very similar ambiguities in *Postnati*.

The legal differentiation is classified by Hale into those territories that were inherited or acquired by the King in his right of the Crown of England, and those territories and jurisdictions in his natural-political capacity. The former included Wales, Ireland, Man, Guernsey, Jersey, Sark and Alderney, Berwick, Calais and later acquests such as the Bermudas, Barbados, Virginia,

New England and the East Indies; the latter included Normandy, Aquitaine, Guinne and Gascony, among others. Wales and Scotland were perceived to have been in a 'feudal' relationship with England, with their rulers initially having rights over their subjects but in turn subject to the Kings of England until, in varying circumstances and with time, they were 'joined' to the Crown of England. Jurisdictions such as the plantations and those acquired by conquest were cases where the King had 'sole authority' to make laws, which he could institute through commissions. They were not subject to the laws of England or parliament, until a King's proclamation. Hale observed that laws in such terrains appeared very different from the laws of England, and he compares this situation to Ireland and its history thereby raising the question as to whether English law could negate Irish laws or raise taxes in Ireland without the consent of the latter. This is a question that is never satisfactorily resolved or explored.

Closely related to conquest was martial law, which too worked to reiterate the King's laws lying beyond existing laws and jurisdictions. Hale speaks of martial law as that which concerns both the army (a particular kind of jurisdiction over them) and the laws of war (concerning the enemy, and therein another jurisdiction). Yet he affirms a particular kind of 'intermixture' between the two which characterizes both; both are distinct but inevitably 'touched' by one another.[110] War ensures that power lies with the commander and ultimately the King, over both the person and the property of the enemy. Martial law at the same time may continue after the immediate fighting, since it is only in conjunction with such a law that one is able to treat critical issues emerging from war such as the treatment of prisoners and the disposal of booty.[111] Though Hale does not expend much energy over these aspects, it is important to note that there was a general discourse over many issues pertaining to the laws of war when it came to booty and the disposal of the property of the enemy. All these issues formed a branch of martial law concerning the treatment of hostile aliens, and in turn might involve the admiralty laws (and the law of the marshall), forming a terrain distinct from jurisdictions such as that of parliament and common law. This entire field of problems in emerging from war reiterated the fundamental recognition of conquest as a title which fell exclusively under the King's domain, beyond that of parliament, and involving questions of subjects and aliens.

The Fictions of Conquest and Consent: The Natural Law Tradition in the Context of Common Law

In all of the above discussions, allegiance and sovereignty were considered 'natural' in the common law perspective. It is this duplex structure that Hobbes transfigures through what he believes to be a science. For Hobbes, the making and maintaining of commonwealths required skill and therein consisted in rules, like the sciences of arithmetic and geometry. That is to say, they were a science and it was his intention to unravel such a science for the betterment of all. Political life could not be improved with mere practice, as in tennis-play, but required an understanding of and conformity to the rules.[112] Notwithstanding points of convergence between Hobbes and the common law understanding of issues such as the role of the King or the peculiar conjoining of conquest and consent, the motivating rationale and theoretical matrix that undergirds each are fundamentally different.

Much like the common lawyers, Hobbes recognizes the title conquest, in which all other types of title appear to be subsumed.[113] At the same time a theory of the institution of sovereignty is outlined through the familiar argument of the state of nature, too well known to be recounted here. It is nevertheless worth underlining that Hobbes saw both the 'rights' and the 'consequences' of the instituted and conquest forms as identical.[114] Conquest gave one proprietorial rights over the conquered, and here Hobbes supplies his own historical examples in which he includes William the Conqueror, thereby differing from Hale.[115] Admitting that estates may by and large be left alone, the victor all the same, says Hobbes, had the right to redistribute lands and rights in the blazing aftermath of victory. However, the waters are significantly muddied when Hobbes argues that it was not conquest that gave the rights to the conqueror but the consent of the conquered that bestowed such rights,[116] here echoing Hale's 'mixture' of conquest and consent in theoretical terms. For the conquered could always have fought unto death, and that he surrendered and found his life dearer than his freedom – to adopt the Hegelian idiom – meant that whatsoever he owned was in fact owed to his lord who had spared his life.

Hobbes insists that this 'consent' was the origin of the conqueror's right, rather than the brute fact of conquest. The nature of consent is thus in dissociable from fear and difficult to isolate from the brute (f)act of conquest. It was precisely the fear-propelled consent that also constituted the famous instituted form of sovereignty, taking the form of a 'social contract'.

Consent thus signified the end of war and the enabling condition of peace. Unlike the lawyers, Hobbes argues that the sovereign directly constituted law in parliament and it was statute that confirmed customs, since no custom had force without being sanctioned by an authoritative court or institution like King-in-Parliament.[117] This was in direct contrast to Bacon's claim that common law was 'more worthy' than statute, or the suggestions in *Postnati* about the common law interpretability of statute, an issue we will take up in some detail in the conclusion of this part. Nevertheless Bacon was at one with *Postnati* in his understanding that in England, even in his public acts and legislation, the political and natural capacity could not be divided because in the assent which made a bill a law, the King acted in his natural capacity.[118]

The similar results in terms of entanglement of conquest and consent, natural and political capacity in the institution of sovereignty do not detract from the fundamental differences from common law argumentation, because it must be reiterated that Hobbes's argument emerges from the hypothesis of a state of nature where the equality and liberty of individual men is postulated; in Hobbes's case, as argued by Pateman's classic work, this was a rare instance where one could possibly speak of individual women too.[119] There is no evidence for such a postulate in the common law tradition where one is born being beholden to father and King. The conceptualization in the common law conception of sovereignty and subjecthood is thus almost Aristotelian where action requires the act and the acted upon, hence *both* sovereign and subject partake in the action even if the action is that of the sovereign. On the other hand, for Hobbes, sovereignty is the result of the action of two or more distinct entities in the form of a contract or promise. While he wishes to derive the actions from each, in the final analysis it becomes difficult to see this through without altering what one conventionally means by action or consent. The conqueror's action in conquest and the 'consent' of the vanquished are seen to be distinct actions, the latter seen to be the ground of title.

From an Aristotelian perspective, it would in fact be but *one* action which expressed one as sovereign and the other as subject. By way of contrast, for Hobbes, the contract or compact is primary, requiring the postulation of *a priori* distinct and individualized entities endowed with inherent freedom, whereas for the common law judges, one is born to a bound relation which always expresses a subject and a sovereign – what in physical terms would be called a mover and a moved.

This difference between the fundamental theoretical matrices of the common law tradition and Hobbes results in specific politico-legal differences. For Hobbes, the treatment of the rebel and the open enemy took place according to the natural law and martial law.[120] In both cases not only the person, but the property of the challenger was confiscated. For the common lawyers, a much more finely graded and differentiated response was required to the question of conquest. Thus, certainly in such a case, the person and the property were subject to the will of the victor (martial law), but it was also posited that such was the situation until the establishment of (municipal) law, as discussed in the previous section. In Hobbes, any political condition involving consent also involved conquest – the sovereign ultimately had proprietary right as sovereign.[121] This was in contrast to the common lawyers who gave a certain centrality to conquest but simultaneously traced a legal route to the translation of the will of the conqueror in conquest to the settlement in law, whether by assemblies or common law. While there is no time-frame given that is meant to regulate the coming into being of (municipal) law in the wake of conquest, the almost moral demand to effectuate such a situation is undeniable.

This problematic of defining and distinguishing conquest and consent haunts the work of John Locke too, and one can trace a series of impasses in which it ends. While Locke is clear about the right of the victor over the person of the aggressor in the context of the invoked state of war, he is less clear – or strategically confused – about the precise status of the right over property of the vanquished, in such a context. Towards the end of the part on 'paternal, political and despotical power' in the *Second Treatise*, he characterizes 'despotical power' as the power over captives in a just war, which moves close to the Hobbesian position.[122] And he further argues that nature gave 'despotical power to lords for their own benefit, over those who are stripped of all property'.[123] The point is hammered even more clearly when it is stated that despotical power implied the absence of property (in the vanquished). By property Locke meant, here as elsewhere, that which men have in their goods as well as persons. Therefore, it is clear that the victor in a just war has rights over the person as well as the property (estate and goods) of the conquered.

Yet, the very next chapter on 'conquest' in the *Second Treatise* appears to take great pains to argue that while conquest in just war gave one the right over the person and life of the aggressor, it did not give title over the property or estate of the conquered. While in an unjust war, the defeated always retained the right to 'appeal to heaven' and continue the war, in a just war, the victor had a 'perfectly despotical' authority over the vanquished. At this juncture, however, Locke makes three important qualifications which are entirely absent in the previous chapter on 'paternal, political, and despotical power': the first qualification is that despotical authority is not to be exercised on those allies with whose aid conquest is made; second, power may be exercised only over those enemies who actually consented, concurred and assisted in waging aggressive war against oneself; and finally, and most importantly from the broader perspective of this chapter, conquest gives title only over the person and not over the possessions of one's enemy.[124] The last clause appears to clearly contradict the previous chapter where title over possessions was subsumed in the title of conquest that granted powers over the person.

While acknowledging that the recovery for damages incurred by the battle may well be extracted as recompense, Locke emphasizes that there is no right to the goods and estates of the vanquished because this would be a violation of the claimants to those goods and estates, i.e. the children and other heirs of the defeated party.[125] Moreover, Locke narrows the right of conquest over the lives of the aggressor by giving an analogy with the rights against a robber, whom one may kill in self-defence but whom one may not rob in turn.[126] There can thus be no just right, he argues, over the land or country of the vanquished, unless the latter consents to the victor's rule– a consent that therein forms the basis of political right.[127] In this sense, Locke seems to be arguing both against Hobbes and against the very existence of Hale's category victory *in populum*, which granted personal rights and proprietorial rights over the vanquished. Locke here is also going against the well-established legal precedent of the attainder, where rebels and others could not only be punished but also have their heirs deprived.[128]

This strong, and in certain ways unprecedented, argument regarding the rights over the life of the aggressor that did not amount to rights over his property is perhaps intelligible only in the particular historical context of the time. The argument invoking the appeal to heaven as a call to war, as much as the 'strange' doctrine of conquest over people and not property, requires to be interpreted against the backdrop of renewed threats of civil war in the 1680s. It might be argued that the celebrated Lockean theory of property must be seen as a way to defend and preserve property rights in the context of an anticipation of civil war and/or invasion. It was an attempt to maintain the proprietorial order – codified as a system of laws – when there was the strong possibility that a change in Kings, and a change in Crowns, would take place. Did Locke wish to ensure that any such change would involve, to use Hale's terminology, only a victory *in regem* and not a victory *in populum*? There could be no other way to ensure this than by simply denying the validity of the latter category, which was well established in the laws of war.

More concretely, this peculiar Lockean argument appears to be an anticipation of possible 'conquest' by William III. The argument that the conqueror would have no rights over property implied the illegality that would mark any attempt by William III to expropriate or disturb the proprietorial order of England, even if he were to acquire the Crown of England by conquest. In fact Locke admits that his argument regarding the conqueror's right as not extending to the possessions of the vanquished is a 'strange doctrine', and not to be found in practices across the world.[129] Thus it is the laws, the proprietorial order, that 'require' to survive any change in political authority, and which therefore forms the substance and ends of political rights. Let alone 1066, in making such an argument Locke completely ignores the consequences of the rights of conquest on the proprietorial order as applied to Ireland or the Americas, brought to notice by various lawyers and court judgments. In mobilizing an argument about the foundational importance of laws and property, Locke can characterize princes as creatures made like any other, thereby going against the legal characterization of English kingship and the importance of 'royal blood', as clearly enunciated by *Postnati* and as would continue to mark English kingship well after 1688–89.

This severing of a 'political' change of Kings from an enduring state of the propertied (nation) becomes clear in the fact that Locke is unable to respond to, let alone acknowledge, Filmer's central argument, notwithstanding the painstaking detail that characterizes his engagement with the latter. Filmer's central wager was that those who maintain 'the natural liberty of mankind' will also have to, in turn, examine 'their own charters, deeds and evidences by which they claim and hold the inheritance and freehold of their liberties'.[130] In other words, the very structure of the propertied order would be rendered uncertain if the partisans of natural liberty wished to be truly consistent and serious about their arguments. Locke's entire *Second Treatise* is caught in the contradictions that disable any response: contradictions formed by attributing the determination of property to 'natural right' on the one hand, and 'positive constitutions' on the other. It is the latter that appears to be the dominant one, such as when Locke famously argues about property involving the right over the labour of servants.[131]

This concern regarding the propertied order is discernible in the detailed arguments of the *First Treatise* if we were to reflect again upon some of the torturous distinctions that Locke attempts. Claiming a natural liberty of mankind, with scarce evidence of such a state in the scriptural record otherwise accepted as infallible, Locke argues that God had ensured that no one could have just power over the life of another by virtue of a right to property, land or possessions. From here it is argued that justice required that one help someone in want, such as one nearing death by starvation, through the property one had. The starving man had a *title* to charity.[132] This point is strengthened by Locke's argument that to take (unfair) advantage by subordinating one who was in desperate need was no different from subordinating someone through physical means.[133]

On the other hand, Locke runs against himself by conceding that if indeed one enslaves or subjugates another either by brute force or by taking advantage of someone's necessity, even then such a title to property could not be the basis of authority over men. This authority is to emerge only from a 'compact'. In a distinctly Hobbesian vein, Locke argues that in such a case, authority arose not from brute possession but from 'consent' to authority by the one who preferred 'being his subject to starving'.[134] Consent is here detached from any substantive normative horizon and merely indicates the acceptance of the person, *whatsoever* his context – whether he is overwhelmed by necessity or sheer brutal force. According to Locke, it is immaterial if such consent emerged from the fact that one person took advantage of another person's desperate need,[135] completely contradicting the earlier argument on the title to charity and the denial of any right to take advantage of the desperate need of another, Locke here affirms that sovereignty and property emerged from and were based on the consent of the individual, even if such consent were to be extracted in the most unequal of conditions. In a Hobbesian vein, conquest and consent are indiscernible since any action resulting from the threat of fatal violence is all the same rendered as 'consent'. That is to say, the cost of servitude resulting from the unwillingness to simply die is construed as an act of choice and therein consent, not necessity. Strangely, Locke joins Filmer in combining property and sovereignty as ultimately emerging from the same source, even if such a source remains paternity for Filmer but is conquest construed as consent for Locke. The right of property is therein both entrenched and rendered precarious by force. But the denial of the right to charity, and the sanction of appropriating as property what is another's necessity, leads directly to the famous chapter on property in the *Second Treatise*, where the master has ownership over the servant's labour.[136]

Moreover, Locke also admits that parental power, as derived from begetting, is a divine gift and grant that cannot be abridged by any inferior power or prescription. When trying to limit this natural power by distinguishing it from the magistrate's (political) power, Locke does not address the host of Biblical examples that Filmer gives of parental power being simultaneously the basis of political-juridical actions such as capital punishment and war- and peace-making authority – arguments that were to be found in the discussions and ruling around *Postnati*.[137] Locke does not account for such examples from scripture; he merely describes the existence of such powers, as when he speaks of the war-making powers of bands in the Americas or slavery. This description in itself is meant to convey the title of property and appears no different from Hobbes's discussion of force, consent and title.

Finally, Locke constantly accuses Filmer of turning everyone into slaves of Kings, but does not quite dwell on his strange affinity with Filmer in the invocation of James I's and James IV's statements on royalty and consent.[138] Filmer repeats an old trope, seen in *Postnati* too, which treats Kings as above the laws, but at the same time requires Kings to bind themselves to the laws in their treatment of their subjects, the primary objective always being the well-being of all.[139] He at the same time recognizes tyranny and usurpation, thereby allowing for the fact that the replacement and deposing of Kings had divine sanction in history.[140] However, he does not recognize any legal form by way of which subjects or peoples had rights to depose their King.[141] Locke's famous discussion of prerogative similarly made it clear that there was no legal – terrestrial – procedure to weigh the difference between the King and the legislative body, and to adjudicate between them.[142] This meant that he in effect was part of a long legal tradition in holding that there was no (municipal) law by way of which one could legally proceed against the King.

However, as is well known, Locke did recognize the right to resist the King on the basis of the more fundamental right to property, since the latter was construed as the basis of the contract which founded political society.[143] Rather than an enlarging, this was in fact a narrowing of the right to rebellion, since it only appeared to give such rights to the propertied. While there is a rich debate on the extent to which Locke supported the increase in franchise, there seems to be no doubt about the fact that there is nothing like an argument of universal franchise irrespective of property in Locke.[144] Part of the problem in interpreting Locke lies in distinguishing between the 'state of nature' (natural rights) and 'civil society' (positive constitutions). But on the question of property franchise in the state of civil societies, it seems clear that Locke does not support an individual natural rights-based approach to the question of appropriation of property through labour, and the concomitant acquisition of franchise. In fact, while unhappy with the state of the electoral laws regarding franchise in relation to territory, he makes it clear that this legal situation is not to be changed by even the legislature, let alone individuals, on the basis of any natural right to labour and property. Rather, he argues that it is through princely prerogative that such alterations in franchise can be made. In this context he suggests that the rule of '*salus populi supremalex*' lies with the princely executive.[145]

If Locke had earlier left no legal room for a conflict between prerogative and a legislature perceiving a violation of their property rights, this argument about the rights of princely prerogative regarding franchise makes it clear that he did not support any 'radical' alternative regarding the mere extension of franchise. This abridgment of the right to both legislate and resist on the grounds of property could be distinguished from the Filmerian argument. In Locke's discussion of the rights of the propertied over their servants no such natural liberties were given to the servant, and in no sense could the latter inquire into or resist the claims of the former, whose property rights were treated as invulnerable. This leads to tensions and contradictions which force themselves upon Locke's treatment of conquest and the emergence of rights and authority. If property itself could emerge from force, on what basis could Locke have sanctified a propertied order – right to the aggressor's person and not his property – in a just war? Whatever the difference between Locke and Filmer on the matter of the King and the laws, it must be recognized that in England, no legal action could be initiated against the King, a principle that has worked its way until the present.

What is sometimes seen as Locke's inconsistencies can be moulded into a more specific interpretation in the light of concrete history. That he had no problems with the navigation laws, slavery in the American colonies or the treatment of the Irish, may well point to the fact that the *Treatises of Government* were directed towards a very specific moment in English history anticipating and reflecting on a crisis, which was a change in Kings through conquest, and the very real threats of war and civil war. The consistency and inconsistency of the Lockean line of argument can be better discerned and understood when one traces the appropriation of his argument in a context that he might well never have approved of, i.e. Ireland.

In the late seventeenth-century philosopher William Molyneux's appropriation of specifically Lockean arguments, one witnesses an exacerbation of the more theoretical and historical problems of conquest, settlement and a propertied order. Molyneux's arguments for the essential independence of the jurisdiction of Ireland from England in its subjection to the King followed a long tradition of debate from the early 1640s to the 1690s.[146] Early on in his *The Case of Ireland being Bound by Acts of Parliament in England, Stated* (1698), Molyneux drew from Henry Spellman the fact that a conquest could either mean a 'hostile subjugation' or a 'peaceable acquisition'.[147] This might well be related to Hale's distinction, discussed earlier, between conquest *in regem* and *in populum*. Molyneux, all the same, forcefully argued against Hale's position when he saw Ireland as a distinct kingdom and equal to England – subordinate to the King but in no way to the English parliament (the English kingdom). Hale had derived the subordination of Ireland from its historical origins in the title of conquest, although as discussed, there were some ambiguities, reflecting *Postnati*, on the precise relationship between Ireland and England. In sharp contrast, Molyneux argues vehemently using both historical example and legal argument to establish that such subordination had no legal standing, and was in fact forced upon Ireland only in recent times by legislation regarding commerce such as the Navigation Acts. Molyneux was building on a long-standing tradition on the equality of the kingdom of Ireland, and from such a perspective, it was this putatively recent subordination in the form of the Navigation Acts that he wished to challenge. He was nonetheless one with the main strand of the common law tradition, exemplified in *Postnati*, which had declared the subordination of the kingdoms to the King.

The legal infirmity of Ireland's recent subordination is established by giving a history of the relations between the two kingdoms, and the super ordinate position of the King over the two. In the first place, using historical records and statutory precedents, Molyneux argues that neither hostility nor wars between the Irish and Henry II led to the annexing of Ireland to the Crown of England. 'Conquest' was achieved peacefully with the consent of the people of Ireland, who accepted parliamentary and other institutions along with the laws of England. Inverting Hale's narrative, Molyneux argues that the Irish case was to be explicitly distinguished from the conquest of England in 1066.[148] In comparison to Ireland, 1066 was a violent singular battle that was clearly inscribed in the records. This argument is therefore an implicit challenge to the common law argument that title ultimately emerged from William's acceptance of the ancient English laws, as well as the consent of the English people in accepting William as ruler.

From the time of Henry II, Ireland was a distinct kingdom with its own laws, subject only to the King and in no way under the jurisdiction of the English parliament.[149] Various statutes are cited to establish that all laws in

Ireland were confirmed by the Irish parliament and the King (with his Privy Council), leaving no role for the English parliament.[150] And if historical questions were raised about the precise 'modus' whereby Henry II 'settled the laws of England' in the kingdom of Ireland in directing the institution of parliament, similar questions, argued Molyneux, might be more justly raised regarding the role of the King in the establishment of the English parliament. There was, all the same, a consensus over the fact that Ireland did indeed 'settle' into a separate and distinct kingdom with its own laws, always subject to the King.

Having tried to establish that there was consent and not conquest in the Irish case, Molyneux also dwells on the juridical terrain by arguing that conquest itself had to be divided into a just and an unjust conquest. While the former had a just cause, the latter did not. Notwithstanding the distinction, in neither case, Molyneux argued, could the victorious party claim the estate and property of the vanquished by right of conquest.[151] Just as the victor had no rights over the property of his companions, he did not have any rights over the property of those who did not assist in the resistance, i.e. who did not directly aid the enemy. As to those who resisted and actually took part in the battles as opponents and enemies, while their lives could be taken, their estates could be appropriated only so as to recompense damages incurred by the victor in battle. Here, Molyneux cites and echoes the arguments of the *Second Treatise* discussed above, echoing the possibility of the 'strangeness'[152] of an argument that protects the property of the enemy. While such conduct was not practised in most places, this is how things ought to be, it is said.[153]

After attempting to undermine the historical and juridical arguments which were to have subordinated Ireland to England by the conquest argument, Molyneux acknowledges the fact that recent laws did in fact subordinate Ireland – laws which, he argues, themselves had no basis in precedent.[154] Thus, the 'Navigation' Acts which forced all ships from the colonies to first stop in England, or the laws which forced all of the Irish wool trade first into England, were characterized as examples of this recent ('illegal') subordination.[155] Significantly, Molyneux sees such interference from the English parliament as an encroachment into both the liberties of the Irish and the *prerogatives* of the King.[156] Such English parliamentary legislative acts which affected the property, in the broadest sense, of the people of Ireland without their consent was held to be an egregious violation of the people's rights, conferred and confirmed by the King and the Privy Council. It was the King, through his prerogative powers, the Privy Council, his Courts and

(Irish) parliamentary institutions (embodying the consent of the people), that together upheld the liberties of the Irish people. Here, Molyneux argues that any comparison between Ireland as a distinct kingdom and the colonies in America was totally inappropriate, since Ireland had its own parliament and laws. Of course, this did not stop the colonists from using precisely the kind of arguments that Molyneux employed. One might even argue that such arguments could be derived from *Postnati*, which held that rights to taxation emerged from the 'place' where one lived, and ultimately the King.

Finally, Molyneux strongly repudiates the argument that it was the expenses for putting down rebellions in Ireland that formed the basis for the interference of the English parliament. In the first place, he makes a general argument about the numberless 'rebellions' witnessed in England from Richard to the War of Roses through to the recent civil wars, all of which did not entail any special expropriation. He then builds on this with reference to a current and sensitive English example. Concerning rebellion and compensation, he states that the precise nature of the expenses incurred ought to be decided by the Irish parliament, not the English parliament. And this was indeed what happened, as he points out, in the recent 'revolution' of William III, where the English parliament decided to reimburse Holland an amount of 600,000 pounds, the amount demanded by Holland in this context.[157]

Molyneux then takes a step further, asking whether it would have been just or legal for Holland to dispose of estates and properties in England as claims for the damages incurred by William's undertaking.[158] This many-sided refutation of the justification of English statutory interference on the basis of Irish rebellion steps on an array of delicate fingers. The analogy between the current conjuncture and the Irish case involved characterizing the settlement of 1688–89 as a 'conquest', thereby implying the possible legitimacy of expropriation of estates as part of its title. This was exactly what Molyneux accused his opponents of, i.e. expropriating Irish estates by the English and deriving such expropriation from the title of conquest. All he did was to turn the gaze back, once again to England, just as he did when he spoke of the title of conquest pertaining much more certainly to England in 1066 than Ireland in the period of Henry II.

Molyneux's set of arguments also explains the difficulty in defending the Lockean analogy between a robber and the conqueror, which formed the basis of the Lockean position that in just war, while the aggressor could be punished or killed, his estate could not be appropriated. For in the case of the robber there existed a terrestrial judge, but between sovereigns there existed no such judge, as Leibniz had argued in his remarks on William Sherlock.[159] There was also the implicit threat – and logical deduction – that if such a legal-proprietorial order was not maintained, the people could appeal to heaven. There is no other way to explain Locke's self-admittedly 'strange' doctrine of not allowing proprietorial right in conquest when it came to England, but recognizing the historical and legal origins of property in force – the allowing of such forcible appropriation in Ireland as much as the slavery of the Americas.

Contemporaneous political argument against James II, across the Whigs and the Tories, accepted conquest as a legitimate title. Yet, as is evident from above, it was far from clear as to whether, and if so in what sense, conquest implied proprietorial right over the vanquished. While Mark Goldie and J.G.A. Pocock[160] have demonstrated the vitality of conquest as title in 1688–89, with Pocock going so far as to argue that in a certain sense a civil war took place in 1688, neither of them sees Locke's doctrine of conquest as being in fact an argument about the way to regulate the possibilities of impending war and civil war – particularly the point that such fears of property or proprietary right may well be the basis for Locke's celebrated doctrine of property, which was indeed an attempt at voiding the victor's power over the property of the vanquished. The 1688–89 settlement was finally attributed to the action of James II, even if as an abdication it was an action of a negative sort.

It was an abdication that took place in the wake of William's claim to the title of the throne through inheritance, but also in so far as he had landed on the shores of England with arms, therefore invoking the title of conquest. As shown above, jurisprudence across the spectrum, from a judicially effective common law to a philosophically speculative natural law, had irretrievably muddied the lines between conquest and consent. In Hobbesian terms, both were driven by fear, and it was not actual violence but consent in the face of fear that grounded sovereignty, whether of the acquisitive or inherited sort, while the common law traditions allowed for species of conquests to be, in time, perfected in law. That James II was meant to have abdicated, and that William III who had arrived with arms and made claims was recognized as the new sovereign, makes it clear that the fact that the constitutional settlement provided for consent could not be taken to imply that it was a repudiation of conquest, in the light of the above discussions. For in no sense did the transfer of crowns declare the source of sovereignty to lie with the people's elective power, as was the argument made by a minority of writers, including a Locke in hiding and an unafraid Sidney, whose fate is well-known. The constitutional settlement did not deny the prerogative power of the King nor his various jurisdictions.

The King's Prerogative and the Branches of Prize Laws: Situating the East India Company

The Case for Prerogative and the East India Company Franchise

The above discussions have established the central role of the King in the constitution of the body-politic, as well as war that might lead to the incorporation of territories and peoples. The close nexus between war and 'foreign' trade was not merely expressed in the practices of the day with a militarized commerce, but their interconnections simultaneously raised constitutional questions on the nature of royal prerogative and on the subject's rights and liberties. It is in such a context that one may interpret the royal prerogative as having as one of its channels, the East India Company, and territorialization of seas, islands and scattered regions of the subcontinent. The Company, as a corporation, was constituted by a royal grant, and was given exclusive rights to trade in the east. From its very inception questions were raised about whether it was indeed benefiting the public, and whether it was not abridging the Englishman's right to trade. The first set of issues that emerged from these questions went on to become an important site and early instance of what one might call the discipline of economics, where the relations between trading rights and the public benefit, money and labour, were analysed.[161] The second set of questions concerned the very legality of the grant to the Company, claiming that the royal charter to the Company violated a (universal) and natural right to trade that was the right of every Englishman, particularly in the light of statutory prohibitions on monopolies.[162]

This issue of the legality of the royal grant simmered for long, reaching the King's Court in 1684 in a celebrated case that discussed, and legally settled, a whole range of questions around monopolies, right to trade and royal prerogative. One of the longest legal cases, it involved the best legal minds of the time. Its significance was indicated by the Chief Justice, who pronounced that it was one 'of great weight and consequence, perhaps as ever any case that has come into Westminster hall'.[163] The question was brought to the court by the East India Company, which claimed that Thomas Sandys had traded in areas in the east, regions that were out of bounds for all except the East India Company – this was a privilege granted to them by the King in his charters. Sandys and his lawyers questioned both the legality of the grant given by the King through his prerogative, as well as the right of the Company to initiate legal action against so-called violators of the charter in such a context. When it arrived at the King's Court, two questions therefore needed to be settled: the first concerned the legality of the royal grant to the Company, the second concerned the right of the Company to sue for damages on the basis of this grant.[164]

The case directly involved the nature and extent of royal prerogative through which the Company was constituted and given its rights and privileges, parliamentary statute, common law, and most importantly, their inter-relations. The main arguments put forward by Sandys's lawyers were that statute and common law allowed Englishmen to trade across the seas as a matter of right, and therefore any sort of royal grant that excluded this right was void in law;[165] only a parliamentary statute could abridge such a right.[166] Moreover, it was argued that such a specific royal grant which gave exclusive rights to a corporation amounted to a monopoly and was therefore, in yet another sense, void in law.[167] It must be recalled that the royal charters to the Company not only gave it exclusive trading rights in the east, but also gave it the power to grant licences to individuals to trade, and in turn allowed for the confiscation of the ship and goods of those who were found trading in these prohibited areas. After confiscation half the share of the ship and goods went to the King, and the other half went to the East India Company. The grant further gave the Company powers to grant to others the right to trade in the east.[168] Such a 'monopoly', as it was termed, was said to be void in law since it not only restricted another Englishman's right to trade, but in fact punished him.[169]

The attorney and solicitor general, on the other hand, argued that the East India trade was a 'foreign' trade, and there was no particular right to a foreign trade recorded anywhere. And even if there existed such a right, it was not meant to be a universal right but one that could well be restricted by the King in his political capacity. The prerogative writ of *Ne Exeat Regnum* allowed for this in the name of defending the realm.[170] In fact they argued that foreign trade as such came within the exclusive domain of the King, where he reigned supreme. As a subset of this argument, the lawyers cited authorities from the Bible to *Postnati*, among various statutes and historical precedents, to argue that 'infidels', i.e. those whom the Company traded with in the east, were regarded by law as 'perpetual enemies', and therefore no English subject could trade with them without special licence from the King.

Once again, the argument was that in the foreign domain, especially when one was dealing with non-Christians, Englishmen had no unmitigated right. This was grounded in the King's powers, in his capacity as the defender of religion and therefore part of the *Jus Publicum.*[171] If the King's licence was said to be required even for enclosing a castle or fortress within the realm, or transporting coin, there certainly could not be any doubt about his rights in the case of foreign trade.[172] The case of the East India Company could not be categorized as a monopoly because this was not a case where existing liberties of others were being restrained as in the case of a monopoly; such liberties in the foreign domain did not exist in the first place.[173] Parliamentary critiques of monopoly took place in the context of charters given to the Company, and never was the latter therein denied, proving that parliament did not consider the trade a monopoly. Similarly, there were several past instances of monarchs giving special licences to trade, as those given by Queen Elizabeth in the context of China or the Americas, or in other such domains where infidels ruled.[174]Particularly when it came to infidels – the domain where the Company carried out its trades – who were legally defined as 'perpetual enemies' by *Postnati,* the King's powers were deemed unquestionable.[175]

The counter-arguments to such a position pointed to the current trades with the Ottomans and other 'infidels', as well as statutory acts such as the Navigation Acts which did not appear to discriminate on the basis of religion. The 'perpetual hostility' towards infidels had to therefore be interpreted as being restricted to the 'spiritual sphere', having no application in the temporal affairs of trade.[176] The Jews were also mentioned as people who could not be classified as 'perpetual enemies' merely because they were not Christian, and the fact that the Jews had their properties before their general expulsion meant that one could not strictly adhere to the classification of non-Christians as infidels *qua* perpetual enemies. Such a status would have made any kind of property right impossible, something contradicted by the historical existence of the Jews, their properties and their estates.[177]

In countering this point, the attorney general reaffirmed aspects of *Postnati* which had delineated the determining role of the King in matters of allegiance. The King did have the power to make denizens out of enemy aliens, and the exercise of this power explained the status of both Jews[178] and 'infidels'. Jews were under special protection of the King and so could not be treated by any subject as an alien enemy.[179] This only established that the King had the power of determining subjecthood and therefore legal status. It was the King who had the prerogative powers to enter into public leagues and treaties with other sovereigns, thereby having the powers to alter their status, resulting in the possibility of trade with these 'infidel' nations.[180] The thrust of the argument was again that 'foreign' matters pertained to the King as matters of war and peace, and it was the domain in which he was supreme and therefore was allowed in law to make such a grant to the East India Company.

Citing a number of statutes and precedents to establish such a case, and particularly echoing *Postnati*, the lawyers reaffirmed the powers of the King to determine the status of the subject. It appeared true, they argued, that according to ancient statutes the goods of a pagan or Jew – as 'alien enemies' or 'perpetual enemies' – could be seized by anyone, just as the lord could beat his villain and a husband his wife; such alien enemies could not initiate legal actions because of their status.[181] But the attorney general clarified that this could be done only if the King had already declared an open war on the sovereign to whom these aliens were subject, thereby rendering these aliens as alien enemies. Only in such an open war declared by the King could subjects seize as Prize the goods of an alien enemy.[182] Any alien enemy, including infidels who were declared as 'perpetual enemies' according to common law, most recently in the shape of *Postnati*, could be rendered into alien *amis* (friends) if the King chose to give them such a status or safe passage – as clearly recorded as far back as the Magna Carta.

Thus, when it came to both alien friends and alien enemies, the King's actions had the power to change their status.[183] The right to Prize in an open war was enabled only by the declaration of the King, just as an alien enemy, even the infidel as perpetual enemy, could be given protection by the King disabling the rights that subjects would otherwise have had in seizing as Prize the goods of an alien enemy. All this established the fact that the King, through his prerogative, had exclusive rights when it came to foreign trade and establishing leagues with both alien friends and alien enemies, and therefore the legality of the patent granted to the East India Company, concerned as it was with trade with infidels, was to be considered good in law. While naturalization required an act of parliament, the King could grant denizenship which in effect gave the same rights.[184]

Moreover, the rights of the King in such respects were confirmed by past precedent, such as the Michelborn case, which showed that the King had the powers to give special commissions and letters of Prize and marche to individuals to 'spoil' and attack enemy infidels in and across the seas.[185] This was seen as particularly relevant in the case of the East India trades, because here trade was eminently 'political' and militarized involving 'pagans', and the

Company had to be given the rights to such reprisals in case they were injured or attacked. The fact that there was no public league entered into with the rulers of India[186] meant that such powers of war- and peace-making, as well as the right to reprisals, had to be granted.

If the trade were opened to all individuals, by the conventions of the time, in case any individual injured the subjects in Asia, reprisals would be taken by the princes of India on all other traders including those of the Company. Pragmatism, the lawyers argued, therefore required that the Company be given sole authority, so that the trades built over several decades, which had brought great prosperity to the public in England, not be brought to nought in catering to the interests of individual adventurers such as Thomas Sandys.[187] On the other hand, they reiterated, the fact that no public league had been entered into by the King with the princes of India meant that no right to trade could be asserted by English subjects, as might be claimed in those trades where such leagues and treaties were entered into.[188] Common law had no jurisdiction in these areas beyond the seas where other jurisdictions such as the Admiralty Courts (and imperial civil law) directly under the King held sway. Common law could not hold sway because all such foreign trades were regulated by the law of nations and civil law; foreigners could not be expected to know and adhere to the municipal and common law jurisdictions of individual kingdoms.

In outlining the King's powers, the lawyers pointed to the fact that even fairs and markets internal to England were given by the grant of the King, and therefore certainly no question could be raised when it came to foreign trade. All fairs, rights, staples and corporations within the country derived from a King's grant, and even in cases where no such grant was found and claims were made on the basis of prescription, it was assumed to have been originally granted by the King.[189] It was this fact that enabled the forfeiture of such rights to the Crown, held the lawyers. In the realm of foreign trade, there were too many such special privileges and grants to mention, from individual commissions such as those given to Raleigh, to the Russia, Turkey and Barbary companies.

Trade could not take place without treaties or delegated powers such as those given to the East India Company. The rationale behind many of these special grants lay in the fact that only in this manner could new trades be encouraged. Thus, the charters and commissions should be treated as exclusive rights that were given to patents and other such inventions.[190] The grant to the East India Company needed to be construed similarly and therefore could not be characterized as a monopoly, which was acknowledged as void in law. Moreover, in the case of the Company, the trades had been carried on for several decades without any parliamentary disapproval, and these decades saw the building up of material and political infrastructure on the basis of which adventurers like Thomas Sandys could trade. These several years therefore, in themselves, created a kind of property right, which could not be extended to others without causing injustice.

Interestingly Thomas Sandys's lawyers, while questioning the application of prerogative to the case, simultaneously insisted that the grant to the Company indirectly amounted to abridging this very prerogative. They argued so because by the terms of the royal grant the Company could grant licences to others to trade, but the King apparently could not.[191] On this matter, the attorney general merely stated that the King was not 'bound up by his grant', but the fact of the matter was that Sandys was given no such grant by the King and therefore this question was not the issue.[192]

After listening to all the arguments and counter-arguments, the judges agreed that it was the 'inherent prerogative in the crown that none should trade with foreigners without king's license'; matters relating to war and peace came under the dominion of the King.[193] Moreover, years of trade by the Company itself created a right they held. Chief Justice Jefferies, in clarifying the prerogatives of the King, also emphasized the fact that the terms of the charter allowed the King to void the grant after giving three years' notice.[194] Although not directly relevant to the case, the chief justice further held that the King could indeed grant a licence to others by his prerogative powers notwithstanding the terms of the charter. Upholding the argument of the attorney general, he held that it was within the sole prerogative of the King to enter into treaties with foreign princes or grant corporations the licences to trade with them.[195] The same prerogative extended even to manufactures and corporations within England, which prohibited engrossing and forestalling in local trades. And that which was called prescription and custom had their 'commencement by royal grant', and corporations might claim 'liberties and privileges by prescription, yet these originally proceeded from the crown, and are therefore forfeitable to the crown'.[196]

Moreover, common law did not extend to matters of 'foreign trade', for here it was the law of nations and 'imperial civil law' that provided a legal and regulatory framework, all of which came under the King through the Admiralty Courts and the Court of Chancery.[197] Foreign trade and commerce came under the '*inter jura regalia*' power of the King's undoubted prerogative, which also had the authority to give letters of mart and reprisal, as it did, to the Company.[198] The judges unanimously held the right of the King to grant the Company good in law, as well as the Company's right to proceed against Thomas Sandys. Thus, the Sandys case firmly established the close juridical link between the Crown and Company, making it clear that the Company's trades and powers were derived firmly from the King's prerogative.

In the preceding debate and discussion between the government and Company lawyers there was an ambiguity about the relations between (King-in) parliament and the chartered rights of the Company. In the course of the debate, the attorney and solicitor general did not deny the powers of parliament on matters of trade and rights to trade. In fact, in defending the validity of the Company's charter, they pointed to the fact that parliament had never in the past several decades, since the origin of the Company, challenged its charter on the grounds of any general right to trade. Notwithstanding the strong ways in which they emphasized the role of the King and his prerogative, this dimension of the importance of parliament was simultaneously stressed. That is to say, no clear (King-in) parliamentary act could be found that articulated a general denial of the King's rights in such matters, nor did there exist on record a specific denial of the legality of the East India Company charter. Similarly, as discussed, the King's lawyers were at pains to argue that the Company's trade could not be categorized as a monopoly, conceding that such a monopoly was not good in law since it abridged rights held to be common and universal.

The East India Company was empowered by royal charters in the 1660s and thereafter to conduct war and peace with non-Christians, as well as enforce martial law in its territories. This included letters of marche to try pirates and seize the goods of 'interlopers', a case of which provided the pretext for the Sandys decision. Specific interventions by the powers of the King and his commissioners played a crucial role in the conduct of the East India Company. For instance, in the same year of the trial, 1684, Bombay was seized by Captain Kweigen in the name of the King. It was only after a specially commissioned officer, Thomas Grant, intervened that peace was restored.[199]

Several petitions were made to parliament pleading for enabling a greater participation, beyond the East India Company, in the lucrative East India trades. In 1693, the set of issues on the relationship between the common and universal rights of Englishmen to trade and the Company's exclusive privileges resurfaced, and were discussed in the House of Commons. The

House then passed a resolution to the effect that all Englishmen had the right to trade in the East Indies unless denied such a right specifically by parliament. It then went on to petition King William to dissolve the Company. The King, in consultation with the Privy Council, made clear that it would not be good in law to immediately dissolve the Company, and stated that such an act of dissolution could be done only with a notice of three years according to the charter. He also suggested that for the House of Commons to fulfil its intention to regulate the East India trade, it would be best for it to formulate a bill to such a purpose in three years.[200]

In the meantime the Company, by not paying a particular tax, had forfeited its privileges and therefore was lobbying hard to reconfirm its charter. This charter was acquired from King William, who gave it under the great seal because of, in his words, the Company's 'industrious application'.[201] More charters were issued subsequently, and in all, four charters were granted by William III between the end of 1693 and the beginning of 1698.[202] These charters were passed despite the House of Commons resolution, a resolution which took statutory effect only some time later in 1698 when an act was passed denying the exclusive rights of the East India Company, and in turn enabling the formation of a new regulated Company whose subscribers would be granted the right to trade in the East.[203] The same statute also allowed persons subscribing to the new corporation to themselves form into a distinct corporation to trade in the east. The year 1698 therefore witnessed the first parliamentary statute directly applicable to the East India trade.[204]

When speaking of statute, parliament and royal prerogative, it must be remembered that it was the King through his assent who made a bill a law, and he could unilaterally disallow a bill from becoming a law. King William used this power a few times, and though such a power was rarely, if ever, used thereafter, it was never formally annulled. The 1698 Act which regulated the East India trade was affirmed by two royal charters issued by King William III. Together, all three in effect enabled Englishmen to trade in the form of a new corporation whose subscribers could themselves form a distinct corporation. Thus the 'older' Company remained as a separate joint-stock company continuing to trade in the East, and in fact this particular company's distinctive identity and rights to trade – no longer exclusive – were renewed by a parliamentary statute in 1701.[205] The branch of the prerogative that uniquely enabled the King to constitute corporations was affirmed in the 1698 Act, and exercised in the constitution of the corporations as a regulating company which was called the 'New Company'.[206]

In its constitutive capacities, the King's specific powers to enable a corporation to govern by creating laws, by-laws and ordinances were affirmed.[207] While (King-in) parliamentary acts henceforth renewed charters which enabled the Company to retain its trading privileges in the east, it was specifically from the King that the legality of 'governance', the enactment of laws, by-laws, courts and regulations issued. Thus, for instance, in 1726, the corporations of Bombay, Calcutta and Madras,[208] as well as the Mayor's Courts, were established from such specific authority of royal charters and letters-patent.[209] These specific royal patents not only gave juridical powers, but also reconfirmed the powers of martial law that had been delegated to the Company in the charters of the seventeenth century. Moreover, as a branch of war, Prize jurisdiction issued forth from royal prerogative, as signified, for instance, by the letters-patent regarding Prize issued by William III in 1693.[210] Other specific rights, such as the right to attack pirates, emerged from this very same royal prerogative in the form of specific charters or empowerment though royal commissions

The King's Foreign Domain: The Laws of Prize Nesting East India Company Trade

While the King's prerogative powers were in various ways confirmed in the granting of various rights and privileges to the East India Company, it is necessary to investigate Prize laws as a branch of this prerogative which framed and authorized the Company's military–commercial actions in the East. While in 1693 (King-in) parliamentary statute regulated the East India trade for the first time, both before and after 1693, the East India Company was governed by specific charters and privileges issued specifically from the King in his prerogative powers. To better understand this, this section analyses the King's Prize jurisdiction in its historical emergence, ending in an analysis and documentation of its specific manifestation in the East India trade.

The question of Prize law and the rights of the captor in relation to the rights of the sovereign were much discussed in Greek and Roman law as well as scripture.[211] Grotius gives us a detailed history of this juridical problem in his *Rights to War and Peace*, which fundamentally amounted to the following question: In war or hostilities, did the property of the conquered lie with the immediate captor or did it lie with the sovereign under whose jurisdiction the captor lay?[212] Many layers of this problem – growing into an entire ethical –political discourse – were already in existence during Roman times where there was evidence for both arguments on record, as well as a calibration of various qualifications. For instance, it was asked, if war placed one in a 'natural state', was the right over the vanquished and his property a natural right or could the latter be governed by civil law? Some legislation sanctioned to the soldier a certain amount of the spoils, but he was meant to give the rest to the commander. There were many cases where commanders refused such booty since it was glory and not riches that they were said to value.[213] And at other times, the taking of lawful Prize by generals and soldiers was seen as akin to robbing the public, who, it was argued, had the real right to enemy property.[214] On the other hand, according to some, allowing the soldier his booty was a way to encourage his dedication to the country and ensure that such justice would only encourage and induce him to fight harder and stronger.

This jurisprudential backdrop is essential to consider the operationalization of Prize law in European and specifically English history, that may be seen to begin in the later medieval period. A history of Prize laws from the twelfth to thirteenth centuries is simultaneously a history that unveils the absolute claims by sovereigns to any captured property, as well as the recognition that the actual captors had some right, howsoever undefined, in the share. This absolute claim of Kings was not always the case. For instance, in the eleventh and twelfth centuries there is evidence of merchants forming associations to defend themselves against pirates, with an 'admiral' – the word derived from the Saracean *amir* – to lead them.[215] An early example from Denmark records the practice of a commercial association having the right to defend and attack ships on sea, and divide the plunder and booty without any specific sanction from the proprietor, who was left with one-eighth of the share. Christians were to be released, but no such definite rule restrained the treatment of non-Christians, reiterating and anticipating the legal categorization of non-Christian religious communities, as 'perpetual enemies' in *Postnati*.[216] This was an example which testified to the absence of a juridical process or sovereign assent to such captures, in which lives were taken and property acquired.[217]

However, in England, soon after the Norman conquest, in the thirteenth and fourteenth centuries, the King's right to ships, goods and captures clearly appears on record. Grants for such captured objects show that the legal title to them required the authority of the King.[218] Before the formalization of an Admiralty Court – beginning from the fourteenth century – it was the King's Council which declared whether the captured object was Prize or not. Condemning and declaring it to be Prize was recognition of its legality, after which claims to it in concrete could be made.

Captured objects would thus have to be understood and evaluated at two levels: first, in the existential–categorical sense, i.e. the determination as to whether it was Prize (lawful Prize) or not; secondly, as to who could claim rights to Prize. From very early times, the King established the right to decide the first question. This could be seen not only in the functioning of the King's Council in determining Prize, but also in the existence of letters of marque that enabled privateers and merchants to capture ships and goods on ships. As early as 1293, there is evidence of subjects soliciting letters of marque from King Edward the First.[219] This needs to be read as a departure from treaties between France and England in the early thirteenth century where the rights of private subjects to attack other sovereigns or their subjects without any specific authorization was acknowledged.[220] The thirteenth century also saw the emergence of admiralty jurisdictions, and admirals had the right to give letters of marque.[221] By the fourteenth century it seemed to be necessary to apply for such letters.[222] These were signs of the King assuming absolute forms of sovereignty within their realms, and thus requiring that their subjects be denuded of any authority of their own to war among themselves (within the kingdom) as well as war between kingdoms (private subjects fighting private subjects of another sovereign or another sovereign directly). The latter dimension – the denial of private subjects of one country to fight another without sovereign sanction – was codified in several treaties between rulers.

In England during the fifteenth century, at the time of Henry V, legislation enabled safe passage to foreigners in specific contexts through treaties.[223] Yet treaties also specified that aggrieved parties ought to apply to their sovereigns first and not initiate action on their own.[224] The extent of unregulated warfare in the seas by privateers is indicated by emerging legislation which required that privateers provide security deposits to their own sovereigns before they set out to sea.[225] However, to ensure that subjects had the right of reprisals against any attacks from foreigners, they were given the right to apply for specific sanction from the 'keeper of the seals'.[226] In 1414, legislation specifically stated that private ships which may have taken any property from enemies were required to bring their Prize to the port and subject it to the Admiralty Court, which would determine whether it was lawful Prize and decide on the manner of the property's disposal.[227]

While private actors were deprived of authority of their own, it was by no means the case that sovereigns did not use such private actors against each other, whether in open war or in hostilities and undeclared wars. In fact it was precisely these authorizations from sovereigns which distinguished privateers and non-public actors from being designated as pirates, and therein 'enemies to all'. Privateering amounted to the outfitting of a ship to attack the enemy and prevent anyone, including 'neutrals', from assisting or engaging in any kind of commerce with the enemy. Such practices clearly developed and flourished in the sixteenth century.[228] Specific instructions were given that enabled them to search and seize even neutral vessels during times of war. This was rationalized by the argument that the commerce of neutral vessels aided the enemy.[229] In the fifteenth and sixteenth centuries, greater commerce across the globe expanded, and with it, war, hostilities and rivalries between the great powers. In such a context, the increasing menace of privateering was well reflected in the growing regulations and laws around it. Privateers were encouraged and since they were not under the regular pay of the state, specific inducements in the forms of Prize and plunder were given.[230]

Maritime warfare thus lost all the constraints that a land war might have imposed. In land wars, in general, the peaceable subjects of the enemy were to be left unmolested. In the case of the seas, however, there existed no such category of 'peaceful subjects', and the property of 'neutrals', which would have been protected in a land war, lost all sanctity.[231] The privateer could be induced only by promises of plunder; glory was for those who fought directly for the public. The long wars between the Dutch and Spain and then the coming of the English into these militarized forms of commerce during the reign of Queen Elizabeth saw much maritime-cum-commercial conflict, particularly against Dutch privateers and later against Spain.[232] During the reign of Elizabeth, the Admiralty Court is to have become completely formalized and run a brisk business, reaffirming the rights of the King.[233] An example of royal power reiterating its sovereign rights in these matters is the invalidation of the Warden of the Cinq Ports, and the many commissions granted to privateers empowering them with rights of reprisals and recaptures.[234] Kings granted commissions to establish colonies – commissions which included the right to exclusive trades, and therein the powers to prevent others from trading. Simultaneously, an increasing number of commissions to capture the ships of pirates, enemies, and those aiding and trading with enemies in war were issued.[235]

While the sovereign right of the King to determine the category of plunder through his judicial procedure and courts seemed settled, there appeared some ambiguity on the relationship between the shares to be divided by King and captor. From the earliest times on record, there does not seem to have been any uniformity in the matter, even as the King always staked a claim to a share of Prize and booty, since it was considered legal only if sanctioned by him.[236] It was legal either through a commission before the seizure or by the decision of an Admiralty Court after. The laws of war were regulated by civil law in the Admiralty Court, as well as the Courts of Marshall and Constable which were directly under the King.

However, there existed previous statutes, as discussed in the Sandys case, which suggested 'natural right' of the captor. In Finch's *Common Laws*, it was stated that 'every man may seize the goods of an alien enemy for his own use'.[237] However, the same work speaks of the Courts of Marshall and Constable as regulating the treatment of alien enemies, thus clarifying the supremacy of the King in matters of war.[238] Coke's reports also made clear that in matters regarding martial law, civil law was followed, and all this remained within the King's domain. In fact the domain of martial law was the limit that distinguished the kingdom(s) from the King, while at the same time subjecting the former to the latter. As the attorney general in the Sandys case argued, the natural right of an individual to seize the property of an alien enemy as Prize could proceed only if the King had declared an open war.

In the sixteenth century, the rising formalization of the Admiralty Court, which adjudicated Prize, outlined a terrain of jurisdiction that was to be clearly distinguished from that of common law. These courts, insofar as they dealt with foreign princes and their subjects, operated in terms of civil law or the laws of nations. Prize jurisdiction and the laws on captures were closely entangled with treaties from very early times. It is at the site of the Admiralty Courts that we see the development of what might be called a law of nations. In an important case in 1612, twelve judges designated and recognized the Admiralty Court as the King's Court, and Prize was condemned in his name.[239] The navigation laws of the commonwealth era allowed any violators of the Navigation Acts to be designated as pirates, and their ships and goods as Prize. Admiralty Courts seemed overworked with Prize being available among a range of entities including enemies, those who aided them, those violating the navigation laws, as well as those individuals and states who were not formally in public league with England. 'Turks' and other sovereigns and peoples with whom no formal treaties existed could also be characterized as 'pirates'.

Prize jurisdiction was adjudicated by the Admiralty Courts, and while the latter often competed with the common law courts, this competition concerned the domain of instance not Prize. Prize was one point on which even Coke recognized the jurisdiction of the Admiralty Court.[240] Since the very nature of Prize was determined by the King's Courts, the King's share appears to have been derived therein. Simultaneously, the captor's right to the property of the vanquished was also acknowledged both as his inherent right as captor, as well as a reward and stimulus to aid the King/Queen in his/her ventures. Much like in Grotius's discussion of Roman law and the practices of antiquity, Prize law and the civil law as practised by the Admiralty Courts also appeared to recognize the right of the captor over its 'prey' if the latter was recognized to be an alien enemy. This right acquired a statutory dimension, however, only in the 1690s, even while all Prize was ultimately to be subsumed within the rights of the royal sovereign.[241]

By the late seventeenth century, a very concrete commercial policy was etched with a sophisticated legal apparatus that included courts and commissions. This was along the vector of the developing discourse of a law of nations. Admiralty law had to be seen in conjunction with the very specific circumstances of treaties and wars. More uncertain – in a conscious strategic way, one might add – were the relations between actors such as the East India Company who were formally commissioned by the King, and the foreign political entities who did not enjoy any legal status from the perspective of the English in not having formed any treaties with the latter. Such political entities therefore did not have access to the Admiralty Courts or any procedure recognized by English law. While one may not wish to agree with Grotius, his characterization of the English, as those who saw it within their right to plunder anyone with whom no formal treaties existed as they sailed across the seas, seems unerringly accurate and forcefully prescient. This was indeed English law since an earlier Henrican statute did not allow legal action against the English on the seas, and they had to be brought to land to be judged – a situation that was changed only in 1700 when, under William III, parliamentary statute allowed for their trial abroad.[242]

It is in this light that one may situate and read the specific history of the East India Company, which always enjoyed a special relationship with the King.[243] It was governed, and in turn governed, on the basis of charters which were regularly renewed by the King in the seventeenth century. The Company was, by royal charter in the late seventeenth century, explicitly given war- and peace-making as well legislative authority, apart from martial law.[244] It was also specifically given letters of marche and reprisal as well as commissions to capture pirates.[245] These powers were specially occasioned by rebellions, interlopers, and conflicts with native powers in the course of their militarized trades. The specific nature of these charters and the rights bestowed needs to be read in conjunction with a whole range of other legislation that revealed, as much as concealed, the nature of English sovereignty as much as Indian territory.

For instance, the commercial and military formation that was the Company from very early on partook in claiming Prize, among other forms of jurisdiction, in the eastern waters. There are early instances of claims of Prize by James IV that were consented to by the Company, even as it resisted other claimants, such as the Lord Admiral, to such Prize.[246] Prize law operated at the tender ligament that joined the primordial right to capture by the actual captor and the sovereign, in whose idiom the subject-captor achieved legal legibility. From very early on, as discussed above, the legitimacy of the King's claim could not be denied; after all it was such a claim that rendered the Prize legal. Attaining legality however also meant that Prize was now fundamentally seen as the King's, even as it was customary for the King to only claim a particular share, leaving the rest to the captor. Understanding Prize is equally to enter into the deep and unpredictable currents of martial and maritime jurisdiction. For instance, in 1683, the East India Company was itself granted admiralty jurisdiction and not just rights to Prize in 'countries within their limits', which would allow them to 'seize and condemn' ships deemed interlopers.[247]

In the 1680s, the precise historical moment of the Sandys case and thereafter, the Court of Directors of the East India Company decided that the only way to improve and secure their trade was to become an 'Indian power'.[248] Its clear ambition was to become a political power with its own specific territory, enclaves, revenues and armies, which could form the basis of domination and expansion. The attempt was to make its stations in India militarized regencies and assert power so as to be no longer dependent on the local powers for rights and privileges. In part, this was to imitate the Dutch who had outmanoeuvred them in Bantam by placing upon the throne their own candidate as King.[249] Other reasons included the need to act on 'interlopers' and secure trading privileges through force of arms – privileges that otherwise, they argued, were subject to the whims and wishes of native rulers. In pursuit of this aggressive military–commercial policy the Court of Directors of the East India Company encouraged war with the Mughal emperor as well as with the King of Siam towards the end of the seventeenth century.

In an attempt to realize its larger ambitions of wars with the local rulers across territories from the subcontinent to South East Asia, as well as help quell a local rebellion by its own officers who rebelled in the name of the English King, the Court requested King James's help, who obliged generously. Many officers, such as Thomas Grantham and Captain Nicholas, were granted commissions by the King, and were directed to proceed in armed ships to help the Company against interlopers as well as establish fortified settlements.[250] Dr St John was commissioned by the King as 'Judge Advocate',[251] and the rebels, who were defeated, would therefore be tried under him in what was construed to be a 'King's Bench'. While the King had earlier granted 'Admiralty jurisdiction' to the Company within its territories to prosecute interlopers, under the advice of St John, John Child[252] was made the Company's president by the King's patent. His title was president, 'Captain General and Admiral' of territories from India to the Gulf of Persian.[253] The Company retained its powers to try interlopers, and they did so through the 'King's Bench' – for instance in 1685, when forty-eight were principally charged.[254]

The concerted nature of the plan to aggressively consolidate and expand is further indicated by the fact that the Company applied to the King to issue a royal proclamation, which he obliged. In the proclamation, it was held that all Company servants and English subjects had to return to Company settlements[255] or face punitive consequences. The seriousness of encouraging such concrete settlements can be gauged by the fact that soldiers were urged to marry native women in the Bombay region so as to promote colonization. For every child with these women, they were promised a gold pagoda each as reward.[256] In pursuit of its larger plans of expanding its militarized trades, the Court decided to have a fortified station in the 'mouth of the Ganges' by capturing Chittagong.[257] Dictated by the belief that success in war would enable an enforcement of favourable terms of trade on concrete issues like the lessening of duties, the Court hoped to replicate the Dutch model in the subcontinent. Armed ships by royal commission were outfitted to capture vessels from the Persian Gulf, and kept as bargaining counters to ensure claims and privileges of the Company's trade.[258]

While the Court was making its plans, certain events took place in Bengal that was to have important consequences.[259] In what was a clear dispute between local weavers and the Company, the local *faujdar* forced the Company to pay the former. In this context, the Court decided to express its aggressive policy. With the approval of the King in England, instructions were sent to commence hostilities with the Nawab and the Mughal emperor, in a reassertion of 'trading' rights. For this, an expedition was fitted out from England consisting of ten ships. Captain Nicholas and eighteen others were given King's commissions, and were to join forces with those of Fort St George. Disembarkation would take place in Chittagong, which was to be taken possession of, treaties signed with amenable local rulers, and 'the Mogul's ships of every description, were to be seized, and a Court of Admiralty appointed in Bengal (Captain Nicholas to be Judge Advocate) to condemn the Prizes'.[260] In effect, war was to be declared on the Nawab, the Mughal emperor and the King of Siam. Fearing that Aurangzeb would attack Surat in the west, Child, the Company president, got the royally-commissioned ships to seize the vessels trading to Moccha and Basra as Prize.[261]

Another flashpoint erupted on 18 October 1686, in which a quarrel by English soldiers in the bazaar had led to the killing of 60 persons of the Nabob's troops. A large number were wounded, guns were destroyed and 500 houses burned by the Company.[262] The Nabob in turn seized the English factory at Patna, imprisoning all those residing there. An armistice ensued. But this armistice was not something the Court in London was happy about. They wrote that there ought to have been more plundering in the area since that would be the only way in which the English could claim some dignity.[263] In their continued efforts to obtain Chittagong, they sent Captain Heath, who arrived in Bengal in 1688 with a frigate. There were attempted negotiations, in the meantime, in trying to get the release of the English who had been held captive by the Nabob. Notwithstanding a *parwana* of peace which had been received by the English from the Nabob, the Company 'landed the troops and seamen attacked and took a battery of thirty three guns and plundered the town of Balasore'.[264] In return, the local governor burned the English factory and took the captive English up country. Attempts at negotiating a peace continued, but before any denouement, Captain Heath set sail for Aracan, attempted to interfere in local politics, and then all of a sudden deciding to return to Fort St George. Complaints were immediately made to the Court that Heath did not do what he was sent out for, i.e. capture Chittagong or any fortified station suitable to trade in Bengal.

In the meantime, John Child had the unenviable job of commencing hostilities with the Mughals. He was to claim that the Company had attributed the causes of war to interlopers who were said to have had the support of the Mughals, even though clearly, the cause lay in the 'rash and indecisive conduct' of Company officials in Bengal.[265] Child wrote to the Dutch and the French asking them not to interfere and to abide by treaties between their countries.[266] Meanwhile the governor of Surat, Mr Harris, was detained as feared, and in the face of the local governor's powers in the land and the Mughal fleet under Sidi Yaqub, attempts at reconciliation were initiated. However, at exactly that very moment, the Company ships had returned from

Persia with Mughal ships as Prize. Hostilities could no longer be concealed.[267]

Even so, the arrival of a new local 'Governor', Shaistha Khan, who was predisposed to peace, led to a convention being negotiated between Child and him. That was the time when the armistice was broken in Bengal. As part of the attempted settlement, Mughal Prize ships were returned, despite the Court's specific instructions against this from England.[268] The convention with the governor gave the Company the right to mint coins. However, Shaistha Khan in the meantime imprisoned Company officials Harris and Gladman in Surat, and sold off the Company's properties. Child had by now captured forty trading vessels off the coast of Bombay, and a conflict with the Mughal fleet seemed imminent. Recognizing his own precarious position in the face of Aurangzeb marching victoriously across the Deccan, Child attempted to open negotiations with the emperor.[269]

At this crucial juncture Child died and the mantle was passed on to Vaux, since the second in command, Harris, was imprisoned in Surat.[270] Desperate for peace, Vaux moved to Surat from Bombay to negotiate. While Harris was released, the terms of the negotiation, ultimately acceded to by the English, were seen as deeply humiliating. In the words of the chronicler John Bruce, rather than a negotiation between equals, Aurangzeb treated the English 'as a prince pardons a criminal whose labours might be useful, but whose character was no longer respectable'.[271] In the meantime, Aurangzeb's admiral Yakut Khan's fleet and army had invaded Bombay and got possession of English territories (Mahim, Mazagaon and Sion). The goods taken by the English were restored, but they were to pay a large fine as a punitive measure. Thus, only in May–June 1690 did Khan vacate Bombay and other English possessions.

From Fort St George, the Company officials prayed for Aurangzeb's protection, saying that the happenings in Bengal were but an attempt to retrieve ancient privileges that were granted, and should not be taken as an attempt at war. Aurangzeb was not very far off. Having conquered Visiapore he was approaching Golconda, which was very likely to succumb.[272] The English, afraid of Aurangzeb's successes in the Deccan, pleaded for peace, and were given another 'pharman' to trade in exchange of gifts and presents of money.[273] They were also invited to settle in Bengal in their factories.

At the same time, in the context of the momentous happenings in England, the Court of Directors of the East India Company experienced the very concerns prevalent in England regarding the impending 'conquest' of William III. They all the same sent instructions through their ships that they had the rights to make Prizes of interlopers as well as native powers that were seen to threaten their interests; the charters of Charles and James were appended as proof.[274] Battling the Dutch in the dangerously tropical and maritime environs of the East Indies, the Company officials were being told by their Dutch enemies in stray encounters that William III, the Dutchman, had landed in England with large armaments.[275]

How would William III adjudicate between his subjects and his countrymen, it was wondered. Putting such concerns to rest, William III was proclaimed King jointly, accepted as monarch by the Company as much as the rest of England. In fact it was not long before William claimed 100,000 pounds as Prize from the Mughal ships captured by the East India Company.[276] The claims of the King over the seas were however not restricted to Prize. The first statutory legislation on Prize in 1692 has to be read alongside both the Piracy Act of 1698 and the East India Company Act of 1698, all of which indexed the legislative penetration of the seas and trade. Since the earlier Henrican act required that juridical actions had to take place on *terra firma* – difficult in a time of continuous war – the new act of 1692 ensured that Admiralty Courts could act and condemn at sea.

While the parliamentary act of 1698 henceforth served as the basis for the establishment of a 'New Company' to trade in the East Indies, the King's specific powers of constituting the corporation as well as serving as the bases for its juridical and military powers were only emphasized by the said act. These powers of the King to delegate to the Company the powers to make laws and by-laws, and enact martial law, were emphasized by the royal charters of 1726 as well as subsequent parliamentary statutes relating to the East India Company in the early eighteenth century. And thus, a distinctive royal channel of jurisdiction remained unaffected, its manifestation being the constitution and military–commercial actions of the East India Company. In the concluding section below, an attempt is made to analyse the changing role and place of the King in the constitutional arrangement across the seventeenth century, so as to return to the question as to whether the East India Company's history sheds any light on forms of royal jurisdiction that are distinct in their own right.

Conclusion

If there has been silence above on the raging conflicts of the civil wars and the Cromwellian period, it is because the discourse produced during those tumultuous times is explicitly refuted by the Restoration and post-Restoration settlement. If this is simply an undeniable fact, the question to be inquired into is whether, and in what sense, the 'revolutionary' settlement of 1688–89 affirmed the constitutional principles of the early 1600s while repudiating the civil wars and interregnum. While this is no doubt a broad question and the subject of variegated and rich scholarship, it might not be uncontroversial to begin by stating that the essential postulates of *Postnati* were reaffirmed in settlement of the last decade of the century.

The principle of hereditary kingship as the source of jurisdictions survived intact.[277] Two anachronisms might obscure this fact. One is the clear-cut distinction between the legislative and the executive, and the treatment of the first as primary and the second as derivative. The other is to confine the problematic of kingship to the question of individual powers in relationship to specific institutions that are seen as independent of the King, rather than inquire into the theoretical account of the continuity of the body-politic and/as jurisdictions. Even after 1688–89, while the King could be conceived as distinct from parliament, the latter could not be conceived of as distinct from him, and it was allegiance to the King and his heirs that defined allegiance, therefore accounting for the unity and identity of the body-politic/jurisdictions across space and time. Finally, in a conceptual-Aristotelian sense, action/execution is not to be conceived of as either derivative of or dependent on a law-making parliament, since the latter could enact its laws only through the King, retrieving the Aristotelian argument that actuality was prior to potentiality. The King was distinct because in him lay the principle of action, and no (human) law could judge him.

Kingship was therefore defined so as to mean that the King remained in his natural person the object of allegiance, remained essential to statutory and common law, and at the same time remained a distinctive source of jurisdiction of his own right – whether in the context of war, the military or colonial settlements, as is shown below. In this context, it bears reiterating that the judicial decision of *Postnati* clearly rejected the prior and contrary resolution of the House of Commons, and the understanding that though Scotland and England were united in the person of the King, allegiance lay towards the laws and therein the laws-territory. In other words, allegiance was 'diverse'.[278] In sharp contrast, the judges of *Postnati* declared that it was 'between sovereignty and allegiance that laws were begotten', and sovereignty was owed to the natural person of the King.[279] Such a conceptualization of allegiance was simultaneously a particular articulation of the body-politic in its diverse jurisdictions. In concluding this part of the book, interpreting the post-Restoration settlement in the light of the long seventeenth century and *Postnati* will be undertaken, first, through an engagement with the question of allegiance, before moving on to then examine its implications for understanding the integrity and diversity of the imperially differentiated body-politic.

The confirmation of allegiance as owed to the natural person of the King even in the revolutionary settlement has to be placed in its historical and ideological context. The so-called convention parliament was enabled by writs issued by William III for an election by an assembly that he had called – until which time he assumed government, on petition from the same assembly.[280] After much debate and discussion, the (pseudo)parliament resolved that James II, having 'endeavoured to subvert the constitution of the kingdom by breaking the original contract between King and people', having violated fundamental laws by the advice of 'wicked people', and having withdrawn himself out of the kingdom, had 'abdicated the government', leaving the throne 'vacant'.[281] That the characteristic act was 'abdication' made it starkly clear that no claim was being made about any resistance by anybody – whether parliament or the people – which had resulted in the deposition of King James II.

Debate over the characterization of the 'vacancy' of the throne arose because such a characterization would indicate that a genuine transfer of crowns had occurred, raising questions of title. The abdication of James II and the proclamation of William and Mary was nothing but a 'transfer' of crowns, because the non-consideration of the heirs of James had effectively repudiated the hereditary principle of monarchy. That is to say, if the hereditary principle was followed, no 'vacancy' could exist; the heir would inherit directly without any intervening 'vacancy'. However, such a clear repudiation of the hereditary principle was not to be understood to mean the introduction of an elective principle in the institution of monarchy. This was made amply clear by attributing the 'vacancy' to James's own 'abdication', rather than the resistance and deposing power of any particular body endowed with such rights and liberties. The only legally coherent explanation and description for the transfer of crowns from James II to William and Mary was conquest, as was well recognized by several contemporaries.[282]

From the perspective of *Postnati* as well as subsequent jurisprudential literature, sovereign title was acquired either by conquest or through inheritance. That William III had arrived in England with armed forces and was jointly crowned with Mary meant that such a transfer could only be interpreted as a title by conquest; adherence to the hereditary principle would have resulted in Mary inheriting and no joint crowning, without any intervening 'vacancy'. Constitutional principles from *Postnati* onwards had recognized that allegiance and protection were reciprocal, what in the 1688–89 context might well have been worded as 'constitution' or 'fundamental laws' in the declaration of the (pseudo)'parliament'– the 'constitution', 'original contract' and 'laws' which were to have been violated by James II. That this 'parliament' could not be considered sovereign was clear, not merely because it did not take the responsibility of deposing James II, and was called and therein enabled by the writs of William III, but also because the proclamation crowning William and Mary had no conditions attached. The Declaration of Rights constituted no such condition.[283] It confined itself to speaking of James's abdication, of the throne being vacant, and of the fact that it was 'the Prince of Orange, [who] had been raised by God to be the "glorious instrument of delivering this Kingdom from Popery and Arbitrary Power"'.[284]

It was thus clear that allegiance remained towards the King (and Queen) and not the laws (as expressed in any particular body such as parliament). To have claimed to represent the fundamental laws or constitution would have meant claiming the right to depose James and crown William and Mary, something never entertained by anyone or anybody, including parliament. This allegiance as owed to the King in his natural person remained a constitutional principle that continued well into the nineteenth century, if not thereafter, and was signified, among other things, by the statutory definition of treason which referred to the natural person of the sovereign and his/her heirs. The King as 'corporation sole' and his powers to 'enact' law in parliament survived intact, as did the King's authority and jurisdiction, in certain cases, as distinct from parliament, such as that of the military personnel or conquered territories.[285] But before entering into the jurisdictional-territorial implications of the 1688–89 settlement, a moment may be spent on the question of allegiance, and its history from the perspective of a contemporary.

In April 1695, in the aftermath of the 'settlement', the German philosopher Leibniz, known for his arguments about plural sovereign rights, had written to Mr Burnett approving of the main arguments of William Sherlock's *Allegiance Due to Sovereign Powers.*[286] Sherlock justified his acceptance of the new dispensation of 1688–89, basing his arguments on theology and Bishop Overall's *Convocation Book* (1603), apart from copious scriptural citation;[287] we might add the *de facto* Act of Henry VII and *Postnati*'s affirmation of *de facto* allegiance. This important Church of England document spoke of the allegiance due to *de facto* authority, authority which was always ultimately derived from the divine. Sherlock forcefully made the argument – through scripture and reason – that allegiance was due to the King who possessed such actual authority. Laws such as treason referred to *de facto* authority, and such authority, even if illegally obtained, required to be obeyed.[288] Moreover, even if a lawful King was dispossessed and banished, the subject was required to show allegiance to the existing actual and settled authority, rather than work against the latter in the name of the overthrown ruler. Changes in crowns were a mark of providence and with these, allegiance too had to be seen as altered. The legality of earthly, political authority could never be justified or understood by humans. Such legality could not be derived from consent or choice, since this naturally led to contracts and laws of force according to such an understanding – implications of contracting which were neither denied by nor lost on Hobbes and Locke.

Does Sherlock's 'Tory–Anglican' discussion unpeel the radical possibilities, sometimes termed 'Whig', of the common law doctrine of allegiance that was expressed in *Postnati*? Does not Sherlock exploit the 'reciprocal' nature of protection and allegiance, implying that the loss of protection allowed for the withdrawal of allegiance? Leibniz certainly thought so, and argued that the relationship between government and the people was to be characterized as a 'quasi-contractus'.[289] Reiterating common law arguments, Sherlock makes the distinction between a 'natural allegiance' and a 'legal allegiance', subjecting the latter to the former. Natural indicated the immediate existing palpable actual power of administration;[290] that is to say, actual possession, much as in *Postnati*, indicated sovereign right. Attentive to the possibility of being accused of 'Hobbism', Sherlock attempts to distinguish between Hobbes, where power determined right, and his own argument, in which power was a sign of right.[291] While this may well turn out to be an obscure distinction and not necessarily applicable to Hobbes,[292] the further claim is made that one need not assist Kings in their illegalities even if one was prohibited from actually resisting them; one might even accept situations where nations replaced Kings. What remained important for Sherlock was hereditary monarchy, even if it was not necessary for hereditary monarchy to be confined to one family. In fact he pointed to concrete instances in English history, from Richard II to Henry VII, where conquest and force determined power. A transfer of crowns was possible as long as the crown remained a hereditary monarchy, this might well be an accurate characterization of the settlement and post-settlement monarchy. All these arguments regarding *de facto* sovereignty, as much as the necessity of 'hereditary' monarchy and the legitimacy of conquest, could well be derived from the principles enunciated in *Postnati*.

While Sherlock formulaically stuck to a doctrine of passive resistance, his historical examples and emphasis on *de facto* sovereignty showed how passive resistance was congruent with the common law principle of conquest as a title to sovereignty. This was not necessarily theologically suspect, because arguments against tyrannicide while familiar theological tropes merely reflected the deadly seriousness with which they had taken political form in Europe. The problematic entanglements of the *de facto* and *de jure* could easily be translated into the problem of conquest and consent, in their obscure discernability, as formulated by Hobbes and Locke. Any argument that Locke's distinctive contribution lay in an appeal to the people at large on grounds of law and property needs to be confronted with his simultaneous argument that property was established by 'positive constitutions' and subsumed rights over persons. How could this impasse between the natural law and positive constitutions be translated into the peculiarly English discourse on kingship and law?

This can be seen in Locke's doctrine of prerogative which might be exercised against the law, and was in fact exercised before the law in the state of nature which knew no such law. If law is more fundamentally defined in terms of a direction towards freedom, there is no better embodiment of it than in prerogative, whether in the state of nature, in positive constitutions (in the person of the King) or in the threat to a return of the state of nature (the individual prerogative of the King as challenged by the collective prerogative of the people, with only heaven to decide). If executive action has such overriding importance in the larger structure and telos at a time of civil society outside of the state of nature, it must be reiterated that only the King's (executive) act in consenting makes a bill law in King-in-Parliament, whereas the King's executive action in prerogative also lies outside and possibly against the (legislative) law. It is in such a context that courts and judgments might be seen as forms of executive power.

Yet, in the fundamental emphasis of executive and prerogative power, that is also to be found in Hobbes's more direct subsumption of property in sovereignty, no reference is made to the importance of the royal line or the corporation sole. To have accepted the importance of executive and prerogative power without binding it to questions of inheritance meant that both Hobbes and Locke veered towards the very republican arguments which had been repudiated by Bacon in *Postnati*. It also meant that their arguments were of no relevance to the peculiar difficulties of monarchy as they took personal, territorial and jurisdictional expression. After all, republican arguments denying the importance of a natural royal line, amounting to a clear distinction between the person of the King and the institution of kingship, did not emerge in the 1640s but could be traced further back to the Spencers in the fourteenth century, if not Richard II, which was vehemently repudiated by *Postnati et al.* It is no wonder that the arguments of Hobbes and Locke found no resonance in the post-Restoration settlement, neither in the (Hobbesian) affirmation of a 'mortal god' nor in the (Lockean) denigration of royal blood. Common law, Whig and Anglican–Tory arguments had an idiom for the transfer of crowns and conquest, but all the same affirmed the immortality of the royal line. This is what made them inassimilable to the republican arguments – foreshadowing Hobbes and Locke – where the sovereign was itself a result of a contract and artificial, not grounded in the natural line or law of the King as corporation sole. The one point where Hobbes comes close to the corporation sole idea is when he speaks of the natural capacity of the King doubling as a political capacity, in his ability to give land away.

By attenuating the distinction between the natural and the artificial, Hobbes and Locke did not confront the precise contours of the relationship between sovereignty and territorial jurisdiction, and the jurisprudential dilemmas therein nested – such as differences and conflicting jurisdictions whether on the question of slavery, colonial assemblies or corporate sovereignty in the East Indies. And hence their irrelevance to the history and structure of English kingship in the Restoration and post-Restoration periods, as much as the problems under investigation here. The recurrent problem, flagged off by *Postnati*, after all was to conceptualize and frame the King in terms of his multiplying bodies-jurisdictions. Whatsoever the idiom regarding the King's sovereignty and the laws, neither of them was to be determined simply by the unilateral determination of a particular people, i.e. a nation intelligible only in terms of a propertied order. Fortescue is still salient: nations come and go, what is sought as a raft in the whirlpools of time is the law – more particularly, the law begotten by sovereignty and allegiance. Yet, since the body-politic was formed of distinct and different jurisdictions, the problem remained of defining one in relation to the other, and it is this that we now turn to.

If the constitutional position of allegiance owed to the natural person of the King through conquest remains intact in the aftermath of the glorious settlement of 1688–89, the question of the relationship between allegiance and sovereignty as expressed in its territorial–jurisdictional differentiation arises. The precise function of conquest was manifest in the articulation of the relationship with Ireland, as (once) acquired by conquest. The ambiguities around this in *Postnati* and Hale have been discussed, and several constitutional arguments were put forward thereafter regarding the distinctiveness and equality of Ireland as a jurisdiction owing allegiance to the King. This was afterwards denied by underlining the legal subordination of Ireland to England, a subordination that was owed to its status of having (once) been conquered. An important illustration of this subordination was in the judicial decision of *Craw v. Ramsey* (1681), where it was held that subordinate jurisdictions like Ireland could not make laws binding on England.

However, there was a consistent counter-perspective to the subordination of Ireland that could well be seen as building on the ambiguities of *Postnati*: ambiguities particularly pertaining to the division of jurisdictions, and their relations, being embedded in allegiance to the same King. This was clearly enunciated and reiterated with great force in the time of the 'settlement' of 1689–91. Soon after the proclamation of William and Mary as jointly sovereign, James II reached Ireland and called parliament in May. The King-in-(Irish) Parliament, while proclaiming James II as sovereign and calling William an 'execrable usurper', reiterated a long-held position that Ireland was a distinct kingdom which was not subordinate to England.[293]

This denial of subordination was formally enacted into a law. The Navigation Laws and appeals to the King's Bench in England were set aside as precisely such signs of bondage, and further confirmed the kingdom of Ireland's equal and distinct status. The Irish parliament also affirmed the hereditary principles of the monarchy, declaiming on the illegality that would stain any attempt – by anybody, including parliament – to coerce the King. Soon thereafter, however, the defeat of James II at the Battle of Boyne and the Treaty of Limerick led to the proclamation of William and Mary as sovereign. However, the experience of Ireland only confirmed, as was remarked upon by commentators of the time, that the title to sovereignty by William and Mary was one of conquest.[294] This was not merely because of the full-fledged battle which had just taken place at Boyne. Rather, the question was of legal consistency. That is to say, even going by the English position that Ireland was historically and legally subordinate to England, since the English convention parliament had declared the throne 'vacant', this entailed a return to an original condition with no sovereign or body-politic, where Ireland could no longer held to be subordinate.[295] It was only in such an 'original' context that

William acquired sovereignty by conquest, which repeated in terms of title his acquisition of England by conquest.

If William III's title was one of conquest, the question of the relationship between sovereignty and territorial–jurisdictional differentiation remained. If the post-settlement period confirmed fundamental monarchical principles such as allegiance to the natural person of the King, and the essential role of the King in 'enacting' a bill thereby making it law, in what sense, if any, had monarchy been transformed? Maitland, in his canonical *Constitutional History of England*, draws attention to the fact that while the Bill of Rights declared, with reason, that 'suspending powers' were never lawful, the King did in a sense (continue to) enjoy 'dispensing powers'.[296] And yet, rather than engage headlong with the question of the significance of the Bill of Rights, one might narrow the issue to ask whether the King, as distinct from King-in-Parliament, remained a distinctive source of jurisdiction post-1689. Once again, one might examine this in the light of the long seventeenth century beginning with *Postnati.*

In the conception of the jurists of the early 1600s who had asserted that allegiance was diverse and owed to the laws, Scotland was not a subordinate kingdom-jurisdiction like Ireland, Gascoigne, etc., where the 'great seal was passable' and 'parliament had power'.[297] Since allegiance was owed to the 'laws–jurisdiction–kingdom', while the King may naturalize a Scotsman by law, it could not be construed as natural or inherent that a Scotsman, by virtue of being the King's subject, could inherit in England.[298] In other words, allegiance to the laws of a place meant that only those living there could enjoy the benefit of the laws, even if the special powers of the King in naturalization by law was recognized. Such a position was repudiated by the judges of *Postnati* both in terms of the larger argument about allegiance being owed to the natural person of the King (and his heirs) and the specific interpretation of the laws. Thus, these jurists declared – in what would become the constitutional position – that while royal remedial writs ran according to place and jurisdiction, the great seal also had a 'preceptorial power over the person' of the subject who owed allegiance to him and not the place-jurisdiction.[299] In other words, all subjects as the subjects of protection enjoyed the benefit of all the laws even if it was well recognized that the King governed according to place. Subjects bore the 'burdens and taxes' of the place where they lived, 'but living in one for his livelihood in one, he is not to be taxed in the other, because laws ordain taxes, imposition and charges, as a discipline of subjection particularized to every particular nation'.[300] This was at once an emphasis on the sovereignty of the King and the implicit equality between territory-jurisdictions by virtue of the principle that one was taxed *in* the place where one lived (where one as propertied represented oneself in an assembly in which such decisions were taken). Place was defined in terms of its channel of jurisdiction to the King, whether a King-in-Parliament or King-in-Council and the King's Courts.

The question could thus be seen to turn on the relationship between parliamentary statute and common law. *Postnati* commented on the relationship between the House of Commons and common law by claiming that it was investigating the 'truth' and not what was 'good' – the law as it existed and not a matter of what might be considered policy based on considerations of the beneficial. This was a point introduced by Francis Bacon and reiterated by Lord Chancellor Ellesmore. In fact, Bacon in his argument about the 'natural law' basis of allegiance to the natural person of the King, held common law to be superior to statute: 'common law is more worthy than statute'.[301] In Coke's report, the importance of the mode of interpreting written law through natural reason and custom pointed in the same direction, and was thus consistent with his *Doctor Bonham's Case.*[302] Thus the limitation of place and statute in favour of sovereignty and common law, a legacy which lies at the heart of the contestation over the line between parliament and courts, historically and in many jurisdictions today.

Such an emphasis on both allegiance and the limitations of (English) parliamentary statute was further enabled by the constitutional consideration of conquest as title in *Postnati.* Here, too, was outlined a delimitation of parliamentary statute. Illustrative is Bacon's argument against the notion that conquest meant introduction of the laws of England. He held that conquest meant continuation of the old laws of the conquered territory unless and until the King, by proclamation or letters patent, changed them. In fact Bacon held that these laws might even be altered to the extent of being repugnant to the laws of England.[303] Differentiation of place may imply differences in, even contradictions between, laws – not allegiance and sovereignty.

On the paradigmatic relation between conquest and jurisdiction, i.e. Ireland, Bacon held that it was not conquest but John's charter which introduced the 'laws of England', leading to Ireland carrying the 'marks of sovereignty in their [Irish] parliaments and coins'.[304] According to him there was no meaningful distinction between Scotland and Ireland, and he thereby rejected the idea that Ireland was 'subordinate'. Moreover, Bacon affirmed not merely diversity in jurisdiction, but clarified that it was not necessary that these diverse jurisdictions were under the 'government of England'.[305] The limits to English statute were testified to in relation to other territorial–jurisdictional examples. As illustration, Bacon held that even when one found English parliamentary statutes 'ordering matters' in Gascoigne, a close look at them confirmed that they either referred to English subjects in Gascoigne, or the subjects of Gascoigne in England.[306] Such jurisdictions and their subjects were thus not under the 'government of England' even while they owed allegiance to the same King.

Much later in the century, Mathew Hale, much like Coke's report in *Postnati*, affirmed the powers of the English parliament to bind Ireland in naming them. All the same he had written, as discussed above, that neither could the English parliament impose taxes on Ireland, nor could it negate laws made by the Irish parliament. In explicating the broader jurisprudential issues at stake, Hale explained that the King could act purely in his individual capacity or in his capacity as King of England. In places like Virginia, even when the King acted in his latter capacity ('the King in right of the Crown of England') while he issued commissions to take possession of such lands, the laws of England were not operational there until he decided so by proclamation.[307] That is to say, echoing *Postnati*, in Hale, the King had the sole power of making laws until he decided to make it subject to the laws of England, and this was exactly what was to have happened in Ireland, where English laws were slowly introduced. As discussed above, the equality of the kingdom of Ireland and its subordination to the King, not to English parliament, was an argument that was taken up forcefully at various points in the seventeenth century. One might say that the legal ambiguity around this question is indexed by the fact that one had to wait until the declaratory Act of 1719, which definitively affirmed the subordination of Ireland to the British parliament, even if this act was rescinded later in the eighteenth century, returning Ireland to a jurisdiction that was owed distinctively to the King and his Courts.

This account of kingship as essential to an understanding of the British Empire in its differentiated jurisdiction might well appear to resonate with strands of Charles McIlwain's famous thesis on the arguments of the American colonists against parliamentary jurisdiction close to a century ago. McIlwain affirmed the constitutionality of the American colonial arguments of the 1760s and 1770s, among other things, on the basis of the discourse around the independence of Irish jurisdiction.[308] He rooted this constitutionality in an imperial paradigm where the King ruled over diverse jurisdictions –

the realm and the dominions – on the principle that each jurisdiction owed allegiance to the King but was not to be considered subordinate in relation to the other. Dominions (such as the colonies) were therefore not to be considered subordinate to the realm (England). McIlwain argued that first the interregnum, and then the settlement of 1689–90, repudiated this imperial paradigm by giving supremacy to the English nation as represented by the English parliament (the realm) in its capacity to bind other jurisdictions such as those of the colonies (Ireland and the dominions).[309] While he noted that historically the English parliament did reach beyond the realm and into the dominions, he found it important to clarify that such statutes were merely declaratory of the law and did not introduce anything new – something that would often be used to define statute in distinction from the courts' judgments.[310] Therein lay the grounds for the argument that the English parliament could not legally bind the colonial dominions until the cementing of the English parliament by the settlement of 1688–89. Yet there was no reason to accept the constitutionality of such an arrangement that subjected the dominions to the English nation, and hence the legality of the American colonial argument of the eighteenth century.

The colonies and their legal basis derived from royal grants, and were therein subordinate to the King and his Privy Council, not (necessarily) the English parliament. An early case regarding fishing rights in Virginia suggested that these dominions were exclusively part of royal jurisdiction and not English parliamentary statute.[311] In repudiating the claims of parliament over the dominions, McIlwain emphatically points out that the American colonists had a clear precedent in the Irish case, although he does not discuss the Irish parliament's legislative programme to the same effect under James II or the legal issues analysed above on the nature of conquest as title in the case of William III.[312] In less than a decade after its publication, the McIlwain thesis faced its first serious challenge in the form of R. Schuyler's critique in *Parliament and the British Empire.*[313] This critique took the form of a documentation of the reach of English statutes into the dominions, beyond the realm-territory of England before either the interregnum or the settlement of 1689–90, thus aiming to question McIlwain's thesis about the significance of either as definitively introducing the subordination of dominion jurisdictions to the English nation and English statute.

As subsequent scholarly discussions of the set of legal issues involved showed, Schuyler did not focus either on the specificity of the seventeenth-century moment (most of his examples being of earlier centuries) or on the constitutional-doctrinal issues that were at stake in the seventeenth century (such as *Postnati* and the ambiguities surrounding the subordination of Ireland), thereby leading to debilitating weaknesses in his critique.[314] As Barbara Black has persuasively argued, Schuyler's own 'conciliar theory', where an act of parliament was an act of the King and the two could not be separated, undermined any clear-cut affirmation of the powers of English parliament, as such, to bind dominions. That is to say, since parliamentary statute itself was indubitably part and parcel of the King's power, evidence of parliamentary statute to bind the dominions could be interpreted as a sign of the King's powers and not a sign of the inherent powers of the English parliament – particularly because it was recognized that the King did and could, in a variety of cases including conquest, govern through channels distinct from the English parliament.[315] One might add to this the interesting fact that the House of Commons resolutions and the arguments therein put forward against Calvin's right to inherit in England as the King's subject – to which *Postnati* was a response and repudiation – presented arguments similar to those of Schuyler on the reach of the English parliament and its inherent powers. Schuyler also did not take into full cognizance the precarious and ambiguous relationship between statute, law and sovereignty on questions of titles such as heredity and conquest, as elucidated by *Postnati* – in other words, the principles that emerged when the allegiance towards a particular jurisdiction, such as England, was repudiated in favour of hereditary kingship.

While the argument of this part of the book is congruent with that of McIlwain in emphasizing the role of the King in the constitution of the differentiated body-politic, it does not endow, as shown above, the settlement of 1689 89 with the same significance. A history of the military and legal branches of war, including that of Prize, affirms the fact that kingship, apart from parliament, could channel a distinctive jurisdiction of its own. While the implications of the 1688–89 settlement in terms of military and martial law will be analysed in the next part, this part has shown that the King, apart from parliament, remained a source of jurisdiction when it came to the East India Company and its settlements, both before and after the settlement of 1689–89. In other words, a history of the East India Company fortifies the argument about the capacity of the King to form government – legislative and judicial – independent of English parliament, irrespective of the 1688–89 settlement.

Royal charters empowered the legislative and judicial activity of the East India Company. These very charters until 1698 empowered the Company to make laws and by-laws, as well as undertake war with non-Christian polities or those who were not in league with the King. While (King-in) parliamentary statute intervened in 1698 for the first time in denying the older Company's exclusive trade, it was simultaneously declared that nothing but the specific powers of the King's charters of incorporation enabled the Company to exist in its corporate capacity as well as trade and govern by laws. This was not surprising, since even while it was admitted earlier in the century that parliament could pass statutes regarding corporations, it was the King's definitive powers, exercised through charters, that in fact 'made' them. Once again, Coke had clarified this exclusive function of the King in the Sutton Hospital Case, a function and power that was maintained by jurists and jurisprudence well after the settlement of 1688–89.[316]

It is therefore not surprising that distinct from statute, it was specifically the King's charter of 1698 which empowered the Company to undertake wars with 'heathen powers', and make laws and by-laws with powers of punishment, apart from being empowered to erect courts of judicature which were under the superintendence of the King and his Privy Council. Something not dissimilar took place in the East India Company settlement where the charters of 1726, as discussed, established Mayors' Courts and the corporations of Bombay and Madras. Here too the governance of the Company settlements was clearly under the superintendence of the King and Privy Council, with no role for parliamentary statute. While parliamentary statute provided the broader conditions for maintaining a trade, what might be called the political dimensions of governance were grounded specifically in the King and his Privy Council. This was with reference to the very distinctive identity of the 'corporate settlements', as much as their powers to 'legislate', hold courts in judgement and undertake war. Appeal beyond a certain amount lay with the King-in-Council, and the powers to enforce martial law and raise troops were also granted in these royal charters. The reach of martial law beyond the martial law statute, the justiciability of courts and laws independent of statute, powers of war and peace, civil law, were all distinctive features of Company governance. In denominating the powers of the Company in relationship to non-Christians, *Postnati* no doubt functioned as one source of relevant jurisprudence.

This distinctive channel of royal governance was even stronger in the East India settlements than was the case with the American colonies where (King-in) parliamentary statute operated in relationship to general matters of trade, the most significant of which was no doubt the Navigation Laws. In the case of the east there were no such broad statutory restrictions, and the Company was therefore governed in matters of trade as much as land revenue by its charters. This distinction would explode at both the western and eastern ends of the royal spectrum in the eighteenth century, where American colonists, while accepting general restrictions on trade, would deny parliamentary statute to unilaterally determine questions of revenue.[317] The conquests in the east and ensuing modes of governance would explode into contention in its own way, and is the subject of the next part. For now, in this late seventeenth-, early eighteenth-century moment, it is sufficient to note the fact that the enduring significance of *Postnati* and royal jurisdiction – illustrations of which would include judicial decisions such as *Dutton v. Hall* (1693) and *Smith v. Brown and Cooper* (1702) – confirmed that as conquered territories there existed a channel of jurisdiction from these settlements to the Privy Council and King, untrammelled by the parliament of England.[318] Holt had in fact confirmed that Virginia 'being a conquered country their law is what the King pleases'.[319]

In 1722, however, with regard to 'foreign plantations' in the Americas, it was held that in cases of 'uninhabited countries' the English carry their laws with them, whereas in the case of conquered countries, the conquering King 'gains a right and property in such [vanquished] people, in consequences of which he may impose upon them what laws he pleases'; in this context, clearly the American colonies were being interpreted as 'uninhabited' and bound by English parliamentary statute when named. Notwithstanding which, in the case of 'conquest', not only was the King's rights reaffirmed as in *Postnati*, but even the centrality of 'religion' was upheld in the Privy Council, holding that

> Until such laws given by the conquering prince, the laws and customs of the conquered country shall hold place, unless where these are contrary to our religion, or enact anything that is malum in se, or are silent; for in all such cases the laws of the conquering country shall prevail.[320]

The distinctive channel of royal jurisdiction, apart from parliamentary statute, was therefore undeniable in the jurisprudence of the title of conquest. In the cases of the east,[321] did the denial of status of 'heathen' law, from Coke to the charters and such judicial opinions, amplify the ambiguity about the King, parliament and conquest?[322] Even now, English parliamentary statute cannot be mistaken as the univocal source of law.

As has been sought to be established in this part, the growing number and strength of the American colonies and the territories under the East India Company require to be perceived as two important channels of this form of royal rule, on a historical soil that includes Wales and Ireland as much as Calais and Gascony. It would be a mistake to simply view the seventeenth century as putting an end to prerogative powers and their effects, or treat prerogative and parliamentary statute as competing in a zero-sum game. The ghosts of Richard II and Charles I would put to rest any celebratory claims of ascending parliamentary power over the royal person from the late seventeenth century onwards. In fact, it is the extension and intensification of royal prerogative as such through Prize charters, and in combination with statute, in the East Indies during the eighteenth century that is the focus in the next part. The contorted and contested questions between conquest and the laws, allegiance and equity, sovereignty and settlement, acquire a new salience when examined from the perspective of the millions being ruled under implied royal jurisdiction in the East Indies. The prolixity of the discourse around these conquests is equalled only by their orchestrated lack of resolution and the resounding silence of the violence against those populations designated 'Indians' in the west[323] – a silence that contrasted with wildly gesticulating, if ineffective, concerns when it came to the east, where too 'Indians' struggled to find both voice and status.

Notes

1 I have used the anachronistic term 'British' merely for the sake of convenience, to describe the formation of an empire in the seventeenth century that would otherwise involve a listing of the various jurisdictions. See note 2 to the introduction.

2 While there is rich scholarship on the English East India Company in the seventeenth century from various perspectives, there is very little on the relationship between English jurisprudence and the legal basis of the Company, and more particularly the royal basis and channel of Company government. While it may be held that Philip Stern's *The Company State* (2011) is an exception, from the perspective of this part and its arguments, Stern's understanding of the basis of the Company is faulty precisely in its failure to take into cognizance fundamental jurisprudential issues such as the relationship between kingship and law, as already discussed in the introduction.

3 https://web.archive.org/web/20100105161033/http://home.freeuk.net/don-aitken/ast/h8a.html#145

4 Howell, ed., *State Trials*, Vol. II (1816) [Mores Report]: 567–68. This is analysed in detail in the main sections of the part as well as in the conclusion.

5 See *Commentaries or Reports of Edmund Plowden* (1816), particularly the case of the Duchy of Lancaster that forms the point of departure of the detailed analyses of the King's natural and political bodies in Kantorowicz's classic study, *The King's Two Bodies* (1957). Stern's study (*The Company State*, 2011) fails to take seriously such royal powers and capacities, and therein misconstrues the autonomy of the East India Company.

6 The importance of *Postnati* can also be gauged by the fact that it 'settled' the doctrine

of hereditary monarchy and of conquest, thereby negating other possibilities that had already existed in English history, such as the Henrican statutes that empowered the King to choose his own successors as well as exclude the Scottish line from succession– as much as the Elizabethan statutes which prohibited the questioning of statutes on succession. See Figgis (1896): 85–87.

7 See Richard Burns's argument on the possible novelty of seventeenth-century absolutism lying in hereditary succession for monarchies. He reminds us that all the same the 'two most notable monarchies' of Europe during this time – the empire and the papacy – were elective; Burns (1990): 31. On the diversity of political arrangements, see also H.G. Koenigsberger (1978): 191–217. Jean Bodin also believed that there were very 'few' hereditary monarchies in Europe, practically only the English and the French. See the citation of Bodin to this effect from his *On Sovereignty*, in Richard Tuck's *The Sleeping Sovereign* (2015): 25. Grotius's *The Laws/Rights of War and Peace* gives an acute sense of the various kinds of polities from patrimonial to elective Kings and republics in the seventeenth century.

8 Richard Burns recognizes that Hobbes's argument in the *Leviathan* specifically goes against hereditary succession; see Burns (1990): 39. But what he does not note here is that the Hobbesian natural law argument was in effect reiterating the Henrican statute that gave the sovereign King such powers, and goes against the elaborated theory of *Postnati* – issues that are analysed in this part.

9 For a sustained argument regarding on the relationship between Irish arguments and the arguments of emerging from the American colonies on subjection to the King and the limits of English parliamentary statute, see Charles H. McIlwain's *American Revolution: A Constitutional Interpretation* (1923). See also Barbara A. Black's 'The Constitution of Empire: The Case for the Colonists' (1976).

10 Ibid. This is no doubt a rich a complex field, but from the perspective of seventeenth-century English jurisprudence, an important study, including an engagement with the relevant literature, may be found in James. R. Stoner Jr., *Common Law and Liberal Theory* (1992): 179–223.

11 Howell, ed., *State Trials*, Vol. II (1816) [Bacon's Speech]: 598; Coke's 7th Report, http://www.law.harvard.edu/faculty/cdonahue/courses/lhsemelh/materials/CalvinsCase.pdf: 389.

12 Howell, ed., *State Trials*, Vol. II (1816) [Mores Report]: 569

13 See note 98 from the Introduction.

14 See *East India Company v. Thomas Sandys.*

15 For a detailed analysis of the issue see, C.H. McIlwain's *The High Court of Parliament and its Supremacy* (1910). See also J.G.A. Pocock's *The Ancient Constitution and Feudal Law* (1987).

16 https://web.archive.org/web/20100105161033/http://home.freeuk.net/don-aitken/ast/h8a.html#145

17 This is analysed in Part III.

18 In the words of Lord Chief Justice Popham, the laws of England 'continued as a rock without alteration in all the varieties of people that had possessed this land namely the Romans, Britons, Danes, Saxons, Normans, and English, which he imputed to the integrity and justice of these laws, every people taking a liking to them and desirous to continue them and live by them, for which he cited Fortescue's book of the laws of

England'; Howell, ed., *State Trials*, Vol. II (1816) [More's Report]: 569. Judge Popham used such an argument for the primacy of laws as opposed to the King.

19 On F.W. Maitland's argument regarding the 'parsonification' of the King, see his essays, 'The Corporation Sole' and the 'Crown as Corporation', in Runciman and Ryan, eds (2003). Kantorowicz's important study, *The King's Two Bodies* (1957), explicitly builds on, and critiques, Maitland's insight on the King's bodies. On the explicit refutation of the parson–King analogy, see F. Bacon's speech and Coke's report for *Postnati* and its discussion later in this section.

20 Howell, ed., *State Trials*, Vol. II (1816) [Bacon's speech]: 598.

21 Coke's 7th Report, http://www.law.harvard.edu/faculty/cdonahue/courses/lhsemelh/materials/CalvinsCase.pdf: 382, 388.

22 Howell, ed., *State Trials*, Vol. II (1816) [Mores Report]: 565–68.

23 Ibid.:567.

24 Ibid.

25 For instance, Dodridge, the king's solicitor, Lawrence Hyde, Brook, Crewe and Hedley, professors of common law, gave nine reasons against automatic naturalization into England of those born in Scotland since James inherited the Crown. This question was itself framed in terms of 'whether naturalization proceed from the King or the laws'. The first among the several reasons urging for naturalization as proceeding from the laws spoke of the etymological link between allegiance and the laws. Ibid.:567–68.

26 '. . . allegiance and laws were not of equiparation for six causes. 1. Allegiance was before the laws 2. Allegiance is after the laws 3. Allegiance is where laws are not 4. Between sovereignty and allegiance laws are begotten 5. Allegiance extends as far as defence, which is beyond the circuit of laws 6. Allegiance followeth the natural person, not the politic.' Ibid.: 570.

27 Ibid.; 'If a king be expelled by force and another usurps, yet the allegiance is not taken away, though the law be taken away.'

28 Ibid. Also see Howell, ed., *State Trials*, Vol. II (1816) [Bacon's speech]: 596–97.

29 Howell, ed., *State Trials*, Vol. II (1816) [Mores Report]: 570.

30 Ibid.: 571. Ireland was classified as a dukedom but then became a kingdom.

31 Ibid.: 572.

32 Ibid.: 573.

33 Ibid.: 575.

34 Ibid.: 576.

35 Ibid.:, Howell, ed., *State Trials*, Vol. II (1816) [Bacon's speech]: 578. It is thus important to emphasize that notwithstanding Maitland's argument about the compatibility between 'commonwealth' and 'prince', the conceptual distinction was well recognized and insisted upon by the English jurisprudence of the King as corporation sole; it is not accidental that Maitland misconstrues the enormous significance of the latter concept. See Runciman and Ryan, eds (2003): 38.

36 Howell, ed., *State Trials*, Vol. II (1816) [Bacon's Speech]: 578.

37 Ibid.; '. . . but in monarchies especially hereditary; that is when several families or lineages of people do submit themselves to one line imperial or royal, the submission is more natural and simple, which afterwards by laws subsequent is perfected and made more formal; but that is grounded upon nature'.

[38] Ibid.: 578–79.

[39] For a study of the philosophico-political significance of the shepherd analogy in Plato, see, amongst other studies, Castoriadis's *On Plato's Statesman* (2002).

[40] Howell, ed., *State Trials*, Vol. II (1816) [Bacon's Speech]: 579. 'And therefore both amongst heathen, and amongst the Christian, the word "sacred" hath been attributed unto kings, because of the conformity of a monarchy with a divine majesty never to a senate or people. And so you find it twice in the Lord Coke's Reports; once in the second book, bishop of Winchester's case; and his fifth book, Cawrie's case. And more anciently in the 10 of H 7 fl 18 "rexest persona mixta cum sacredote"; an attribute, which the senate of Venice, or a canton of Wisses can never challenge . . . and therefore other states are creatures of law; and this state subsisteth by nature.'

[41] Ibid.: 580.

[42] All these four submissions [paternity, admiration of virtue, conduct in war and conquest] are evident to be natural and more ancient than law; ibid.: 580. And later, 'Allegiance is of a greater extent and dimension than laws or kingdom, and cannot consist by the laws merely; because it began before laws, it continueth after laws, and it is in vigour where laws are suspended and have not their force'; ibid.: 596. The points of the Kings being more ancient than law and the importance of 'natural equity' before law are reiterated here. The patriarchal element is once again stressed, for 'the allegiance of subjects to hereditary monarchies can no more be said to consist by laws, than the obedience of children to parents' – allegiance even after the laws, the context of the defeat of the King and conspiracies against him could be tried after his return to power; ibid.: 596.

[43] Ibid.: 581. 'And although the king, in his person, be solutes legibus, yet his acts and grants are limited by law, and we argue them every day'; ibid.: 580. 'Even so it is of allegiance of subjects to hereditary monarchs, which is corroborated and confirmed by law; but is the work of the law of nature', 'so surely I shall hardly consent, that the king shall be esteemed or called only or rightful sovereign, or our lawful sovereign, but our natural liege sovereign'.

[44] Ibid.: 581; 'and therefore you shall find the observation true, and almost general in all states, that their law givers were long after their first kings, who governed for a time by natural equity without law'. See also Coke's 7th Report: 392–93; 'And it is certain that before judicial of municipals laws were made, Kings did decide causes according to natural equity, and were not tied to any rule or formality of law. Government and subjection were long before any municipal or judicial laws. For it had been in vain to have prescribed laws to any but to such as owed obedience faith ligeance before in respect whereof they were bound to obey and observe them.'

[45] Howell, ed., *State Trials*, Vol. II (1816) [Bacon's Speech]: 581–82.

[46] Ibid.: 582; 'he [the alien enemy] can have no remedy in any of the king's courts; but he must complain himself before the king's privy counsel; there he shall have a proceeding summary hour to hour; the cause shall be determined by natural equity, and not by rules of law; and the redress of the counsel shall be executed by aid of the chancery as in 13 E. 4'.

[47] Ibid.

[48] Ibid.: 583.

[49] Ibid.: 'subjects obtained from conquest are naturalized'; later arguing that, 'therefore to

proceed now to overthrow that distinction of descent and conquest' (ibid.: 591). This has important implications with regard to the nature of the jurisdiction of Ireland, as will be analysed.

50 Ibid.: 594; 'There is one and the same reason of naturalizing subjects by descent and subjects by conquest and that is the union in the person of the king; and therefore that the case of Scotland is as clear as that of Ireland and that they that grant the one cannot deny the other.'

51 Ibid.: 592.

52 Ibid.: 593.

53 Ibid.: 585–88.

54 Ibid.: 595. 'Statute 25 ed 3 all children born in any parts of the world, if they be of English parents continuing at the time as liege subjects to the king and having done no act to forfeit the benefit of their allegiance, are ipso facto naturalized . . . therefore law of England can operate or confer naturalization outside of England'; ibid.: 585.

55 Ibid.: 595; 'Humans are naturalized to one another . . . law of naturalization as branch of law of nature . . . either place or parents . . . law of England opens her lap to receive people to be naturalized and that it is the law of a warlike and magnanimous nation fit for empire. . . . Littleton alien is he who is born out of the allegiance of our lord the king. Allegiance cannot be applied to the law or kingdom but to the person of the king; allegiance more latitude and comprehension than law or kingdom.'

56 Ibid.: 590–91.

57 Ibid.: 596.

58 Ibid.

59 Ibid.: 581.

60 Ibid.: 589.

61 Ibid.: 594; 'The natural body of the king hath an operation and influence into his body politic, as well as his body politic hath upon his body natural: and therefore that although his body politic of king of England, and his body politic of king of Scotland, be several and distinct yet nevertheless his natural person which is one hath an patio upon both and createth a privity between them.' See also Coke's 7th Report: 388–89.

62 Howell, ed., *State Trials*, Vol. II (1816) [Bacon's Speech]: 597–98. 'Let us see what operations the king's natural person hath upon his crown and body politic. Of which the easiest and greatest is, that it causeth the crown to go by descent, which is a thing strange, and contrary to the course of all corporations which ever more take in a succession, and not by descent; for no man can shew them all the corporations of England, of what nature soever, whether they consist of one person, or of many, or whether they be temporal, or ecclesiastical, any one takes to him, and his heirs but all to him and his successors. And therefore here you may see what a weak course that is to put cases of bishops and parsons and the like, and to apply them to the crown. For the king takes to him and his heirs in the manner of a natural body, and the word, successors, is but superfluous; and where that is used, that is over duly placed after the world heirs, "the king, his heirs, and successors".'

63 Ibid.: 598–99; 'for it proveth plainly that the natural person of the king hath such a communication of qualities with his body politic, as it makes the subjects of either kingdom stand in another degree of privity one towards the other, than they did before'. This was based on an interpretation of acts of parliament and common law.

[64] Therefore the charge against the Spencers was that according to them, homage and oath of the subject is 'more by reason of the crown than by reason of the person of the king'. 'So that if the king doth not guide himself by reason by right of the crown, his lieges are bound by their oath to the crown to remove the king.' Bacon continues, 'by which act doth plainly appear the perilous consequence of this distinction concerning the person of the king and the crown', and later, 'for it is the inference that they make, which is, that the king may be deposed or removed, that is the treason and disloyalty of that opinion'; ibid.: 599. In Coke's 7th Report, the position of the Spencers is similarly condemned as a 'damnable and damned opinion' (ibid.: 390).

[65] See note 20 above.

[66] Howell, ed., *State Trials*, Vol. II (1816) [Bacon's Speech]: 599.

[67] Ibid.: 601.

[68] On the union of Scotland and England, Bacon says that 'this is by now, by the providence of god the fourth time that the line and kings of England have had dominions and seigniories united unto them as patrimonies, and by descent of blood; four unions I say, there have been inclusive of the laws'. First was Normandy in the person of William; second was Gascoigne, and Guienne and Anjou in the person of H2; third was the crown of France in the person of E3; and fourth the kingdom of Scotland in his majesty. Ibid.: 601.

[69] 'And if any do conceive that Gascoigne and Guienne were governed by the laws of England; first that cannot be in reason; for it is a true ground that whenever any prince's title unto any country is by law, he can never change the laws, for that they create his title; and therefore no doubt those duchies retained their own laws; which if they did, then they could not be subject to the laws of England. And next again the fact or practice was otherwise, as appeareth by all consent of story and record; for those duchies continued governed by the civil law, their trials by witnesses and not by jury, their lands testamentary and the like.' Ibid.: 605.

[70] Ibid.

[71] Ibid.: 605–06.

[72] Ibid.: 606.

[73] This is repeated in Coke's 7th Report too, where it is clarified that 'neither the climate nor the soil, but ligeantia and obedientia that make the subject born' (ibid.: 384).

[74] Howell, ed., *State Trials*, Vol. II (1816) [Bacon's Speech]: 591–92.

[75] Ibid.

[76] Ibid.

[77] Ibid.: 605–06.

[78] Ibid.: 590.

[79] Coke's 7th Report: 382.

[80] Ibid. Several statutes are cited as authoritative in this regard. 'Ligeance is the true and faithful obedience of the subject due to his sovereign. This ligeance and obedience is an incident inseparable to every subject; for as soon as he is born he oweth by birth-right ligeance and obedience to his sovereign.' And later, 'for as the subject oweth to the King his true and faithful ligeance and obedience so the sovereign is to govern and protect his subjects'.

[81] Ibid.: 394; 'The oath of allegiance involved the observation of 5 things. Temporally it was indefinite, from the moment pronounced, it was true and faithful, it was sworn

in general to the King and his heirs, and not the King as the King of Scotland, King of Ireland etc, it was sworn until death, allegiance was not limited by space and owed wherever one was.' Ibid.: 385; 'And therefore thus were directly and clearly answered as well the objections drawn from the severalty of kingdoms, seeing there is but one head of both and the postnati, and us joined in ligeance to that one head, which is *copula et tanquam* oculus of this case.'

[82] See Bishop Overall's *Prayer Book* (cited in William Sherlock's argument in the 1690s and analysed in the concluding section of this chapter) and Hooker's *Law of the Ecclesiastical Polity*: 128–58, which recognize the right to tyrannicide. Apart from this there was also statutory sanction in the form of 11 Henry VII c1, which gives 'protection to all the supporters of a *de facto* King, and even attempts to prohibit future parliament from attempting its repeal'. See Figgis (1896): 85.

[83] Willion V. Berkley, in *Commentaries or Reports of Edmund Plowden* (1816): 238. Kantorowicz, in *The King's Two Bodies*, traces to the case of the Duchy of Lancaster the elaboration of the King's bodies, natural and political; available, similarly, in ibid.: 212.

[84] Coke's 7th Report: 399; 'though the King of England hath absolute right to other kingdoms or dominions, as France, Aquitain, Normandy & c., yet seeing the King is not in actual possession thereof, none born there since the Crown of England was out of actual possession thereof are subjects to the King of England'.

[85] Ibid.: 385; the categories being, Natural born, Denizen, local and legal, all of which are due unto the King. 'Denization of an alien' could also take place by conquest; ibid.: 384. '[I]f an alien enemy come to invade this realm, and be taken in war, he cannot be indicted of treason; for the indictment cannot include contra ligeant sue debitum, for he never was in the protection of the king, nor ever owed any manner of ligeance unto him, but malice and enmity, and therefore he shall be put to death by martial law'; ibid., cited statute 15.H7 in support. '[N]ot common law, but before the constable and marshal (who had special commission under the Great Seal to hear and determine the same according to martial law)'; ibid.

[86] Howell, ed., *State Trials*, Vol. II (1816) [Bacon's Speech]: 597–98. The jurisprudence of the King's bodies has been traced to the *Commentaries or Reports of Edmund Plowden*; see note 83 above.

[87] Coke's 7th Report: 389; 'it was due to the natural person of the King (which is ever accompanied with the politic capacity, and the politic capacity as it were appropriated to the natural capacity) and it is not due to the politic capacity only, that is, to his Crown or kingdom distinct from his natural capacity, and that for diverse reasons. First, every subject . . . is presumed by law to be sown to the King, which is to his natural person, and likewise, the King is worn to his subjects..which oath he taketh in his natural person: for the politic capacity is invisible and immortal; nay, the politic body hath no soul, for it is framed by the policy of man. 2. In all indictments of treason, when any do intend to compass mortem destructionem domini Regis [which must needs to be understood of his natural body, for his body-politic is immortal; and not subject to death], the indictment concludes . . . body politic being invisible can as a body politic neither make nor ask homage . . . the King holdeth the kingdom of England by birth right inherent by descent from the blood Royal, whereupon succession doth attend' – not requiring any special ceremony or act.

[88] Ibid.: 393.

89 Ibid.

90 Ibid.: 399–410.

91 Ibid.: 397; 'Every man is either alienigena, an alien born or a subditus, a subject born. Every alien is either a friend that is in league or an enemy that is in open war. Every alien enemy is either temporary for a time, or perpetus, perpetual or permitted specially.'

92 Ibid.: 'for if you derive denize from deins nee one born within obedience or ligeance of the king, then such a one should be all one with a natural born subject'.

93 Ibid.

94 Ibid.: 397–98.

95 Ibid.: 398. There has been the debate on the crucial question as to whether Coke meant the English or the Irish parliament with this reference. The arguments in this part on the Irish case – and therein the crucial importance of the King, build on Barbara A. Black's insightful discussion in 'The Constitution of Empire: The Case for the Colonists' (1976). On the basis of these arguments and their logic it does seem that Coke was referring to the Irish parliament, as Black argues (ibid.: 1182).

96 Coke's 7th Report: 398.

97 Ibid.

98 Grotius in his *De rebus belgicis, or, The annals and history of the Low-Countrey-warrs*: 869; https://quod.lib.umich.edu/e/eebo/A42214.0001.001/1:6.16?rgn=div2;view=fulltext. Compare this with Coke's 7th Report: 397–98, on the distinction between subject and alien enemy (defined as one with whom no public league existed).

99 Sir Mathew Hale's *The Prerogatives of the King*. Hale here speaks of two kinds of territories, 'first such as the King hath in right of the crown of England, as parcel thereof or annexed thereto and therein we reckon England itself, Wales, Ireland, Man, Guernsey, Jersey, Sark and Alderney, Berwick, Calais, and our later acquests viz, Bermudas, Barbados, Virginia, New England etc. Secondly, such as though the same person that is king of England hath them, yet he hath them not in the capacity of the Crown of England, as Normandy, Aquitaine, Guiennes and Gascony, France, Scotland. First, therefore, concerning England. It is an ancient kingdom: though possessed successively by several nations viz. Britain, Romans, Picts, Scots, Saxons, Danes, Normans'; Hale (1976): 19.

100 Ibid.. 11; Hale holds that the titles and styles of the King include *rex, basileus* and *imperator* 'since the coming in of King William'. In his words, referring to statute, 'it is not a recognition of the king's sovereignty only over particular persons distributively, but over the very three estates of parliament collectively and over all the people represented by them'.

101 Ibid.: 54–61.

102 Ibid.: 8–10.

103 Ibid.: 32; 'For the manner of its [Ireland] acquisition to England, it was by conquest, and that not only a conquest in *regem* but a conquest in *populum* whereby clitor is acquisition *guit universalis.*' On the status of Ireland, see ibid.: 32–40.

104 Ibid.: 63; 'It is most apparent by the book of Doomsday compiled by his command that the former laws were then in force, and that the former owners held their possessions and those that were ejected from them recovered their possessions by assise of mort dancestor and the king contended himself with those demesnes that were terrae *regis Edwardi*. And if it be said that he disposed of mens lands *juxta habitum conquestoris*, as Easmerus and some others express it certainly it infers nothing of a conquest upon the people; but

possibly they might be of such as were actually opposite to him, and therefore by him reckoned no better than traitors; and if it went farther, yet after so great a concussion by such a war, it is not wonder if there were some acts of violence done by him as a prince or captain, not as a conqueror.'

105 Ibid.: 9; 'That though there were oppressions, rapines and usurpations upon the people after the Norman victoria, which is always the consequence of a victory, yet it was not *victoria in populum* but *in regem*, for neither the laws nor lands of the people were taken from them.'

106 Ibid.: 8.

107 Ibid.: 34; 'Although the victor gets by right of conquest up the conquered, yet these English planters and colonies were free Englishmen and carried with them their rights and liberties of Englishmen, though into a country acquired not only in point of superintendency but in point of propriety, by the conquering king. Indeed the *jus victorumcedit in jus et patrimonium vincentis* but not the *jurasubditorum*.'

108 Ibid.: 34–35; 'Capitulations, laws and establishments whereby now that people even the very native Irish descended from the first conquered inhabitants are now no longer under the unlimited power of a conqueror, but under the legal and regular government of a king and all those acts of parliament preceding 10 H. 7 are now as much the birthright of the native Irish as they are of the subjects of England, if they do not forfeit them.'

109 This issue of Ireland's subordination is further analysed in later sections as well as in the conclusion.

110 Ibid.: 119; 'So that now there falls in aptly the consideration of martial law which properly concerns the army, and *jus belli* which properly concerns the enemy, though there is an intermixture of both in *each* of these jurisdictions.'

111 Ibid.: 122; 'In matters civil, for which there is no remedy by the common law, the military jurisdiction continues as well after [the] war as during the time of it, for that part of the jurisdiction of the constable and marshal stands still notwithstanding the [war] determines, as concerning right of prisoners and booty, military contracts, ensigns &c.'

112 See Thomas Hobbes, *Leviathan* ([1651] 1994): 135; 'The skill of making and maintaining commonwealths consisteth in certain rules, as doth arithmetic and geometry, not (as in tennis-play) on practice only.'

113 Thomas Hobbes, *Dialogue Between a Philosopher and A Student of the Common Laws of England* (1681): 'After the first manner, which is by war, grew up all the greatest kingdoms in the world. Viz., the Egyptian, Assyria, Persian and the Macedonian monarchy; and also did the great kingdoms of England, France and Spain.' War was how the specific 'growth' of the English body-politic was historically described.

114 Hobbes ([1651] 1994): 127; 'And this kind of dominion or sovereignty differeth from sovereignty by institution only in this, that men who lose their sovereignty do it for fear of one another, and not of him whom they institute; but in this case they subject themselves to him they are afraid of. In both cases they do it for fear, which is to be noted by them that hold all such covenants as proceed from death or violence void; which if it were true, no man in any kind of commonwealth could be obliged to obedience.' Much rich scholarship has noted the significance of conquest in Hobbes, moulding this to their own important theses. A particularly insightful deployment for a reconsideration of the entire 'social contract' may be found in Carol Pateman's *The Sexual Contract* (1988).

115 Hobbes (1681); 'Is there at this day among the Turks, any inheritor of land besides

the Sultan? And was not all the land in England once in the hands of William the Conqueror? Sir Edward Coke himself confesses it. Therefore it is an universal truth that all conquered lands, presently after victory are the lands of him that conquered them.' And later, after making a distinction between the King's political and individual capacity so as to argue that those lands that were had in the King's political capacity could not be disposed except for the benefit of the people, or by Act of Parliament, Hobbes nonetheless states, 'But where do you find that the Conqueror disposed of his lands . . . by Act of Parliament?'; ibid. Compare this with Hale's attempt to distinguish between patrimonial and the royal as well as Grotius's discussion of the same.

116 Hobbes ([1651] 1994): 131; 'It is not therefore the victory that giveth the right of dominion over the vanquished, but his own covenant. Nor is he obliged because he is conquered (that is to say, beaten, and taken or put to flight) but because he cometh in, and submitteth to the victor.' Later, it is clarified that the victor has therein the right over the property of the vanquished. Here it is important to note that Hobbes classifies both the acquisitive and instituted forms of sovereignty as 'despotic' and 'paternal', drawing the parallel between the master–servant relationship and the sovereign–subject relationship. In his words, 'In sum the rights and consequences of both paternal and despotical dominion are the very same with those of a sovereign by institution'; ibid. This position should be contrasted with the argument of Hale who wishes to distinguish between patrimonial and monarchical forms, and argues that the former was not applicable to England.

117 Ibid.: 175–77. See also, Hobbes (1681).

118 Ibid.

119 While this is the well-known argument of the *Leviathan* (Hobbes [1651] 1994), in the *Dialogue* (Hobbes 1681), a more historical approach too might be found in evidence. Here too the 'paternal', familial origins of sovereignty are traced, which might be seen as veering towards the kind of argument that was traced earlier in this part in Bacon.

120 Hobbes (1681). See also Hobbes ([1651] 1994): 208

121 See note 114 above.

122 Hobbes ([1651] 1994): 383; 'And thus Captives taken in a just and lawful War, and such only, are subject to a Despotical Power, which as it arises not from Compact, so neither is it capable of any, but is the state of War continued.'

123 See P. Laslett, ed. (1988). Distinguishing despotic from paternal and political power, Locke writes, 'Forfeiture gives the third, Despotical power to Lords for their own Benefit, over those who are stripp'd of all property'; ibid.: 384.

124 Ibid.: 387–88; 'Let us see what Power a Lawful conqueror has over the Subdued; and that I say is purely Despotical. He has absolute power over the Lives of those who by an Unjust War have forfeited them; but not over the Lives or fortunes of those, who engaged not in the War, nor over the Possessions even of those who were actually engaged in it.' And later, 'The Power a Conqueror gets over those he overcomes in a Just War is perfectly Despotical: he has an absolute power over the Lives of those, who by putting themselves in a State of War have forfeited them: but he has not thereby a Right and Title to their Possessions. This I doubt not but at first sight will seem a strange Doctrine, it being so quite contrary to the practice of the World; There being nothing more familiar in speaking of the Dominion of Countries, than to say, such an one Conquered it. As if Conquest without any more ado, conveyed a right of Possession.'

[125] Ibid.: 392; 'Nor has the Conqueror any right to take them away by the bare title of having subdued him, that by force attempted his destruction; though perhaps he may have some right to them to repair the damages he has sustained by the War, and the defence of his own right, which how far it reaches to the possessions of the Conquered, we shall see by and by. So that he that by Conquest has a right over a Man's person to destroy him if he pleases, has not a right over his Estate to possess and enjoy it.' 'His [the aggressor's] force and, and the state of War he put himself in, made him forfeit his Life, but gave me no Title to his Goods. The right then of Conquest extends only to the Lives of those joyn'd in the War, not to their Estates, but in order to make reparation for the damages received, and the Charges of the War, and that too with reservation of the right of the innocent wife and Children.'

[126] Ibid.: 392–93.

[127] In a long passage refuting the title to dominion based on conquest with examples from the Americas, where he argues that 'conquerors take little care to possess themselves of the Lands of the Vanquished', Locke writes, 'even in a just war, hath by his conquest, no right of Dominion'; ibid.: 392.

[128] Compare this with Hobbes's discussion in *Dialogue* (Hobbes 1681).

[129] See note 113 above.

[130] See J.P. Sommerville, ed. (1991): 55; 'If such as maintain the natural liberty of mankind take offence at the liberty I take to examine it, they must take heed that they do not deny by retail that liberty which they affirm by wholesale; for if their thesis be true, the hypothesis will follow, that all men may examine their own charters, deeds, or evidences by which they claim and hold the inheritance or freehold of their liberties.'

[131] Laslett, ed. (1988). As Locke writes, 'thus the grass my horse has bit, the turfs my servant has cut, and the ore I have digged in any place where I have a right to them in common with others, becomes my property, without the assignation or consent of any body'. See the important use made of this passage by Neal Wood (2021): 72–93 and Ellen Meiksins Wood (1992): 657–89.

[132] Laslett, ed. (1988): 170.

[133] Ibid.; 'A man can no more justly make use of another's necessity, to force him to become a vassal by with-holding that relief, God requires him to afford the wants of his brother, than he that hath more strength can seize upon a weaker, master him to his obedience, and with a dagger at his throat offer him death or slavery.'

[134] Ibid.

[135] Ibid.: 171; 'And anything by this rule that may be an occasion for working upon another's necessity to save his life or anything dear to him at the rate of his freedom may be made a foundation of sovereignty as well as property.'

[136] In the same way, while there is a show of the denial of Adam's lordship over Eve, Locke nonetheless affirms such lordship in making use of a distinction perhaps too subtle to ever be gleaned. He writes, 'God in this text, *gives not as I see, any authority to Adam over Eve, or to men over their wives, but* only *foretells what should be the woman's lot, how by his providence he would order it so, that she should be subject to her husband* as we see that generally the laws of mankind and the customs of nations have ordered it so; and there is I grant *a foundation of nature in it.*' Is not Eve subject to Adam after all by divine providence and natural law? See ibid.: 174. For a fine analysis of such problems in the

instituting of gender as a powerful heuristic to diagnose the theoretical idiom of modern politics, see Pateman (1988).

137 See Sommerville, ed. (1991): 58–60.

138 Laslett, ed. (1988): 399–400.

139 Ibid.: 96; 'For as Kingly power is by the law of God, so it hath no inferior power to limit it. The father of a family governs by no other law than by his own will, not by the laws or wills of his sons or servants. There is no nation that allows children any action or remedy for being unjustly governed. And yet for all this every father is bound by the law of nature to do his best for the preservation of his family. But much more is a King always tied by the same law of nature to keep this general ground, that the safety of his kingdom be his chief law. He must remember that the profit of every man in particular, and of all together in general, is not always one and the same, that the public is to be preferred before the private and that the force of law must not be so great as natural equity itself.'

140 Ibid.: 397–98.

141 See Sommerville, ed. (1991): 93–94, 66–73; see Filmer's discussion and critique of Grotius. The Filmerian argument about the King's powers being before laws mirrors the common law discussions in *Postnati* that have been earlier discussed.

142 Laslett, ed. (1988): 379.

143 Ibid.: 360–61, 418–19.

144 See Neal Wood (2021) and Ellen Meiksins Wood (1992). N. Wood and E.M. Wood convincingly critique the arguments of James Tully and Richard Ashcraft on the relationship between franchise and representation in Locke, through historical and textual evidence. Among much else, E.M. Woods's discussion of 'tacit' consent and its relationship to Hooker sheds light on this set of issues.

145 Laslett, ed. (1988): 372–75. These passages have been much discussed and debated in the literature around the question of franchise and representation. Their implications for Locke's thinking on prerogative have been less attended to.

146 For a discussion of these earlier arguments, see McIlwain's *American Revolution: A Constitutional Interpretation* (1923). The immediate context of Molyneux's arguments in this vein could well be the Irish parliamentary legislation under James II immediately prior to the Battle of Boyne in 1689, where the case for the independence of Irish jurisdiction was clearly declared. These issues will be revisited in the concluding section of this part.

147 W. Molyneux, *The Case of Ireland being bound by Acts of Parliament in England, Stated, with anew Preface* (1770): 16.

148 Ibid.: 16–17; 'Nay, *England* may be said much more properly to be *conquered* by *William* the First, than *Ireland* by *Henry* the Second: For we all know with what Violence and Opposition from *Harrold* King *William* obtained the kingdom, after a bloody Battle near *Hastings.* Whereas *Henry* the Second received not the least Opposition in *Ireland,* all came in peaceably, and had large Concessions made them of the like Laws and Liberties with the People of *England,* which they gladly accepted, as we shall see hereafter.'

149 Ibid.: 32; 'In conclusion of all, if this *Superiority* of the Parliament of *England* have been *doubted* a great while ago, so it has been as great a while ago strenuously *opposed,* and absolutely denied by the Parliaments of *Ireland.* And by the way, I shall take Notice, that from whencesoever this ancient *Pretence of Ireland's Subordination* proceeded in those

Days, it did not arise from the *Parliament* of *England* itself: For we have not one single Instance of an English Act of Parliament *expressly claiming* this Right of binding us: But we have several Instances of *Irish* Acts of Parliament *expressly denying this Subordination,* as appears by what foregoes.'

150 Ibid.: 23; 'From all which it is manifest, that there were no Laws imposed on the People of *Ireland* by any Authority of the Parliament of *England,* nor any Laws introduced into that kingdom by *Henry* the Second, but by the *Consent* and *Allowance* of the People of *Ireland.* For both the civil and ecclesiastical State were settled there, *Regiæsublimitatis Authoritate,* solely by the King's Authority *and their own good Wills,* as the *Irish* Statute, 11 *Eliz.* c. 1. expresses it. And not only the *Laws* of *England,* but the Manner of *holding Parliaments* in *Ireland* to make Laws of their own (which is the *Foundation* and *Bulwark* of the People's *Liberties* and *Properties)* was directed and established there by *Henry* the Second, as if he were resolved that no other Person or Persons should be the Founders of the Government of *Ireland,* but himself and the *Consent* of the People, who submitted themselves to him against all Persons whatsoever.'

151 Ibid.: 19.

152 Ibid.

153 Ibid.: 20; 'From what has been said, I presume it pretty clearly appears, that an *unjust* Conquest gives *no Title* at all; that a *just* Conquest gives Power only over the *Lives* and *Liberties* of the *actual Opposers,* but not over their *Posterity* and *Estates,* otherwise than as before is mentioned; and not at all over those that did *not concur* in the Opposition. They that desire a more full Disquisition of this Matter, may find it at large in an incomparable *Treatise,* concerning the *True original Extent and End of civil Government,* Chap. 16. This Discourse is said to be written by my excellent Friend, John Locke, *Esq*; Whether it be so or not, I know not; this I am sure, whoever is the Author, the greatest Genius in *Christendom* need not disown it.'

154 Ibid.: 39–41.

155 Ibid.: 42–45.

156 Ibid.: 60; '*Sixthly,* it is *against the King's Prerogative,* that the Parliament of *England* should have any co-ordinate Power with him to introduce new Laws, or repeal old Laws established in *Ireland.*'

157 Ibid.: 53–54.

158 Ibid.: 54; 'We have an Example of this in Point between *England* and *Holland* in the glorious Revolution under King *William* the Third: *Holland,* in assisting *England,* expended 600000 Pounds, and the *English* Parliament fairly repaid them: It would have looked oddly for *Holland* to have insisted on disposing of Lord *Powis*'s and other Estates by their own Laws, to reimburse themselves.'

159 See Patrick Riley, ed. (1988): 214–17.

160 For studies that have richly documented and argued for the centrality of conquest as a way to frame the settlement of 1688–89, see J.G.A. Pocock (2007) and Mark Goldie (1977 and 1983).

161 This was the subject of a previous study; see Govind (2015).

162 However, there remained the contentious issue of whether those jurisdictions that came under the immediate grant of the King, such as the ones established in the Americas, were subject to parliamentary statutes against monopolies in the same way. For a discussion, see Harvey Wheeler (1956).

[163] See Howell, ed., *State Trials*, Vol. X (1816): 454.

[164] Ibid.: 385.

[165] In the words of Sir George Treby's argument, 'the king cannot by his letter patents take away the subject's property and I do not know of a greater property than freedom of trade and labour'. Ibid.: 387, 421–23.

[166] 'It cannot be inferred that the king may restrain his subjects from trade; for my lord Coke, in his Comment. Fol. 57, says, that this prohibition must be intended by an act of parliament, for that it concerns the whole realm, and is implied by the word "public".' Ibid.: 389; see also 387–89, 404, 453.

[167] 'I shall lay for my foundation, that this patent as to restraining the trade, and excluding all other subjects, has the nature of a monopoly and is therefore void in that particular'; ibid.: 386. Several cases from Magna Carta are referred to; ibid.: 421–42.

[168] Ibid.: 418.

[169] Ibid.: 403–04.

[170] In the words of Mr Holt, 'My lord I think it is plain by the writ of Ne exeat Regnum, that says the king may prohibit any person from going beyond the sea. Why? For the defense of the realm; that is a sufficient reason, it is not in the power of the party to litigate it with the king, but he must submit. Now always religion is first to be regarded; secondly, the defence of the kingdom; and thirdly, the trade thereof.' Ibid.: 375; see also 406–07.

[171] Ibid.: 408–11.

[172] Ibid.: 378–79.

[173] Ibid.: 380; this argument that the Company could not be characterized as a monopoly is reiterated (in ibid.: 406), for instance, by the solicitor general, and may also be found later (in ibid.: 424–30).

[174] Ibid.: 381; see also ibid.: pp. 476–77 on the argument that other companies were not denied such privileges.

[175] Ibid.: 375–76.

[176] Ibid.: 391–92. On Coke's argument about infidels being 'perpetual enemies', the lawyers of Sandys argue, 'It seems by these words, that it is to be understood of a spiritual discord with respect to religion, and not a temporal between nations'; 'A Pagan, Turk or Jew, may maintain an action of debt or battery or other personal action here; were it otherwise, there could be no trading of the Jews here, nor of the Turks; the contrary whereof is implied and admitted in the Act of Navigation 12 Car 2 c 18 par 18. By the like reason that there should be no trading with infidels there ought to be no foreign trade at all, for there is no country where the religion does not differ in somewhat or other from the religion established in the church of England'; see ibid.: 443.

[177] Ibid.

[178] Ibid.: 408–09; see also 486–87. Legally it was held that a Christian marrying a Jew was a felony and therefore incurred the punishment of burning.

[179] Ibid.: 445–47.

[180] Ibid.: 446; 'The charters that they have cited to Barbary and other places, some of them are before the last of these statutes, that is the statute of king James; and yet there is no difference taken notice of there between Christians and Infidel countries; so that, my lord, taking all together the light, or at least the weak authorities of these sayings and occasional discourses, for this distinction of infidel and Christian, in point of trade, will

signify but little; and the constant practice of our time, wherein we have any sort of trade.' See also ibid.: 449, 486–88.

[181] Ibid.: 443; 'Then for 12 H 8 4 they also cited, that is only this. The original case in an action of trespass for beating his servant, taking away his dog, called a blood-hound. And there it is said "if a lord beat his villain, or a husband beat his wife, or a man beat one out-lawed, or a traitor or a Pagan; they shall have not action, because they are not able to sue an action".'

[182] Ibid.: 483–86

[183] Ibid.

[184] Ibid.: 486–87.

[185] Ibid.: 442; see also 516, 518, 531–32.

[186] Ibid.: 486.

[187] Ibid.: 478.

[188] Ibid.: 488.

[189] 'No assemblies could be held for the traffic of buying or selling, without the king's licence; for though some markets and fairs are held by prescription (the original grants not appearing) yet these were derived for the crown, by some royal licence before the time of memory; they all depend upon the same crown, and may be forfeited to the crown . . . and here the prerogative of the crown had a great stroke. The inland traders, in buying and selling might buy and sell in private places could not be restrained but they could not hold assemblies for trade without the king's leave and licence; marts, fairs, and markets, in their true notion being no other than royal licences to assemble for trade and traffic'; ibid.: 459. 'And the managery of the principal part of the home traffic, which consists in the marts, fairs, and markets of the kingdom, depends upon the king's prerogative, and is managing under the law having entrusted the king with that power for the benefit of his people, and the peace of his kingdom'; ibid.: 459–60, 472 (on butter and cheese), 524.

[190] Ibid.: 428–29.

[191] Ibid.: 496–99, 520–21.

[192] Ibid.: 457.

[193] Ibid.: 516.

[194] Ibid.: 522.

[195] Ibid.: 530.

[196] Ibid.: 524. This doctrine of the unique royal powers of making corporations has been documented in the Introduction. In the context of the above arguments it is therefore surprising that recent histories of the seventeenth-century East India Company do not take cognizance of the crucial role of the King in constituting the Company; the critique of Philip Stern's argument (in *The Company State*, 2011), that Justice Jefferies 'introduced' the 'Crown' as a 'third side', has already been made in the introduction. Jon Wilson too, in an attempt to characterize the East India Company as completely anomalous with no roots in English institutional and legal history, writes (in *India Conquered*, 2016), 'Sharply at odds with the mainstreams of domestic commercial life, the East India Company's governors needed a theory to explain why they had created such a strange institution to trade with Asia. They did so by appealing to religion, and arguing that Asia was different.' Yet, as has been demonstrated in this section, the Company's lawyers, the attorney general as well as the judges rooted their decisions in

readings of English constitutional history and jurisprudence and no less a celebrated case than *Postnati.* None of this is referenced in either Wilson or Stern's analysis of the matter, thereby participating in the old venture to separate the Company's history from its roots in empire. See note 98 from the introduction.

197 Ibid.: 525.

198 Ibid.: 530.

199 See John Bruce (1810): 541.

200 *An account of some transactions in the honourable House of Commons, and before the right honourable Lords of the King's most honourable Privy Council, relating to the late East India Company together with the said companies new charter*; https://ota.bodleian.ox.ac.uk/repository/xmlui/bitstream/handle/20.500.12024/A38195/A38195.html?sequence=5&isAllowed=y. This role of the King is not analysed or mentioned in Philip Stern's argument (2011: 154), who largely follows the lead of Ilbert's *Government of India Being a Digest of the Statute Law Relating Thereto, With Historical Introduction and Explanatory Matter* (1898), who himself depends of Macaulay's history. Stern participates therefore in an old attempt to treat the 1690s in terms of the false teleology of the House of Commons as heroically embodying the story of liberty by moving away from royal control.

201 *An account of some transactions in the honourable House of Commons, and before the right honourable Lords of the King's most honourable Privy Council, relating to the late East India Company together with the said companies new charter*; https://ota.bodleian.ox.ac.uk/repository/xmlui/bitstream/handle/20.500.12024/A38195/A38195.html?sequence=5&isAllowed=y.

202 *Charters Granted to the East India Company from 1601*; https://indianculture.gov.in/reports-proceedings/charters-granted-east-india-company-1601-also-treaties-and-grants-made-or: 141–87.

203 9 & 10 GULIELMI III, Cap. XLIV.

204 In a sense this was anticipated by the Scottish parliament which passed an Act allowing Scotsmen to trade in the East Indies.

205 *Collection of Statutes Concerning the Incorporation, Trade and Commerce of the East India Company*: 39; 12 William III, XXVIII.

206 Ibid.: 19, 9 and 10 William III, Cap. XLIV (1698), section LVI on the letters-patent of the King constituting companies/corporations: 15.

207 Ibid.: 25; section LXVII.

208 Madras had been incorporated earlier by the East India Company, with the 'approbation' of the King.

209 *Charters Granted to the East India Company from 1601*, letters-patent issued in 1726: see 368–99.

210 *Charters Granted to the East India Company from 1601*, 11 (under the appended section 'list of the several charters and letters-patent granted to the East India Company which are not present in this collection').

211 See, for instance, Grotius's discussion of several precedents in H. Grotius, *Rights of War and Peace*, Vol. III ([1625] 2005): 1303–59.

212 As Grotius writes, there is the difficult question regarding the spoils from the enemy got in a public war, about whether they belong to 'the people in general, or to private persons'. And he goes on to say that while in Roman law they belonged to the 'captor',

canon law suggested that they were to be divided by 'public distribution', though the captor had the 'original right' (ibid.: 1327). He later distinguishes between 'private wars' and 'public wars': whereas the former remained with the private people, the latter remained with the 'people' (ibid.: 1330). And Grotius further distinguishes between acts undertaken in a private capacity, where the lawful Prize remained with the captor, and acts undertaken in a military expedition, where 'every soldier represents the Body of the state' and 'the state acquires both the possession and property of things taken' (ibid.: 1333). See also P.Q. Wright (1913): 1–16, for Prize in classical antiquity.

[213] Grotius ([1625] 2005): 1343.

[214] Ibid.: 1350.

[215] See M. De Martens (1801): 17.

[216] Ibid.: 6.

[217] Ibid.

[218] See R.G. Marsden (1915–16), Vol. I: ix, 8, 12, 69 (for the documents).

[219] Ibid.: ix–x, 19; Martens (1801): 10.

[220] Ibid.: 10–11.

[221] Marsden (1915–16), Vol. I: xiii; Martens (1801):17–18.

[222] Ibid.: 10.

[223] Ibid.: 13.

[224] Ibid.: 13–14.

[225] Ibid.: 14.

[226] Ibid.: 13.

[227] Ibid.: 18.

[228] Ibid.: 21.

[229] Ibid.

[230] Ibid.: 24.

[231] Ibid.: 23.

[232] Ibid.: 25–26.

[233] Ibid.

[234] Marsden (1915–16), Vol. I: xvii, 168.

[235] Marsden (1915–16), Vol. II: xvi. Commissions given to the East India Company to capture pirates are also documented.

[236] Marsden (1915–16), Vol. II: ix; Martens (1801): 36–37.

[237] Finch (1759): 20.

[238] Finch writes here, 'the Court of the Constable is for matters of law. See here the Statute 13 Richard 2 cap. 2. And if an alien enemy enters into the realm, and levies war here against the King, he shall be tried by this court and not by the Common Law'; ibid.: 386–87. See https://books.google.co.in/books/about/A_Description_of_the_Common_Laws_of_Engl.html?id=4e8yAAAAIAAJ&redir_esc=y

[239] *Brymer v. Atkins*, https://books.google.co.in/books?id=6bs2AQAAMAAJ&pg=PA173&lpg=PA173&dq=1612++Admiralty+Court+as+the+King%E2%80%99s+Court&source=bl&ots=MYbNf1ALeB&sig=ACfU3U09JpUeorZ9rVSJA88dWiU-fBU5ng& hl=en&sa=X&ved=2ahUKEwiXje7InOv0AhWiSWwGHei2ClcQ6AF6BAgtEAM#v=onepage&q=1612%20%20Admiralty%20Court%20as%20the%20King%E2%80%99s%20Court&f=false: 174.

[240] See H.J. Bourguignon (2004): 1–31.

[241] Martens (1801): 176.
[242] Marsden (1915–16), Vol. II: xx.
[243] For a historical study on this, see Robert Brenner (1993).
[244] Charters giving war- and peace-making authority. It is not surprising that in James Mill's celebrated 'official' history of the East India Company (*The History of British India*), none of these powers regarding Prize are detailed. In fact the word Prize does not occur even once. The same may be said for the contemporary treatment of the subject by Philip Stern (2011) and Jon Wilson (2016).
[245] Marsden (1915–16), Vol. II: xvi–xviii.
[246] R.G. Marsden (1909).
[247] John Bruce, *The Annals of the Honourable East India Company* (1810), Vol. II: 496.
[248] Ibid.: 567; see also John Bruce, *The Annals of the Honourable East India Company* (1810), Vol. III: 73–74.
[249] Bruce (1810), Vol. II: 492.
[250] Ibid.: 500, 506.
[251] Ibid.: 538.
[252] Ibid.: 539.
[253] Ibid.: 552.
[254] Ibid.: 551.
[255] Ibid.: 569.
[256] Ibid.: 572.
[257] Ibid.: 575.
[258] Ibid.: 501.
[259] For a modern historical account of the East India Company's early conflicts with native polities, see Bruce Watson (1980), and for particularly this many-cornered war described in the following section, Bruce Lenman (1987).
[260] Bruce (1810), Vol. II: 559.
[261] Ibid.: 605.
[262] Ibid.: 579.
[263] Ibid.: 596.
[264] Ibid.: 647–48.
[265] Ibid.: 600.
[266] Ibid.: 604.
[267] Ibid.: 631.
[268] Ibid.: 613.
[269] Ibid.: 631–35.
[270] Ibid.: 638.
[271] Ibid.: 641.
[272] In the ensuing war, the English factory at Visagapatnam was destroyed, four men killed and the Company's stock seized and plundered.
[273] Bruce (1810), Vol. II: 639–50.
[274] Ibid.: 627.
[275] Ibid.: 663.
[276] R.G. Marsden, *Early Prize Jurisdiction and Prize Law in England* (1909): 55.
[277] When referring to kingship, it must be stated at the outset that there was a very old discourse that attempted to distinguish lawful kingship from despotism, and hence

paradoxical formulations such as the King being both above as well as under the law; or the idea – closely linked to parliamentary institutions – that the King's reason referred to the counsel of his Courts and assemblies. For a detailed study on these matters see E. Kantorowicz's *The King's Two Bodies* (1957). The present study, while cognizant of this line of argumentation, has sought to flesh out the role of the King through a study of the spatial and temporal conjoining of allegiance and jurisdiction.

[278] Howell, ed., *State Trials*, Vol. II (1816): 567.

[279] Ibid.: 570.

[280] Timothy Harris, *Revolution: The Great Crisis of the British Monarchy 1685–1720* (2006): 312–13, 312. See also the detailed discussions in Howard Nenner, *The Right to Be King* (1995): 120–219.

[281] Harris (2006): 324.

[282] While Harris states, 'however arguably the most radial act of 1689 – and certainly the most unequivocally Whiggist – was the transfer of the crown itself from James to William and Mary' (ibid.: 321), he does not see this as necessarily leading to the title of conquest, even though in his rich study he recognizes that the theory of abdication was a formal denial of parliament either electing or deposing the monarch, and therein an acceptance of the monarchical institution. This *a priori* non-consideration of conquest leads to the following, 'The Convention did not claim to have deposed James, although one might argue that the mere fact that the Convention imposed this particular interpretation of events meant that, in effect they had' (ibid.: 329). The fact that this actually amounted to a conquest, as was recognized by several including the Earl of Nottingham (ibid.:333), is not taken seriously into cognizance. For recent scholarly arguments on the centrality of conquest for the settlement, see J.G.A. Pocock (2007) and Mark Goldie (1977 and 1983).

[283] Harris (2006): 346.

[284] Ibid.: 335.

[285] The 'Act of Settlement' cannot be construed as novel in the sense of intervening in the terrain of royal inheritance (recognizing biological 'heirs' but excluding Catholics). It also merely continued to enable the King to require his own assent for removal and the declared principle of 'good behaviour' was already accepted by Charles I. See C. McIlwain's argument – and the evidence therein adduced – that, 'So far as parliament's power goes, the words of 1701 seem merely declaratory of existing law'; McIlwain (1913): 217–29. On the other hand, the statutory 'limitation' of heirs was hardly novel either; see note 6 above.

[286] Letter to Burnet De Kemney, April 1695, in Patrick Riley, ed. (1988): 214–17.

[287] W. Sherlock (1691): 3–13.

[288] Ibid.: 21–36.

[289] Riley, ed. (1988): 214.

[290] Sherlock (1691): 19.

[291] Ibid.: 10.

[292] For a discussion of 'natural reason' in Hobbes that militates against any simple equation between power and right, see R. Govind, 'Equality, Right and Identity: Rethinking the Contract through Hobbes and Marx' (2011), 'Criminalizing unto Death, Act of Judgment, Act of War' (2021), and 'The Haunting Image of the Frozen Jew (in Christian Self-Understanding), the Self-Determining Universality of Human Reason

and Anticipating the Secular Nation-State: From Hobbes to Kant and Beyond' (2023).

293 Harris (2006): 439, 443–44.

294 Ibid.

295 This was the argument of Charles Leslie; ibid.: 460–62.

296 F.W. Maitland, *Constitutional History of England* (1908): 303.

297 Howell, ed., *State Trials*, Vol. II (1816).

298 Ibid.: 567–68.

299 Ibid.: 575.

300 Ibid.: 576.

301 Ibid.: 581.

302 Ibid.: 641. For a discussion of Bonham's case, see James R. Stoner Jr., *Common Law and Liberal Theory* (1992): 48–69. As has been pointed out, there is sufficient scholarship that has made the connection between aspects of *Postnati* and Bonham's case to justify the (American) colonial critique of (English) parliamentary statute. As Barbara A. Black puts it (in 'The Constitution of Empire: The Case for the Colonists', 1976: 1175), 'The colonists case, as some of them sensed, took on life at the intersection of Calvin's Case and Bonham's Case.'

303 Howell, ed., *State Trials*, Vol. II (1816): 591.

304 Ibid.: 605.

305 Ibid.

306 Ibid.: 605–06.

307 Sir Mathew Hale's *The Prerogatives of the King* (1976): 43 (citing Hale, 'Rights of the Crown').

308 Charles H. McIlwain's *American Revolution: A Constitutional Interpretation* (1923), 28–66. See also Barbara A. Black's 'The Constitution of Empire: The Case for the Colonists' (1976): 1180–91. More recently, Eric Nelson's *The Royalist Revolution* (2014) has reiterated the importance and validity of McIlwain's thesis, even though he takes the argument about 'royalism' in a different direction. Nelson is interested in showing that not merely were the American colonists arguing as King's subjects, such a support for the figure of the King found its way into the formulation of the constitutional powers of the American President. However, in doing so he does not investigate either the specific doctrinal basis of kingship or the problem of sovereignty and jurisdiction, both of which are central to the present study.

309 Ibid.: 1–18.

310 Ibid.: 63. Such an understanding of 'Judgments of parliament by way of law' may be found in *Postnati*.

311 See Barbara A. Black (1976) and Daniel J. Hulsebosch (2003). See also Eric Nelson (2014): 29–66.

312 For a rich discussion on both these dimensions, see Harris (2006).

313 R.L. Schuyler (1929): 1–40.

314 The fact that Schuyler did not account for the specificity of the seventeenth-century moment was a critique made by Harvey Wheeler in 'Calvin's Case (1608) and the McIlwain–Schuyler Debate' (1956). This certainly rings true if one keeps in mind that *Postnati* specifically refuted the English parliamentary position that allegiance was 'diverse', as has been emphasized in this part. For a more detailed review of the debate and a powerful argument on the ambiguities surrounding the status of Ireland in *Postnati*, see

Barbara A. Black's 'The Constitution of Empire: The Case for the Colonists' (1976), on which we have tried to build.

315 Ibid.: 1191–94, 1196–97.

316 See note 98 of the Introduction.

317 See the discussion in James R. Stoner Jr., *Common Law and Liberal Theory* (1992): 179–223.

318 For a detailed study, see Joseph H. Smith, *Appeals to the Privy Council from the American Plantations* (1950). In Daniel J. Hulsebosch's 'The Ancient Constitution and the Expanding Empire: Sir Edward Coke's British Jurisprudence' (2003), an important point is made about the American colonies being considered legally as 'conquered' by jurists and case law in the seventeenth and eighteenth centuries. Black had earlier noted that Coke recognized only descent and conquest as possible modes of acquisition, not therefore recognizing what came to be called colonization, plantation or settlement; see Black (1976): 1177, 1199.

319 Hulsebosch (2003).

320 Coke's 7th Report: 398.

321 One is forced to use such vague appellations, since nothing else indicates the legal latitude given to the Company.

322 It is unclear whether, and if so when and how, subsequent jurisprudence – including important cases such as *Omychund v. Barker* (1780) – affected the status of non-Christians in the context of the laws of war. For an insightful historical interpretation and account of the role of Christian notions in the conduct and practice of war more generally, see Phillipe Buc, *Holy War, Martyrdom, and Terror: Christianity, Violence, and the West* (2015).

323 The massive importance of slavery and enslavement, massacre and domination of native peoples and peoples transported from half-way across the world can no more than be affirmed here. There is much rich scholarship that challenges any celebratory narrative of Anglo-American democracy from the seventeenth to the twentieth century, with which the present investigation works in solidarity; this is an issue that will be taken up in the conclusion.

PART II

The King and the Body-politic in Metastasis

Conquest Perfecting Law in the Eighteenth Century

Introduction

The previous part discussed the crucial role of the King in constituting the nature of allegiance, rights and the degrees of subjecthood. This was the case in the British Isles, the American colonies as much as the British territories in the subcontinent under the delegated sovereignty of the East India Company; unlike judges of the highest courts and eminent jurists of the eighteenth and nineteenth centuries, contemporary historiography has not taken into cognizance the role of royal prize letters-patent in forming the legal bases of the Company's conquests and treaties, i.e. their territorial rule in the Indian subcontinent.[1] If it has been conventional to argue that after the Glorious Revolution and the Bill of Rights the role of the King was diminished, and the King no longer acted through his prerogative or in his distinctive capacity independently of parliament, this cannot be so summarily accepted. There was an undeniable rearticulation of the relationship between King and (King-in) parliament, which cannot be reduced to a simple contest between the two where one gained always at the other's expense.[2] While the King's 'suspending' powers were annulled by the Bill of Rights, his 'dispensing' powers were not so summarily rejected, and war- and peace-making authority, and therein 'foreign affairs', remained very much within his prerogative.[3]

Focusing on the problematic of subjecthood, allegiance and jurisdiction enables one to escape being a hostage to the question of whether parliament or King gained from the settlement of 1688–89. This question is driven implicitly by the conflation between nation and parliament, and embeds the relationship between King and parliament within a grander narrative about the growth of parliamentary powers (taken to represent peoples' liberties) in relationship to a King seen as representing autocratic principles when acting on his own.[4] The falsity of this narrative is demonstrated not only by the fact that parliament was not representative of 'the people' in this period.[5] In addition, parliament necessarily had to work in conjunction with the King, the measure of which is only determinable in relation to the force and violence exerted on peoples and populations completely at a remove from any parliamentary-representative function. Only thereby can any account be taken of the theorization of King and parliament. Imperialism, particularly in places like India, give lie to such claims of representation, both because King and King-in-Parliament were conjointly shaping and mis-shaping vast territories and populations such that the period from the eighteenth to the early twentieth century would have to be seen as one of great disenfranchisement – even if measured by the crudity of comparing those numbers in the metropolis being represented and those elsewhere being deprived. It is to discern this logic in the jurisdictional complexity of spatial incorporation that one has to unpeel the hardened hide that measures growing representation in the ideological *a priori* of the 'nation'; the pustules of imperial violence thereby exposed are not a pleasant sight. Finally, to speak of the growing powers of parliament is slightly ironical considering the explicit parliamentary undermining of royal authority in both the fourteenth and seventeenth centuries, something never attempted thereafter.

Despite this, even in constitutional terms, the King existed in distinction from the parliament, but the latter could not be conceived as independent of the King. Statutory intervention did not necessarily diminish, but often did no more than declare and clarify royal powers. Even while (King-in) parliamentary statute established the rights of the East India Company's trading ventures in the east in the 1690s, its corporate identity as much as its *governance* were derived from royal powers specified in statute, or distinct royal charters establishing judicial institutions as well as those such as that of Prize. While the Mutiny Acts in England clarified the prerogative powers of the King in his government of the army, royal charters had delegated the powers of martial law to the Company until the special Mutiny Act of 1754 similarly granted the King special powers in his government of the East India Company and its army, that were to operate within certain conditions specified in the act, as is analysed below. The specification of royal powers of governance over the East India Company, it will be argued, was reaffirmed in the much better known statutes of 1773, 1781 and 1784. Apart from governance, the war- and peace-making authority derived from the King, specifically his Prize charters, as will be discussed. It is from such a legal framing that one can better understand the nature of East India Company's conquests and rule in the eighteenth century, and the imperial territorialization of a subcontinent.

A central argument of this part of the book lies in the establishment, and analysis, of the fact that the great subcontinental maritime–terrestrial conquests of Plassey and thereafter were grounded in prerogative, particularly the King's letters-patent granting Prize money, while Company governance too had its basis in royal empowerment as declared by parliamentary statute. It is to be underlined that notwithstanding the existence of statutes relating to Prize, the Company derived its rights to Prize not from a statute but from specific royal charters, which formed the basis of the legality of its conquests as well as treaties. The history of Prize jurisdiction and the complexities of the categories of prerogative and conquest are therefore essential ingredients for an understanding of the nature of the East India Company regime in its conquests and governance, raising complex questions regarding subject-formation for the millions vanquished in the wake of war in India. The marine provenance of Prize law was sought to be transferred and translated into the terrestrial order of armed battle in the subcontinent's conquest, and this part therefore begins with a discussion of the way in which the 'revolution' of 1689 rearticulated the relationship between the King and the (terrestrial) army in England as much as the East India Company's armed forces. Building on the rearticulated role of kingship and its government of military forces, the legal position of the King is then analysed in the context of war, conquest and subjecthood, by analysing the celebrated *Campbell v. Hall* within the broader context of Prize law and nationality.

A crucial context is thereby nurtured for the main sections of this part, which involves an analysis and account of the East India Company's wars in India, grounded in the Prize-granting letters-patent of the King (1756–57) and the emerging problematic of subjecthood in the aftermath of the conquest of these territories. Using archival sources, case law and the political trial of Warren Hastings, it is argued that these conquests inaugurate a legal situation so unique as to break out of the hitherto existing rules and norms that governed war and peace in Britain. And yet, it is not merely the 'event' itself but the studied concealing of such legal challenges and their devastating consequences on local populations that seals its singularity. The granting of authority by the King through his letters-patent regarding Prize in one sense legally grounded the Company's conquests, its treaties and its manipulation of the latter. But there was no judicial oversight over Prize and Prize distribution by Admiralty Courts, even though the Supreme Court was granted such jurisdiction from 1774, Prize remaining a matter of the King's grant. Analogously, while the lords in the trial of Hastings recognized that there were no unambiguous rules or laws delineating the Company's precise relations with sovereigns in India, and therefore channels and evaluations of accountability were obscure, they nonetheless did not think it fit to enunciate a clear legal framework that would work towards preventing the repetition and amplification of such anomalies as much as their devastating effects. This allowed for conquest, violence and plunder on an unprecedented scale, in terms of territories and populations. Ironically, precisely the lack of such a detailed transparent framework made it difficult to legally indict anyone for the wars in the east – a lack that was nothing less than an elaborately woven veil.

The discussion of Prize and war below segues into an analysis of governance. King-in-parliamentary legislative intervention in the form of the Regulating Act (1773–74) established the Governor-General and Council of Four as the Supreme Council in charge of governance, empowered to frame 'rules, ordinances and regulations' not 'repugnant to the laws of England'.[6] However, these rules, ordinances and regulations were to be registered in the King's Court (Supreme Court), only after which it was to be considered good in law.[7] In yet another instance of reaffirming the King's powers of governance, it was specifically stated in the statute that individuals unhappy with such rules, whether in India or England, could appeal to His Majesty in Council, who had the powers to set aside or repeal them.[8] Moreover, the King's Bench in England had the authority to proceed against all East India Company officials, including Supreme Court judges.[9] Such a situation led to conflicts between the Supreme Council and Supreme Court on matters of jurisdiction, and so a further statute was declared in 1781. According to this statute, the Governor-General and Council were not liable to the jurisdiction of the Supreme Court if they were acting in their public capacity, and the servants of the Company were similarly immune if it could be shown that they were acting on orders from the Governor-General and Council;[10] this was not applicable to cases where British subjects were involved.[11]

More importantly from the perspective presently adopted, the statute of 1781 once again specified that while the Supreme Court had the authority to frame rules of procedure within its jurisdiction, and the Governor-General and

Council now acted as the final court of appeal for the provincial ('mofussil') courts, and could frame rules and regulations for such courts, all of the latter had to be submitted to His Majesty's principal secretary of state.[12] His Majesty in Council had the powers to disallow or amend any such procedures, rules or ordinances.[13] Finally, in the act, the King's powers of governance, civil and military, were underlined by the fact that he could appoint and revoke, at his will and pleasure,[14] the commissioners (not exceeding six, and including a principal secretary of state and the chancellor of the exchequer) of his Privy Council, who were given full powers to 'superintendent direct and control, all acts operations and concerns which in anywise relate to civil or military government or revenues of the British territorial possessions in the east indies'.[15] In this context, certain trials such as the celebrated case of Nandakumar are analysed below so as to track the surfacing of the problems of rule and subjecthood in the context of a contested and masked sovereignty. All of this testifies to the fact that the only legal rationale for – and channels of – governance of the East India Company remained that of the King, and any incorporation of territories and populations would necessarily have to have the King as referent.

In the concluding section, certain works of Bentham are analysed in terms of the key jurisprudential and constitutional questions that emerge from the above. If the orchestrated overlap between the Hobbes–Lockean categories of conquest and consent, as much as Common Law, serves as a window to the dramatic sequences of Prize, plunder and property in the subcontinent, Bentham's elaborately polemical jurisprudence is more akin to a 'ship of fools' buffeted by an element whose marine depths it can scarcely measure. Without engaging with the concrete legal institutional problems that arise from the massive territorial conquests of the day, he speculates on counter-histories of Britain by tilting against historical reality and hectoring on how it ought to have been, mythologizing on measures of certainty in law. Thus are drawn the perimeters within which much jurisprudence remains confined to date. Like many forms of madness there is an irrefutable consistency and logic, but this has little to do with either the concrete legal-institutional problems present or the past in any analysable form. Instead, what is set up is a legal categorical framework that has succeeded in blinding an awareness of precisely the issues that we are invested in recounting and accounting for in some detail.[16] It is the Benthamite legacy which prevents an acute perspective of the significance of the Company, King and Conquest in a global history of law and empire – not so much either a justification or critique of empire, but the enunciating of a paradigmatic form that can no longer render legible the modes of imperial power and territorialization.

The King, Military Law and Martial Law

In the 1760s, Blackstone's *Commentaries* summed up a constitutional consensus by explicating the powers of prerogative. The prerogative was always associated with sovereignty,[17] and directly related to war and peace as well as justice.[18] Blackstone writes that prerogative, as the word itself suggests, means 'over and above all other persons, and out of the ordinary course of the common law, in right of his regal dignity'.[19] The King has the 'sole prerogative of making war and peace', and the declaration of war is important not merely as a means by which to give advance warning, but to make it clear that it is the sovereign at war and not a private subject. In such a context, it was hardly surprising that the King was traditionally entrusted with the defence of the realm.[20]

The specific war-making powers of the King, however, required his control over the armed forces, which itself had acquired a specific articulation in the first Mutiny Act of 1688. Such an articulation must not be perceived to index anything like parliamentary supremacy over the King. Both King and parliament looked back at the army-led Commonwealth period with dread and suspicion, and so the old question which had led to the terrifying civil wars regarding the rights over the armed forces, the so-called militia question,[21] irresistibly surfaced again. The Restoration period witnessed sustained public polemic against any possibility of a 'standing army', which was diagnosed as a sign of the growing powers of the royal prerogative and parliamentary corruption.[22] And yet it was precisely such a standing army that was virtually established from the time of the first Mutiny Act in 1688. To better comprehend the specific significance, contours and implications of the act, some historical background is necessary so as to elucidate the shifting contours of categories such as martial and military law, the army and the militia. It is from such a framework that the nature of the King's exclusive and absolute powers *beyond* the realm, and over the East India Company's civil and military establishments, will also gain clearer legibility.

Prior to the civil wars, the King's powers to defend the realm were achieved through the 'county' system, which took on the name of a 'militia' in discussions of the Restoration period.[23] This system was enabled by military tenures[24] (where lords were responsible for providing armed men in times of war), governorships (commissions granted by the King for the upkeep an governance of fortifications)[25] and statutory provisions which enabled the King to empower lord lieutenants to raise forces in the case of eventualities such as rebellions, invasions and unlawful assemblies.[26] The militia was therefore not a permanent body of soldiers, but required that the entire population, divided county-wise, was armed and available for mobilization at the local level by commissioned officers for limited periods when the need arose.[27] Distinct from the militia was the body of armed personnel that formed the guard of the King for his personal protection.[28] This was an armed body which he directly governed and was raised through impressment, a power inherent to his prerogative that was not denied even in subsequent centuries.[29]

While the militia was subject to the civil magistrate, the armed forces were directly governed by the King and his royally commissioned soldiers.[30] These armed forces were billeted with the civil population and subject to a distinct legal framework. This was called Martial Law and the written rules were called the 'Articles of War', both of which were applied to soldiers as well as those civilians who associated with the former in their criminal conduct.[31] Martial law, its application in times of peace, as well its application on civilians, led to protests which culminated in the Petition of Right (1628–29). The petition, accepted by King Charles I, found such royal commissions and martial law to be illegal when declared in times of peace (without parliamentary consent) or when applied to civilians.[32] Billeting too was questioned on the grounds of the individual's right of property, which was seen to be invaded by the requirement that soldiers be provided for by civilians. Reiterating the principle that a standing army in a time of peace was a violation of the constitution, the petition declared that martial law was a law of necessity and existed only when the common laws were literally not functioning – i.e. a time of actual war.[33] Though he accepted the Petition of Right, Charles I some years later attempted to raise an army in peacetime, in anticipation of a Scottish threat rather than an actual invasion. This led to a dispute between King and parliament over the control over the armed forces, and as is well known, this was one of the causes that contributed to the great civil wars.

Before dealing with the constitutional and statutory developments of the Restoration period, it is important to underline the fact that the right to raise, maintain and govern military forces had as their object the keeping of peace amidst both internal as well as external threats. Early statutes had declared that the King could by royal commission empower the lord lieutenant to raise armed forces in the event of a riot, unlawful assembly, rebellion or war, without therefore providing any statutory discrimination between what one might consider war, rebellion and civil war.[34] The Edwardian statute on such unlawful assembly enabled Queen Elizabeth to raise forces against foreign invasions and their threats.[35] It was the voiding of this statute in the reign of James I which laid the basis for the dispute between parliament and King on the latter's legal powers of raising the militia and armed forces.[36]

After the civil wars, the Restoration statutes disbanded the army and confirmed the King's 'sole and supreme command' over the military forces, explicitly denying parliament any authority to raise forces or levy wars.[37] Those acting under royal commission were granted indemnity while it was also asserted that there could be no transportation of subjects or armies outside the realm except by the recognized procedures of the law. The army was disbanded, and the militia of each county was placed under a lieutenant over whom the King had powers of appointment and dismissal. While this armed force was therefore local, it could be moved around to any county in the event of insurrections, rebellions or invasions. The act laid out the proportions according to which horse and foot soldiers were paid for by owners of property, and no limit to the numbers for such a military body was specified.[38] These soldiers of the militia were subject to the civil magistrate, while the lieutenant was allowed to exert some minor powers over them.[39] This formal establishment of a militia under the control of the landed powers and the civil magistrate is to be clearly distinguished from the army, which was wholly dependent on the King. While the Restoration Acts had disbanded the army, the latter remained in the attenuated form of guards and within garrisons under the direct payment of the King[40] – ostensibly for the latter's personal safety, rather than as a standing army for the defence of the realm.

Tensions between parliament and King crystallized because the former wished to strengthen the militia and weaken the guards/army over which the King exerted direct governance, whereas the latter worked in the opposite direction. Parliament could exert no specific control over the King's payment of the army, since at the time it merely granted a stipulated annual sum to the King who had the freedom to defray expenses in any way that he thought fit. Moreover, even though the army was ostensibly disbanded, the fact that statute did not specifically lay any limit for the King's guards enabled the King to retain and increase this number at will.[41] The tensions of the pre-civil war period resurfaced regarding the specific relations between the militia and the army, and the nature of their difference. This was particularly true in connection to quelling civil disturbances, because this was a task left to military forces. While the militia was made up of a body of men who were not professional full-time soldiers with other incomes, the army consisted of professional soldiers wholly dependent on and financed by the King.[42] This ended in frictions between the powers of the militia and the army, because while the House of Commons wished to employ the militia to put down civil disturbances, they realized that they had no such powers by statute except through the King's consent – a consent that was hardly forthcoming and immediately parried as an attempted invasion of the King's prerogative.[43]

The pre-civil war controversies over the governance of military forces and its implications for the civilian population remained unresolved by the fact that military forces under the King enjoyed immunity from the civil magistrate (unlike the militia) and were under the jurisdiction of their military superiors. They could appeal to no legal authority but the King.[44] On the other hand, paradoxically, these forces could not be legally subject to penalties over life and limb even by military superiors to whose jurisdiction they were subject. A case during the time of Charles I indicated this seeming legal paradox.[45] Charles I had empowered a general to shoot a soldier for the crime of mutiny, but this action was legally challenged. The unanimous opinion of the judges and lawyers on the issue was that such an action was illegal because martial law could only be employed during actual war or when the enemy was literally near the King's army. While a special commission of oyer and terminer[46] could always be employed for such trials of 'military' crimes such as mutiny, there was a large-scale apprehension among many over the effect that such a legal ruling would have on the discipline of soldiers who knew that they could not be punished by their military superiors. These problems of jurisdiction between martial law and common law festered in analogous cases such as the recovery of debts from soldiers or their criminal actions on civilians with whom they were billeted.[47]

Several such cases of 'non liquet' with grave consequences, in the Restoration period, fed into the growing demands to reduce what inevitably appeared as a virtual standing army of the King's guards. Eminent jurists such as Coke were invoked time and again to the effect that the old court of marshal (fountain of martial law) was on contracts, deeds of arms and war out of the realm, not within. References to the Petition of Right were made where it was constitutionally declared that martial law was allowed only if an actual war/public calamity had taken place or if the common law courts were literally closed.[48] While parliament recognized the need for speedy trials, it argued that such trials ought to be undertaken by the civil magistrate and not the King. The issue was exacerbated by James commissioning foreigners and

Catholics into the army, as well as arguing that any disbandment of the existing armed forces was not possible because of the ever-present threat of war. That parliament had no right to raise an army had been statutorily established. This in conjunction with several other well-documented causes culminated in the 'revolution' and the arrival on the throne of William the Dutchman.[49]

Upon the arrival of William III, the legal basis of the discipline of the army became acute when a section of English soldiers mutinied in the name of James. The mutineers could not be tried by the common law courts because mutinying was a 'military crime'. To place the governance of the army on a firmer legal footing, a bill was passed which enabled punishment for mutiny for a limited time period, to be renewed on a roughly annual basis.[50] This was the birth of the first Mutiny Act, which declared that the Crown could constitute courtmartials with the powers to punish soldiers even by death for the crimes specified in the act, such as mutiny, sedition and desertion. This enabled William to legally possess powers that Charles I did not have, since the King could now by courtmartial execute capital punishment on soldiers in times of peace and within the realm for the crimes specified in the act. While parliament exerted control over the payment of troops including the power to state a limit to the number of forces to be permanently employed, the 'government' of troops fell under the sole prerogative of the King.[51] The Mutiny Act therefore placed a standing army on a permanent legal footing, which had previously not existed, thereby raising once again the spectre of royal despotism – an anxiety that continued into the eighteenth century and was expressed by its most celebrated figures such as Hume and Blackstone. When it came to the army, the government and judiciary fell to the King even though army personnel in times of peace were to be tried by the ordinary courts of law for non-military offences. The Mutiny Act and its continued renewal thereby subtly undermined what appeared to be the earlier constitutional principle regarding the illegality of 'martial law' during times of peace within the realm without parliamentary consent, even though the preamble had stated that no one may be punished by martial law except by laws of the land and his peers.[52]

The Mutiny Act under Queen Anne added a crucial qualification to the First Mutiny Act – which remained beyond the nineteenth century – which enabled the King to declare martial law by proclamation either in times of war or at any time outside the 'realm'.[53] The Articles of War enabled the destruction of rebel property – a right that while limited within the realm, was unlimited outside of it.[54] As distinct from the question of martial law which affected military personnel as well as non-military personnel, the King's prerogative government over the military forces was not in dispute. Military law applied only to military men who were in the pay of the King, was governed by specific protocols as laid down in the Mutiny Act and Articles of War, and involved positions such as the judge advocate. While the Mutiny Act was not applicable to the militia and did not exempt the soldier from the ordinary course of law, this too soon enough became mired in controversy and ambiguity.

The First Mutiny Act had adopted the principles and procedures of the previous Articles of War in the form of their tribunals/courtmartial, giving the latter a statutory sanctity that it did not earlier possess. A later Mutiny Act of George I explicitly gave the King the power of making Articles of War for better government of the military *within* the kingdoms.[55] While the earlier act during Anne's reign had given powers even when out of kingdom/realm or the seas, the 1717 Act specifically empowered the King to make Articles of War within the kingdom as well as beyond the seas. The Articles of War made in 1717 enabled the trial of soldiers even for ordinary civil offences. Punishments within the kingdom in times of peace were now on a firm legal footing, and in 1748, punishments on life and limb were enabled with reference to the Mutiny Act. To strike or use violence against superior officers in the execution of office was construed as a capital offence in 1728, and neither common law courts nor any legislative authority could challenge the sentence of the military tribunal.[56]

The Act of 1717 allowed the death penalty for disobeying military orders even in times of peace – a provision that remained legal well into the nineteenth century. Difficulties arose regarding the precise mode of distinguishing between military offences (to be tried by a courtmartial) and civil political (ordinary) offences, and therein the boundaries between military tribunals and common law courts.[57] Debates took place in the middle of the eighteenth century on the status of the soldier, and whether military tribunals did not render him a slave to his military superior. The early fears of the Restoration that an army would lead to despotism were amplified in the eighteenth century, with luminaries from Hume to Blackstone expressing their strongest reservations.[58] Fundamental constitutional questions arose as to whether such a status did not have serious implications on society at large. Critics loudly proclaimed that a slave was bound to enslave others. Moreover, such Acts gave the King vast powers of government, which included the legal power to commission and dismiss at will soldiers – powers that appeared to overshadow even those that existed in the previous century. The soldier had to obey or be shot, and had no means of appeal except to the King.[59] There existed no clear forms of procedure when it came to military tribunals and it remained a delicate jurisprudential question as to whether parliament had the authority to make inquiries into such proceedings,[60] and whether they were to remain confidential.[61]

The use of the military to aid in keeping internal peace for long held statutory sanction, whether this took the form of the militia or the regular army. This once again reopened the problems of the boundaries between military and civil jurisdictions, and the principles to be employed in the settlement of justice – precisely the kind of fears expressed from the petition of right to the Restoration period. The Riot Act of George I followed the Edwardian statute on the use of the military to disperse 'unlawful assembly'. In such cases of riots, soldiers in the exercising of their duties were subject to the Mutiny Act even when called in by the civil magistrate, as confirmed in 1796 and 1853. This again was cause for much jurisprudential consternation, since, according to the legal convention, one could not be legally held liable for following the King's command as armed soldiers were duty-bound to do. The soldier's allegiance was to the person of the King, and if he killed another soldier by the King's command, it was not homicide if done in the performance of duty.[62] Only the civil minister could be prosecuted, and he was therefore expected to be present when the military was called in to quell the riot. While the military officer is meant to act under him, the former remains caught in the horns of a dilemma. He is equally liable to be charged with neglect of duty if he is unable to disperse the mob or unlawful assembly for which he has been called. While it was held in 1832 that the soldier was not bound to follow an illegal order, grave fears were once more expressed over the effect that such a principle would have on military discipline. Thus the rule prescribed was a 'rule of the heart',[63] and the key question raised was whether in the exercise of duty the officer acted with malicious intention or not. It was thus not difficult for a commanding officer to legally justify his actions.[64]

The increasing powers of the King were also expressed in the undeniable territorial extension of the Mutiny Acts, which gave statutory form to what were otherwise purely prerogative acts committed abroad. While it was first extended only to the land officers and soldiers within the kingdom, it was later extended to Jersey and Guernsey, then to all officers and soldiers in the marine, then to Ireland and England, and finally to all forces of His Majesty on foot anywhere in the world.[65] The Special Mutiny Act of 1754 enabled its extension to troops of the East India Company serving in India, and later that year it was extended to the King's troops in North America. In 1756, the militia too was placed under the Mutiny Act.[66]

This provides a broad context for understanding the requirement for a Special Mutiny Act in 1754 which was extended to the local army of the East India Company. Until then various letters-patent and charters had specified that the King had the exclusive powers of governance over the Company's establishments, which was delegated to Company officials. While the Company was governed by the King, some law was seen to be required to govern the Company's soldiers who were under their pay because the Mutiny Acts had justified the King's powers of governance over the army with reference to the fact that the latter was employed by the King. The Mutiny Act of 1754 was now applied to the local and English forces of the Company; several acts were passed thereafter on these lines. This act repeated several of the sections of the existing acts regarding the capital crimes of sedition, desertion, mutiny, disobeying a lawful command of a commanding officer, and communicating in any manner or form with rebels and enemies. It however added that His Majesty may grant a commission or warrant under the royal sign manual to empower the court of directors to in turn authorize Company officials to set up courtmartials. Moreover, the King could form Articles of War for the better governance of the East India troops even in times of peace, though no punishment extending to life or limb could be executed except for those crimes specified in the act.[67] From 1813 onwards, statute authorized the Governor-General of India to govern the army by formulating Articles of War.[68]

From Coke to Hale in the seventeenth century to James Mackintosh in the nineteenth century, martial law was defined as that which took place when common law was rendered impossible by actual war.[69] Under martial law, which was no written law, no distinction was made between soldier and civilian. In England there were cases in 1715, 1745 and 1780, and in Ireland in 1798, 1803 and 1833, where the authority of common laws was partly suspended and martial law declared by the King. On opening, parliament sanctioned these acts retrospectively.[70] The King's prerogative in executing martial law was declared time and again, and confirmed several times in the Irish and English parliaments. Martial law, however, took on different forms depending on the nature of the territories, whether in the 'realm', crown colonies or 'settled' colonies. In Crown colonies, resulting from conquest or cession, the King's power to declare martial law was absolute, whereas in the latter case, the liberties of the British subjects who had settled the colonies were to have altered the legal condition – as discussed below in the analysis of *Campbell v. Hall.*

While the King's prerogative, statute and martial law have to be examined and analysed from the perspective of territorialization and territory, and the latter itself determining the specific legal status of the subject-people settled in the said territory, there is simultaneously the important question regarding the relationship between the army, nationality and allegiance. In the context of mercenary armies of a foreign extraction being an absolutist devise, Restoration-period polemicists grew deeply suspicious of James's employment of foreigners and Catholics in his military forces. It therefore soon became the rule that no one born out of the kingdoms or dominions could have the trust of either a civil or military office.[71] This was however relaxed in the eighteenth and nineteenth centuries. While this only serves as a glimpse of the complex and contested nature of allegiance and nationality, it is in the allied and unexpected field of Prize jurisdiction that one can see a much closer discussion and formalization of issues such as allegiance and nationality.

Prize Law and Nationality

Blackstone had written with regard to the relationship between the King's prerogative of war and peace-making authority, and Prize jurisdiction:

> But, as the delay of making war may sometimes be detrimental to individuals who have suffered by depredations from foreign potentiates, our laws have in some respect armed the subject with powers to impel the prerogative; by directing the ministers of the crown to issue letters of marque and reprisal upon due demand: the prerogative of granting which is nearly related to, and plainly derived from, that other of making war; this being indeed only an incomplete state of hostilities, and generally ending in a formal denunciation of war. These letters are grantable by the law of nations, whenever the subject of one state are oppressed and injured by those of another; and justice is denied by that state to which the oppressor belongs. In this case letters of marque and reprisal (words in themselves synonymous and signifying a taking in return) may be obtained, in order to seize the bodies or goods of the subjects of the offending state, until satisfaction is gained.[72]

Henry J. Bourguignon, in his study of Sir William Scott, Lord Stowel of the Admiralty Court, has given us a rich picture of the various decisions regarding nationality and maritime war.[73] A series of cases established certain broad postulates in the late eighteenth century. When deciding the right of condemnation or the question of Prize, it was critical to determine the nature of property as much as the nationality of the person whose property was condemned. The determinant in this case was habitation or place. Notwithstanding the place of birth, if one was making one's livelihood in a hostile country, one's property was liable to lawful capture (Prize) if that country was engaged in hostilities. This was the case even if one was a natural-born subject of the English King. Such a postulate nonetheless posed problems because it was argued that as a natural-born subject of the King, one could not be treated as a hostile national. Moreover, as the previous part of this book has shown, it was established and reiterated that even the progeny of a British merchant living in foreign lands was to be considered a natural-born subject; allegiance could never be disavowed. Despite all of this, English admiralty case law did not make a distinction when it came to Prize, and it was not seen as a contradiction to have another nationality – where one resided and earned a living – while owing permanent allegiance as a natural-born subject to the English King.

Bourguignon, citing the relevant case law, argues that considerations of mercantile policy often determined the reasoning of crucial judicial decisions.[74] And the over-riding objective of this policy, often accomplished in fact, was the destruction of the enemy and their trade. Thus, in the context of hostilities or war, the properties of all those aiding the enemy nation was considered lawful Prize. This meant that irrespective of birth, anyone seen as contributing to the commerce of the enemy was seen as a lawful object of aggression and his property was construed to be liable as lawful Prize. This also meant that any initial ambiguity regarding 'neutrals' was, with time, resolved in favour of this aggressive argument. That is to say, any neutral aiding an enemy was also subject to the laws of war. Nationality based on locality did not deny that subjecthood was about allegiance, could not be thrown off and was linked with (sovereign) protection, in reiterating arguments going back to *Postnati*. Due to the importance given to commerce in the strengthening of one's state and destroying and weakening the enemy, including the properties of one's subjects found involved in the commerce of the enemy, legal concessions and immunities were granted to armed personnel engaged in war, even in relationship to natural-born subjects. A particularly important illustration of this impingement of commerce and war on such (even 'natural') subjects is *Le Caux v. Eden*.

In *Le Caux v. Eden*, Mansfield's judgment makes it very clear that the reasoning regarding Prize required to be rested on matters of policy as much as judicial precedent.[75] The case concerned the capture of a ship and its trader Bee, a British subject, by a (private) ship-of-war captained by Le Caux who had a letter of marque. The Admiralty Court in England stated that the cargo and ship were restored to the owner, and the captor was condemned to give damages and costs. Bee and others however wished to pursue the case in the common law courts on the issue of trespass and assault, which as criminal charges did not come under the Admiralty Court. Here the judges, including Mansfield, made it clear that such a case could not be pursued since it would have very deleterious effects on the 'sea services'.[76] If cases such as this were pursued, it would deter any attempt at taking Prize. It was taken as self-evident that Prize was an essential component of the commercial–military policy of the state. Notwithstanding which, in the course of the case, it was reaffirmed that the court for matters of Prize was the Admiralty Court. And even though, factually, trespass and imprisonment did occur, because they occurred in the course of the taking of Prize, these were to be judged by the Admiralty Court. That it was not lawful Prize did not alter the nature of the action of trespass as consequence of Prize. The nationality of the captive did not affect the proceedings because the Admiralty Court worked according to the law of nations.[77]

In the course of his judgment, Mansfield also gives a history of the Admiralty Court and clarifies that Prize was not to be restricted merely to the sea. It might well be the case that the 'prey was killed at sea but taken in the land'.[78] The reference was to the conquest of St Eustius by sea, even if plunder took place on the land. Many such examples were given as illustrations of the entanglement of land and sea in matters of Prize. In the course of his reasoning Mansfield distinguishes between what appeared to be the well-established rules, conventions and laws with regard to Prize, with the complete absence of any such equivalent in the case of a 'merely continental war'.[79] In such a land war there appeared to be no clear laws, and all booty or plunder were to be cleared by the commander on the spot. 'There is no instance in history or law, ancient or modern, of any question before any legal judicature, ever having existed about it, in this kingdom.'[80]As opposed to Prize law, where the navy was involved even if captures stretched into land, in a mere continental land war, there is 'no light to go by' with regard to booty.[81]

While throwing his hands up in the air on the question of plunder in the course of a land war, Mansfield had all the same, in a recent case, pronounced very strongly on the elusive point at which war settled into peace. The other side of this evanescent transition point between war and peace is the story of subject-formation as allegiance to the sovereign who in turn was protected in the context of conquest. This was the most important case since *Postnati*, which was the last case that had dealt with the issues of sovereignty and subjecthood exhaustively, particularly in matters of conquest, and is now be taken up for analysis.

Campbell v. Hall: The Ever-receding Line between War and Peace, Outlaw and Subject

Postnati, which had remained the key reference point for the jurisprudence around conquest and subjecthood, was put to the test again in 1774, during *Campbell v. Hall. Campbell v. Hall* arose to determine the issue not of prerogative as such whose constitutional position was unassailable; rather, the question was whether a particular action by the King in his prerogative powers in a particular case was good in law. The case concerned Granada, which had been conquered by England from France. After the capitulation in 1762, a treaty was signed which secured certain particular rights for the vanquished inhabitants.[82] Subsequently, in February 1763, the Treaty of Paris enabled defeated subjects to retain their liberties, including the practice of their (Catholic) religion. The inhabitants were also permitted to sell their properties to British subjects and emigrate elsewhere if they so wished. A royal proclamation was issued on October 1763 inviting British subjects to emigrate, but also promising the constitution of a government by commissioning a governor and council. The governor would also be empowered to call assemblies, until which time the government remained his and ultimately that of the King-in-Council.[83] Other rights and liberties promised included the preservation of local laws and properties, as well as the practice of religion, until the specific decisions were made and conveyed by King George III. The King issued a second proclamation thereafter on March 1764, directing a land survey for the division of the settlement into administrative units such as parish and district.[84] A governor was commissioned by the King, through letters-patent, in April 1764 to constitute an assembly of free-holders and planters, and he was tasked to attend to matters of trade and the plantations. With his negative vote and powers of adjourning, proroguing and dissolving the council, the governor would have the authority to constitute laws, statutes and ordinances 'not repugnant, but as near as may be, agreeable to the laws and statutes of [this our kingdom of] Great Britain' – ultimately subject to the King-in-Council.[85]

Before the actual establishment of a legislative assembly, a natural-born British subject, Mr Campbell, arrived in Granada, purchased land, indulged in trade and was charged a duty in the export of his goods. Prior to the governor's arrival on December 1764, the King by his letters-patent in July 1764, after the signing of the Treaty of Paris and the issue of the royal proclamations, had directed a duty of 4.5 per cent in lieu of the duties which had earlier been paid to the King of France.[86] The question arose as to whether the King had the authority to issue such a tax after promising the constitution of a legislative assembly which would be given such powers. The lawyers for Mr Campbell argued that the locus of legislative authority was (King-in) parliament, which included the right to tax. Therefore the King could not in his own prerogative capacity have such a legislative authority to tax after the cessation of war and his royal proclamation promising the constitution of an assembly. In such post-conquest circumstances, authority either had to be of the English parliament or the local legislative assembly.[87] It was thereby argued that the duty/tax imposed by the King was defective in law.

It is important to note that Mr Campbell's lawyers accepted the fact that the King had prerogative powers in conquered lands. However, they argued that the royal proclamations signalled a 'waiving' of these prerogative powers by the King himself and the ceasing of conquest. Such a ceasing of conquest was to have indicated the shifting of the locus of legislative authority to (King-in) parliament.[88] Prerogative powers were 'waived' and therein were to have resulted in an alteration of the legal status of Granada. From a conquered country it had become a territory governed by the laws of England. The royal proclamation inviting subjects to colonize testified to such an interpretation, and it was in the context of this shift in legislative authority that a natural-born subject like Mr Campbell reached Granada. His arrival was motivated by the understanding that he was no longer in 'conquered' territory under the sole power of the King, but that his rights were now protected by the British constitution which only gave (King-in) parliament the authority to tax subjects. Taxation in the post-conquest condition required 'an act of legislation'.[89] This was the argument put forward by Campbell's lawyers for whom the King's proclamation inviting British subjects to colonize had to mean that they were to be given, on arrival, the benefit of the laws, i.e. the parliament or (local) assemblies.[90]

The question raised was thus again about the nature of the King's authority as such, in relation to parliament with respect to certain categories of political entities and/or territories. It was jurisprudentially recognized that in conquest the King's powers reigned through natural justice and equity. However, when Mr Campbell was charged the tax, was Granada to be considered a conquered territory or was it to be considered as already 'annexed' to the Crown and incorporated into the territory of Great Britain? An answer to this question involved not only the specific rights of Mr Campbell as a natural-born British subject and his relationship to King and King-in-Parliament, or the precise political status of Granada at the time that he paid the tax, but the more general one of the relationship between the King's prerogative powers and King-in-Parliament. Elucidating the latter would involve further distinctions such as territories acquired by descent and those acquired by conquest.

The *locus classicus* on this issue remained *Postnati*, where Coke's report had distinguished between territories acquired by descent and territories acquired by conquest. The question therein concerned not only the limits of the prerogative, but also the limits or role, if any, of the English parliament in relationship to conquered territories. In *Campbell v. Hall*, the historical examples of Ireland, Wales, Calais and the American colonies, among many others, were discussed as illustrations of the fact that the King initially did govern in his sole capacity, without interference from the English parliament. Other places such as Brittany, Gascoigne and Calais were also mentioned, where the (British) parliament appeared to have no legislative authority. But not surprisingly, the colonies in the Americas occupied pride of place as stellar instances of territories acquired by virtue of royal grant, which enabled the rise of local assemblies and other such governing institutions independent of (King-in-British) parliament. By 1774, a rich discourse was already developing around the theme – well established even in the seventeenth century – of the royal grant and commission, rather than (British) parliament, as the ground of law. Rights to taxation could only be local and in a sense originally derived from the King's grant and charter or commission, not English parliament.

In *Campbell v. Hall*, though the arguments did not stretch so far as to completely exclude parliament, it appeared clear to all the disputants that the rights of subjects as settled in the American colonies were 'secured' by the charters of the King and had little to do with the British parliament. However, while Campbell's lawyers accepted this fact by arguing that 'legal acts of prerogative' and the Crown may by proclamation and inherent rights promulgate, enforce, communicate and secure rights, such charters and patents are 'accommodated to protect the *anterior* rights of the colonists, and not to convey those rights, as dependent on those charters and derivatives from them'[91] (emphasis added). A fine distinction was sought to be made between the acts of prerogative and the 'anterior' rights of subjects, even while it is unclear by what institutional principle these rights emerged or existed – particularly since only the King and not parliament is mentioned in the histories of these constitutions. Even while recognizing the historical fact that the charters to the American colonies signified that the ultimate judicature lay in the King and not in his 'right of the crown', yet this entire history is interpreted as one that does not alter the 'constitutional law or the principles of the law of empire', where rights are seen to be inherent to British subjects[92] and any conquest is understood to be a conquest of the *state*. A conquest was therefore defined to be a situation where the conquered 'owe obedience to the laws of the conquering state and hold their property from them'.[93]

That the King was constitutionally instrumental in the setting up of the colony meant that colonization as a process had a close legal affinity with conquest. In both cases the King in his sole authority – without the English parliament – determined the legal characteristics of the territory that was acquired. With colonization, as with conquest, the establishment of (local) governing assemblies appeared to derive from the authority, grant or commissions of the King. For the lawyers of Campbell, however, the role of the King was one of a supreme *executive* who merely secured or allowed for already existing British constitutional rights possessed by colonizing British subjects. Using some of the contemporary philosophical and legal literature of the time such as Vattel, they made the argument that colonization meant that the natural-born (British) subject took his laws with him wheresoever he went.[94] In this reading of the British constitution, a 'law of empire' is envisioned where English laws were to seamlessly extend wherever English subjects went, whether in cases of colonization or conquest. In the words of Campbell's lawyer, 'If therefore the political laws are co-extensive with the territory of the state, however disjoined in space, as this excellent author decides they are, then every constitutional right of the subjects of that state is co-extensive with its territory.'[95] While in the case of a colony the English carried their laws, liberties and privileges with them, in the case of conquest, after the capitulation, the conquered were to be understood as 'British subjects', *in the sense* of subjects who wished to be governed 'by the laws and constitutions of England'.[96]

Yet one might argue, this line of argumentation was precisely the one that was explicitly refuted in *Postnati* and Bacon's argumentation, according to which the legal specificity of place/territory was not to be conflated or confused with sovereignty or allegiance (subjecthood), *both* of which referred to the *person* of the King. Since the British Empire allowed distinct juridical orders, even kingdoms, it was the King and not an individual parliament that could be their unifying locus. On the other hand, Campbell's lawyer grounded his 'law of empire' in natural principles that were to undergird British subjects, and the authority of prerogative was recognized as only in the fulfilment of such ends. These natural principles which took the form of the law of empire and constitutional principles were to trump any past precedents of royal authority in cases of colonization and conquest. On factual matters Campbell's lawyer, Alleyene, was corrected by Wallace and Mansfield,[97] but this did not deter him from arguing his case on (so-called) principles. In fact, the prosecution accepted that whatever one wished 'ought' to be the case when it came to the relationship between King and parliament, prerogative and legislation, the case had to be decided on existing and past principles.[98]

Since historical precedent was all the same so absolutely crucial in a common law tradition, Campbell's lawyers found strategies to circumvent them. While, on the one hand, they referred to the importance of the 'glorious revolution', insisting on the impossibility of directly citing precedents such as James I/IV where the King was indeed absolutely powerful,[99] on the other hand, they reinterpreted past cases in innovative if somewhat forced ways. For instance, they argued that the reference to 'King' in *Postnati* referred to 'King in Parliament' or absolutist kings and not the English King.[100] In the same way, they interpreted the conquest of Ireland as one that was in fact nothing but the carrying of laws into Ireland by English subjects, denying the foundational role of the King. It was precisely in this way that colonization in the Americas was also described, wherein royal grants were once again (rc) interpreted merely as confirming the already existing rights of the English colonizers.[101]

All the same, these historical examples and their jurisprudential import were mobilized to refute Campbell's lawyers by arguing that precedent had made it amply clear that 'the power of imposing laws upon a conquered country belongs to the king as part of his prerogative'.[102] They pointed out that the role of the (English) parliament in many 'acquisitions' was practically non-existent, whether Ireland, Wales, the colonies in America,[103] ceded territories such as Calais and Minorca (where the previous Spanish laws were allowed to continue in some form notwithstanding the sovereignty of the English King), or conquered territories such as St Christopher.[104] In all these instances, there was certainly no seamless extension of 'English laws' when territories were 'acquired'. Sensitive to the question of history and the importance of the glorious revolution, the lawyers cited instances of the King exercising his right to tax even after the revolution, putting to rest the argument that no such instances could be found. The year of the revolution saw the *Soomers and George Treby* case establishing the King's sole right to revenue, and in 1702 this same right was exercised in St Christopher. The King's Bench had held that if a territory was considered conquered, it was under the sole authority of the King. The same therefore was to apply in Jamaica. Such royal powers were also underlined in the recent charters given in Massachusetts Bay.[105]

The more general critique of the immediate and indefinite extension of English laws by English subjects was meant to cater to the particularities and peculiarities of the conquered place and community. It was on these terms that the King's lawyers argued that once conquered, the treaty of capitulation meant that the vanquished became subjects and were in turn offered protection, in the sense of their being allowed to follow their own laws as far as possible. The argument of the imposition of English (civil) laws – with its peculiarities on inheritance and contract – on conquered populations following distinct laws would be a 'total and unnecessary' change, it was forcefully argued, echoing Bacon.[106] Thus the laws of the conquered were legally enabled to remain until altered, accustomed as the conquered community would have been to such laws as 'modes of regulating and disposing property'.[107] Whether in cases of conquest or colonies, the constitution had 'intrusted' the King with such powers, and 'there has not been an instance in which the king has not exercised the disposition of the laws and property of the conquered country'.[108] From here a constitutional settlement was reached, allowing for local participation through local assemblies. This included the rights to taxation as argued in *Postnati,* where it had been legally affirmed that the right to tax lay only in the (local) representative institutions of the place of one's livelihood. Granada was a good example of this where after the conquest the treaty indicated that locals were now British subjects who took the oath of allegiance. They were also distinguished, in contrast to other subjects, by the fact that though they were British subjects, they were not to be compelled to fight against their erstwhile sovereign, the French King. This would continue until a formal treaty with France was inked which ceded the territory and thereby established a formal peace. After the treaty the King issued proclamations about the imminent setting up of a representative assembly. Lands were surveyed, taxes and imposts announced, and a governor empowered to help establish the assembly, which would be subject to governor and King.

The events in Granada seemed to mirror previous cases of conquered colonies such as that of Jamaica. Like other colonies, the King did initially act in his sole capacity in cases where territory was acquired through conquest. This was not unlike colonization where too political institutions were set up through the King's charters in his sole capacity, and not through the institution of King-in-Parliament. The logic of *Postnati* and *Sandys* was followed except for the distinction between Christians and pagans that was made therein. This aspect was explicitly set aside as a wholly irrelevant distinction when it came to the rights of the subject or King (or parliament).[109]

Justice Mansfield intervened several times in the course of the arguments and at one point made it clear, in opposition to Campbell's lawyers, that it would be 'absurd' to assume that the English carried all the (English) laws with them when they colonized. He affirmed that not only was the Crown necessary for any colonial settlement, but only such laws were carried which were applicable or expressly enacted.[110] He further explicated the constitutional processes of colonial governance by holding that it was not by (proprietorial) grant but by the King's commission and the instructions therein added, which might include the formation of an assembly, which formed the constitutional order of the colony.[111]

At the conclusion of the case, Mansfield in his judgment appeared to accept the King's special and specific powers in cases of conquest and therein the fundamental distinctions in the legal nature of territories. There were, however, irrepressible conceptual tensions in his judgment, in which may be found a subtle modification of *Postnati*. On the one hand, Mansfield held that a conquered country was 'a dominion of the King in the right of his Crown, and therefore necessarily subject to the legislative power of the parliament of Great Britain'. That is to say, the King exercised a power of 'subordinate legislation', 'subordinate to his own authority, as part of the supreme legislature in parliament'.[112] On the other hand, it was clearly affirmed that the King's powers in such contexts of 'subordination' were (also) part of his 'prerogative'.[113]

In Mansfield's words,

> Taking these propositions to be granted, he [the King] has a legislative power over a conquered country, limited to him by the constitution, and subordinate to the constitution and parliament; and a power to grant or refuse capitulation. If he refuses, and puts to the sword or extirpates the inhabitants of a country, obtaining it by conquest, the lands are his; and if he plants a colony the new settlers share the land between them, *subject to the prerogative of the conqueror.*

> He is *intrusted* with the terms of making peace *at his discretion*; and he may retain the conquest or yield it up, on such condition as *he shall think fit to agree. This is not a matter of disputed right*; it has hitherto been *uncontroverted that the king may change part or all the political form of government over a conquered dominion.*[114] (Emphasis added.)

It may be remarked that the prerogative that enables the rights of conquest and 'legislative power', even when 'subordinate to constitution and [King-in-] Parliament', does not negate the same prerogative as it exists in relation to Parliament. Mansfield amplified the point about the King's sole power of legislation and governance, independent of the British parliament, in the historical examples that he cited of Ireland, Wales, Berwick, Gascony, Guyenne and Calais, Gibraltar and Minorca. Then, taking the example of Jamaica and the colonies, he held that in the Restoration period the King had invited settlers by proclamation, promising them protection. He first appointed a governor and council, and only thereafter did he grant a commission to the governor to call an assembly. It was in this manner that 'every province immediately under the king has arisen'.[115]

How was *Postnati* both reaffirmed and simultaneously modified? While the historical examples indicated the King's sole power independent of (English) parliament in both conquered and colonized settlements, Mansfield had clarified that all this was subject to the 'supreme legislature [King-in-Parliament]'. Yet, notwithstanding such pronouncements, it must be reiterated that in actual historical fact, the first royal proclamation of October 1763 had specifically stated, independent of parliament, that 'said [colonial] governments' were constituted by royal letters-patent, which empowered governors to call assemblies, until which government would lie in the governor and council.[116]The proclamation also made clear that this form of (colonial) government in structure was like that of the existing 'colonies and provinces of America – which are under our *immediate government*' (emphasis added).[117] No mention was made of parliament, and the sole independence of the King in the colonies and provinces were emphasized.

At the time of the hearings of *Campbell v. Hall*, the British parliament debated and ultimately passed what was to be known as the Quebec Act. The act declared the King to have the powers to commission a governor and council for the governance of the province. It was much later, only in 1791, that an elected assembly was constituted. Recognized thereby was the constitutional space for the King's government through Privy Council, governor and council; this took place in the temporal 'lag' between the conquest and the commissioning of an elected assembly. In relationship to Ireland too, the King and Privy Council briefly returned the position of a supreme government through the 'constitution of 1782' wherein the supremacy of the British parliament was negated, thereby almost returning to a pre-1719 situation. It is this structure of royal governance through commissioned governors declared by statute that best provides the legal grammar for understanding the East India Company regime in the aftermath of the great territorial conquests of the 1750s and 1760s in India. Unlike other settlements originating from royal grants and commissions, however, it would take well over a century for anything close to an elected local legislative assembly to be formed in the subcontinent, a 'lag' of truly continental proportions. The absence of an elected legislature was the absence of representation and the ability to participate in the making of rules regulating property and taxation in India. Company governance was therefore the inauguration of a despotic proprietorial regime, and the destruction of the very principle of property and law for the people being governed. It is only in this context that one can speak of royal-imperial governance – despotic in the denial of legislation and representation – of India.

The East India Company's Conquests: The Subject of the Law of Plunder and Prize

Conquest may involve complete extermination, but peace emerges when a settlement is made, evolving into a legal situation where law and property were defined and protected, and representative assemblies introduced. How do these thundering injunctions from the mouth of one of the most eminent judges in the highest court apply to the vast, in terms of peoples and lands, territorial conquests being made by the East India Company? The year 1774 saw not only *Campbell v. Hall* and the Quebec Act, but also the East India Company Regulating Act. The question naturally arises, in what sense do any of the principles and laws of conquest, peace and subjecthood, discussed from *Postnati* to *Campbell v. Hall*, 'work' in the case of the East India Company regime in India? If there was 'no light to go by', according to Mansfield, in *Le Caux v. Eden* in the legal determination of land wars, and if Prize laws could offer but very limited protection even for natural-born subjects, what kind of effects do they have in places so far removed, in every possible sense?

In making the case for the King's prerogative in *Campbell v. Hall*, the attorney general Lord Thurlow had stated,

> when I refer to corporations in England invested with powers to provide laws over part of the dominions of the king of England from which they were distant and not natives or inhabitants, I shall think myself entitled to contend that a power which he can delegate he can exercise in his own *personal* authority.[118] (Emphasis added.)

It was settled that the East India Company was established by royal charter and governed by the King, even as statute had enabled the Company's trading 'monopoly' at the end of the last century. This could serve as an entry point to analyse the blazing conquests from the mid-eighteenth century which were grounded in specific Prize laws granted to the Company by royal letters-patent, completely independent of parliament. With respect to India, the first statutory intervention with regard to Prize came as late as 29–30 Victoria C. 47 (1866).

Most works on the East India Company and its conquests in the eighteenth century appear to give little thought to Prize, Prize money and plunder. The crucial legitimizing and governing law on Prize money, sealed by His Majesty King George the Second, could be traced to September 1757 and January 1758, where the Company was granted powers to 'cede, restore or dispose of any fortresses or any fortresses districts or territories, acquired by the conquest from any of the said Indian princes or governments'.[119] The letters-patent of September 1757 and January 1758 did not emerge *in vacuo*, but was the response to applications that the East India Company had made in 1756 to the attorney and solicitor generals, the pre-eminent law officers of the Crown, who in turn had forwarded the application with suitable recommendation and comment to William Pitt, one of the secretaries of the Crown, to be in turn forwarded to the King.[120] With the application the law officers appended their own draft of what would become in essence the letters-patent of 1757 and 1758. In the applications of the East India Company, and the response of the attorney and solicitor general, one might glean the germ of the problems that collected again in the dispute between Company officials and the Court of Directors, and of course the fraught contested tendons of the British Empire.

The Company had written to His Majesty on 11 October 1756 with a request.[121] Alluding to the war with the kingdom of France and the collusion – possible, actual and imaginary – between the latter and the local rulers in Bengal, the petitioners pointed to the fact that in the course of such war that has or may occur, in so far as all conquests were vested directly in him, His

Majesty in his sovereignty kindly grant the right, to capture and recapture, 'for their own [the Company's] use, all such plunder and booty, ships, vessels, goods, merchandize, treasure and other things whatsoever, which may be taken by any of your petitioners land or sea forces from any of your majesty's enemies, or from the Indian enemies of your petitioners'.[122] Unless such right was granted, the petition argued, it would be difficult to maintain the armies that were required for the carrying out of such trade in the east. Encouragement to trade was conditional on the encouragement that could be given to those engaged in the arts of war.[123] This requesting of powers over the use and disposal of territories and objects acquired in the course of war, treaty or grant with local principalities, was of course always subject to His Majesty's 'right of sovereignty'.[124] The Company in its applications had more concrete questions regarding the norms to be followed, specifically in the distribution of Prize between Admiral Watson, as representative of His Majesty, and the Company officers in the recent case of Gheria and Calcutta.[125]

From the response and considered suggestions of the law officers, it is clear that the Company asked whether its actions were governed by the lately promulgated Act of 1756, passed in the context of the war with France. Writing on 16 August 1757, the law officers were responding to requests regarding the re-taking of Calcutta, and not a post-Plassey settlement.[126] They wrote that in their considered opinion, the said Act of 1756 referred only to the war (with France) and could not be applicable to the case of the Company's relations with powers in the subcontinent. And so, the most apposite way to deal with the Company's question regarding its authority in such relations with local powers, in the event of war and with regard to Prize, would be to apply and request the requisite letters-patent from His Majesty. With regard to what is re-taken, the law officers took the view that as far as the territory of Calcutta was concerned, it would be restored to the Company. However, 'All places newly conquered accrue to his sovereignty and is vested in his majesty by right of conquest.'[127] All movable goods that had been altered while in the possession of the enemy as well as newly acquired movable goods would belong to His Majesty, 'in whose name and under whose protection, and by the assistance of whose fleet, the same is regained'.[128] These suggestions led to the letters-patent issued in September 1757. The Company in the meantime had written to Fort St George that they had been given a specific grant by the King, commending the agreement between Admiral Watson and the Secret Committee which stated that all plunder and booty would be deposited until His Majesty made his pleasure known. The result – the letters-patent of September 1757 – was therefore sent to the subcontinent. However, in response to further petitions and requests for further clarifications, on 24 December, the law officers elaborated on the urgent questions of sovereignty and Prize.

While making no specific reference to Plassey although writing in a vein that would encompass actions such as the Battle of Plassey, the law officers reiterated that all conquests as such were vested with His Majesty, as also specific goods and items acquired therein. However, '*in respect to such places as have been or shall be acquired by treaty or grant* from the Mogul or any of the Indian princes or governments, your majesty's letters-patent are not necessary, *the property of the soil vesting in the company by the Indian grants, subject to only your majesty's right of sovereignty over the settlements as English settlements, and over the inhabitants as English subjects, who carry with them your majesty's laws, wherever they form colonies and receive your majesty's protection, by virtue of your royal charters*'.[129] This was an important and fine distinction whose intelligibility can be traced to the discussions in *Postnati*, Mathew Hale and *Campbell v. Hall.*[130] While laws and customs could, and did, vary with place/territory and/as property, the Company as English settlements and English subjects were subject to His Majesty's right of sovereignty. Allegiance was owed to the King despite the possible diversity of place and law. The law officers clearly wanted to deny the Company the sovereign authority to carry out conquest and make peace, which ultimately vested in His Majesty – specifically, His Majesty's prerogative. Perhaps more significant however is the fact that the rights of the Company were being derived exclusively from a royal charter and not from any Prize statute.

Responding to the questions posed by the Company in the unfolding situation in the subcontinent, it was recorded that the Company was petitioning His Majesty for directions and rules, and such petitioning was evidence of their 'honourable intentions'.[131] His 'majesty's right of sovereignty' over the subjects and settlements as being English applied to those contexts that have, or would have, been acquired by treaty or grant. Not for conquest, where 'the property as well as the dominion vests in your majesty, by virtue of your known prerogative and consequently the company can only derive a right to them, through your majesty's grant'.[132] This notwithstanding the fact that His Majesty had on previous occasion, through his charters, empowered the Company to make war in defensive circumstances – i.e. 'only to recompense themselves for loses or to repel invaders'.[133]

The question to be settled is not who is sovereign as defined by the authority to make war and peace, but whether in the circumstances that the

Company finds itself, there may be some way in which the latter would not have to apply to His Majesty after each and every acquisition of place, whether by treaty, grant or conquest. It is to obviate this that the letters-patent of 1757 and 1758 were granted, that closely followed the drafts prepared by the law officers of the Crown. In the meantime, the Court of Directors had written to Fort St George in the light of the King's grant, clarifying the fact that the grants of Prize and their principles applied to any and all hostilities and expeditions that the Company may engage in. The only condition was that they had such rights in full when they were the sole actors, but if a conquest or capture was made in conjunction with the King's forces, half of the share would be rendered to the King. The Court then moved on to make a finer distinction that is a familiar one in matters of Prize jurisdiction, and one that continued to haunt the Company's actions well into the nineteenth century.[134] From the legitimate share of the Company, in case of a conquest, they would give the actual captors half of this share and would retain the other half. However, yet a further division/exception turning on the distinction between land and sea was made. In cases of land wars, cannon and ammunition and military stores were to be reserved to the credit of the Company. However, at sea, in cases of ships and cargo, there would be an equal division between the captors and the Company.[135] The Court further ordered that the plunder of the forces be divided according to rank and station, leaving it to the discretion of the Company's forces. In the same breadth they stated that when the King's forces were involved, the plunder ought to be divided between the Company forces and the King's forces, as was earlier decided. The Court would all the same wish to be informed about exactly how the plunder was distributed both among the Company's forces as well as among the King's forces.[136]

But the full story of His Majesty's forces and their role in the Company's conquest was far from over. The disputes between Aldecron as representative of the King's forces, and the East India Company before the recapture of Calcutta, do not leave in doubt the fact that his position as King's representative ensured his superiority over the Company's soldiers.[137] After the capture of Calcutta by Nawab Siraj Ud Dowla, when an expedition and recapture were being planned in Fort St George, the Council of War had requested that Aldecron not lead the expedition. The reason given was that as commander-in-chief, he was not subject to the Company's command. The select committee of the Company conveyed their view that they would rather send an employee of the Company to re-take Calcutta, so as to have greater control over the expedition. It was also made clear that if, in the re-taking of Calcutta, the

Nawab refused to pay for the damages demanded, the Company would have to engage in 'reprisals'; these expeditions would best be undertaken by a Company officer. Piggot, Clive, Orme *et al.* then wrote to Aldecron that they hoped that the Nawab would come to terms with the Company, but they expected rather that he would come with his army and attack, in which case the Company should be prepared to war with the Nawab:[138] 'We are of the opinion that the expedition should not finish until whether he comes to terms or that his capital or Murshidabad be destroyed.'[139]

As discussions proceeded in Fort St George it was realized that they would need the help of Admiral Watson as part of the military operations. The admiral was to help land the troops and then, if required, carry out attacks on the 'moor towns' as part of the reprisals. The ships of the moors could be taken as Prize by anointing commissioners on the spot. Any Prize or booty would be deposited as such until His Majesty's pleasure was known, even if a certain gratuity may be given to privates and others as part of encouragement. The admiral's position was specifically that of one who is vested with the King's powers.[140] The expedition to Bengal was then initially likened to the expedition against those perceived as sea pirates, a sort of classical framework for articulating Prize law. It was argued that the Prize money should be divided just like it was done when Gheria was captured and plundered in 1756 by Admiral Watson and Clive;[141] while Gheria was seen as the preserve of 'sea pirates', in fact it was under the control of the Maratha leader Sarkhel Tulaji.[142] But naming enemies as pirates allowed the legitimization of unmitigated access to property; this was an old precedent and inherited practice. All the same, it was also suggested that this expedition of re-taking Calcutta was qualitatively different, since the object of the expedition was to retrieve 'ancient rights and privileges'. Unlike the standard cases of Prize, here the East India Company as a corporation was responsible; one could not simply divide the booty among captors. Notwithstanding a discussion on the (alleged) customary right to the captor, it was finally resolved by the committee and Admiral Watson that all plunder and booty would be deposited with the Company, and ultimately the King, until any specific grant was given.[143]

It was at the same time that application was made to the secret committee in England for legal sanction. And the distribution of Prize which was sent in 1756 (before the re-take of Calcutta) was received in London when the law officers of the Crown discussed the requests. In this application demands were made in relation to: (1) what was re-taken and (2) reprisals. While the settlements and effects of that which is re-taken was to lie with the Company, one half of the reprisals was to be deposited with His Majesty until his pleasure be known; the other half was to be distributed as Prize money. All this was of course in the form of an application to His Majesty. It was these applications routed through the Court that then took up the attention of the solicitor and attorney general, the pre-eminent law officers of the land, leading ultimately to the letters-patent of 1757 and 1758.

To better understand this more general problem of sovereignty through Prize money as well as the initial petition of the Company in 1756 that wished to be governed by the Act of 1756,[144] it would be incumbent to study the said act. This act was proposed to encourage the seamen of Great Britain to participate in the war against the French in April 1756, prior to an official declaration of war. The earlier Act of 1739 (the Naval Prize Act) had ensured that British seamen in His Majesty's vessels or privateers in their own ships had the sole right to Prize money in their captures, subject to the commissions that were granted by the Courts of Admiralty after a war had been declared. The application for such commissions and the payment of a fee guaranteed such a right. However the bill under discussion in 1756, before the outbreak of actual war with the French kingdom, suggested that Prize could be claimed and (re)distributed in the context of 'reprisals' without the formal declaration of war. Such a law, it was believed, would help counter or minimize the violence of the press gangs that were at large – necessary as they were during wartime or in anticipation of war. Captured ships from France or captured goods re-taken from the French would therefore not merely lie idle at the ports awaiting formal clearance, but could be legally redistributed to those involved in the expedition even without war being declared. While parliamentarians saw the merit in such a bill, which they deliberated upon in a context of what they perceived as unmitigated French aggression, especially in the Americas, they also pointed to the fact that such a bill, if made an act, might itself be construed as a declaration of war and might not in itself withstand legal scrutiny from the larger European community. Among the acts of hostility mentioned – indications of the existence of a war already underway – was the construction of garrisons and fortresses by the French in British territories in America.[145]

One of the issues discussed was the issue of 'reprisals' and its exact nature before a declaration of formal war, i.e. whether a legal distribution of the Prize or plunder could take place before the declaration of war. Welbore Ellis, a parliamentarian, argued that reprisals per se were not to be treated as acts of war, and that there were firm procedures in place to be taken into account for reprisals to be initiated: for instance, letters of reprisals could only be issued after four months of the demand for satisfaction. The working of reprisals into treaties ensured that they had a status within the European community of sovereigns.[146] On the other hand, the argument against pressing as one of the merits of bill was countered by the assertion that pressing was coeval with monarchy, an assertion that was backed with historical evidence.[147] It was also held to be in conformity with common law and statute. Charles Townshed, another parliamentarian, added a new angle to the discussion by arguing that reprisals were to be understood as acts that were undertaken in response to injury done to a private party, and only when the state was involved in such circumstances could such an act be construed as an act of war.[148] The bill was finally rejected, and among the many reasons for its final rejection was the argument that for the legality of the distribution that was Prize, a formal declaration of war would have had to have been announced. Almost confirming this position, within a month, when formal war was declared, the act was passed.[149] It was this very Prize Act under which the Company had requested its rights for Prize, but were in turn granted on the basis of specifically royal charters.

In the light of the above, one is in a better position to appreciate the Company's demand for legal sanction from the King for the distribution of Prize after the reconquest of Calcutta, a sanction in its wording that could then continue seamlessly to sanction the conquest of Bengal and other provinces, subject of course, as always, to His Majesty's 'right of sovereignty'. The law officers were keen to specifically add a clause in the letters-patent to ensure that the rights to make peace would not only be entailed in the distribution of Prize, but would also give the powers of ceding (transfer) to the Company, in treaty, grant or conquest with the native powers. The transfer to the terrestrial of what conventionally had its dominion in the maritime element of the seas, Prize money, is what was expressed acutely in the record of the Company's actions since 1756; this 'transfer' from sea to land was recognized and formalized in *Le Caux v. Eden*. The initial applications for Prize of the Company in 1756, in the case of the re-taking of Calcutta, is not cause for surprise because the Company's forces were operating in conjunction with Admiral Watson's *naval* command, the latter directly representing His Majesty's forces. Watson's cooperation as a naval force was in fact crucial for the recapture of Calcutta.

It was not only Prize but the recapture or re-taking of Calcutta that needs to be uniquely kept in mind for an understanding of this gravid moment in history. None of these terms – whether Prize or recapture – is used in a conventional sense, and we have to probe them to better apprehend the lexicon of such politicio-military terminology. Towards this end, we enlist Marten's *An Essay on Privateer, Captures and particularly on recaptures* (1801) and T.H. Horne's *A Compendium of the statute laws and regulations of the court of admiralty relative to the ships of war, privateers, prizes, recaptures and Prize Money* (1803). To begin with, Martens argues that 'privateers', who came up in the discussion on the legislation with regard to the 'encouragement' of seamen, were to be strictly distinguished from pirates in that they had commissions from their sovereigns to conduct war with enemies, which in turn accorded them the right to Prize after following due process. Pirates, as conventional and legal wisdom of the time had it, were the common enemies of mankind, i.e. the enemies of a common mankind.[150]

Other than details regarding the application for sanctions of Prize money and their various forms, there were also procedures regarding the evaluation of Prize that had to be followed. Furthermore, in Europe, as Martens shows, the King often claimed deductions that were progressively reduced over time. In Holland it was reduced from 30 per cent to 10 per cent, to none at all. Britain, according to recent legislation, did not make any deduction for the sovereign when its own forces were not involved.[151] However, according to English law, privateers had to receive legal sanction from the sovereign for making any claims on captures or recaptures.

In all cases there was a distinction made between capture and recapture. This distinction will have relevance for the applications made by the Company – in their preparation to recapture Calcutta – to the King via the Law officers. According to Martens, in cases of recapture, the sovereign had the right to decide; this was the position of the law officers in 1756–57. Yet, neither the rationale of such decisions nor the exact procedures was at all clear. To further examine this question, he takes resort to the natural law, derived from Roman law, of war: that the captor derived the right of that which he has captured from the capture itself. Ambiguities remain. For it is not clear from which point in time the captor has acquired 'full property' or legal title. Would it be from the time of acquisition? The time of reaching the port? Or after a certain specified duration? These lines of pursuing the question are jettisoned because Martens argues that time, or rather the arbitrary segmenting of time, cannot define natural law. The only reasonable way out of the impasse, he argues, would be to say that while war gives the capturer the right to dispose of property, it does not give full proprietorship of the sort that erased every trace of the right of the original proprietor. This extinction of every trace can only be achieved through, and in the establishment of, peace (and 'law'). Documenting this discussion with reference to statute, Martens writes,

> The first law which I could find on this subject and which has served as a basis to many succeeding laws, is the act of parliament of 1692 which enacts that if any ship vessel or bark belonging to their majesties subjects who continue to live under their protection and obedience, after having been captured by their majesties enemies shall be recaptured, that ship and its cargo or part of it shall be restored by *decree of the court of admiralty* to the first proprietors, who shall pay for salvage, if the recapture is made by a ship of war, one eighth of the value which shall be delivered to the captains, officers, seamen of the said ship of war to be divided among them agreeably to the present act of parliament concerning the share of prizes belonging to them. (Emphasis added)[152]

The statutes were very clear that all persons had to apply for commissions and had to apply in writing, reflecting the fact that all captures could acquire title only through authority derived from the sovereign. In Horne's *Compendium of the Statute Laws and Regulations*, detailed specifications of Prize money and its distribution are given.[153]

One is now perhaps in a better position to understand the circumstances under which the Company applied for Prize and the distribution of Prize before the recapture of Calcutta. An important aspect of this expedition was that this would be a joint operation with Admiral Watson of His Majesty's naval forces. After 1757, the next major battle in Company history, the Battle of Buxar, was led by Hector Munro, also of His Majesty's armed forces and commander-in-chief. After victory, Munro was offered the *diwani*, which he refused. But he did take one-eighth of the Prize money, which consisted of 4 lakhs of rupees, from the merchants of Benaras, as well as 80,000 rupees from Balwant Singh, the 'raja' of Benaras. Lieutenant George Harris, over three decades later, in another major victory at Srirangapatnam, was also from His Majesty's service. Prize money and its maritime habitat, while having something to do with the recapture of Calcutta where the naval fleet was required, have imperceptibly and indiscernibly come to rove the terrestrial order: Murshidabad, Buxar, Srirangapatnam and all the captured places in-between.[154]

The precariousness and complexity of deciding Prize and its legitimate claimants is evident in the attack, capture and plunder of the properties in Fort Vidyadurg in Benaras in 1776, amounting to 300,000 pounds. This incident received a great deal of publicity in the trial of Warren Hastings, linked as it was to what was called the charge of Benaras. After attempting to arrest Raja Chait Singh, the English attacked his fortress, Vidyadurg, where the raja's mother and wife lived. It was believed to have housed much of Chait Singh's property and money. The course of the trial revealed that Hastings had allowed Major Popham to capture, plunder and divide whatever property was found in the fortress. This was indicated in a private letter to Major Popham which sanctioned the plunder.[155] Later Hastings tried to retrieve the divided plunder but did not succeed. While recognizing the right of soldiers to plunder, Hastings believed that the distribution should have been done under the aegis of the Company. Yet the fact of plunder and Prize was not denied, even though Hastings argued in his defence that he did not give any direct order to plunder the fortress. On the other hand, Major Popham stated before the House of Lords that Hastings's private instructions were well known, and it was understood by the army to mean that they did indeed have the right to plunder. In this context, it was argued that Hastings would have to take responsibility, since plunder could be recognized as Prize only if it followed a legal procedure, whereas in the case of Vidyadurg no such procedure was followed.

There is evidence that the Company believed that the actual captors, Company forces, were often taking Prize money that had in fact been granted to the Company as a corporate entity, as part of the royal grant. In 1782, the solicitor general gave his legal opinion that the Company was the body that had been entitled by the royal grant, and individual soldiers or forces of the Company could not assume to have been so entitled. He made it clear that the claim of the 'captors' to the Prize would have to include, in fact, the entity that authorized it, i.e. in this case, the Company. So it was in Roman law and the law of nations, where the 'captor' was taken to mean the 'state' that enabled and carried out the expedition. Citing Puferdorf, the solicitor general also stated that when soldiers were regularly paid, they certainly could not claim Prize money beyond a very miniscule amount. If they were not paid and were not regular forces it might have been different, but this was not the case, since the East India Company did regularly pay its soldiers. Therefore, in the case of Nagapatnam, the soldiers were held to have no justifiable claim since all Prize was inherent in the Crown, and rights to plunder were given to the Company as a corporation by letters-patent. Share in the booty by the Company was also based on the fact that it bore the principal share in the expedition in the first place.

In the context of the Battle of Srirangapatnam in 1799 too, the commander-in-chief of the troops was accused of having taken more than his share of the Prize money involved. When intimated of the Company's reservations in 1804, Lieutenant-General George Harris, of Srirangapatnam fame, sat down to write to the president of the Board of Control and the Court of Directors of the East India Company, in defence of his past conduct. Harris was accused of illegally apportioning to himself one-eighth of the Prize money, i.e. 3,24,907 *pagodas* or what came to approximately 130,000 pounds, that was acquired in the Battle of Srirangapatnam in 1799.[156] To get a sense of perspective, one may say that this amount was slightly over .04 per cent of the *entire* revenues collected from Bihar, Bengal and Orissa in the highly revised and inflated rental amount of 1793; the entire Prize money amounted to approximately .34 per cent of the latter. Lieutenant Harris, in defence of what he considered his right to one-eighth of the Prize money and filled with righteous indignation, wrote,

> . . . thus devoted to the cause of my king and country you my lord may judge of my feelings when I accidentally learn that the Court of Directors think fit to draw me from that shade to which I had retired, to impeach the propriety of my conduct in regard to the prize money of Srirangapatnam and to question my right to the share allotted to me.[157]

Harris referred to the long history of Prize distribution amongst the land forces in the subcontinent, also highlighting the fact that he had recourse to such precedent only because he was unable to initially ascertain what precisely was meant by the 'established usages' of Prize money and its distribution. He wrote to the Court of Directors that he could not initially find an instance that did not involve the navy, even if the one-eighth share was uniformly taken by commanders-in-chief, in the various wars on subcontinental land. The Court of Directors, on the other hand, cited the 1793 law regarding the naval Prize distribution as well as His Majesty's letters-patent of January 1758, to argue that property captured by joint operations of His Majesty's and the Company's forces was solely reserved for His Majesty's pleasure. The Battle of Srirangapatnam was conducted by the joint forces of His Majesty and the Company. This was the case even in the crucial Battle of Buxar, where commander-in-chief Hector Munro had apportioned to himself one-eighth of the Prize/booty.[158] This contention about the shares of Prize money came to the fore in the context of the Battle of Srirangapatnam, where much booty and treasure was looted. After getting the ratification of the Prize shares from the King, the Company came to the view that the distribution was not in order. Since the war was conducted by a conjunction of the King's and the Company's forces, it was believed that half of the shares would be reserved for the Company, the other half being divided by the captors. However, in the Srirangapatnam case the commander-in-chief, General Harris, reserved to himself one-eighth of the entire Prize. The Company felt that this was not in line with the contemporary usage or custom, and that the Harris had reserved to himself more than his share and therein had deprived others amongst the forces. At the end of the wrangling it was decided that since the grant was already ratified, there was no court of law that could be approached for settling matters. The advice of the attorney general and solicitor general to the Company was that in such a case, only a bill of equity be filed by those soldiers who felt themselves aggrieved. This was not taken recourse to, and General Harris kept his Prize.

While the Prize money and its distribution were recognized in right and practice, the point of contention was whether the claim that Lieutenant Harris as commander-in-chief had the right to one-eighth of the plunder followed the established norms. The dispute lay in clarifying the rules of Prize distribution where 'established usages' were invoked, even while it was not entirely clear what these were. The Court of Directors of the East India Company held that the 'established usages' had to refer to the rules found in the distribution of naval Prize, where, if there was more than one commander, then the one-eighth share had to be divided amongst the commanders. Whereas for Lieutenant Harris, the 'established usages' stood for the actions of British land forces in the subcontinent where from 'immortal Clive' onwards, one-eighth of the share fell solely to the commanding officer.[159]

In the Battle of Srirangapatnam, while the commander-in-chief was awarded over 3.5 lakh *pagoda*s as Prize, 'private native troops' were awarded 12 *pagoda*s, the European rank-and-file 18 *pagoda*s each, the general officers on the staff 27,000 *pagoda*s each, and the generals got a third more.[160] Other than citing precedent in the many wars fought in India as well as the recently concluded conquest of Delhi by Lord Lake, Harris argued in his defence that not only had Governor-General Wellesley explicitly delegated to him the task of Prize distribution after the war, he himself had followed strict protocol in constituting a committee that was elected by officers and the rank-and-file which had taken charge of Prize distribution. Moreover, he suggested that to be governed by the precedents in naval Prizes did not take into account the fact that the wars in the subcontinent involved native troops, and the strict application of naval Prize procedures would in effect erase the distinction between native troops and the British, notwithstanding the fact that according to him British soldiers were, rightly, more highly paid than the native sepoys.[161]

We might speculate on the origin of the proportion of one-eighth as a share of the commander. After acquiring *diwani*, Clive as a governor claimed one-eighth of the revenue, although we do not know on what grounds.[162] While many historians have argued that the *diwani* was a sign of the Company ruling as a native power, this would be a mistake with serious implications. Not only is the historical context of defeat important, even the legal wording of the treaty mentions the *diwani* as a 'free gift', renouncing all monetary claims except for a 'tribute'. Both the practice of the one-eighth share as well as the tribute was put to an end by Hastings. To mistake Clive's stated policy of double government, where the Company deceptively gave rulers merely nominal power while retaining for itself all real power as historical reality, would be to ignore the historical facts and forces at play. That it was a policy was confirmed negatively when Hastings reversed this by stopping the tribute and thereby explicitly asserted English sovereignty, an action that he did with the full support of his superiors in London.

The King's Justice in the Calcutta Supreme Court

Condemned to the twilight between conquest and the formal inauguration of subjecthood, how was one to characterize various kinds of people subject to the Company's policies? It is this problem that was well-articulated by the establishment of the King's Court or the Supreme Court in Calcutta, to regulate and restrain the abuses of the Company. The extent of its jurisdiction was necessarily a question of the determination of subjecthood. We therefore turn to this Court and its early functioning.

The Regulating Act of 1773 was expressly enacted to bring order ('regulation') and prevent violence and injustices carried out by the East India Company upon natives, and to regulate the trade and politics of the Company so as to ensure that the latter was a financially viable instrument of power and profit for the English public at large. The role of the King was unmistakable in the establishment of the Supreme Court as a King's Bench, invested with civil, ecclesiastical and admiralty jurisdiction – a role that was explicitly recognized by Hastings who interpreted the act in terms of the King's explicit participation in governance.[163] They could try Europeans without a jury, and assess damages. They had a 'local' as well as 'personal' jurisdiction. The former was literally well-defined in so far as it referred to territory, whereas the latter was a source of contention since it referred to whosoever was a 'subject' of His Majesty. Returning to the wording of the law commissioners above in relation to the applications for Prize money, the Company was to be treated as subject to His Majesty's 'right of sovereignty' as 'English settlements' and 'English subjects'. The latter naturally included officials of the East India Company, but it also included those who could be characterized as being in the 'direct or indirect' employment of the Company.[164] Proleptically, one might say that Bahadur Shah Zafar was accused of treasonous behaviour on the basis of the fact, or further claim, that he was under the employment of the Company.[165] By focusing on the Supreme Court in India and its inter-relations with Company governance, in this section, the measure and scope of sovereignty as emanating from the King, and the nature of the 'subject' in its status and differentiation, are analysed. It is found that the nature of the subject can by no means be abstracted from the prior and primary question of sovereignty.

The first series of confrontations between the Governor-General and Council, and the Supreme Court,[166] flared up in precisely deciding the issue of whether natives such as zamindars could be said to be *subject* to the Court and its jurisdiction. This was a complex issue on many counts. First, the Hastings plan of 1772 had already explicitly laid down the judicial structure of an appellate court system. The plan had specified that for the purposes of civil issues (inheritance, debt, religion, caste), the relevant scriptural authority would be resorted to.[167] In the case of the inheritance of zamindaris and *talukdaris*, the president and council would directly make the determination. Clearly, this provision would be a blatant violation of property right if zamindari rights were seen as a form of inheritable property rights. Already by 1772, Company practice had denied any such right by its annual farming of zamindaris, and a rich discourse developed attributing the crisis of the economy, including the devastation of the famine, to such a policy and practice.[168] The resistance from several zamindars has been well-documented and Hastings's five-year plan was an attempt to mitigate precisely such a situation.[169] The Company's practice of auctioning and denying any inheritable property right of the zamindar to his zamindari was formalized in the judicial plan of 1772. This clause of the direct determination of zamindari inheritance was distinguished from property rights in general, which were to be determined by the appellate court system, and follow native religion and custom. Hastings's patronage of the formation of the first Hindu 'code' is to be interpreted in such a light, but the crux of the issue is the manipulated distinction between the revenue rights claimed by the Company (which involved the question of zamindari), which was absolutely discretionary, and the civil and property rights of the people, which was ostensibly dependent on local religion and custom.[170]

That Hastings wished to portray his scheme as consistent with the highest principles of British law and justice is testified to by his letter to Lord Mansfield in 1774.[171] In this letter he strongly argues in favour of allowing the local population to be allowed to follow their own laws, which, he argued, were of a well-developed nature, and could not be characterized as savage or barbarous. This argument seems consistent with the principles embodied in Mansfield's judgment in *Campbell v. Hall*, where he held that in cases of conquests, local inhabitants ought to be allowed to continue with their laws and be guaranteed property on such terms to the extent possible. It is in this context that Hastings seems to be arguing strongly against the idea that English principles or laws be introduced in India in the name of protecting native religion, law and property. It was in this context that he sent Lord Mansfield the recently formulated 'code' of Hindu laws.[172] However, in making the argument that natives ought to be left to their own laws and institutions, Hastings crucially leaves out the close nexus between revenue demand and property, as well as the fact that notwithstanding the use of local pundits, decisions were ultimately made by British officers who were employees of the Company, and therefore bound to be guided by the Company's interest. That is to say, the precise right on the basis of which revenue could be demanded was unclear, particularly if royal charter had indicated that the 'property in the soil' was attributed to a local grant. In addition, the close link between revenue arrangements and personal law and their management for achieving the Company's aims at the cost of the property and rights of the native has been decisively demonstrated.[173]

Yet, the plan of Hastings in the 1770s was obstructed by the newly established King's Court at Calcutta, and the exact determination of the zamindari as a form of property would be open to the clash of jurisdictions of the East India Company (from governor and council down to the provincial courts) and the Supreme Court. Any vestige of local authority in the form of the Mughal emperor or Nawab had been definitely repudiated by stopping the payment of tribute, as well as the very establishment of the judicial plan of 1772 in which the Nawab played no role. It might be reiterated that the *diwani* was bestowed as part of the treaty requiring tribute and only concerned revenue matters, not criminal matters which were also addressed in the plan of 1772. All of this showed that the Company had gone far beyond the scope of the *diwani* grant, *de jure* and *de facto*.

Simultaneous with the cases of the zamindars was the *cause célèbre* of Raja Nandakumar, who in August 1775 was sentenced to death by the Supreme Court on account of fraud, i.e. forging a bond. The arguments that Governor-General Hastings initially used against the Supreme Court's jurisdiction – as one that was held to interfere with the judicial system established in 1772 –was that the Supreme Court was not cognizant of or conversant with the laws of the natives and so it would be unjust for the latter to be subject to its jurisdiction, notwithstanding the fact that the control exercised by the Company over the court system established in 1772 was exercised by Company (English) officials almost wholly untrained in law, Indian or English. For the plan of 1772 had made it clear that there would be two parallel hierarchies of courts divided by subject matter: one for 'civil causes' and the other for 'trials of crimes and misdemeanours'.[174] Apart from all this, when it came to the inheritance of zamindaris and *talukdari*s, the president and council's decision would be supreme;[175] this too is clearly traceable to the King's prerogative in English history,[176] and English history was replete with precedents for this establishment.[177] And this juridical power has to be directly linked to the revenue settlements that Hastings was intent on making. The juridical power cannot be traced to the emperor's grant of *diwani* since no such power was granted,[178] and its only possible source could be the anointing of the president and council as Justices of Peace by the King's charter of 1729. It was the supremacy of the president and council, which had even exercised control over the Mayor Courts, that would be challenged by the establishment of the Supreme Court in 1774.

In the light of the above, the argument cannot be one where the Company stands for and supports native custom against the 'foreign', and therein unjustly imposed English laws by the Supreme Court. This was because of the simple reason that the Company in fact controlled the juridical system that was established in 1772. Derret and, more recently, Nandini Bhattacharya-Panda have demonstrated conclusively that what came to be known as 'Hindu scriptural law', or the bastardized Anglo-Hindu law, served the commercial and governmental agenda of the Company.[179] On the other hand, in late eighteenth-century English legal culture, it was not necessary that a specific religious or cultural identity meant per se exclusion from the King's Bench. One must also remember that Glannvil's dictum of the King making laws and customs that was common law, was in theory and practice relevant for the eighteenth century.[180] Mansfield had recently allowed non-Christians to participate in English juridical processes, just as 'aliens' could well be 'subjects' in that they could appeal for protection to the King.[181]

Jenks, Baker, Hussain and most recently Halliday[182] have amply demonstrated the fact that when it came to the King's prerogative – especially that of habeas corpus – no specific national or cultural identity per se disqualified one from being a subject to the King's laws. Thus, while the Nandakumar instance is often used as justification for the argument that English laws should not be applicable to natives – and therefore the synecdoche for culture is a qualification or disqualification for the application of the King's law – things turn out to be more complicated when looked into. That there was no perceived contradiction between the juridical rationale of the Supreme Court and local custom and/or religion is fully congruent with the way the law was understood and practised in England, as well as evidenced by the fact that two years after its establishment, native pundits were attached to it for providing advice on matters relating to Hindus.[183] For instance, Impey's initial correspondence makes it clear that natives were all too eager to use the Supreme Court to defend themselves against the rapaciousness of Company officials and their agents. Before getting ahead of ourselves, however, let us return to Maharaja Nandakumar.

Nandakumar, placed in confinement in the custody of the Supreme Court, in response to a charge[184] had pleaded that by the customs and religion of the country, since he was confined in a place that included Muslims and Christians, he would lose caste and would have no option but to starve himself to death. This was communicated to the Supreme Council (Governor-General and Council) and in turn conveyed to the judges of the Supreme Court. After conducting his own investigations, Chief Justice Impey concluded that no such demands on the 'natives' were made by their religion or customs. Basing this conclusion on consultations with natives, Impey wrote to the Supreme Council that 'they [the natives] added it was no easy matter to lose caste, a Brahmin must eat 8 times of the meat of a musselman before he can lose his caste'.[185] Impey further argued that indeed the law would take into account the religious sentiments of the natives, but not to such an extent as to, in effect, annul the very course of justice. If this were done, he wrote, the very rationale for setting up the Supreme Court of judicature would be defeated. There were many of a higher caste than Nandakumar who had been confined without such a complaint, and taking Nandakumar seriously would render ineffective the law in relation to the Brahmans who were a numerous caste in and around Calcutta. To this, the Supreme Council in its reply stated that according to its own investigations the claims of Nandakumar were true, and were confirmed by the head of a local caste council. Impey however remained confirmed in his views, writing that he had himself read the relevant extracts of the *shastras* and there was nothing in them to authenticate the claims of Nandakumar; also, the president of the caste council who was to have allegedly advised Hastings in fact did not support Nandakumar's views. When Impey demands written evidence for the views of those native dignitaries that Hastings's (and the Supreme Council) claim had supported Nandakumar's position, he is met with silence. In reply to which Impey exclaims, surely such evidence would have to be submitted if it were expected to take effect.[186]

As justices of the King's Bench, the Supreme Court judges were also Justices of Peace, and therefore invested with powers of magistracy. Nandakumar was confined as part of a case that was a civil suit, but insofar as it involved the accusation of forgery, it was a criminal case. While this case originated years ago, only subsequent to the establishment of the Supreme Court were forged documents allegedly found, and therefore it was in the said court that Nandakumar was brought to trial. While Nandakumar was taken into the custody of the Supreme Court in May, just two months previously, in March, he had approached Philip Francis and handed him a letter accusing the Governor-General, Warren Hastings, of embezzlement. Francis brought the letter and charge to the newly established Supreme Council. Hastings, as Governor-General, refused to take cognizance of the charge, and ended up dissolving the Council. James Fitzjames Stephen, who had studied the case in detail at the end of the nineteenth century, writes that this was not the first time that the Governor-General had used his power to dissolve the council in response to a charge; 'on a previous occasion there was a charge that he and his banyan (*baniya*) between them received 40000 rs a year of the salary of 72000 rs paid by the company to the foujdar or native head of the criminal justice and police at Hoogley'.[187] Hastings had then similarly dissolved the council. While very soon Nandakumar himself was accused of forgery, tried, found guilty and hanged – in all of four months – it is not clear whether Impey and the Supreme Court judges did know of his charges against Hastings. Stephen, in his detailed study of the subject, concludes that there was no evidence of a conspiracy between Impey and Hastings, and that the trial was fairly conducted following due procedure without malice.[188] Here is reversed the narrative dramatized by Burke and Macaulay, that Impey and Hastings had colluded and conspired in the 'judicial murder' of Nandakumar.[189]

While the Nandakumar case has at times been taken as the paradigmatic sign of the absurdity and injustice of transferring English laws to Calcutta, an absurdity that was to have been expressed by native resentment, the issues brought up are significantly more subtle and elusive. On at least one previous occasion, in 1756, Radhachandra Mitra was pronounced guilty of forgery and given the death sentence, even though he was finally granted mercy after a petition by a group of eminent natives. Derrett, in his own study of the Nandakumar case, argues that Calcutta and its denizens would have believed, even if erroneously, that the statute on forgery would be applicable in Calcutta.[190] In the Nandakumar case, in the month of July, no less than four addresses to the Supreme Court judges expressed their appreciation of the court, one of which was signed by 'natives' and the other by Armenians.[191] The issue to be examined is whether the idea for the Supreme Court legislating was all that absurd, or whether it was well within the scope of a legal culture that recognized the King's laws to determine and protect custom. It was in such a context that Impey writes – in lines cited by almost every recent study on the subject – the natives are ultimately under the protection of the laws, more fundamentally than that of the Company's government.[192]

Two things may be kept in mind. The King's Bench, where the King was to be virtually present, was by its very nature not to be limited by custom. This was the case as much in England as in any of the other dominions or beyond. Impey in his initial correspondence had made this clear. On the other hand, the Company's claim that it protected and represented native custom – and this in no way was meant as a disavowing of its own subjection to the King – has been successfully refuted at various levels. In this context, the claims that the Supreme Court was merely fulfilling its function in protecting natives from the illegal authority of the Company may well be examined.

On 1 April 1777, the Chief Justice had written to the Lord Chancellor,

> The court is increasing daily in business we are beginning to make the vultures of Bengal disgorge their prey – cases kept back by the timidity of the natives which had been much increased by assurances from those who should have supported the court that the foundation of it was unstable should be destroyed and therefore that they could receive no permanent protection from it are now bringing forward and I am now convinced we shall in a great measure give redress for the past injuries.[193]

Impey goes on to outline a rather frightening state of affairs where Company officials and their native subordinates appear to hold all else in thrall through their 'cruelties and extortions'. As indicative, he reports an instance where a native of 'uncorrupted integrity' and 'diligence', who was assisting the court with petitions of various sorts, had been offered money to keep away from his duties, which he refused. He however paid with his life, for he was found murdered with none of his ornaments stolen, by one who had disguised himself as a sitar maestro and was teaching this man lessons in the art.[194] Such an incident was by no means unique, and Impey goes on to detail the rapine and loot that, according to him, had become second nature to British officials, drunk with power. In another letter to Lord Weymouth, Impey continues to complain about the 'despotic principles to which British subjects long resident in this country have been naturalized from early youth'.[195]

In such a context, Impey argued, it would be most unjust to accept the demands of certain elements within the British population of demanding a trial by jury or by their peers, who would naturally be other Englishmen. For this demand to be tried by a jury, by one's peers, was made in the name of the rights of an English subject. The organizers of this demand included those charged with acts such as assault, battery and the illegal confinement of natives. And it was clear in Impey's mind that the demand for rights as an English subject and the rights to a jury were merely attempts to support and protect what cannot be distinguished from institutionalized and unjust discrimination. Speaking of those tried and convicted of assault, battery and illegal confinement as 'prickly' Englishmen demanding their rights, as has been done in a recent study, is a simplification so gross as to amount to inaccuracy.[196] Rather, here might be found one of the sources and points of origin of the argument that as freeborn Englishmen, Englishmen in India would not submit to Company governance, which resulted in a historical record where they did (and would) commit the greatest of violence on natives with impunity in a system where 'rule of law', that is to say, 'equality before the law', did not prevail.[197]

Chief Justice Impey also claimed that the judicial system established by the Company was corrupt and manipulated by Company officials so as to exploit the native population, just as he was keen to argue that in its conquests of new territory, London should be sure to establish new courts so as to ensure justice.[198] This general indictment of the nature of the Company rule was clearly articulated by all the King's judges in a case that swiftly followed the Nandakumar case, also involving him, which deserves analysis on these grounds. This was the trial of Joseph Fowke, Nandakumar and Roy Radhachuran[199] for a conspiracy against Warren Hastings. In the course of the trial, the Governor-General and Council sent to the King's Court a memorial by Radhachuran, in which the latter claimed that he was a 'Vakil' and 'public minister' of Nawab Mubarak Ul Dowla (the Nawab of Bengal), and therefore entitled to the 'rights privileges and immunities allowed by the law of nations and statute law of England to the representatives of princes'.[200] As a foreign dignitary with such immunities, and in no way subject to the laws of Great Britain, to conduct such a trial as was presently taking place under the Supreme Court would be an 'infringement of the laws of nations, and of the established rights and privileges to which he is by law entitled in the character aforesaid'.[201] The Governor-General and Council supported Radhachuran's claim, in their communication to the court, that as an important public minister of a sovereign prince he did indeed enjoy such ambassadorial privileges. Moreover they argued that the East India Company, under express sanction of British laws, had entered into a treaty with the Nawab and therefore could make such claims of exceptions for foreign dignitaries.

The court first expressed surprise at the fact that this claim for immunities by Radhachuran was not made at the outset of the trial. While recognizing the rights of ambassadors and the laws of nations in general, the court raised the question as to whether the Nawab of Bengal was indeed an 'independent sovereign prince' who therein possessed the authority to send an ambassador. To determine this question the court asked the Governor-General to state in a formal affidavit, what they appeared to be claiming. That is, they demanded that the affidavit state that the Nawab was an independent sovereign prince who could appoint ministers and act independently of the Company government, and that he could independently make war and peace as well as carry out negotiations.[202] The counsel for the Company argued that the Nawab was indeed a sovereign, and the evidence for this lay in the fact that he exercised criminal jurisdiction in his provinces, signed death-warrants, sent ambassadors, possessed a royal mint and coined money, and was accepted as sovereign by all European nations; the claim that the Company was the real sovereign would be nothing less than a provocation to European nations that could lead to war.[203] In order to substantiate this set of claims, the treaty between the Company and the Nawab was placed before the Court.

In its response, the counsel for the prosecution argued that the treaty only confirmed the fact that the Nawab was not an independent sovereign since, according to the provisions of the treaty, he could not independently undertake war and peace, and was in fact supported by the Company with an armed force and a stipend whose sanction came from the Court of

Directors. Even the claim of criminal jurisdiction and capital punishment was illusory, since such jurisdiction – and the court system – was established by the Company in 1772 without any consultation with or concurrence from the Nawab.[204] Citing authorities such as Grotius as much as early English statute, the prosecution argued that ambassadors could be sent only from one sovereign to another, and hence ambassadorial immunity was wholly inapplicable in this case where the Nawab was clearly not an independent sovereign. Finally, it was argued that

> the late act of parliament, and the charter by which the supreme court is established clearly evince, that in the eyes of the British legislature, the provinces of Bengal, Bihar and Orissa, are considered as conquered country, in which the conqueror hath a right to introduce his laws, and make them obeyed.[205]

There was no question of the Nawab possessing sovereignty.

That the Company had established courts for criminal justice on their own authority without consultations with or even the concurrence of the Nawab, and that the Court of Directors had recently reduced the annual stipend of the Nawab, was confirmed by an affidavit of Governor-General Hastings in the course of the proceedings. George Vansittart in his affidavit confirmed the facts presented in Hastings's affidavit, and explicitly stated that the Nawab was not a sovereign independent ruler. Yet, the Company's counsel continued to argue that the fact that the Nawab was 'divested' of power did not mean that he did not possess the right of sovereignty.

The Court did not agree with the Company's counsel, and affirmed the prosecution's argument that the treaty between the Nawab and Company indicated that the former had surrendered all power to the latter, and therefore was divested of sovereignty. Citing the law of nations, Chief Justice Impey argued that ambassadors were granted immunities because they represented the 'person of the prince', who was sovereign, and the role of ambassadors was indelibly incident to the sovereign rights of making war, peace and treaties. Since the Company was unable to either provide an affidavit confirming that the Nawab was a sovereign prince or that it had always treated Radhachuran as an ambassador, neither could be accepted in the face of the facts. Without speculating on the specific rights or status of the Company, Justice Impey remained content in affirming that the Nawab

> had surrendered his power entirely into the hands of the East India Company [and] cannot himself, nor can the East India Company in his name protect

> delinquents, subject to the jurisdiction of this court, from being punished by the laws of Great Britain; that the agents of the East India Company cannot, by making him the instrument, do indirectly what they would not do directly.[206]

Not only was the Nawab therefore not sovereign, the Company was directly accused of masking its sovereignty in the name of the Nawab to escape accountability.

Justice Chambers, while agreeing entirely with the Chief Justice, made clearer his position on the status of the East India Company by stating that the Company had the powers of making war, peace and treaty as 'delegated by the Crown', as happened elsewhere, such as in cases of generals and viceroys.[207] It was once again reiterated that the question was not one of not recognizing ambassadorial privileges, which, according to Justice Chambers, Islamic empires too recognized, but rather of determining whether the Nawab was indeed sovereign and capable of exercising his sovereignty in sending ambassadors. Justice Lemaistre, while agreeing with the findings pertaining to the lack of sovereignty in the Nawab, offers a slightly varying opinion from Justice Chambers on the status of the East India Company. Stating that ambassadors were always sent from one sovereign to another, Justice Lemaistre states, 'I cannot admit any right of sovereignty in the East India Company; in every charter granted to them by the crown, there is an express reservation of sovereignty to the king of Great Britain, his heirs and successors'.[208] While both recognize the supreme powers of the Crown, differences appear on the question of 'delegation'. Directly invoking the relationship between Prize and sovereignty, as well as the Prize charters issued to the Company as evidence for the sovereignty of the King, Justice Lemaistre goes on to state, 'When the East India Company had taken plunder it was doubted if that plunder could be vested in them, without the King's grant. A charter was therefore applied for, and granted for that purpose.' Thus, notwithstanding the Company's protestations, Radhachuran[209] was not recognized to have ambassadorial privileges, and incident to this was the clear establishment of the Company masking its sovereignty in the name of the Nawab. Despite his repudiation of Clive's doctrine of 'double government', Governor-General Hastings came around very quickly to understand its use.[210] This fiction was at root because sovereignty manifested itself as that which dissimulated so as to avoid accountability. Rather than detail the subsequent career of Impey, the accusations against him and the judicial reforms of the 1780s,[211] this section ends with a court case in London more germane to the subject of our investigation: the 'fact' of double government, and its propensity for injustice and violence that was screened from accountability.

If one could characterize law as having its function in scrutinizing the authority by which an act was committed, we find in the metropolis too the important recognition of the violence ingrained in double government. The specific case concerned the illegal confinement of Rafael, an Armenian merchant, by Henry Verelest, governor of the Company. This case, not unusual for the time, had originated in the subcontinent but reached Chief Justice De Grey in London. Rafael accused Henry Verelest of illegally confining him and forcibly bringing him from Oudh, territory (nominally) under the sovereignty of Nawab Shuja Ud Dowla, to Calcutta. The judges, including Blackstone, found Verelest guilty of 'trespass'. That Rafael was an 'alien' did not matter since this was an injury against the person, i.e. trespass. Whatever the defendant's arguments about the suzerainty of the Nawab, these did not apply because it was recognized that Shuja Ud Dowla was subservient to the English, as there was a company of soldiers in Oudh under the command of Colonel Harper though under the pay of the Nawab.[212] Since the Nawab was not seen to be an actor in the case – being in awe of and under the influence of Verelest – the latter would need to be seen as the principal actor, i.e. the one who commanded or procured the act.[213] What the King's Bench in London, in a reiteration of Impey's finding in Calcutta, was prepared to admit and act upon in an individual case was nothing less than the recognition of as much as a demand for a more open declaration of British sovereignty. Whether it was Impey or Francis, both wanted a clear declaration of His Majesty's sovereignty over the regions of Bengal that the Company had power and delegated authority over. Even Hastings in effect did this when he stopped the tribute due to the Mughal emperor, pronouncing that such sovereignty or right was not Clive's in the first place to have been given away.

The clear-cut manipulation of sovereignty backed by military force enabled continuous extortion. Earlier the Company had asserted the absolute sovereignty of the Mughal ruler when they wished to trade on the basis of his *dastaks*, but later officials like Clive were keen to argue for the independence of the nawabs so as to extract military and land revenue assignments from them without sanction from the Mughals. After defeat in battle, the Treaty of Allahabad which granted *diwani* was also unprecedented, because it specified that the *diwani* was given as a 'free gift', with an exemption from the payment of customs which used to be paid to the Mughals.[214] However, the Company was to stand surety to pay 26 lakhs of rupees in exchange, and all revenue that was acquired after this payment was allowed to remain with the English. Acting under instructions from the Court of Directors, Hastings did away with this crucial treaty obligation, and went on to establish a criminal justice system completely outside the ambit of *diwani*. This system was indirectly recognized by the Regulating Act of 1773–74, when it empowered the Governor-General and Council to frame laws, ordinances and rules. It was only thereby that the Company's rights to revenue could, even if only indirectly, be affirmed.

However, this did not prevent natives from contesting the justice of Company revenue collectors at the Supreme Court. In the light of the disputes over jurisdiction, the threat emerged of the entire revenue-engorging process being brought to a standstill; something had to be done. This is the context of the enunciation of the Act of 1781, which clipped the wings of the Supreme Court by declaring that it could not interfere with matters of revenue and did not serve as the court of appeal for the provincial courts. Rather, the Governor-General and Council were regarded as the final appellate authority, thereby establishing its authority over provincial ('mofussil') areas in matters of revenue. Agents of the Company following directives were granted immunities from the Supreme Court. This statute enabled the Company to impose its revenue policies through laws and penalties that were now immune from supervision by the Supreme Court and only ultimately subject to authorities in London and the King-in-Council.[215]

According to legal precedent from *Calvin* to *Campbell*, while conquered territory remained within the authority of the King, such was not the case after capitulation. It was throughout recognized that taxes and revenue were to be based on local legislation, and legislation itself required representation from the locality. In the case of the subcontinent, 'legislation' emerged from Governor-General and Council, with the possibility of appeal to King-in-Council. The complete occlusion of the local population from any decision regarding revenue demand was the clearest sign of a conquered territory that was being ruled despotically. The 1784 Act reaffirmed the powers and immunities of the Company from the Supreme Court at Calcutta, and made it clear that His Majesty's subjects and the servants of the Company were amenable to the jurisdiction of the English courts for

> all acts, injuries, wrongs, oppressions, trespasses, misdemeanours, crimes, and offences whatsoever by them or any of them done or to be done or committed in any of the lands or territories of any native prince or state or against their

> persons or properties or the persons or properties of any of their subjects or people *in the same manner* as if the same had been done or committed within the territories directly subject to and under the British government in India.[216] (Emphasis added)

'In the same manner' takes us back to James's grant to the American colonialists, but the Act signifies a form of 'personal' jurisdiction over the territories of India, thereby at once undermining local sovereignty as well as exercising power over its own officials. In clearly enunciating the judicial accountability of native populations serving the Company whether as military or civil officials, it once again left completely obscure the status of other natives who could always appeal but in fact had no inherent liberties that could only take shape in forms of self-representation in legislative assemblies. The Company could claim statutory sanction as well as rights from royal charters with little definite being left for the natives.

This was a situation of strategized and discretionary ambiguity that, perhaps unprecedentedly, carried on for well over a century, if not more, over vast populations. Since justice and revenue demand – law and property – were interdependent, the Company's precise juridical basis was always obscured. If the Regulating Act placed the Company's 'regulations' under the jurisdiction of the Supreme Court, the Act of 1781 construed the Governor-in-Council as a Court of Record, lording over the provincial councils and subject only to King-in-Council, immune from the Supreme Court in matters of revenue.[217] King-in-Council – not parliament – was once again the channel for authority and appeal. And if the 1781 Act on the one hand legitimized regulations based on the religion and caste of the natives, the principles of adjudication in the hands of non-native judges who were always supreme were to be the common law principles of 'justice, equity and good conscience'.[218] Cornwallis's 'reforms' in the 1790s, which did away with the requirement for the Nawab's signature on death warrants, did away with the last vestige of this fiction on the basis of Hastings's judicial plan of 1772. In his minute of 1791, he made it clear that the basis of his own interventions and alterations of local religious law lay in Hastings's alterations of the then existing native religious laws by the judicial plan of 1772 – alterations that were ultimately based on and recognized by authorities in London and parliamentary statutes.[219]

Finally, despotism lay not merely in the complete exclusion of the populations from the decision as to the revenue they owed, but rather in both the immunities and powers granted to the Governor-General and Company officials in the carrying out of their day-to-day functions. While the 1781 Act specified that the Governor-General and Council was immune from any liabilities in the carrying out of actions in his 'public' capacity, Company officials were guaranteed the same immunities as long as they could establish that they were following the orders of their superiors. If such immunities were codified in law, a terrorizing provision was introduced in the Act of 1784 which enabled the Governor-General to indefinitely keep in custody, without trial, individuals suspected of threatening peace. This was no doubt an early instance, if not the origin, of what now flourishes under the name of preventive detention law.[220] Once again, the only forum where all these immunities and powers could be appealed to was His Majesty-in-Council.

The East India Company and the Hastings Trial

This section raises the question as to how, if at all, one could legally account for the actions of the Company through a study of the infamous trial of Warren Hastings. The trial proceedings archive the difficulties involved in judging Hastings, but simultaneously establish yet again the unimpeachable fact that the East India Company and its officers were subject to British laws, principles and institutions. It is another matter that at the end of the trial, in the face of the enormity of issues that remained unresolved, the question may be asked whether any principles or procedures were left in the wake of the Company's actions, and whether indeed it was not true that actions in India were consciously screened from thorough constitutional and legal scrutiny at the altar of the financial, commercial and military-strategic interests of empire.

In 1773 parliament had passed – in the midst of a great deal of investigation and discussion – the Regulating Acts, which indirectly conceded that it was the violent abuse and excesses of the Company's ventures that urgently demanded fundamental administrative and structural reform in the form of such regulation. The resulting statutory acts however invoked antinomies of their own making. On the one hand, as demonstrated above, it was strongly reaffirmed that Company officials were subject to legal scrutiny for their actions in India, *including* in territories that were (nominally) under local sovereigns. On the other hand, the Governor-General was excused from local judicial scrutiny for actions that were performed in his 'public capacity'. No clear criterion was given for the determination of such a capacity.[221]

It is perhaps ironical that Warren Hastings, the first Governor-General, a position born in the attempted reforms and regulations of 1773, was subject to the longest, perhaps the most spectacular and acrimonious political trial ever seen at the House of Lords, charged with crimes ranging from rapine, plunder, corruption to the rampant abuse and misuse of authority. To fully understand the meaning and import of this trial of Hastings, one cannot but interpret it from the perspective of *Campbell v. Hall* and case precedent such as *Postnati*, as much as the history that we have attempted to unravel. These cases definitively outlined the constitutional position of the King in relationship to the East India Company, the King's powers in relations to corporations, as much as his position in relation to that of (King-in) parliament and therein the legal procedures and processes that were laid out in the contexts of conquest and cession. This section outlines the stakes of the court case, and the constitutional and jurisprudential questions involved, through an examination of specific charges – particularly those related to Raja Chait Singh, the Nawab of Awadh and the Begums of Awadh.

While Warren Hastings was impeached by the House of Commons, it is well known that he was also acquitted by the House of Lords. And yet the principle on which he was acquitted is not always acknowledged, let alone analysed. This principle was stated in the following way: acquittal was to follow if 'whenever he appeared to have acted clearly for the public service or whenever any doubt arose so far in point of law, as that the most learned authorities in the House differed in their construction of the law upon the subject'.[222] If the record of the long tumultuous proceedings revealed anything, it was this paradox: precisely because there was no consensus amongst the august lords about what the legal rules were to be followed by the Governor-General in the Indian subcontinent, it was found impossible to hold Warren Hastings culpable by the terms and principles of the trial. This lack of consensus on even legal principles to be applied is documented below. For now it might be stated that in his last address to the House, Burke anticipated this conjuncture, thundering to the assembly that after dragging on for so many long years, the dispute did not lie any longer in the realm of facts but had entered the realm of law.[223] On the facts of war, plunder and extortion, there was no denial.[224] The question was narrowed to whether such conduct was carried out in the exercise of lawful authority and ultimately in public service (to the Company and Britain), or was it merely a case of personal aggrandizement.[225] In fact even here, in framing the question, dissension arose, since it was also held, on the contrary, that as someone in whom 'great power [was] lodged', his actions could not be judged merely by his intentions, 'howsoever pure they might be', but had to be judged according to principles of morality and justice such that not everything could be excused with reference to matters of public exigency.[226] And since no consensus on the precise rights – or the rules for their adjudication – that the Company possessed over native kingdoms and natives existed, all doors to culpability were solemnly shut.

Warren Hastings in his defence of many of the charges brought together several strands of argument. He defended his actions as grounded in the rights of government that were delegated to him, and in the context of the specific charges, he employed the principle that in circumstances of necessity such as war, governments are empowered to act in the ways that he did. Moreover, he emphasized that his actions were undertaken with the knowledge of or under the direction of his superiors in London, the Court of Directors and the 'King's ministers', and the fact that he was reappointed to his position of authority and never reprimanded was clear evidence of their consent and approval of his actions. This set of defences was particularly emphasized in response to two charges. One was the charge that he had illegally extorted money from Chait Singh who was a zamindar under the Company, and whose zamindari had been guaranteed by the Company in an earlier treaty with the Nawab of Awadh, which was subsequently transferred to the Company. And when such money was not forthcoming, he once again illegally – in the sense that no legal procedure was followed – attempted to arrest Chait Singh. The second charge referred to his 'prevailing' over the Nawab of Awadh to dispose the Begums of Awadh of their *jagirs*, even though the Company had earlier guaranteed to secure these very *jagirs*. Hastings argued that both Chait Singh and the Begums were involved in a rebellious plot against the British, and therefore his actions were justified on the principle that governments had the right to arrest, extort money from subjects and violate treaties in such circumstances.[227] Though it was at times admitted by the defence that strict legal proof could perhaps not be found, the prosecutors including Burke demanded evidence for the following of some legal procedure as would be required in cases such as rebellion.[228]

Necessity and right were collapsed together because Hastings argued that he was delegated the absolute and discretionary powers of government, which formed the basis of actions in times of great emergencies such as war.[229] Unlike the neat outline stated by Mansfield in *Campbell v. Hall*, that in a conquest the King had the power to either exterminate or offer protection on his own terms, in the case of the millions of people in the subcontinent there were no clear terms of subjecthood even while massacres and wars were routinely and continually carried out by the Company's arms. Treaties existed, but since war- and peace-making authority were seen to have been delegated, and none of these treaties were explicitly ratified in England by King or parliament, their standing or their ability to legally bind was never clarified. In fact Hastings reiterated the argument that from the position of having been given absolute powers, the East India Company government could abrogate treaties when they thought it necessary, particularly in circumstances such as hostilities and wars.[230] His actions were therefore defended not merely from native precedent, but from what he saw as the rights of a government in relation to subjects and foreign sovereigns.

In relation to the charge regarding Raja Chait Singh of Benaras, the question was also raised as to whether Hastings's demand for money and his attempt to arrest Chait Singh, who held a zamindari under the East India Company at the time, followed any lawful procedure – particularly because the Company had itself initially promised to secure the status of this zamindari, when Chait Singh's father Balwant Singh held it under the jurisdiction of the Nawab of Awadh. This Benaras zamindari was transferred to the Company in 1774 and the specific charges related to the subsequent treatment meted out to Chait Singh by Hastings in the form of monetary exactions and attempts to arrest. Hastings argued in his defence that the Company was sovereign over Chait Singh, who was a subject of the Company as a zamindar. In its capacity as a sovereign government, the Company therefore had the right to require money and aid in the form of cavalry of its subject Chait Singh, and arrest or fine him if he refused such sovereign commands. Such actions were apparently well recognized in the subcontinent, and Hastings argued that such powers of government were even presupposed by British law.[231]

The managers (of the charges) in the House of Lords, on the contrary, first argued that Hastings himself personally had no such right, and that he acted on his own without the mandate or specific permission of the Supreme Council.[232] Furthermore, in his attempt to arrest Chait Singh, Hastings was accused of not following *any* legal process or procedure in terms of which his demands might be justified. These demands themselves, the managers argued, were unreasonable and illegal, and beyond the terms which had secured Chait Singh's zamindari to be transferred to the Company. In so far as there was no due process in his actions when he arrested Chait Singh, Hastings was to have violated all laws, whether 'feudal', British, 'Muhommadan' or 'Gentoo'.[233] His actions could not be justified by any principles of morality or justice, and were therefore culpable. In turn, Hastings insisted on the sovereign rights of the Company as delegated by the Court of Directors, statute and the King's ministers. He defended his actions by claiming that Chait Singh was involved in a rebellion and in such contexts government as such had rights over subjects, whether it be a demand for money or criminal punishment.[234] 'Fining' was an act that the Company government considered legitimate and continued to use, and the instance of Cornwallis's treatment of the Raja of Burdwan was mentioned as evidence.[235] Hastings also made it clear that on all these matters, as a matter of record, he was in constant communication with the Court of Directors, who were superintended by the King's ministers, and therefore their acquiescence to his actions was undeniable.[236] Moreover, even if he were to accept his error in conducting the arrest, no criminality could be attributed to him since there was no definitive proof that criminality characterized his intention, or that he acted for personal and not public benefit, even if mistakenly.[237] Here Hastings was taking advantage of the same statute that granted him legal immunity for his actions in India undertaken in his public capacity. His defenders pointed to the glaring fact that there were no existing laws to regulate conduct and no agreement even on norms or laws that might be established for the future conduct of Company officials. If British governors were usually given strictly defined powers with a set of instructions, nothing of the sort existed with regard to Hastings,[238] who in his position along with that of the Council, combined all civil and military powers. From the ruins of the Company's actions, no guiding spirit of the law could be evoked.

The attempted arrest ended in Chait Singh attacking the British troops and fleeing. This led to an expansion of conflict, with the British attacking his Vidyadurg fortress where his mother and wife lived. In the siege to this fortress, Hastings makes it clear, as discussed above in his private correspondence with Colonel Popham who led the siege, that the army was entitled to the booty as reward. The plunder of the fort and the ill-treatment of the women once again form a major charge against Hastings – as discussed in the previous section. Moreover, ultimately the charge falls not because of a denial of the facts of the case, but because it was held that there was nothing to prove that all these actions were undertaken not motivated by 'public service' but for private aggrandizement. This construal is also put on the Company's role in getting the Nawab to resume/appropriate the *jagirs* of the Begums. The plunder of the jewels and treasure of the Begums, another charge in the trial, are justified because they are meant to have 'rebelled' and been involved in a campaign, along with Chait Singh, to attack the Company.

Once again, the complexities refer to points of law rather than fact –

points of law which had no stated rationale or resolution. What rights did Hastings have over Chait Singh? Could the King's Board of Commissioners, which superintended the Company, be implicated in the Company's actions which had forced the Nawab of Awadh to 'resume' and thereby dispossess the *jagirs* of the Begums so as to repay the 'debt' he owed to the Company? On these issues, and the norms and laws to govern them, there was a wide variance of opinion among the lords of the House. According to one of the judges, since Hastings as Governor-General had not been given any specific mandate, his rule had to be measured by local circumstances, and it would have to be the people of India and Mohamedan judges who would really have the right to try him in the circumstances.[239] This seemed to be a minority position, with most other judges affirming that as a British subject he was entitled to British laws and could only be judged therein – as was indeed testified to by the trial of impeachment.[240] And yet fundamental differences refused to die. Even if Hastings was considered to have a right over Chait Singh not different from that of a sovereign over his subject, could he exercise it in the way that he did without any legal process? Could any legal state, while having rights over subjects, treat them in absolutely any way that they pleased, was a question that was raised time and again in the course of the proceedings. Hastings's defence was that in the light of the war and the rebellion that was looming, in the face of a delicate and dangerous situation of conflict with a range of native powers, at a time when the entire empire seemed to be slipping, he was entitled, even duty-bound, to act precisely in the way that he did.[241] The managers argued that there was no evidence to prove any such rebellion, and in fact, until the attempt at arresting Chait Singh and the actual dispossession of the Begums, the Company appeared to enjoy the best of relations with them.

If the rebellion, apart from other reasons, was used by Hastings as a justification for his actions, a related constitutional-jurisprudential question which had a clear bearing on the dispossession of the Begums involved the determination of actions by the Company in relation to local political entities. The question pertained to whether Hastings's actions as a 'minister of the British Government' was criminally liable in British law, if he were to 'prevail' over a foreign prince in violating the rights of the foreign prince's subjects.[242] The general principle raised therein concerned the question as to whether Hastings could be judged by British laws in his act of prevailing upon the Nawab of Awadh to unjustly acquire the *jagirs* of the Begums, particularly when the *jagirs* had been guaranteed to the Begums by the Company. While, on the one hand, it was held that British laws did not allow the culpability of a British minister if he was to prevail over an independent sovereign to act unjustly on the latter's subject, on the other hand, it was held that in this particular case the Nawab of Oudh could not be construed as an independent sovereign since he was clearly dependent on the Company, militarily and otherwise.

The recent case of *Rafael v. Verelest* in the King's Court was invoked and held to have clarified that Rafael as a native Armenian of Bengal could indeed bring charges against Verelest, a British subject and East India Company governor, for 'prevailing' upon the Nawab of Awadh in wronging him. Citing this precedent, it was considered beyond doubt that Hastings and the British did have power and influence over the Nawab of Awadh, not least because it was British troops that held power in the region. Documentary evidence was also placed on record to show that Hastings had exerted pressure on the Nawab, which indeed had resulted in the dispossession of the Begums' *jagirs*. In such a context, using the precedent of *Rafael v. Verelest* (1774), it was argued that Hastings's actions were not only justiciable but in fact culpable.[243] Other relevant legal precedents would include the observations and conduct of the King's Court in Calcutta regarding the non-sovereignty of the Nawab of Bengal, discussed above, as well as the Act of 1784 which specified that the actions of Company officials in the territories of the native powers were subject to the courts and laws of Britain. Notwithstanding all of this, Lord Thurlow affirmed that Hastings could not be held culpable for the actions of an independent sovereign, a sovereign whose independence was recorded in correspondence and treaties.[244] Thus, once again, a dispute in the very form of law ensured that no legal process could in fact be triggered with the defendant being given the benefit of doubt.

The King, by his patents in 1756 and 1757, had explicitly given the Company rights to Prize as well as conquest and cession, which has already been discussed. One specific constellation of charges against Hastings directly demonstrated the crucial role of Prize money. While in the House of Lords, the Vidyadurg case was discussed, earlier in the House of Commons, Hastings was charged with using the Company's forces as mercenary troops for the Nawab of Awadh in the latter's conquest of the Rohillas. In the course of the war with the Rohillas there is a significant correspondence between Hastings as Governor-General and Colonel Champion as commander-in-chief of the Company's troops.[245] Colonel Champion wrote to Hastings to say that he had heard of a great deal of treasure in the fortress of Pilli (Pilibhit), and that he intended to see precisely how much it consisted of so that the Board and the Nawab may give the soldiers a share of the same as part of their right to plunder, i.e. Prize money. Hastings replied that the very idea of Prize money was disagreeable, but in case of conquest and capture the course that the colonel intended to follow – in applying to the Board and the Nawab – was indeed a lawful one. Colonel Champion replied, in turn, that Prize money was indeed a right that soldiers did have according to the custom and usages of British law, and that it would be both unfair and against sound policy to discontinue it. He further argued that if this custom of Prize money was not followed, chances of the soldiers resorting to indiscriminate plunder might well ensue, especially since the Nawab and his troops had (allegedly) amassed great wealth and treasure on the back of the efforts of the British brigade. In the meantime, the Nawab had written to Hastings and the Board that Colonel Champion and the troops had entered Pilli, and were demanding treasure and money and threatening to plunder the riches that were there. While the Nawab tried to insist that the Company troops had no right to this wealth, he did concede that if indeed they did take away such riches from Pilli this would have to be considered to be in lieu of the payment that he, the Nawab, was to make to the Company for their military-mercenary services.[246]

The Board meanwhile had written to Colonel Champion in no uncertain terms that since the Nawab was the principal in the war, he had a right to every captured fortress and city, and the Company troops could not extort money from those places. Moreover, Prize money was only that which was taken 'by storm', and the soldiers were in any case being paid for their services and therefore not entitled to anything more. Colonel Champion, in his reply to this communication, makes a distinction between the payment of services and the rights that soldiers had to Prize money, which he considered unrelated to any payment that they may receive. He simultaneously writes to Hastings that the Nawab, out of his liberality and gratitude to the British, had paid the soldiers 7 lakhs, even though Hastings makes it clear that he believed this to have been mere extortion during a time of war. The Board sanctions the 'donation' from the Nawab even while expressing misgivings regarding the donation, since it appeared to violate the recently passed Act of Parliament (1784) which explicitly prohibited such donations from country powers. In reply to these stated misgivings, Colonel Champion writes to the Board that in such a context, it might be best to get the Nawab to write another letter. Rather than frame it as a donation, the Nawab might be induced to state that he was merely returning a debt that he owed the British. All the same, Colonel Champion vehemently defends the British soldier's right to plunder, stating that no parliamentary act could undermine such a right. Ultimately, apart from the 7 lakhs of rupees for the brigade, the Nawab ends up paying 3 lakhs of rupees to Colonel Champion personally (which he reveals only later when he returns to the Presidency), and 50,000 rupees to each of the field officers. The Company makes it clear that none of this would be counted as part of the repayment of the Nawab's debt towards itself.[247]

The above gives some sense of the relations between the Company and the Nawab of Awadh in addition to all the material provided to the House of Lords on the dependent status of the Nawab, and the manipulation of such a status in the conquests and governance of the Company. The long and arduous trial spectacularly showcased fundamental differences in points of law. But ironically, nowhere did it lead to a resolution of the difficulties and questions that were raised. If one had expected that, at the least, the long drawn-out trial would lead to the articulation and implementation of a system of laws and channel of accountability whereby the actions of Company officials could clearly be judged, one would be sorely disappointed. To cite one example particularly relevant to this study, in the discussion of Prize money, it was held that there was a *law* of plunder, and the mere taking of the property of individuals during war without the following of a legal process amounted to a criminal act.[248] However, nowhere was this legal process or procedure outlined or followed in the numerous Prize cases in the subcontinent. Disputes arose as to the share or Prize, not to the criminal culpability of actions, as will be demonstrated in the next part of this book too. The Company followed its own rules, only subjecting itself to the King, and grounding its right in the letters-patent of 1757–58. This appeared to be a unique instance of the use of Prize laws for a subcontinent with no judicial process or scrutiny as were clearly laid out in the procedures of the Admiralty Courts. Prize law was applied in a fundamentally new way so as to specifically legitimize the land wars and conquests of the East India Company which were governed and regulated by the letters-patent on Prize awarded and reaffirmed by the King in 1758. Prize as incident to war-making and peace-making remained within the King's prerogative in the subcontinent.

The awarding and distribution of Prize through the Governor-General and not the Admiralty Court ensured that the East India Company's government did not subject itself to any kind of judicial review. This was justified very early on by the argument that relations between two sovereign entities could not come under municipal judicial review. In the case *Nabob v. East India Company* (1793), it was held that the relations between sovereigns could not come under a municipal court without taking into cognizance the possibility of the instrumental fictionalization of sovereign power to screen accountability that had been recognized by several authorities even in England; this case concerned sums of money that the Company was said to owe the Nawab of Arcot.[249] However, nothing prevented a review by the Supreme Court or an Admiralty Court which was to have been adjudicating on the 'law of nations'. Yet no such court was established, notwithstanding the fact that nothing could be termed more urgent, reasonable or just, in the face of the vast territories and innumerable peoples being subjected to the relentless laws of violent plunder.

From the constitutional position outlined by *Postnati* and *Campbell*, since the King did not explicitly avow the treaty, there was no clear stated promise of protection to the people. As discussed above, even the King's Court, in the context of Radhachuran, had explicitly underlined the fact that treaties were used as instruments of oppression and concealment, specifically to exclude accountability. There was certainly no question of the formation of assemblies or representative institutions in relation to the fundamental issue of taxation and revenue which involved property right; issues were to be despotically and unilaterally determined by the Governor in Council. Subjecthood for the natives, as promised in Granada and as seemed to be implied in Mansfield's statement on the consequences of conquest, remained a chameleon-like presence and divorced from the most fundamental quality with which it was otherwise associated, i.e. representation. Wars did not lead to a proclamation by the King, as happened in Granada, to seal a more formal peace. It would be a long time, decades later in 1857, before the Queen promised to guarantee peace and protection. Until then there was little that could be called law in the subcontinent, even in the stated terms of English constitutional principles. There is little doubt that the Company was subject to the Crown, and that it was meant to benefit Britain. Hence, whether by common sense or law, the hand of the Crown (and parliament) in the actions of the Company, even when not visible, was blindingly discernable.

Jurisprudence and case law until Mansfield had a name for this state that seemed an extension of war and stopped short of peace. It was rule by 'natural equity' of the King, which meant that no *settlement* – the framework of law within which the rights of property and protection were embedded – existed. This legal position, if one can call it that, was certainly an apt description of the history of the Company where treaties were abandoned at will, representative institutions denied and clear-cut subjecthood never even promised. Nothing better explains or describes the actions archived by the

Company, including the Hastings trial, which was never denied by Hastings or his lawyers. Finally, if there was one paradigm that could legally form the basis of judging actions, it was 'martial law' under 'civil jurisdiction'. That is to say, when military commanders were judged by civil courts regarding their actions it was to be assumed that they were acting under the best of intentions – unless it could be proved that they acted out of malice, as shown above in the section on military and martial law. Their actions in themselves could not be judged, and this was precisely the argument made by the defenders of Hastings. Ultimately, the condition of martial law as a perpetual state may well be the best legal description of the condition of the conquered regions of the subcontinent.

Jeremy Bentham: Of Kings, Conquests and Colonies

While Bentham's broad critique of common law is well-known,[250] that he closely identified common law with the King, and that he discerned the powers of the King in colonization and conquest, is less analysed. In this context, it is imperative to dilate on his critique by noting that while he critiqued the role of the King in common law and colonization,[251] he believed that one could 'reform' and 'rationalize' law without confronting the historical and inherent diversity of jurisdiction. It is this utopianism – the inability to characterize power as place-making – that sets a paradigm of jurisprudence free of any grounding. The above sets of inter-related arguments, in what Bentham manages to say and what he does not, are now explored through a study of the interweave of three texts: *The Influence of Time and Place in Matters of Legislation* (1781–82), *Emancipate Your Colonies* (1793) and *A Plea for the Constitution* (1803–04). It is important to foreground this critical dimension of Bentham's work so as to evaluate his critique of certain forms of colonization which were accomplished by nothing less than an obfuscation of the very nature of imperial conquest.

In his *Plea for the Constitution*, Bentham forcefully argues that Governors had no legal powers – legislative or juridical – in the recently colonized New South Wales, because no such express powers were given to them by parliament.[252] The argument went that the King could not delegate any such powers since the constitution did not give the King any legislative powers except when sanctioned by parliament, and all legislative powers were vested in that supreme body. Any recognition of the powers of the Governor would in effect be a tacit acceptance of the King's legislative powers independent of parliament. This would be nothing less than a direct violation of the fundamental principles of the constitution, with a result that would imperil hard-won freedoms from the days of the Magna Carta.[253] A specific argument about the King's powers in relation to a specific colony thereby became the site where broader constitutional principles were raised.

Notwithstanding the constitutional arguments with regard to New South Wales, Bentham recognizes that at least until the middle of the eighteenth century, the American colonies were jurisdictional domains where the King did in fact exercise legislative powers through delegation, independent of parliament. Though he questions the principle on which this was based, he admits that the sheer historical fact of royal jurisdiction was undeniable.[254] In the course of the discussion of the King's powers independent of parliament and colonization, Bentham also recognizes the importance of conquest as a legal category. As illustration, much like in *Campbell v. Hall*, he alludes to Jamaica, where the King's right to taxation would be legitimate only if it was considered as conquered territory; the right could not be held valid if it were to be characterized as merely a colony. Here he follows the attorney general's argument in *Campbell v. Hall*, as well as the reasoning of Mansfield's judgment in the case. Bentham argues that none of these arguments could be applied to New South Wales, which was not considered conquered territory. Nor was there any promise of an assembly as was the case in Granada.

Notwithstanding the historical facts and implied constitutional principles, Bentham explicitly argues against the juridical and constitutionalist position on the independent rights of a King in conquest. He proceeds to state that even this 'right' could be open to question.[255] Mounting a speculative counter-history, Bentham charges that the Bill of Rights, the Magna Carta as well as the judicial pronouncement of the St Alban's case (1603) had established the fact that the King could not as such, on his own, legislate without sanction from parliament.[256] In the St Alban's case,[257] Lord Coke had argued that the mayor of the incorporated town St Albans could not arrest the individual Clark under the ordinances because of clause 12 of the Magna Carta, which affirmed the necessity of due process in the case of imprisonment. However, it was held that the mayor had a right to impose a reasonable fine because of Clark's breach of the pronounced ordinances. Bentham interprets this specific judgment to mean that the King could not independently charge a free Englishman and that parliamentary sanction was required for any legislative act of the King.[258] It is not clear how such an inference is to be made as the St Alban's case was limited to voiding the imprisonment of the individual burgher by the mayor as punishment for not abiding by an ordinance requiring a payment, while the decision upheld the right of the mayor (and corporation) to charge a 'reasonable fine'.

Yet Bentham interprets the *common law decision* to mean that parliament had sole legislative power and that the King had no such power independent of parliament. Building on this, he argues that since the American colonies were to be treated as English land, like any manor, there too the King had no right to exercise independent legislative authority.[259] Bentham was reiterating the very arguments that had been definitively voided in *Postnati*, which held that laws could not be uniform and homogeneous across territory, and the diversity of jurisdiction in fact found authority in the King and not the (English) parliament.[260] In making his argument Bentham simply refuses to recognize the existing diversity of jurisdictions and laws in the British Empire, whether through colonization, 'inheritance' or conquest, let alone the unprecedented forms of the Company in the east. The histories and laws of Ireland, Wales and Calais, among several other colonies and outposts, have marvellously vanished in Bentham's deductions. His untenable presumption requires the homogeneity of laws, which is in turn to cause the operationalization of a code – so essentially a part of the Benthamite ideal. Such homogeneity was never to be found. Rather, what jutted unevenly for all to see was the tangled morass of juridical differentiation constituted through bloody wars and contests of the past.

This desperate desire to insist on uniformity, against the facts and laws, is most clearly established in the absence of any serious consideration of the East India Company, the forms of its jurisdictions and the legitimacy of its conquests in the subcontinent – conquests which had been the source of scandal and intense debate within and outside the confines of parliament; and it is not surprising that Bentham refers to the violence of the Hastings regime in only the most fleeting of ways.[261] As discussed above, the entire trial of Hastings made clear that there were fundamental differences even in point of law as to how to judge or apply laws to governors who were directly or indirectly implicated in the devastation and destruction of the lives and properties of millions. Considering this situation, it might appear notably odd that Bentham waxed so eloquently on New South Wales and the illegitimacy of the Governor's actions as the jumping point for his speculative jurisprudence, rather than the massive wars and scandalous corruption that characterized the East India regime of the subcontinent.

In fact Bentham seems to have maintained a studied silence on the issue, even though one would have thought that here was a prime example of the violence of conquest being combined with the powers of the King, the very issue he indicted as a scandal on the constitution. Something on the issue may be gleaned from *Emancipate Your Colonies*, in which Bentham recognizes the close bond between the East India Company and the King. He polemicizes that these colonies might well be beneficial to the Company and the King of England, and this could not be a reason for the French to conquer them, at the cost of 'rapine bloodshed and devastation'. While imploring France to emancipate its colonies, he refuses to promise giving up those of Britain. The Company's conquests are kept out of any scrutinizing ambit by indicating that even if France did give up its colonies, the Company could keep its own. Rather, such conquests are taken as a *fait accompli*, for Bentham argues, 'if it is determined they must have masters . . . and I question whether you would find any less bad ones than our English Company'.[262] In the concerted strategy to repress the rights and nature of British conquests in the east, Bentham joins his illustrious contemporaries, Edmund Burke and Adam Smith.[263]

In addition to the above, perhaps the most stunning screening of the Company's conquests, and their naturalization, can be seen in his *Essay on the Influence of Time and Place on Legislation*. While this text is dressed as an abstract study on the role of place and particularity in matters of legislation, it is in fact, much like *Plea for the Constitution*, a fundamental critique of the King and common law in England. Bentham translates the more abstract question of the role of particularity in matters of legislation into a presupposition and a question. He presupposes that there are the laws of one country that are taken to be the 'standard' and assumed to have the best laws. The more concrete inquiry now is to determine the variations and alterations that would be required to be made to the 'standard' laws to make them into the best possible laws for another country – 'best' not in an abstract sense but in relation to the other country. Becoming even more specific, Bentham assumes that England is the standard country and Bengal the 'target' country to which English laws must be altered so as to best benefit Bengal. Bengal is chosen precisely because it is so different in its particularities of 'climate, mixture of inhabitants, natural productions, face of the country, present laws, manners, customs, religion of the inhabitants',[264] and can therefore serve as a good test.

Bentham is clear that 'complete perfection' is impossible since 'universal accuracy requires infinite detail',[265] and he is well aware that even the same individual event in one place will not produce the same effect in another place. Hence the challenge for the legislator who is concerned with laws has to work on the principles of causes and effects. He would therefore have to construct two tables of the standard and target country, and see the different effects of different offences and punishments such as corporal injuries, confinement, offences in relation to person and property, etc. The different factors influencing these differences would include the physical (climate, topology) and moral (government, religion, manners, etc.). In considering the question as to the suitability of altering the target country's laws in the image of the standard country (which is assumed to be superior), Bentham assumes that any such attempted change would involve 'evils', and so the question raised is whether it is worth it. And even if one were to say that such change is worth it, since the 'evil of the remedy' (of altering laws) is temporary, to let the inferior country's laws remain as it is would be permanent ('evil of the disease'). If convinced by such an argument, another question is in turn raised regarding whether there was indeed any way in which one could assess the loss of present comfort that would necessarily emerge from such suggested alterations, in the face of a future uncertain benefit. Bentham then raises a more radical scepticism when he avers that it might well be possible that the laws of the target country were in fact better suited to it than the laws of the standard country on any one issue. But he once again shows himself to be open to the possibility that the 'inferiority' of Bengal as the target country may with time disappear, and the differences between the two countries – standard and target – might be bridged.[266]

Yet, from these difficult issues assailing the question of the alterations of law to suit place and particularity, that are peppered with concrete examples from several places including England and Bengal, Bentham goes on to make a most surprising turn. While he had begun with the assumption that England as the standard country had the best laws, and argued that to ensure that they could be successfully transferred to another place they had to be so altered as to suit the latter, towards the end he raises the question concretely whether indeed England could be taken as a standard possessing the best laws. Beginning the essay with a proposition about choosing English law as the standard (and the best) since he knew it best, he ends up with a damning critique through a demonstration of this very knowledge. While acknowledging the value of the constitutional branch of English common law, he is excoriatingly critical of the procedures of common law. He then makes the point that the English were not completely aware of the irrationality of their law since they had simply accepted it or been told that they did not understand its intricacies. However, it is in the attempts at transplanting it to

Bengal that Bentham argues about its grave faults which became undeniably visible to everyone, particularly when applied to a people who were not habituated to its absurdities.[267] In making this case of the inherent defects of English common law, Bentham strongly refutes the position that English laws were inapplicable to Bengal as the laws of a free country could not be applicable to a country used to despotic principles. Rather, it is his argument that English laws were full of defects even as they existed in England, and he shows this through specific examples, many of them related to the royal centre of common law.[268] It is in relation to these inherent defects – and not merely to their suitability to Bengal – that 'Asiatic' laws and customs may well fare better, he avers.[269]

Bentham does therefore return to his life-long critique of the King and common law, but does so with scarce cognizance as much as utter indifference to the nature of imperial jurisdictions and their effects on subject populations across the globe. A beginning is thereby made by an abstract critique on principles and the false self-provincialization of analysis, both held to be sufficient to 'reform' the law. But one can find neither an anti-imperial critique as Pitt's interpretation of Bentham would have it, nor an anticipation of 'comparative government' through a discourse of improvement as Chatterjee suggests in his interpretation of *Essay on the Influence of Time and Place on Legislation*. To ask whether his work did or did not support imperialism only serves to occlude the question of how one is to even understand the nature of empire. It is in this sense that the significance of his work and method lies: in the inauguration of an analytic jurisprudence which takes shape in the epistemic screening of the form and long-standing damaging effects of empire,[270] making it impossible to actually confront, let alone critique, the fulcrum of imperial conquests. What are perceived to be inconsistencies in relation to empire are in fact a function of the inability to see its foundational and constitutive role in the making of England, and the attempt to treat the latter as separable from its imperial infrastructure. In both method and concrete critique Bentham anticipates, in damaging shallowness, those contemporary Americans and non-Americans who thought they were being radically anti-imperialistic in demanding that their military troops return from Afghanistan in the name of economic calculations and anti-militarism, without a moment's reflection on the profoundly violent, historical and structural effects of American empire in the very shaping of the region.

Conclusion

Neither the consistencies nor the failures of Bentham's reasoning helps to uncover or engage with the histories of war or justice that form the matter of imperial jurisdiction traversed in these parts of the book. In this he is far from the writings of Locke and Hobbes, and even his nearer contemporaries, Blackstone and Adam Smith. Bentham's critique of the King is bereft of the cognition of the stakes of the matter, and is far removed from the concrete institutional arrangements and their sustaining legal rationalizations. It therefore functions as a blind. The blinds are closed on Blackstone's *Commentaries*, which carry the tensions between the prerogative of the King and the absolute authority of parliament, and manifest in Mansfield's judgment in *Campbell v. Hall*. These tensions shape and conceal the forms of jurisdiction, historical and otherwise, which testified to the independent powers of the King – and this was to be seen not merely in terms of distinct territorial orders, like the East India Company or the American colonies, but also substantively on questions of military and martial law.

Yet Bentham is certainly building, even when fictively, on Mansfield's and Blackstone's attempts to subordinate the King in his sole capacity to the institution of the parliament of Great Britain. A comprehension of this attempt cannot be located within a larger abstract competition between King and parliament, but has to account for concrete territorial-jurisdictional orders. If *Postnati* had confirmed that in the person of the King lay the unity of the diversity of territorial-jurisdictional orders, Blackstone and Mansfield embodied the attempt to place the parliament of Great Britain as the ultimate legislature. This was no easy task given the territorial orders that were initially unrelated, or only obscurely so, to the English parliament and what later became the parliament of Great Britain. Not merely the colonies but also conquered territory, and therein the ambiguity in Blackstone and Mansfield, which took the form of pertaining to the specific question of the forms of law required in territories conquered or colonized. Particularly in cases of conquered populations, how was one to recognize and accommodate the property and laws of native populations?

Postnati had framed the problem of jurisdiction by recognizing the King's powers in conquest but at the same time abridging it through subjecthood that could only take shape in the form of consent. The authority to tax could only emerge from the specific place in which one lived, since only thereby was consent in the form of assemblies enabled. No doubt, this was only for the free, and in Coke's ringing words, 'What a word is that franchise? The lord may tax his villain high or low, but it is against the franchises of the land, for freeman to be taxed, but by their consent in parliament. Franchise is a French word, and in Latin it is Libertas.'[271] As is well known, this conceptualization of the propertied having this right guaranteed through legislation on matters of taxation formed the basis of the House of Commons and its power in the eighteenth century; laws were therefore formulated through King-in-Parliament. Only a miniscule proportion from Britain – and there remained no conception of the nation as a self-governing unit that can only emerge with democratic principles of equality – was represented. And people were disenfranchised on religious grounds. In order to make sense of the power and effects of the English parliament working in conjunction with the King, one cannot remain confined to the regions of Britain and take full account of the workings of King and empire. It is in this context of the nexus between liberty, property and representation that the American colonies resisted British parliamentary taxation. The idea that liberty and property required local self-representative legislation, in conjunction with the King, could be traced back to the fact that it was ultimately the King who was to uphold the unity of diverse jurisdictions and not the representative assembly of one locality, namely Britain. It was this distinction made in the American discourse up to a point regarding the restraints on trade, such as the Navigation Laws and the direct extraction of revenue in the form of taxation, that gives one an insight into the problems of law, property and representation, shedding some light on the scandal of the East India Company. Needless to say, it was such diversity in jurisdiction that enabled a flourishing slave trade as much as the violent conquest of native populations that unfortunately cannot be addressed here, even if they must be flagged as critical registers on which to evaluate the more totalitarian stories of Euro-American liberties and their march.

While the letters-patent of 1757–58 recognized the 'property in the soil' as derived from local grants, the King's distinctive powers of sovereignty over subjects and settlements were asserted. However, the statutes of 1773, 1781 and 1784 declared the authority of the Governor-General and Council as a court to be able to frame laws that would affect the revenue of local populations. Even the territories under native princes were territorialized as specific jurisdictions of the King and King-in-Parliament. While framed as 'judicial regulations', these were in fact the basis of the so-called revenue settlements notorious for their devastation of the lives and livelihoods of the populations subject to them, most clearly visible in the famines of the period.

While the defining feature of property – as that which involved representation and legislation through which the right could exist – was extinguished, even so locals were anointed proprietors responsible for paying revenue. Not only was any 'consent' and representation missing, even the government authorities in the form of the East India Company and their agents were granted legal immunities from 'local' authorities including the Supreme Court. Appeal could only be made to King-in-Council, and there was no place for parliament in this chain of authority. The nexus between King and King-in-Parliament as forming the basis for the Company's governance and conquests on a subcontinental scale renders any plot about the growth of representative principles and parliamentary authority at the expense of the King and autocracy nugatory.

Moreover, the framework of Prize jurisdiction and military government added to the destruction of any form of property for the natives and the legal immunities for the government noted above. As will be shown more clearly, the indefiniteness between war and peace, as must be the case as long as the King does not announce the peace through proclamation or enter into a treaty, meant that the legal condition of the subcontinent could be construed as one of perpetual war. This is directly articulated in the court cases discussed in the next part, where the highest authorities declared that Prize or the appropriation of property could not be challenged if there was no clarity about the termination of war, and therein Prize jurisdiction – yet another way in which the Company imperilled and annulled property in its rule. In short, Prize enables one to liberate the true history of property from the myths of the nation and state as *sui generis* entities.

If there is a discernable attempt in subjugating the King to King-in-(British)Parliament, what in effect was being instituted is a sect and property limited '*national*'-*imperialism* that might well be directly contrasted with the ideas of national-popular sovereignty that emerged in the time of the French Revolution. The King remained central, even in his sole capacity and not merely as an essential constituent of King-in-Parliament. He retained prerogative, war- and peace-making powers. He had a quasi-legislative authority over the army and could declare martial law. Allegiance was owed to his person, and treason and sedition once again referred to his person. Nothing but the King could be seen as unifying the diversity of territorial jurisdictions that composed the empire. This meant that no other doctrine except that of the 'corporation sole', the King's bodies, corresponded to the facts of the matter. There was little else that could work as a conceptual language that described both what the empire was and how it conquered.

Bentham's legacy therefore has to be interpreted as epistemological rather than judicial, and it is this legacy of not scrutinizing the origins and formations of juridical terrains that allows the conquests of the Company to slip through the grill of analysis. While economic histories of colonial India generally see the great 'settlements' as revenue arrangements, this misses out on the key juridical and constitutional questions at play. A settlement, as well recognized by jurists, was supposed to be the point at which conquest ended and law emerged. The emergence of law was the recognition of right and property, which itself would have to take the form of some kind of representation. This would also be the birth of a kind of protection and subjecthood, ideally announced by a royal proclamation. Nothing of this sort happened in India until 1857. For about a hundred years, the Company's administration supervised by the Board of Commissioners, the King's ministers, unilaterally determined revenue demand and thereby voided the fundamental principle well codified since *Postnati*, that taxation required a legislative-representative enactment of some kind. In concentrating all powers in the Governor-General, there was no formal recognition of subjecthood, and this was implicitly obfuscated by ambiguities with regard to the claim of sovereignty by the Company. None of this ambiguity detracted from policies and actions that devastated peoples and territories, while greatly benefiting Britain in general and the mass of Company administrators in particular.

Notes

1 While deriving the Company's legal authority to conquer and enter into treaty, in effect its war- and peace-making powers, from what appears to be the seemingly obscure institution of Prize jurisdiction may surprise current historiography; such was not the case in the past. To give just three instances, one may cite a Justice of the Supreme Court, Justice Chambers, in a case of 1775 (discussed and cited later in this part), the eminent jurist of international law in 1856 (see Robert Phillimore 1855, Vol. III: 153, where it is clearly stated that the East India Company's 'delegated sovereignty' is indicated by the Prize charters given to it),and the case of *Lachmi Narain v. Raja Partap Singh* on 19 July 1878 in the Allahabad High Court, which, without mentioning the word 'Prize', saw in the Prize-giving letters-patent of 1758 the 'most important of the several charters granted to the Company' in relation to the question being examined, i.e. the Crown, sovereignty and territory in India. On the other hand, there is deathly silence on this question in contemporary historiography.

2 Julian Hoppit's *A Land of Liberty: England 1689–1727* (2000: 25) interprets the settlement in the following way: 'After 1688 no monarch however popular could rule as Charles II had ruled or as James II had tried to rule. Yet this was not because princely

wings had been clipped by the Declaration of Rights. Indeed, all monarchs after 1688 had more power at their disposal than had James because they were Protestants, had at least the passive support of the bulk of the nation, and because they were prepared to rule through Parliament. This last aspect was especially important, for whereas James had rightly seen Parliament as a potential check to his authority, after 1688 the legislature was a vital means of exercising the royal will (albeit frequently through ministerial intermediaries). Neither Parliament nor monarch were supine after 1688, nor were they always in harmony, but they did develop a way of working together that stood in dramatic contrast to the pre-Revolution order.' While Hoppit goes on to argue that parliament benefited 'disproportionately' in relation to the King, the argument made in the present book is both the problematic nature of such a comparison, and the necessity to examine the relationship in the light of the broader jurisdictional problem of place and allegiance.

[3] See F.W. Maitland (1908): 304–05, 423–24; notwithstanding differences with Blackstone and Stephen, there is a common recognition of the King's authority in matters of war and peace. Stephen's discussion of treason law in *History of the Criminal Law of England* (1883: 267) may also be mentioned here, where he notes that 'after the revolution of 1688 the fictitious [constructive] interpretation of the offence of compassing the King's death was carried much further than it had been under the Stuarts'. This statutory clarification of royal powers was not unusual, as will be seen later in the discussion of the Mutiny Act and military law.

[4] Perhaps an early instance of this attempt can be seen in A.V. Dicey's argument regarding parliamentary sovereignty in his *Introduction to the Study of the Law of the Constitution* (1889). An indication is given early in the discussion of Blackstone's *Commentaries*, where Dicey argues that not only are the arguments made there regarding the King and his prerogative erroneous in relation to the late nineteenth century, but they are not entirely correct even in relation to the eighteenth century. It is Dicey's argument that English history witnessed the decreasing power of the King and increasing power of parliament – which he recognizes is constituted by the King and the two Houses – to reach the situation of the contemporary period which was marked by parliamentary sovereignty. The resilience of Dicey's argument is evidenced by two recent works. David Armitage interprets, in *Foundations of Modern International Thought* (2013: 139), Blackstone as giving an 'account of parliamentary authority almost Diceyan in its scope', even though Dicey had himself recognized the fundamental tensions in Blackstone's *Commentaries* in relation to royal prerogative, interpreting him in his own way. And more recently, Paul Halliday, in 'Blackstone's King' (2014: 169–88), argues, following Dicey, that Blackstone's conceptualization of the King's prerogative in his *Commentaries* was not applicable to the eighteenth century. Needless to say, the parts in this book present a different picture of the King and his importance.

[5] The vast populations disenfranchised even in Britain on the grounds of property and religion need to be constantly kept in mind.

[6] *A Collection of Charters and Statutes Relating to the East India Company* (1817: 153), 13 Geo III Cap LXIII, section xxxvi.

[7] This was analogous to situations in various forms of territorial jurisdiction, whether the colonies in America, Jersey or the Channel Islands. While the American cases have been discussed, until the late nineteenth century, controversies existed on the precise nature

of the jurisdiction of Jersey and the Channel Islands, as discussed in Charles McIlwain's *American Revolution* (1923). An explicit comparison between the jurisdictions in India and Jersey in relation to the King and Privy Council is made by Herbert Cowell, *History and Constitution of the Courts and Legislative Authorities in India* (1936): 49.

[8] *A Collection of Charters and Statutes Relating to the East India Company* (1817: 153), 13 Geo III Cap LXIII, sections xxxvi, xxxvii.

[9] Ibid., section xxxix.

[10] Ibid.: 204, 17 Geo III Cap LXX, preamble and section 1.

[11] Ibid.: 204, section iii.

[12] Ibid.: 206, sections xix, xx, xxi.

[13] Ibid.

[14] Ibid.: 222, Geo III 24 Cap XXV, section v.

[15] Ibid., section vi.

[16] The concluding analysis of Bentham in this part is very much undertaken in an Ambedkarite spirit which is best captured in his own words: 'Jeremy Bentham was a great legislator; he was a man who indulged in formularies; he was a man who indulged in symmetrical classification of things; he wanted to reform the English law on the basis of pure rationalism. The South American colonies thought that a man who believed in nothing but applying reason and who believed in doing things a priori was a proper person who would be asked to frame a constitution for themselves. They sent emissaries with briefs, I believe, marked, as they usually are for counsel, to draft the constitution. There were innumerable colonies in South America, all spilt out of the old Spanish empire. Jeremy Bentham jumped at the opportunity of drafting constitutions for these new countries in South America. He took great pains and framed the most elaborate documents. I see the Prime Minister laughing, because he knows the facts. And, Sir, they were shipped all these documents, constitutional documents framed by Jeremy Bentham, were shipped over to South America, for the protection of the life and liberty of the people and for the intonement, if I may say so, of the democratic principle. When they went there, they were tried by the South American people for a few years. And afterwards every constitution that was framed by Jeremy Bentham broke to pieces, and they did not know what to do with the surplus copies that had arrived; and all the South American people decided that they should be burnt publicly.' V. Moon, ed., *Dr. Babasaheb Ambedkar: Writings and Speeches* (2014), Vol. 2: 245.

[17] Maitland (1908): 418. As Blackstone writes, it was a fundamental judicial maxim that the King is not only incapable of doing any wrong but even of thinking any wrong (http://avalon.law.yale.edu/18th_century/blackstone_bk1ch7.asp). This maxim was part of the jurisprudential literature well into the nineteenth century, and J. Austin in *Province of Jurisprudence Determined* (2012: 95–105) reaffirms the same.

[18] Maitland (1908: 419–20) notes that prerogative included the authority to make courts of law. More recently, Paul Halliday, in *Habeas Corpus* (2010), has underlined the judicial powers that emerge from the prerogative of the King.

[19] See William Blackstone, *Commentaries on the Laws of England*, Book 1, Chapter 7, http://avalon.law.yale.edu/18th_century/blackstone_bk1ch7.asp

[20] For broad histories and legal justifications of 'martial law' in England, see W.H. Holdsworth, 'Martial Law Historically Considered' (1902) and H. Erle Richards, 'Martial Law' (1902), apart from the references given below.

[21] C.M. Clode, *The Military Forces of the Crown* (1869): 52–53; J.G.A. Pocock, *Machiavellian Moment* (2016): 410–11. Clode was a recognized authority on matters of military and martial law, and cited as such by jurists across the spectrum from A.V. Dicey to Carl Schmitt.

[22] Pocock (2016): 410–11, 459.

[23] Maitland (1908): 455–58.

[24] Clode (1869): 7.

[25] C.M. Clode, *The Administration of Justice under Military and Martial Law* (1874): 50–51.

[26] Blackstone, *Commentaries* (1765), Book 1, Chapter 13; Book 4, chapter 11 Maitland (1908): 455; Clode (1869): 6–7, 31–32.

[27] Maitland (1908): 455–56; Clode (1869): 31; 34–35.

[28] Ibid.: 54–55.

[29] Blackstone, *Commentaries* (1765), Book 1, Chapter 13; Book 4, chapter 11 Maitland (1908): 453–54;Clode (1869):26–27.

[30] Ibid.: 35, 52–55.

[31] Clode (1874): 4–5.

[32] Clode (1869): 19–20, 5–6, 177–78.

[33] This was the standard argumentation formulated by Coke and reiterated by Hale.

[34] Clode (1869): 32.

[35] Ibid.: 31–32.

[36] Ibid.: 33.

[37] Ibid.

[38] Ibid.: 34–35.

[39] Ibid.: 35–36.

[40] Ibid.: 36–37.

[41] Ibid.: 53.

[42] Ibid.: 53.

[43] Ibid.: 37.

[44] Ibid.: 54–55.

[45] Ibid.: 56–57. Other cases had existed prior to the civil wars where no legal penalty was attached to insubordination to superior military offices. See H. Prendergast (1855): 4.

[46] These were commissions authorizing judges to hear and determine criminal cases at the assizes, courts which sat at intervals.

[47] Clode (1869): 56–57.

[48] Ibid.: 76.

[49] Ibid.: 79–82. Every King's minister was responsible to parliament. Parliament decided the number of men in the army in times of peace.

[50] Clode (1874): 19, 142–43; Clode (1869): 4–5.

[51] Ibid.: 84; Clode (1874):21.

[52] Ibid.: 20–21.

[53] Ibid.: 25–26, 177; Clode (1869): 143.

[54] Clode (1874): 177; Clode (1869): 143.

[55] Ibid.: 146–47.

[56] Ibid.: 155–57.

[57] Ibid.: 158.

[58] According to Henry Hallham's *The Constitutional History of England*, Vol. II (1884): 259, in the early eighteenth century, in the wake of the Mutiny Acts, one witnessed in the institution of a 'regular military force', the 'most striking acquisition of power by the Crown'.

[59] Clode (1869): 62–67, 174–75.

[60] Ibid.: 176–77.

[61] Ibid.

[62] Ibid., Vol. II: 147.

[63] Ibid., Vol. II: 155. See also N. Hussain's perceptive and rich discussion of the subject and its implication for India, in *The Jurisprudence of Emergency* (2003): 99-144.

[64] Clode (1874): 186–87; Clode (1869), Vol. II: 125–80.

[65] Ibid.: 177–78.

[66] Clode (1874): 32.

[67] 27 George II Cap. ix. See *A Collection of Charters and Statutes Relating to the East India Company* (1817): 112–13.

[68] Clode (1869): 187.

[69] Ibid.: 179; ibid., Vol. II: 161–62.

[70] On at least three occasions in the eighteenth century – 1715, 1745 and 1780 – martial law was to have been effected, thereby assimilating 'rebellion' (1715, 1745) and 'riots' (1780). Ireland and the colonies from Ceylon to the Morant Bay saw this application in different and multiple circumstances too. For the complex legal mechanisms involving King and statute, see Clode (1869), Vol. II: 163–68. From this, it is clear that Hussain's contention that the 'category of martial law was not applied to Great Britain' and it 'fell into domestic disuse from the Restoration onwards' is difficult to accept. See Hussain (2003): 102–03.

[71] Clode (1869): 85.

[72] Ibid. See also Blackstone, *Commentaries* (1764) Book 3, Chapter 5, http://avalon.law.yale.edu/18th_century/blackstone_bk3ch5.asp. It might also be noted here that an Act of Parliament in 1754 extended the Mutiny Acts, and thereby martial law, to the troops of the Company. The Act thereby once again declared that the Company's power over its forces was derived from the authority of the King – specifically, his prerogative in war- and peace-making authority. In the seventeenth century that King had authorized the Company to use martial law, which it did, but as in certain other contexts, here too in 1754, this authority was given a statutory form. See A.B. Keith, *A Constitutional History of India* (1936): 39.

[73] See Henry J. Bourguignon, *Sir William Scott, Lord Stowell* (1987): 115–72. The following two paragraphs are based on this aptly titled chapter, 'Prize Law: Nationality – A Study in Detail', and its documentation and analyses of the relevant cases. For an earlier detailed study on Prize law as well as the laws and court procedures involved, see Francis Upton, *Law of Nations Affecting Commerce During War* (1861).

[74] Ibid.

[75] *Le Caux v. Aden* in Rt. Hon. Sylvester Douglas Baro Glenbervie, *Reports of Cases Argued and Determined in the Court of the King's Bench*, Vol. I (1813): 594.

[76] Ibid.: 594, 596.

[77] Ibid.: 598–619.

[78] Ibid.: 616.

[79] Ibid.: 613.
[80] Ibid.
[81] Ibid.: 614.
[82] *A Complete Collection of State Trials from the Earliest Period to the Year 1783* (1816): 241–58.
[83] Ibid.: 258–59.
[84] Ibid.: 260.
[85] Ibid.: 244, 258–61.
[86] This was the case with other colonies, and such precedent was found to be the case in Granada when it was under the French King. Ibid.: 261–62.
[87] Ibid.: 263–64.
[88] Ibid.
[89] Ibid.: 264.
[90] Ibid.: 262–63.
[91] Ibid.: 273.
[92] Ibid.: 274. He derived this from James specifically designing such charters to ensure his personal rule, in response to a conversation with Seldon, where the latter denies James's claim that since Ireland was conquered territory, it was his to rule personally; ibid.: 75. As the lawyer later argues in one more acrobatic leap, he would be the last to suggest that the 'jurisdiction of the king in council, as the ultimate judicature, is unconstitutional or void'; ibid.: 276.
[93] Ibid.: 310.
[94] Ibid.: 265.
[95] Ibid.
[96] Ibid.: 282.
[97] As for instance, when it was pointed out that the King/Queen did charge a tax when St Christopher was conquered from the French. Ibid.: 283–84.
[98] Ibid.: 301.
[99] Ibid.: 309.
[100] Ibid.: 307, 309.
[101] Ibid.: 282.
[102] Ibid.: 294.
[103] Ibid.: 296–300, 301.
[104] Ibid.: 295–302.
[105] Ibid.: 298–301.
[106] The argument was made that English criminal laws could be allowed since they were deemed lenient, while more freedom was given in civil aspects. Ibid.: 279.
[107] Ibid.: 313.
[108] Ibid.: 314.
[109] Ibid.: 323.
[110] Ibid.: 89. On the Crown being necessary, see ibid.: 87.
[111] Ibid.: 300.
[112] Ibid.: 323.
[113] For instance, where Mansfield held that, 'Taking these propositions to be granted, he has a legislative power over a conquered country, limited to him by the constitution, and subordinate to the constitution and parliament; and a power to grant or refuse

capitulation. If he refuses, and puts to the sword or extirpates the inhabitants of a country, obtaining it by conquest, the lands are his; and if he plants a colony the new settlers share the land between them, *subject to the prerogative of the conqueror.* He is *intrusted* with the terms of making peace *at his discretion*; and he may retain the conquest or yield it up, on such condition as *he shall think fit to agree. This is not a matter or disputed right*; it has hitherto been *uncontroverted that the king may change part or all the political form of government over a conquered dominion*' (emphasis added). Ibid.

114 '[N]o dispute ever was started before upon the King's legislative right over a conquest'. *Postnati* is cited, reiterating the distinction between kingdoms of descent and conquest. Ibid.

115 Ibid.: 300.

116 Molyneux's arguments are constantly referred to and the American colonists' argument could almost be heard in the background. Ibid.: 297–98.

117 '[W]e have thought fit to publish and declare by this our proclamation that we have in the letters-patent under our great seal of great Britain, by which the said governments are constituted, gives express power and direction to our governments of our said colonies respectively that, so soon as the state and circumstances of the said colonies will admit thereof, they shall, with the advice and consent of the members of our council, common and call general assemblies within the said governments, respectively, in such manner and form as is used and directed in those colonies and provinces in America which are under our immediate government – and we have also given power to the said governors with the consent of our said councils and the representatives of the people so to be summoned as aforesaid to make constitutions and ordain laws statutes ordinances for the public welfare and good government of our said colonies and the people and inhabitants therefore as near as may be agreeable to the laws of England, under such regulations and restrictions as are used in other colonies . . . and in the mean time said until such assemblies can be called as aforesaid all persons inhabiting in or resorting to our said colonies may be confide in our royal protection for the enjoyment of the benefit of the laws of our realm of England; for which purpose we have given power under our great seal to the governors of our said colonies to erect and constitute with the advice of our said councils respectively, courts of judicature and public justice within our said colonies, for the bearing and determining all causes as well criminal as civil according to law and equity and as near as my be agreeable to the laws of England; with liberty to all persons who may think themselves aggrieved by the sentences of such courts in civil causes to appeal under the usual limitations and restrictions to us in our privy council.' Ibid.: 244.

118 Ibid.: 313.

119 Letters-patent 14th Jan 1758 in IOR/ Home Misc./83, Asia Pacific and Africa Collections, British Library, London (henceforth APAC). An important exception is herein made for subjects of His Majesty or subjects of a European monarch. This will remain a source of tension for future Company governance. See note 1 for key instances of the legal recognition of the significance of this grant and such grants.

120 IOR/Home Misc./83, APAC, London.

121 Sheila Lambert, ed. (1975): XXVI, item 1; also in IOR Home Misc./94, APAC.

122 Ibid.

123 This was not at all an unusual linkage. Many of the arguments for the East India Company's joint stock structure were based on the further argument that joint stock companies

had greater capital, which in turn could be used to spend on military expenditures.

124 Lambert, ed. (1975).There was nothing particularly novel in this, since the earlier charters, such as that of 1683, granted war- and peace-making authority to the Company when it came to 'heathen nations'

125 This demand, requesting for the clarification of the norms required for recapture and Prize money, is to be found in IOR/ Home Misc./94, APAC, London, letter from the United Company, dated 11 October 1756, received Chesterfield 5 June 1757.

126 For the most detailed argument – fully grounded in the colonial archive – on the rationale for Plassey, see Sushil Chaudhury's *Prelude to Empire* (2000). In this and previous work, Chaudhury demonstrates that the conflicts with the Bengal Nawab did not erupt suddenly in the 1750s but had a history which emerged from disputes over trade and jurisdiction.

127 Letter from C. Yorke and C. Pratt, To the Right Honourable William Pitt one of His Majesty's Sec. of State, August 16, 1757, IOR/Home Misc./83, APAC, London.

128 Ibid.

129 C. Pratt and C. Yorke, 24th December 1757, IOR/Home Misc./83, APAC, London. H.V. Bowen, in *Revenue and Reform* (1991): 54, which is an important study of the East India Company in the context of English political institutions, has noted this document, but omits the crucial phrase '*and over the inhabitants as English subjects, who carry with them your majesty's laws*'. Thus, while Bowen notes the distinction between property and sovereignty, he does not adequately note that even in the matter of treaties and grants, the Company acted as subjects of English laws.

130 See the illuminating discussion by P. Halliday and E. White in 'The Suspension Clause: English Text, Imperial Contexts, and American Implications' (2008), on the relevance of Hale's arguments for the distinction between 'property' and 'sovereignty'.

131 C. Pratt and C. Yorke, 24th December 1757, IOR/Home Misc./83, APAC

132 Ibid.

133 Ibid. This was an old trope going back to the Romans 'who were among the most savage war makers in Antiquity, always justified their wars, as far as we can read the historical record, as efforts to vindicate a lawful claim on property that had been wrongly denied to the Roman people, and the ancient records of the Roman rituals for the declaration of war required that a Roman priest repeat three times the *rerum repetitio*, the demand that things be given back'. See J.Q. Whitman's insightful discussion of these matters including Isidore of Saville, citing Cicero to this effect, in *Verdict of Battle* (2012): 109–10.

134 General letter from Court of Directors to Fort St George, 3rd March 1758, IOR/Home Misc/226, APAC, London.

135 General letter from the Court of Directors to Fort St George dated March 8 1758, IOR/ Home Misc/226, APAC, London.

136 Ibid.

137 This illustration of the King as the supreme source of jurisdiction in military matters, including the territories of the East India Company, was reiterated by the Supreme Court when it held in the case of John Dalling, the commander-in-chief in Madras, that 'the royal warrant issued to Dalling by the King[was] above all competing sources of law'; it had also held that while both annual British Mutiny Acts and East India Company Acts would operate concurrently, in any conflict between the two with regard to royal soldiers, the former would prevail. See Manu Sehgal's *Creating an Early Colonial*

Order (2021): 105–06, for a detailed account of the broader effects and grounds of militarization and war-making in the context of East India Company conquests, themes on which there has otherwise been insufficient attention.

138 Letter from Piggot, Clive, Orme, Smith, to Aldecron, 3rd September 1756, in IOR/Home Misc./94, APAC, London.

139 Ibid.

140 Fort St George Select Consultations 29th Sept, IOR/Home Misc./226, APAC, London.

141 Ibid.

142 For a historical context of the Anglo–Maratha naval conflicts, see Anirudh Deshpande, 'Limitations of Military Technology: Naval Warfare on the West Coast, 1650–1800' (1992), and Patricia Risso, 'Cross-Cultural Perceptions of Piracy: Maritime Violence in the Western Indian Ocean and Persian Gulf Region during a Long Eighteenth Century' (2001).

143 Fort St George Select Consultations 29th Sept, IOR/Home Misc./226, APAC, London.

144 The full title of the act was 'An Act for the Better Supply of Mariners and Seamen to serve in his Majesty's ships of war, and on board merchant shops and other trading ships and vessels'. It should be recalled here that in 1754, an Act of Parliament was passed that placed the Company under the Mutiny Acts, therein declaring that the Company came under the direct authority of the King's war- and peace-making authority.

145 *The Parliamentary history of England from the earliest period to the year 1903*, Vol. XV, 1753–65: 567–68. Of course this was what Siraj Ud Dowla also construed as a hostile act in 1756.

146 Ibid.: 560–61.

147 Interestingly, in the course of the war with France, Mansfield as Chief Justice allowed for the questioning of the activities of press-gangs by invoking *Habeas Corpus*. See Halliday (2010): 113–14.

148 *The Parliamentary history of England from the earliest period to the year 1903*, Vol. XV, 1753–65: 567–68.

149 Ibid.: 616.

150 This is however not to suggest that there were any clear and self-evident lines between privateers and pirates. On this see, for instance, Lauren Benton, *A Search for Sovereignty* (2009), and the argument regarding 'legal posturing'.

151 The Company's application for Prize is however not unusual since the Company was a chartered company.

152 De Martens, *An Essay on Privateer, Captures and particularly on recaptures* (1801): 176. On the legislative penetration of Prize, see also R.G. Marsden, 'Early Prize Jurisdiction and Prize Law in England' (1909).

153 'The captain or captains of any of his Majesty's ships or vessels of war who shall be actually on board at the taking of any prize is entitled to 3/8ths parts; but in case such capture be made by any of his Majesty's ships or vessels of war, under the command of a flag or flags, the flag officer or officers being actually on board, or directing and assisting in the capture shall have one of the said 3/8ths parts; such 1/8th part to be paid to the said flag officer or officers in the proportions, and subject to the regulations which will be specified in a subsequent page. The captains of marine and land forces, sea lieutenants and master on board, are entitled to 1/8th part.' See T.H. Horne, *A Compendium of the State Laws* (1803): 71–74.

[154] These were of course the most sensational cases documented in IOR/Home Misc./83, APAC, London. One particular case worthy of mention is the Rohilla war, where Shuja Ud Dowla was forced to give the commander-in-chief Colonel Champion, rupees 7 lakhs as a gift.

[155] See *The History of the Trial of Warren Hastings, Esq. Late Governor-General of Bengal* (1796): 19. The letter is cited; the testimony of Fox Clafraft, Aid de Camp to Major Popham, testifies to the same (ibid.: 23). This is discussed in greater detail below in the section devoted to an analysis of the impeachment proceedings at the House of Lords.

[156] Letter from Court of Directors to Governor in Council Fort St George, 24th August 1804, IOR Home Misc./83, APAC, London.

[157] Letter from George Harris to Lord Viscount Castleragh, President of the Board of Control 1804, March 7th, 1804, IOR Home Misc./83, APAC, London.

[158] *First Report from the Select Committee*: 41. In the same report (ibid.), it might be worth documenting Munro's martial spirit in quelling mutiny; in his own words, 'I immediately ordered their officers to pick me out 50 of the worst characters and who they thought might have enticed the battalion to desert to the enemy; they did pick out 50; I told them to pick me out 24 of these 50 worst characters; I immediately ordered a field court marshal to be held by their own black officers, and after representing to the officers the heinous crime the battalion had been guilty of, desired they would immediately bring me out their sentence; they found them guilty of mutiny and desertion, sentenced them to suffer death, and left the manner to me; I ordered immediately four of the 24 to be tied to the guns, and the artillery officers to prepare to blow them away ; there was a remarkable circumstance, four grenadiers represented, as they always had the post of honour, though they were intitled to first be blown away; the four battalion men were untied from the guns, and the four grenadiers tied and blown away, upon which the European officers of the battalions of sepoys, who were in the field, came and told me, that the sepoys would not suffer any more of their men to be blown away; I ordered the artillery officers to load the four field pieces with grape shot and dew up the Europeans with the guns in their intervals; desired the officers to return at the heads of their battalions; I ordered them immediately to ground their arms, and if one of them attempted to move, I would give orders to fire upon them, and treat them the same as if they were Shujahdowlah's army – they did ground their arms, and did not attempt to take them up again, upon which I ordered 16 more of the 24 to be tied to the guns by force, and had them blown away the same as the first was done; I immediately ordered the other four to be carried to a cantonment where there had been a desertion of sepoys some time before, with positive orders to the commanding officers at that cantonment to blow them away in the same manner at the guns, which was accordingly done and which put an end to mutiny and desertion.' Such discipline would of course be repeated, most famously, in the 'Mutiny' and its 'quelling' of 1857–58.

[159] Letter from George Harris to Court of Directors, 15th December 1804, IOR Home Misc./83, APAC, London.

[160] Letter from Court of Directors, 24th August 1804, IOR Home Misc./83, APAC, London.

[161] Letter from George Harris to Court, 15th December 1804, IOR Home Misc./83, APAC, London.

[162] P/A/7 163–64, 278.

[163] See Peter Marshall, 'The Making of an Imperial Icon: The Case of Warren Hastings' (1999): 1–16. While Marshall provides the information regarding the importance of the 'Crown' in Hastings's scheme of governance that is important to note, it will be clear that the present argument is completely at odds with Marshall's own claim that Hastings indeed could be legitimately retrieved as a benign, well-intentioned 'imperial icon'.

[164] A.B. Keith (1922), Vol. I: 45–60.

[165] P.K. Nayar (2007): 1.

[166] See M.P. Jain (1966) and B.B. Pandey (1967).

[167] See J.D.M. Derrett, *Religion, Law and State in India* (1999). Even so there was no necessity that the opinions of the Pandits would be followed, and in this, according to Derrett, the Company courts saw themselves as the court of common pleas or the King's Bench (both royal courts), because other common law courts which adjudicated on issues of inheritance needed to follow the opinion of the Bishop once the latter's view was sought in any manner.

[168] The best discussion remains N.K. Sinha, *Economic History of Bengal* (1962) and Ranajit Guha, *Rule of Property for Bengal* (1963).

[169] See Sirajul Islam (1979).

[170] On the important implications of the inter-relations between civil law, property law and revenue, see Despina Iliopoulou, 'The Uncertainty of Private Property: Indigenous versus Colonial Law in the Restructuring of Social Relations in British India' (2001) and Nandini Bhattacharya-Panda, *Appropriation and Invention of Tradition* (2008).

[171] Letter to Lord Mansfield, Fort William, 21 March 1774, cited in G.R. Gleig, *Memoirs of the Life of the Right Hon. Warren Hastings, First Governor-General of Bengal* (1841), Vol. 1: 399–404. This is cited by Bhattacharya-Panda (2008).

[172] Ibid.

[173] See the references mentioned in notes 169 to 171 above.

[174] *A Plan for the administration of justice extracted from the proceedings of the committee of circuit 15 August 1772*, in G.W. Forrest, ed., *Historical Documents of British India* (1985), Vol. 2: 112–15. The opinions of natives were therefore not independent of the Company in terms of either framework or, ultimately, even substance.

[175] D. Washbrook's influential essay, 'Law, State and Agrarian Society' (1981), is wholly misleading in this context, since the 'public law and the 'private/religious law' could hardly be distinguished but in fact worked as a function of the interests of the Company state which unilaterally determined the nature of property (whether 'permanent' or 'temporary') as much as religion. This nexus being a function of the Company state is insightfully demonstrated in Bhattacharya-Panda (2008) and Iliopoulou (2001).

[176] While the system of courts established in 1772 is familiar to every undergraduate student of Indian history, the supremacy of the President and Council and its control is scarce alluded to in such pedagogy. Recently, Jon Wilson's argument (in *Domination of Strangers*, 2010: 53) about Hastings's 'experiential political epistemology', i.e. the recognition of zamindari right, does not account for the absolute right that the Company had arrogated to itself based on its military might; a fact that, while not recognized by Wilson, was clearly recognized and affirmed by Hastings. This would make an 'experiential political epistemology' an unmitigated despotism, which was in fact the case.

[177] See S.F.C. Milson, *Foundations of Common Law* (1969), which traces the power of the royal courts through various kinds of 'writs'.

[178] The Emperor's grant was a grant of *diwani*; it referred to revenue collection, nothing else. One might also remember that this Emperor, just a few years ago (when he was not yet Emperor), was defeated by the Company's armies in his campaigns in Bihar.

[179] While the Judicial Plan of 1772 had said that certain 'civil' topics were to be administered to Hindus according to the laws of the Hindus, the form in which these laws were applied was dictated by Company interest. Revenue was however unilaterally and directly determined by the Company and Rammohan Roy had early on critiqued the damaging ways in which 'Hindu' inheritance laws and revenue demand intersected, voiding any promised property right to the native, thereby in a sense anticipating some of the arguments of Iliopoulou (2001), as I argue in a forthcoming essay.

[180] As J. Baker (1971): 13 argues, 'The great step forward was in the author's [text attributed to Glanvill] treatment of the fixed customs of the king's court as constituting *jus et consuetude regni*, the law and customs of the realm.' In the eighteenth century, Blackstone defined written law, or statute, as 'either declaratory of the common law or remedial of some defects therein'; see W. Blackstone, *Commentaries on the Laws of England* (1765), Introduction, http://avalon.law.yale.edu/18th_century/blackstone_intro.asp#1

[181] See David Lieberman (1989): 86–94.

[182] See Baker (1971), Hussain (2003) and Halliday (2012).

[183] Thus it would not be accurate to write, as Travers has done in *Ideology and Empire* (2007:185), that 'The judges in Bengal were eventually caught on the horns of a new legal dilemma: how to provide judicial review for colonial administration without being seen to encroach on the indigenous custom and law.' It was Hastings who would pose the issue in this way so as to later accuse the Supreme Court of actual encroachment. Impey, as is shown below, saw no necessary contradiction between law and custom, but thought it to be in the nature of law to provide justice that might have to do away with customs found to be against the interests of justice.

[184] For details of the case, which originated before Nandakumar's accusations against Hastings, and the establishment of the Supreme Court, see James Fitzjames Stephen, *The Story of Nuncomar* (1885) and Pandey (1967).

[185] Letter from Impey, 6th May 1775, *Impey Letter Book*, Vol. 16265, British Library, London.

[186] Letter from Impey, 15th May 1775, ibid.

[187] Stephen (1885): Vol. 1: 78–79. This has been more recently documented by Pandey (1967).

[188] Stephen (1885): Vol. 1: 233–61. This evaluation has been reaffirmed in the most recent detailed studies of the subject.

[189] This critique of the conspiracy theory between Impey and Macaulay has also been convincingly questioned more recently by Pandey (1967): 100–10, a position that also appears to have been accepted by J.D.M. Derrett in 'Nandakumar's Forgery' (1977). Both view Impey's conduct as beyond (judicial) reproach, Derret faulting him for applying a principle ('Equality before the law') which, to his mind, was most 'un-Indian'; ibid.: 252.

[190] Derrett (1977): 250–52.

[191] Stephen (1885), Vol. 1: 228.

[192] '[T]hough the natives without question are under your general protection they are more immediately so under the protection of the laws'; Letter from Impey, 25 May 1775,

Impey Letter Book, Vol. 16265, Add MS 16265–16267, Western Manuscripts, British Library, London. These lines have been cited by Pandey, *Introduction of English Law into India* (1967), Hussain, *The Jurisprudence of Emergency* (2003), and Halliday and White, 'Suspension Clause' (2008).

193 Impey to Lord Chancellor Bathore, 1st April 1777, Impey Letter Book, Vol. 16265.

194 Ibid.: 153.

195 Impey to Lord Chancellor Bathore, 26th March 1779, Impey Letter Book, Vol. 16265. Impey writes, 'after 4 years of experience it is our unanimous opinion that the corruption depravity avarice rapacity and despotic principles to which British subjects long resident in this country have been naturalized from early youth, and which they have been taught by constant examples and in which they have been strengthened by habits as so universal and the distinctions drawn by the most moderate of them, between themselves and the natives are strong and so injurious to the latter'.

196 Robert Travers, in *Ideology and Empire in 18th Century India* (2007: 186), writes, 'Apart from the prickly British inhabitants, the judges also made enemies by their sometimes clumsy interventions in the party disputes which engulfed the Company's administration in Bengal after 1774.'

197 See, E. Kolsky, *Colonial Justice in British India* (2010), which documents the critique – and the rationale of such critique – of Company governance by British traders/planters/freemen into the nineteenth century.

198 For details, see Pandey (1967).

199 The others included Nandakumar and Roy Radhachuran.

200 Howell, ed. (1816): 1101.

201 Ibid.: 1102.

202 Ibid.: 1106.

203 Ibid.: 1107–08.

204 Ibid.: 1113–14.

205 Ibid.

206 'I do not so much blame him [Radhachuran] as the drawer: it is scandalous, it is flagitious, to let him swear to his being a public minister, an idea which is almost impossible to be explained to him . . . it is not to be endured, that the consciences of the natives, swearing in a foreign language, should be thus ensnared.' Ibid.: 1129.

207 'The East India Company can neither wage war nor receive an ambassador by any intrinsic authority of its own; it does both by the authority of the king of Great Britain, and under sanction of his sovereignty'; ibid.: 1130. 'I should not think myself obliged, whatever might be my private opinion, unnecessarily to decide, that the king my master is not sovereign over these provinces; and to decide that he is, I would wish likewise to avoid, because the parliament seems cautiously to have avoided it by founding the jurisdiction of this court, over those who do not reside in Calcutta or the inferior factories, on personal and not local subjection; and because such a decision might engage in quarrels with the French and other European nations who have possessions in Bengal'; ibid.: 1133.

208 Ibid.

209 Radhachuran was ultimately recommended for pardon in the case and granted mercy.

210 Pandey (1967): 70–71. Illustrious contemporaries like Adam Smith also saw the territorial acquisitions of the Company as the undoubted right of the Crown.

[211] For a detailed discussion, see Herbert Cowell, *History and Constitution of the Courts and Legislative Authorities in India* (1936).

[212] This 'policy' was not a new one and can be traced to Arcot in the 1760s.

[213] William Blackstone, *Reports of Cases Determined in Several Courts of Westminster-Hall* (1828): 983–88.

[214] For a translation of the 'Treaty of Allahabad' describing the 'Diwani' as a 'free gift' and the terms and conditions, see Cowell (1936): 30.

[215] For a discussion of the cases wherein the interference of the Supreme Court was seen as affecting the Company's decisions regarding the all-important question of revenue and revenue collection, see Stephen (1885) and Cowell (1936). Detailed economic histories, referred to in the course of this work, have demonstrated the devastation of the revenue policies on subject populations.

[216] *A Collection of Charters and Statutes Relating to the East India Company* (1817), Geo III 24 Cap XXV.

[217] For an important analysis recognizing the importance of the 1781 Act, see Cowell (1936).

[218] See F. Pollock citing the Bengal Regulations in *Expansion of the Common Law* (1904): 133.

[219] F.L. Beaufort, *A Digest of the Criminal Law of the Presidency of Fort William* (1875): 9–10.

[220] This was no doubt the basis of the notorious 1818 Bengal Regulations, which laid the foundations for subsequent preventive detention laws – or laws enabling arrest and confinement without judicial review – right until the present.

[221] *A Collection of Charters and Statutes Relating to the East India Company* (1817), 17 Geo III Cap LXX, preamble and section 1.

[222] This was read out by Lord Walsingham as Chairman of the Committee. See *The History of the Trial of Warren Hastings, Esq. Late Governor-General of Bengal* (1796), Part VIII: 256.

[223] Ibid., Part VII: 122.

[224] In 1781, two committees were appointed to enquire into the 'maladministration of the Company's affairs'. Henry Dundas, chairperson of one of the committees, spoke in the House of Commons about the 'impropriety of the Company's presidencies in undertaking their military operations with a view to conquest only – their breaches of and disregard of treaties – their peculation and scandalous oppression of the native – and the criminal relaxation that prevailed among the Directors at home'; ibid.: vi. Dundas also moved parliament for a specific resolution 'for the recall of Mr. Hastings', because of the 'act of the most flagrant violence and oppression and of the grossest breach of faith committed by the former against Chait Singh, Raja of Benares'; ibid.: vii. However, since this required the Court of Directors to act, they were prevented from doing so by voting against the measure. The reports of the second committee led to the proposal for Fox's Bill which was passed by the House of Commons but defeated in the House of Lords because of the 'secret influence of the Crown'. Hastings finally submitted to the resolutions of recall. He was 'not impeachable for his conduct in relation to the Rohilla war, impeachable in relation to the raja of Benares, impeached for the accepting of presents and "extorting and amassing money"'– Burke moved the motion that he be impeached, which was agreed to; ibid.

225 This was the view of Lord Thurlow; ibid., Part VIII: 159.

226 This was the view of the Lord Chancellor; ibid.,Part VIII: 160.

227 Although Hastings's lawyers did admit that, 'if anyone asked to bring strict legal proof of the existence of a design some time ago to overturn this happy constitution he might not be able to do so yet the fact was of such notoriety that an association had been formed throughout the kingdom to counter the design'; ibid., Part VI: 45.

228 Ibid., Part VII: 125.

229 Ibid., Part IV: 86–101.

230 Ibid., Part IV: 89.

231 Ibid., Part IV: 88; lawyers too argued that Hastings's actions were 'sanctioned by every government in India'.

232 Ibid., Part VII: 125.

233 Ibid.; see also Part VII.

234 Ibid., Part IV: 88–101.

235 Ibid.,Part V: 17.

236 Ibid., Part IV: 88–89, 91, 97, 101. Both Hastings and his lawyers harped on the irrefutable point that Hastings was in continuous communication with his superiors in London, including the King's ministers; ibid., Part V: 5–6, 35.

237 Ibid., Part IV: 98.

238 Ibid., Part VIII: 175–76.

239 Ibid., Part VII: 177–78.

240 Ibid., Part VIII: 175–76.

241 Ibid., Part IV: 101.

242 Ibid., Part VIII: 186.

243 Ibid., Part VIII: 192–93.

244 Ibid., Part VIII: 198.

245 APAC, Home Misc/83 Secret Consultations, Extracts of Correspondence, 1774.

246 Ibid.

247 Ibid.

248 *The History of the Trial of Warren Hastings, Esq. Late Governor-General of Bengal* (1796), Part VIII: 183–86.

249 *Nawab of Arcot v. East India Company*. The judgment held that, 'Political treaties between a foreign state and subjects of the crown of Great Britain, acting as an independent state under powers granted by charter and act of parliament, are not a subject of municipal jurisdiction; therefore a bill founded on such treaties by the Nabob of Arcot against the East India Company was dismissed.' See https://swarb.co.uk/nabob-of-the-carnatic-v-east-india-company-28-jan-1793/

250 For an insightful study, see David Lieberman, *The Province of Legislation Determined* (1989).

251 Eric Stokes's detailed work, *The English Utilitarians and India* (1959), remains the most thorough study of the subject of Bentham and the British in India.

252 J. Bentham, *Writings on Australia, VI. A Plea for the Constitution* (2018): 17–23.

253 Ibid.: 27.

254 As Bentham writes, mourning the fact that history has disobeyed his ideas, 'Be this as it may, what is certain, is – that the question is still open, notwithstanding the decision in the *Granada* case: because in that case, though an opinion was given, affirming the

right of the Crown to legislate in case of conquest, that opinion was not necessary to the decision then pronounced. How much better for this country, as well as so many other countries, would it have been, if instead of fishing for drops of sense out of the extrajudicial ravings of Lord Coke, men of law had attended – on the one hand to the direct decision of the judicial authority as reported, in sober though very energetic language, by the *same* God of their idolatry, in the *St. Alban's* case; on the other hand, to that of the legislative authority, as displaying itself in the *Bill of Rights*! If they had, nothing in the way of legislation would, from first to last, have been done in English-America, but *by* Parliament, or with *express* authority from Parliament. It would not then have been so much as dreamt of, that it was in the power of the King, by confederating with a part of his subjects, withdrawing themselves for this purpose to a vacant territory remote from the eye of Parliament – that it was in the power of his law-servants, by any such management, to oust Parliament of its rights: I mean its exclusive right of legislation, as established in the *St. Alban's* case. Dissension would then have been nipped in the bud: and the American war, with all its miseries, and all its waste of blood and treasure on all sides, would have been saved'. Ibid.: 50–51.

255 'Another point which, being at liberty to speak to it or not, he [Mansfield] thought fit to speak to, was – that *if matters had been otherwise*, such power *would have been* legal. If, in humble imitation of such high and sincerely respected authority, and in precisely the same view, viz. that of seeing important constitutional questions settled on the broadest and most solid grounds, it may be allowable for an obscure ex-lawyer, on this same ground, *to travel*, as the phrase is, *a little way out of the record*, I will venture to state it as a question, which notwithstanding the opinion so distinctly given by that great lawyer in the affirmative, remains still quite open, whether, even in the case of *conquest*, in any colony acquired since the Revolution, *Trinidad* for example, the right of the King to legislate without Parliament – I mean without express authority from Parliament– would, *in case of dispute*, be found maintainable in law.' Ibid.: 50. Here Bentham is not merely hectoring the legal understanding of the early seventeenth century but also the decided case of 1774, finding fault once again with Mansfield's recognition of the King's status and power. He does not dwell on the facts of the proclamation – and the legal and institutional effects thereby unleashed – but merely focuses on the Quebec Act once again to reaffirm the ultimate power of parliament.

256 Ibid.

257 *Clark's Case* (1596) Trinity Term, 38 Elizabeth I In the Court of Common Pleas. First published in the Reports, volume 5, page 64a. It is so brief that the whole text can be cited here. 'In an Action of false Imprisonment brought by Clark against Gape; the Defendant justified the imprisonment, because King Edward the sixth incorporated the town of Saint Alban's by the name of Mayor, &c. and granted to them to make Ordinances; And shewed, that the Queen appointed the Term to be kept there, and that they with the assent of the Plaintiff and other Burgesses, did assess a summe on every inhabitant for the charges in erecting the Courts there; and ordained, That if any refuse to pay it, that he should be imprisoned, &c. and because the Plaintiff being a Burgess, &c. refused to pay, &c. he as Mayor justified; And it was adjudged no plea, for this Ordinance is against the Statute of Magna Charta, cap. 29. Nullus liber homo imprisonetur; 1 which Act hath been confirmed above 30 times, and the Plaintiff's assent cannot alter the Law in such Case; But it was resolved, that they might have inflicted a reasonable penalty, but not

imprisonment, which penalty they might limit to be levied by distress, or by Action of Debt; and the Plaintiff had Judgment.' See https://oll-resources.s3.us-east-2.amazonaws.com/oll3/store/titles/911/0462-01_LFeBk.pdf

258 Bentham (2018): 47.

259 Ibid.: 30. Bentham again cannot help recognize that his interpretation was never deployed: 'The right of thus granting away the powers of Parliament passed (it is true) unquestioned. Why? because nobody ever started up, to whom it had happened to conceive himself as being concerned in interest to question.' But he does not recognize that his interpretation was not followed because it would have been meaningless to the jurisprudence of the seventeenth or even eighteenth century, particularly in this *form* of hectoring to the past.

260 Ibid.: 30–31, 51–52.

261 Bentham (2018). Bentham writes, 'Other reasons against distant dominions may be found in a consideration of the good of the government. Distant mischiefs make little impression on those on whom the remedying of them depends. A single murder committed in London makes more impression than if thousands of murders and other cruelties were committed in the East Indies. The situation of Hastings, only because he was present, excited compassion in those who heard the detail of the cruelties committed by him with indifference'; see https://www.laits.utexas.edu/poltheory/bentham/pil/pil.e04.html. While Jennifer Pitts, in 'Legislator of the World? A Rereading of Bentham on Colonies' (2003), cites the above as a convincing instance of Bentham's critique of imperial rule, several of her other readings have been questioned below, as her more general contention that Bentham was an anti-imperial thinker.

262 Jennifer Pitts, in the context of this paragraph in Bentham's text (ibid.: 211–12), moves from stating that he '*also expresses some doubts* about Indians' capacity for self-government' (emphasis added), to argue that Bentham ends up demanding that 'France sell its Indian possessions to the British East India Company'. Her citation of Bentham stops at the colon and skips the last crucial clause in the sentence which has here been italicized: 'If it is determined they must have masters, you will then look out for the least bad ones that could take them: *and after all that we have heard, I question whether you would find any less bad than our English company*' (emphasis added). Bentham makes a much clearer argument about the unlikelihood of the French being able to 'plant' rights of self-government in India because of the nature of the culture and people there. From here, inferring that Indians 'must have masters', a much clearer and stronger case for the Company is made. Bentham's argument in this text for English imperial colonization is not accounted for in Pitts's argument even while elsewhere she herself cites Bentham's other works, 'Institute of Political Economy' and 'Official Aptitude Maximized – Expense Minimized', where (ibid.: 210–11) she acknowledges Bentham's argument regarding the benefits of British rule. In such a context, her broader argument about the 'turn to empire' being essentially a nineteenth-century phenomenon is difficult to defend.

263 With regard to Smith, Pitts's interpretation conflates the critique of colonization and the East India Company regime with a critique of empire, and therefore sees similarities between Bentham and Smith that do not exist (Pitts 2003: 206–08). In this case too, in her citation of Smith, as I have shown elsewhere, Pitts omits to note a crucial clause which demonstrates the fact that Adam Smith saw the conquests in the Indian subcontinent as the 'right of the Crown' rather than the Company, and that these

territories 'might be rendered another source of revenue more abundant perhaps, than all those already mentioned'. See Adam Smith, *Wealth of Nations* (1999): 1026, and 'Revenue, rent…profit? Early British imperialism, political economy and the search for a *differentia specifica* (*inter se*)' (2011): 183 note 14. Partha Chatterjee describes Jennifer Pitts's arguments and agrees with her conclusion that ideologically Smith and Bentham were opposed to empire; see *Blackhole of Empire* (2012b): 177–79.

[264] J. Bentham, *Essay on the Influence of Time and Place on Legislation* (1843), https://www.laits.utexas.edu/poltheory/bentham/timeplace/index.html

[265] Ibid.

[266] Partha Chatterjee cites this passage in Bentham to make the argument that 'The objective in the longer term was improvement, closing, as far as possible, the difference between England and Bengal' (Chatterjee 2012b: 174). However, in this specific text, notwithstanding what may be found in his other works, Bentham does not suggest improvement as an *objective* of the colonizer, but merely the fact that in time changes might occur. The fact that the form of 'government' referred to by Bentham is implied to be that of the East India Company, and that he moves on to immediately discuss the extortionist and corrupt character of the English in Bengal, as well as the fact that there are instances where Bentham is sceptical of comparisons, such as questions regarding the precise standards to be used in widely divergent settings, makes it difficult to read this passage, or indeed, as is further explored below, this whole text, as one devoted to the project of colonization as improvement.

[267] Bentham, *Essay on the Influence of Time and Place on Legislation*: 'Examine it [English law] piece by piece, we should find it a vast bundle of inconsistencies; the wisdom of one page being constantly disgraced by the folly of the next. But this incongruity does not show itself to the distant and admiring multitude, against whose censure its very immensity, which is one of its greatest blemishes, forms a most effectual defence. Do you comprehend the whole of it? No: then pretend not to sit in judgment over any part of it. Such is the rebuke which the sage professor is ever ready to give to the uninstructed layman: such is the opiate which the uninitiated layman is ever ready to administer to himself. This predilection, how effectually soever it may have veiled from the eyes of Englishmen the defects of English laws, while the dominion of those laws has been confined within the limits of the country which gave them birth, is not so strong, but that the experience of their effects, when transplanted into Bengal, has been able to overcome it: experience too fatal not to be severely felt, and too manifest to be dissembled, has demonstrated their inaptitude.'

[268] Ibid.: 'The most striking feature, in the original polity of that distant country, is the despotism of its leading principles: the most striking feature in that of the English government, is the strictness of its procedure. Hence it seems to have been concluded, and that too hastily, that laws that are competent to a free country must for that reason be incompetent to an arbitrary one. From this observation, an hypothesis has been formed for reconciling the experienced incompetency of the English laws as applied to Bengal, with their supposed competency as applied to England. Laws which are fit for a free country (it has been said) are, for that very reason, unfit for a country where the government is arbitrary and despotical. That this observation is just, as applied to certain parts of the law, is not to be denied: but that it is applicable to the greater part of them, or even to more than a very small part, is what I am much disposed to question. 1st, That

the English law is a great part of it of such a nature, as to be bad every where: 2d, But that it would not only be, but appear worse in Bengal than in England.'

269 Ibid.: 'The points I would rather choose for examples are those in which the inaptitude of the English law must appear the more striking; inasmuch as the practice of the Asiatic courts, in relation to those points, is, or for any thing that hinders may be, less unconformable to the rules of reason.' Chatterjee, in his discussion of this specific text, does not take this critical turn towards the critique of English common law into cognizance unlike Jennifer Pitts, thus making his interpretation of Bentham's 'conceptual innovation' in setting the basis for a 'science of comparative government', intervention and normalization, which itself grounded the 'emergence of the new practices of empire in the nineteenth century' difficult to defend; see Chatterjee (2012b): 172–73. Particularly so in the wake of Bentham's explicit critique of contemporaneous English common law, which even amounts to the recognition that in certain ways law in Bengal may turn out to be more fair and just that English law as such, and not merely in terms of its suitability to Bengal. While I have argued in my doctoral dissertation, 'Antinomies of Political-Economy' (2008), and book, *The Infinite Double* (2015), for the importance of Bentham in inaugurating a new epistemic space of global comparison – the very paradigm of contemporary social-scientific epistemology characterizing Ricardo, for instance – in relationship to the moral philosophy of Adam Smith and David Hume as well as the 'natural right' tradition, this inauguration was rooted in Bentham's philosophical writings on law and epistemology and is difficult to find in the specific arguments contained in his *Essay on the Influence of Time and Place*, as argued by Chatterjee.

270 In this sense this interpretation builds on my previous work on Bentham cited above.

271 This is Lord Coke during a debate in Parliament in 1627, cited in Charles McIlwain's *The High Court of Parliament and Its Supremacy* (1910): 53; its implications for an understanding of the conquests of the East India Company are studied in the next part of this work. Though deeply insightful, the present argument is made to contest the argument of parliamentary sovereignty – and its history – as sketched out in ibid.

PART III

The King and His Epistemic Masks

Empire, Prize and the Making of International Law in the Nineteenth Century

Introduction

The Pitts India Act and trial of Warren Hastings reconfirmed the subordination of the East India Company to King and King-in-Parliament. Notwithstanding disputes and differences in points of law regarding the precise status and powers of East India Company officials in relationship to subjects and sovereigns in India, Warren Hastings himself was finally exonerated. In fact he was exonerated precisely because there was no agreement amongst the highest judicial authorities of the land – members of the House of Lords – on points of law in relation to him. It was constantly bemoaned that no clear legal framework existed that could hold Hastings accountable, but the fact was that such a framework did exist, since channels of accountability led to the King's ministers (the Board of Commissioners) and the King's Privy Council. As Hastings's defenders made clear, the prosecution would have to reach here if they intended to carry through their damning claims – something no one was willing to imagine, let alone follow through. And so, even while recognizing the depredations caused to the native populations, no light was shed on the guidelines for the treatment of native 'subjects' – even if nothing was more needed, considering the wars and devastation wrought in India during and under Company rule. Sovereigns and subjects from the subcontinent were continuously conquered by the Company's armies and incorporated into its exploitative colonial economic system, but their status as juridical subjects was at once clear and murky, articulated but rendered meaningless. Sovereign kings could not easily appeal to authorities in England,[1] because they were treated as sovereigns engaging with the Company as (delegated) sovereigns and therein disabled from appealing to a (municipal) court of justice. Simultaneously, it was extraordinarily difficult for individuals to appeal to the higher courts in England, paralleling the asymmetries of the judicial process in India where natives found it very difficult to appeal to the Supreme Courts when aggrieved by Englishmen.[2] The two were inter-related because, due to the denial of sovereign powers in the staging of their nominal rule, subjects of these countries lived in a legal limbo with no clear channels of appeal. In the life and trials of Rammohan Roy, one sees attempts to appeal to the (British) King in both instances: as a subject of the King critical of East India Company governance, but also as a representative of a sovereign in the form of the Mughal ruler demanding justice from Britain.

Any inquiry into the subject-status of natives in India under the Company can be meaningfully approached only through an investigation into the category of the juridical subject as framed in Britain. This, as we have shown in the discussion of *Postnati* in Part I of this book, was itself a fraught issue. The key dimensions of subjecthood included the ability to initiate an action in law as well as rights to real property. This part traces the ways in which the role of the (British) King remained fundamental to the constitution of many kinds of subjecthood in the nineteenth-century empire, as well as the ways in which a particular discourse – that has become historiographically hegemonic today – conceals and occludes this central fact in its proposition of a civilized democratic parliamentary order. This powerful discourse, as is analysed below, developed in slow measure in the hands of John Austin, Henry Maine and John Stuart Mill, forming incremental degrees of amnesia in relationship to the constitutional place of the King in matters of subject-formation and ensuing kinds of rights. The latter obfuscation of the centrality of the King in turn allows for a distinguishing between 'metropolis' and 'empire', thus enabling the illusion that Britain could have a history independent of the imperial wars of colonization and conquest, and empire as a responsibility to civilize was taken on by Britain after having emerged Athena-like, fully grown before its steps. After introducing the granular deceits of subjecthood as juridically formulated in Britain, this part traces attempts at such a concealment which was already evident in Bentham, but only thickens and curdles in the nineteenth-century discourse.

For, in fact, in nineteenth-century Britain and the British Empire, the principal framework for defining the subject began with the allegiance to the King, just as treason was defined as an act targeting the natural body of the

King/Queen, his/her heirs and those closely associated with him/her, as well as challenging the law. The monarch could through his/her prerogative powers grant subjecthood to any individual, a status that was called that of a denizen, which was a subject-status closely linked to the rights to real property.[3] Real property or property in land was itself framed as various forms of tenure, such as freehold and copyhold, that were held for someone and which was ultimately held by the King, who was defined as one who did not hold land for anyone. This was the legal position on the nature of landed property in the nineteenth century, as explicated by jurists such as Maitland and Pollock.[4] Within the framework of such a 'feudal' legacy of the monarch as supreme lord and landlord there could exist no absolute rights to landed property, and all rights were subject to legal contest.[5] In fact, what was considered 'legal ownership' did not mean absolute rights since they were limited by 'equitable ownership' claims, the logic of which developed over the centuries. In this context, as Pollack argued, it would have been next to impossible for any proprietor to legally prove his right to (his) property, and statutory developments in the nineteenth century were attempts to make land more alienable by making such rights clearer, more absolute and individual.[6]

Certainly, of the property that was ultimately held by the King, the proprietor was guaranteed his property and liberty by virtue of his ability to represent himself in the House of Commons and partake in laws that might affect his property and liberty, i.e. laws concerning taxation and other such 'economic' matters. This population constituted a fraction of the total population; even as it increased in the nineteenth century notwithstanding deep and arguably growing inequality,[7] there was nothing close to universal franchise even in the metropolis. But that such liberties were denied to natives in India is enough to establish that no one can speak of anything like a property right existing under the East India Company regime, or the so-called direct Crown rule thereafter. In the Indian context, until 1857–58, the King remained the highest authority in the judicial framework, which enabled the East India Company through the Governor-General and Council as 'supreme courts' to determine revenue demand without anything like consent. In metropolitan areas such 'laws' in the form of statute were declared in the very same King-in-Parliament which guaranteed to the property holders their property right through representation. This double situation is critical to understand the centralized as well as differentiated nature of empire.

If the King was central to land law, his role was central to subject status too. His prerogatives could make aliens denizen-subjects, and this status should be distinguished from naturalized subjects who were made by acts of King-in-Parliament; but 'naturalization' through acts was not complete until the subject took an oath of allegiance to the King.[8] This difference lay in the fact that while a denizen could not inherit from his alien parent, a naturalized subject could. Otherwise, there was no difference in relation to the right to real property and alienation of property between the two. The denizen as well as the naturalized subject, from 1704, could not occupy positions of high office, but the Act of 1870 removed this constraint for the naturalized subject, preserving such a constraint only on the denizen. Acts of parliament in 1844, 1847 and 1870 concerning aliens defined allegiance in terms of allegiance to the natural person of the King.[9] In 1886, the Lord Chief Justice Coleridge reiterated *Postnati* in *Stepney Election Petition*, as having the 'highest authority' and 'binding'.[10] The judgment ends by stating, to the 'King in his politic, and not personal capacity, is the allegiance'.[11] In what sense this is a departure from *Postnati* is discussed below, but suffice it to say here that one cannot assume that the distinction between the politic and the personal as articulated by the Chief Justice reworks *Postnati*'s distinction between the politic and the natural capacities of the King, because the 'personal' does not map on to and is not epistemically fungible with 'natural'. One need only reiterate the definition of subjecthood as a status that articulates a relationship of allegiance to the King/Queen in his/her natural person (and heirs), and is confirmed by parliament and the courts. And from such a perspective, neither a definitive *a priori* territorial locus nor nationality, howsoever defined, was (yet) articulated as a principle of political legitimacy; nor was it the constituent basis of polities.

In order to gain a firmer understanding of this relationship between kingship and subjecthood as it worked itself out particularly in empire and war, this part tracks the legal framework regulating the Company and its conquests in the right of the King, as much as the 'subject' status of individual natives and sovereigns in the course of these events. From the jurisprudential authorities that have been analysed in the previous part as well as the ones that are discussed here, different kinds of subjects are formulated as differing correlates of sovereignty. In the course of conquest, as held by Mansfield in *Campbell*, there was a time between the vanquished who were subjects as subject to the King's equity, to the time when they were fully confirmed in their subject status by royal proclamation, which initiated the road to liberties in the form of representative assemblies. Similarly, the Privy Council in *Mayor (of Lyons) v. East India Company* (1836), citing *Postnati* and *Campbell v. Hall* among other authorities, had held that conquest in India led to natives being subjects of the King.[12] Legal and jurisprudential pronouncements of the early nineteenth century, from this ruling to Macaulay's draft penal code to Supreme Court justices, confirmed that natives were subjects, even though they explicitly remained agnostic about precisely when or how natives came to be so subject.[13] This reiterates the fundamental refusal of English jurisprudential discourse to explain the legal legibility of both war and conquest, on the one hand, and the urgent question of the precise delineation of the rights of the natives as subjects, on the other. Natives were subjects of conquest, not yet perfected by 'law', unlike subjects in different stages of this process across the imperium from Canada to England.

Victoria's proclamation and the Government of India Act in 1858 declared that the territories in India were being administered by the East India Company prior to 1857 'in trust' for the Queen, continuing the language of the previous charter renewals which spoke of the Company as 'trustees' for the Crown. The Act for the Naturalization of Citizens passed in 1852 by the Governor in Council suggested that individuals could be naturalized in the British territories in India and therein enjoy the same rights as 'natural born subjects', provided they were given such certificates by the Company and were able to 'be faithful and bear true allegiance to the Sovereign of the United Kingdom of Great Britain and Ireland of these Territories as dependent thereon, and [that I will] be true and faithful to the East India Company'.[14] The subject status of the people of India was reiterated by the proclamation in describing the actors of the 1857 'rebellion' as one where 'allegiance' was 'thrown'. The proclamation of pardon clarified even further that 'political offences' such as 'treason, rebellion, mutiny, desertion' were defined as offences against 'her Majesty, her Crown, her Dignity'.[15] But were they subjects when they were denied the representative assemblies by which their liberties and properties could be guaranteed, a principle that was clearly enunciated as far back as *Postnati* and confirmed in *Campbell*?

Prior to Queen Victoria's proclamation in 1 November 1858, the Government of India Act was passed in August, where it was enacted that all powers vested in the Company in relation to territories in India, in trust for the Queen, would now be vested directly with her. It is Victoria's proclamation, not the statute, which promises equal treatment and rights to *subjects* in India. Of particular interest is also the fact that even the 'sovereigns' of India could become subjects or be treated as such. Earlier in the year, in February 1858, a military commission had judged Bahadur Shah Zafar, alternatively titled

King and ex-King of Delhi,[16] to be a subject who had rebelled, throwing off allegiance to the British government. The legal position confirmed in the trial was that not merely Zafar but his father and grandfather too were 'subjects' the moment they entered into the 'protection' of the British after the Battle of Delhi in 1803. The rationale of this 'subjectification' of the sovereign is critically scrutinized in the section below, just as it is argued that such a subject formation, with the (British) King as supreme was recognized with acuity by Rammohan Roy.

If among the kinds of subjects and degrees of subjecthood, the 'natural born subjects' was considered of the fullest kind, and defined as one born within the realm and/or dominions of the King, it might be asked why later generations of natives born in the aftermath of the King's conquest – through the Company – were not to be designated as 'natural born subjects'. Such a question could be asked because natural-born subject was the status of those born within the King's dominions, and the lands conquered by the King were indeed his dominions.[17] In the violent occlusion of this question, while individual natives were legally recognized as subjects, they appear to have acquired the 'full' status of subjects only through Queen Victoria's proclamation where they were promised to be treated equally and according to law. However, even after such a promise, the Queen alienated her dominions in the subcontinent, giving them as rewards to those that were favoured.[18] While the legality of such a transaction was not disputed at the time, it does raise serious constitutional questions regarding the powers of the Queen, her treatment of subjects and territories as patrimony, and the constitutional contradictions in which natives were constantly wrenched: subjects with promised rights, subjects with rights without property right (in so far as there were no representative assemblies through which their property could be guaranteed), and slaves-as-property or subjects without rights or property (when, as discussed below in later sections, dominions were conquered and transferred).

In order to investigate this murky twilight of subjecthood – subjects in equity to 'full' subjects by proclamation – this part is divided into two. The first of these two parts is concerned with the nature and category of the subject in India prior to 1858, and is further divided into two sections. The first section analyses the grievances articulated by Mughal Emperor/King Akbar Shah II regarding what he saw as the violation of an agreement/treaty between him as Mughal ruler and the British government, after the conquest of Delhi in 1803. These grievances were in turn taken up by Rammohan Roy, a self-confessed British subject of the King, who argued the Mughal Emperor/King's case in London; Roy demonstrated an acute grasp of the political formation of empire with the King as its head. The analysis of this legal dispute shows that the Company did not hold even its own agreements/treaties in any sanctity, and was prone to manipulate, deny or annul them unilaterally whenever it thought fit. The 1858 military commission's judgment that Mughal rulers were 'subjects' from 1803 is but one attempt to conceal this sordid history by pretending that Mughal rulers were never rulers but always subjects.

The second part of this Part III goes on to analyse two crucial cases on the laws of war, the rights of the victor and the nature of subjecthood. One was the 'celebrated' *Deccan Prize Money* case, concerning the principles of the distribution of booty/Prize in the course of what are called the third Anglo-Maratha wars. This case, which reached the Privy Council, was considered the definitive case on Prize laws, and the most detailed examination of the laws and rights of war since Richard II by constitutional authorities of the time. The second case, which also reached the Privy Council and was to have a long after-life in legal discussions of martial law, pronounced on the precise question of the legal status of natives in the context of Company conquests – particularly what kind of properties might be categorized as Prize, and the precise rights of natives under Company conquest and rule. As cases decided in the highest courts of the land, they give us an insight into the laws of war, and the rights of the victor and the vanquished. This study complements and supplements the earlier parts by showing the entangled, staged and tensile nature of subjects and sovereigns. It underlines the supreme importance and fundamental role of the King and his Courts in the British legal system in matters of justice as much as the laws of conflict in the nineteenth century.

The second part of Part III analyses, notwithstanding the above, the systematic obfuscation of both the role of the King in general, and his specific role in the legal apparatus of subjecthood and imperialism, in the developing jurisprudential and political discourse of the nineteenth century. The entire logic of conquest, territorialization and rule, documented in the Parts I and II, and in part 1 of the present Part III, is transformed into abstract schemas of the civilized and the barbaric (Austin), the historical logic of custom and contract (Maine) with no place for the King, his bodies or conquest. On the other hand, international lawyers like John Westlake and Indian officials like Charles Tupper reiterate the fundamental importance of the King for the British Empire in India, so as to deprive 'native polities' of all 'international character' once *subject* to the British suzerain. Yet little is done to describe or account for the logic of the Company's conquest, which is recognized to have set the mould for the post-1857 imperial–feudal system. The concluding section draws out the implications of this obfuscation through John Stuart Mill's arguments whose positions on 'liberty', 'despotism' and 'custom' can only be understood in the recalcitrant context of Austin's collapsing of sovereignty and despotism, as much as Maine's unrelenting (historical) critique of political individualism. It is shown that Mill's 'liberal individual' thus emerges as the incontinent precipitate of a despotically designed legal system.

The King, the Subject and the Treaty: The Mughals, Rammohan Roy and the British

The Mughal ruler Akbar Shah II (1760–1837), who had begun his reign in 1806, sent the celebrated intellectual and activist Rammohan Roy to England so as to argue his case against the East India Company.[19] This case involved a set of claims against the Company, including the breach of treaties that were to have been entered into by it in the name of the British government. Treating the Company as the subordinate power and beholden to the British government, this appeal was made to the said government in London. This was not the first time that a Mughal ruler tried to get the attention of Britain in order to complain and accuse the Company of injustice. Akbar Shah's predecessor Shah Alam II, while in Allahabad in 1767, had sent an embassy to England that was meant to convey a letter, gifts and a *nazr* (an amount of 1 lakh of rupees), which was implicitly an acknowledgement of the emperor's subordination to King George.[20] The letter was written on the advice of 'Lord' Clive, who told Shah Alam that he would need sanction from his sovereign King George III if military assistance were to be provided for Shah Alam's restoration at Delhi. However, the money was purloined by Clive and deposited in the Company's coffers in India, and while Shah Alam's envoys, I'stam-Al-Din and Captain Swinton, received no audience from George III, Clive claimed to have given the King the letter while duplicitously gifting King Shah Alam's presents to him as though the presents were his own[21]. It is in this context of an attempt to open a direct line of communication with the (English) sovereign that one must also interpret and understand Rammohan Roy being engaged by the Mughal ruler.

Though accepting the task given to him by the Mughal ruler, Rammohan Roy saw himself as a subject of the British government, King and parliament;[22] clearly, he saw no contradiction. In fact, Roy demonstrated an acute grasp of British law and its subterfuges in his other writings where he makes clear that native subjects were not being given the promised rights of liberty and property. In appealing to authorities first in the Supreme Court and then in London, for the repealing of East India Company regulations restricting press freedom, he showed awareness of the (British parliamentary) statutory provisions that enabled such recourse, even as his failures demonstrated the actual position of native subjects.[23] It was this same knowledge of the delegated sovereignty of the Company that informed his attempt to represent the Mughal emperor, and settle as well as vindicate Akbar Shah's complaints against the East India Company. This specific dispute originated in the differing interpretations of the treaties and promises made by Governor-General Wellesley to Akbar Shah's father, Shah Alam II, in the aftermath of the conquest of Delhi.

However, before entering into this specific set of legal claims in the aftermath of the battle at Patpargunj, it is important to set it in context by narrating the 'prehistory' of the relations between the Company and Shah Alam II. In 1765, in the aftermath of the Company victory at Buxar, it was given *diwan*-ship, as a '*free gift*' '*forever*'[24] in the treaty of Allahabad, whose terms included a payment of 26 lakh rupees to the Mughal ruler. Within six years, Warren Hastings as Governor unilaterally stopped this tributary payment, thus violating the terms of the treaty. Hastings justified his decision by referring to the devastating famine in Bengal and the resultant financial crisis. He also claimed that Shah Alam's march back to Delhi and friendship with the Marathas was an act of hostility. Though a devastating famine had taken place, this did not prevent Hastings from increasing the revenues demanded of Bengal. Moreover, nothing in the treaty of Allahabad appeared as a stipulation denying the Mughal ruler the liberty to leave Allahabad or engage with the Marathas. And yet the Court of Directors sanctioned Hastings's decision to stop the tribute, and violate the treaty.[25] In a more general defence of his actions, Hastings had made it clear that the 'tribute' was not Clive's to give, and the true sovereign title to Bengal was that of the sword and not the Mughal emperor's grant.[26]

Stoppage of the tribute did not prevent Shah Alam's attempts to get redressal. He was in communication with the British in the run-up to the Battle of Delhi, and Governor-General Wellesley promised to settle with him on honourable terms. In the aftermath of the battle while discussing the terms of rule, no mention was ever made about the tribute of 26 lakhs and the treaty of Allahabad. Yet another treaty was drawn up in 1805. The political nature of the Battle of Delhi, as much as the fact that the title to the regions conquered was based on the right of conquest, were underlined when the Governor-General legitimized the Prize money. This money, amounting to 5 lakhs and 40,000 rupees, was acquired by the commander-in-chief Lord Lake for himself and his troops.[27] However, as part of a diplomatic exercise to assure Shah Alam of the government's good intentions, the Mughal ruler was at the same time paid an equivalent amount, and was promised that the stipend – the payment specifically for the royal establishment – would be increased if it were possible as and when the Company's coffers allowed it.[28] Shah Alam died soon thereafter and in 1806, Akbar Shah II became the Mughal ruler.

In the war with the Marathas, who had control over the regions of Delhi and yet kept up the appearance of Mughal rule, the British opened communication with Shah Alam, promising him protection under the power of the British government prior to the military engagement in 1803.[29] There was much discussion amongst Company officials on the terms of the settlement, and the Resident's views were that a fixed amount of money should be paid to the Mughal ruler but no territories should be given to him.[30] The Governor-General suggested that certain territories be given to the Mughal ruler that could also be used as the fund from which a fixed stipend could emerge.[31] Ultimately, in Wellesley's communication with Shah Alam, certain terms were written into a document/treaty which stated the precise terms of settlement.[32] The nature and status of this document became the bone of contention between Shah Alam's son Akbar Shah II and the Company, which soon enough refused to recognize the plain meaning of the terms of the treaty as having any legal validity. This conflict in fact spread over decades, and involved Rammohan Roy and later E. Thompson, as envoys representing the claims of the Mughal rulers to the British. However, before detailing the nature of this conflict, it might well do to outline the terms that were agreed upon in 1805.

According to the document/treaty of 1805, specified territories were 'assigned' to the King of Delhi as his 'Crown lands', and therefore revenue ('peshkush') from such lands were to be considered as his own.[33] One article specifically stated that the expenses of 'troops, police corps, etc employed in the khalisa (crown) shall be defrayed by the honourable Company', thereby suggesting that the King's *peshkush*/revenue was to be understood as the gross income and not the net income, the revenue after the deduction of the expenses of collection and administration which would have required troops and the police.[34] This form of revenue for the King was not a new engagement in the sense that even while under the 'protection' of the Marathas certain lands were assigned to the King, although the exact nature of the amount of the King's revenue and the money that was paid to him by the Scindias is not completely clear.

While the management of these lands 'according to custom' were to remain with the Resident,[35] the Mughal ruler's accountants could attend the Collector's office and report to His Majesty, according to the treaty. Yet another clause made it clear that the Resident would pay specified amounts for the expenses of the royal family and its establishment, 'whether the whole of the amount is or is not collected from the Khalisa (crown) lands'.[36] Any increase in the revenue of the *khalisa* lands would be used to 'augment' the aforesaid amount, i.e. specified payments out of the public treasury for the maintenance of the royal establishment.[37] Specified amounts would also be paid on the occasions of specific festivals, and the expenses incurred for maintenance of troops, police, etc., on the *khalisa* lands would be defrayed by the Company. These specified amounts were therefore to be clearly distinguished from the revenues of the 'assigned lands'.

This treaty was entered into explicitly as one which assured the Mughal ruler protection by the British government. Governor-General Wellesley had made it clear in his communications with the authorities in London that it was important to secure the protection of Shah Alam and enter into such arrangements, because of the possibility of the Marathas or the French pursuing claims in the name and authority of the Mughal ruler. He in fact referred to a previous communication which alluded to the possession of concrete evidence of a 'project for the subversion of the British Empire in India founded principally upon the restoration of Shah Allum under the control and direction of agents of France'.[38] In the same letter, Wellesley made it equally clear that such protection did not at all imply that the rights or claims of Shah Alam as emperor or his prerogatives were to be acknowledged; British protection merely meant supporting the royal family by giving a fixed amount of money as well as revenues over certain assigned territories, which ultimately found their way into the treaty/document of 1805.

There was a crucial difference between the communications that Governor-General Wellesley had with the authorities in London as well as his Resident in Delhi, and the final terms of the treaty. In these communications there existed a clause which stated that 'if the produce of the revenue of the assigned territory should hereafter admit it, the monthly sum to be advanced to his Majesty for his private expenses might be increased to one

Lakh of rupees'.[39] This suggested that one lakh would be a kind of maximum, a ceiling amount, that would be given to the Mughal ruler. However, this crucial clause was not incorporated in the written document/treaty of 1805. Thus, without this clause, the treaty stated that all the revenues from the assigned territories were to be given to the Mughal ruler, and he would be the beneficiary of any improvements of the lands that might lead to increased revenues. No maximum or ceiling amount was mentioned.

Akbar Shah very soon began to complain that his stipend, the income that he was receiving, was not increasing with time.[40] In 1823, Akbar Shah attempted, like his father, to communicate with the King of England. This was thwarted by the Governor-General who deemed 'such correspondence to be inadmissible whether considered with reference to the constitutional character of the British Government in this country or the circumstances and situation of the Delhi Court in relation to that Government'.[41] In 1827, Akbar Shah wrote to the Governor-General sending him the articles of the treaty/document, adding more requests to the same in the hope that they would be honoured. This was sent to Charles Metcalf, the Resident of Delhi, who responded to the articles point by point. Here we find the first clear instance of the Company repudiating a plain reading of its own agreement.

In his detailed response, Metcalf speaks of the treaty/document as but 'an intimation of the *intentions* of the British Government at that time, and *not an engagement positively binding in its future conduct*' (emphasis added).[42] Several attempts are made to undermine the status of the treaty through various modes of argumentation. First, it is stated by Metcalf, as a matter of fact, that the terms of the document were violated almost immediately after they were made, because many of the regions coming under the 'assigned territory' were given away to local chiefs, even though according to the treaty they were to be managed by the Company with the revenue/*peshkush* being given to the Mughal ruler.[43] It is not clear how these past violations, by the Company and not by the Mughal ruler, could be put forth as an argument to undermine the sanctity of the treaty. Secondly, Metcalf argues that since this treaty was entered into in the aftermath of a conquest, and since the Mughal ruler did not have any real power, it was impossible for the latter to enter into a treaty of any sort since he was 'not a master of materials for a mutual negotiation or a treaty'.[44] Such logic appears strange indeed, since it implies that a conquest would ensure that the defeated party cannot even enter into a treaty. This would go against every principle of the law of nations or historical record of every kind. Thirdly, Metcalf argues that one could not precisely ascertain the net revenues of the 'assigned territories', i.e. ascertain which specific regions they referred to. Moreover, he states that even if this were to be done, the revenues from these areas would amount to less than the one lakh that was the maximum promised by the Company.[45] However, in making such an argument, he all the same admits that this crucial clause about a maximum amount was not indeed shared with the Mughal ruler – an admission which, strangely, is in no way seen to undermine his argument.

Later that year, the Governor-General also made a point-by-point response to the articles of the treaty, largely conforming to Metcalf's report summarized above. Regarding the specification of the lands that came under 'assigned lands', the Governor-General merely noted that the provision was not carried through 'for unavoidable causes'.[46] He ended with the declaration that the 1809 increase of the stipend which did not make any reference to any assigned territory – something unilaterally decided upon by the then Company government – should be taken as final. While the treaty had clearly stated that improvements in lands leading to an increase in revenue ought to 'augment' the stipend, indicating that the rights to revenue from the lands ought to be distinguished from other incomes, the Governor-General, rather than addressing the issue, merely referred to his response to the first article, i.e. this provision was not carried through for 'unavoidable reasons' and therefore the 1809 decision remained final.

Nowhere in the above internal communications between the Resident and Governor-General is it said that the terms of the document/treaty of 1805 were formulated by the then Resident without sanction from the Company or authorities in London. It was accepted that there existed such a treaty/document communicated to the King of Delhi with sanction from the requisite authorities. Simultaneously it was confirmed that the Company operated with a clause – of the maximum limit of the King's pension being a lakh – which was not revealed to Shah Alam, whether verbally or in writing, at engagement/treaty of 1805. It was repeatedly stated in response to Akbar Shah's claims from very early on that he was not in a position to dictate terms, and that he was under the protection of the British government which would only fulfil obligations that they considered fit. Thus, in response to a specific claim based on the written agreement/treaty, the Company responded by merely stating that the fact of Akbar Shah's lack of military might did not give him the right to speak of the agreements entered into between the Company and his father.

It was in such a context that Akbar Shah renewed his legal claims by appointing Rammohan Roy as his envoy to the authorities in London. Roy considered himself a British subject and applied to the Company government to recognize the title of Raja that was bestowed by the Mughal King, a capacity that the Company appeared to recognize.[47] This was not the first time that he was appealing to the British King, and he had seen through the Company's fictions accurately by making use of the statutes that enabled direct appeals first to the King's Court in Calcutta and then directly to the King-in-Council.[48] No doubt to prevent what was undeniably a legitimate channel of communication to the King that might well be subversive for the Company's powers, Roy's request was not accepted or confirmed by the local government (East India Company). Therefore, when Rammohan Roy set sail for London, he claimed that he was doing so in his private capacity and not in the public capacity of an envoy or ambassador of the Mughal ruler. However, he did take up Akbar Shah's case while in London, and received a sympathetic hearing from the Board of Control, who communicated with the Court of Directors on the matter.

The legal claims of Mughal ruler Akbar Shah now having reached the highest echelons of government, the Court of Directors was forced to address them. In doing so it repeated the reasoning of Charles Metcalf and the Governor-General. It argued that the referred-to 'document' must be understood to signify the 'intentions' of the Company and Court.[49] This intention was said to be merely limited to ensuring that the King and his household lived with some dignity.[50] On the question of intentions, no mention is made of Wellesley's argument that it was fear of the legal claims and political possibilities of the French and the Marathas reinstating the Mughal ruler that required the British to take him under their 'asylum' and 'protection'. Moreover, the Court of Directors, in response to the Board of Control's questions, introduced a new element by stating that the 'document' of 1805 was formulated wholly by the then Resident and had not received proper sanction from authorities.[51]

In no previous discussion of the subject – and it was discussed many times because of the constant complaints and accusations of Akbar Shah – was it ever suggested that the treaty/document of 1805 was something unilaterally formulated by the then Resident without requisite sanction. This would in any case be difficult to believe, because in the initial correspondence between the Resident and the Governor-General in 1804–05, it was revealed that the Resident did not think it a good idea to give the Mughal ruler any revenue of any lands, since such lands were being managed by him.[52] In this sense it is not surprising that, in the words of Metcalf, the treaty was 'annulled before it even began', because there was a clear interest in keeping the land revenues by the Resident and/or the Company. And finally, while the Court of Directors admitted that an increase may be made to the King's stipend, it requested the Board of Control that this increase should be awarded without any reference to the 'assigned territories' or the case as it was being put forward by Rammohan Roy as envoy of the Mughal ruler.

The Court argued that if any reference was made to the 'assigned territories', this would amount to an admittance of the Company violating the terms of a solemn engagement for all these years, bringing to naught its claims of honour, justice and liberality.[53] In response the Board, in its reasoning, vindicated the persistent stance of the King, most recently articulated by Rammohan Roy, that the Company did indeed owe the King amounts of money in accordance with an agreement that it had solemnly entered into in 1805.[54] The Board stated that the words of the treaty had to be understood for what they meant on a reading of the text, and any 'construction' based on the 'intentions' of one party could not hold. However, it all the same agreed with the Court of Directors that to openly admit as such would amount to a certain embarrassment to the Company, and in practical terms the issue was to increase the stipend – any other reference was held not to be strictly necessary.[55]

As a result of pressure from the Board, the Company offered Akbar Shah an increase in stipend. However, Rammohan Roy in the meanwhile had written to Akbar Shah not to accept the small increase that was offered. Clearly, it was his intention to follow through the case to its logical conclusion. Death cut such an endeavour short, and therefore the Court was allowed to get away with the increase that it had promised. It is not necessary at present to get into the details of the cussedness of the Company in insisting that it would unilaterally determine the manner of the distribution of the increase that it had promised.[56] More significant is the implicit acknowledgement of its own continuous violation of principles in denying Akbar Shah his rightful claims – legal claims which had been recognized in London, thanks to Roy's efforts, which ultimately led to the Company's offer of increase.

The literature on the relations between the Mughals and the British in this period has not paid sufficient attention to the precise and defensible claims of Shah Alam and Akbar Shah with regard to engagements formally entered into with the East India Company. This is obfuscated by focusing on grand and orientalizing claims about the Mughal theories of kingship and English 'misunderstandings' of such ritual, that serves only to block a detailed entry into the nitty-gritty of inter-state and inter-imperial relations.[57] The legal contests discussed above were often also overlaid with contestation over symbolic resources such as modes of address, rituals of incorporation and terms of interaction. The Company constantly warded off attempts by Akbar Shah to project his own superiority over the Company. Perhaps the clearest case is the Company's refusal to accept the *khillat*/robes of honour and incorporation, as well as disallow attempts of the Mughal emperor to send such 'ritual robes' to native chiefs.[58] In the very period discussed above regarding legal claims to the 'assigned territory', the Company also altered the modes of address and the striking of coins, thereby making it clear that no symbolic deference would be carried out in relation to the Mughals. At the same time it must be remembered that since the Company was not sovereign itself but delegated such powers by the British government, it recognized that it could not itself be treated on par with other sovereigns, howsoever limited the authority of the latter might be. In the case of the Mughals, the entire control over revenue as well as punishment was superintended by the Resident. None of this was ever disputed or disregarded, but Akbar Shah indeed expected the British to keep their word etched as they were into written documents.

While the East India Company constantly limited the rights and abilities of the Mughals, it would be difficult to characterize them as 'subjects' in any sense. The treaties discussed and recognized above clearly point to recognition of the sovereign character of the Mughals, even if the latter's authority may not have extended beyond the palatial grounds of the red fort. However, at the 'trial' of Bahadur Shah Zafar, Akbar Shah's successor, after the rebellion of 1857, the premise was that after the battle of 1803, the Mughals were subjects.[59] The 'legal' basis of both the trial and the prosecution was that as subjects they had thrown off allegiance, and hence were being prosecuted. From the above discussion it becomes clear that such a position is difficult to sustain. The plasticity of the subject under force of arms was thus little more than a convenient, cynically manipulable instrument of rule.

The utter disregard towards formal engagements entered into by the British as much as the susceptibility of the subject to political-legal design turn up in a place not conventionally expected but completely in line with the concerns in this book.[60] They turn up in the most celebrated case regarding Prize money in the early nineteenth century, called the *Deccan Prize Money* case. In the discussion of cases related to Prize in both this section and in the section that follows, the indistinguishability between subject and not-subject, whether foreign sovereign or foreign populace, becomes nothing less than an art form – an art form veiling sordid butchery and brazen deceit in the form of Prize jurisprudence.

The Interlocking Cases of Prize and Martial Law in the Maratha Wars

What are called the Anglo-Maratha wars (1817–18)[61] gave rise to two interlocking judicial cases on Prize, which forms the subject of this section. The first case studied here was known as the *Deccan Prize Money* case, and was much celebrated in its time. The issue to be decided was who precisely was entitled to Prize money: the actual captors directly involved in the war, or even those military divisions who played a more indirect role in victory? Implicitly, this legal dispute also sheds light on the responsibility, if any, of the victors towards the vanquished, and therein the rules of engagement between parties during a war and thereafter. The second case involved an issue that emerged directly from one of the battles within the Anglo-Maratha wars, i.e. the capture and conquest of Poona. Here the issue to be decided was the exact limits of the rights to acquire Prize. More specifically, since Prize was linked to war, the question to be decided concerned the moment when the right to take Prize was to have ceased, which in turn involved the question of how one was to discern the end of war. The second case is analysed first, before moving on to the first case.

The more precise issue to be determined regarded the claims put forward by Ammerchund, executor of Narrabo Outia, against the United Company and the Company officers Elphinstone and Robertson (defendants) in the Supreme Court of Bombay; a case that was later heard on appeal by the King-in-Council (Privy Council). The Supreme Court of Bombay heard the case for twenty-two days, examining witnesses and evidence from both sides. From this the following facts were inferred by the court.[62] On 17 July 1818, Lieutenant Robertson got his men to bring Narrabo Outia from his home in Poona, and had his men search Outia's house. Robertson had been appointed provisional Collector and Magistrate of Poona and the adjacent country in February 1817, a position that was delegated to him by Elphinstone who was himself appointed as Commissioner in December 1817 in the aftermath of the conquest of Poona which had just taken place in November 1817. Narrabo Outia was an important official in the Peshwa administration and had held the position of a treasurer. Robertson was in charge of civil and criminal matters, and his men confiscated twenty-eight bags of gold mohurs and venetians (forms of currency) which were found in Outia's house. While Outia was detained under duress, along with his *gomastha*, Robertson claimed that the money found in the house was the Peshwa's money. Outia and his *gomastha* were released only after close to four months, at the end of which the venetians were given to Robertson. While they were being detained, Robertson was approached by the Prize agent about the money that he had found in Outia's house. Robertson in his response appeared to be uncertain as to whether the confiscated money could be characterized as Prize or not. While Outia, under detention, had written in his own hand that the money was the Peshwa's, the judges of the Supreme Court did not consider this statement as having any value, since they inferred from the facts of the case that it was extracted under conditions of duress.

The properties seized from Outia were to be characterized as Prize, according to the defendants, because this was the same money that Outia had brought with him to his house in Poona from the fort of Rygheur where he had surrendered to the Company's forces. Thus, the defendants claimed, Outia, on surrender, had broken the terms of the capitulation and the treaty then entered into by fleeing the fortress and reaching Poona with the money of the Peshwa. That it was the Peshwa's money meant that it could be treated as the enemy's property and Prize money; as the proceeds of war it was a rightful and lawful acquisition. In one sense, the defendants argued, that since the state of war did not end by July 1818 even though the Peshwa had surrendered in June, the seizure from Outia's house constituted an act undertaken in the course of war. This argument was justified because notwithstanding the surrender at Poona by the Peshwa, hostilities still existed in the countryside, and Outia's money, seized in Poona, was to be understood as enemy property.

These assets included treasure (gold coins, jewels, shawls and property) from the fort of Rygheur which had been taken by Colonel Prother after the capture of the fort; the treasure confiscated in Poona had five bags of venetians which were subsequently taken by Robertson. In the course of the proceedings, the claims regarding the assets confiscated at Rygheur were given up. The value of the entire confiscated properties calculated with interest amounted to 36,560,007 rupees. In response, the Company as well as Elphinstone and Robertson argued on the principle that the properties seized were lawful Prize by right of war and conquest. This was an issue as matters of war and Prize directly concerned His Majesty, and the Supreme Court of Bombay had no proper jurisdiction over these.

On what was presented before them, the Supreme Court of Bombay judges commented on the lack of any evidence that the money and properties confiscated from Outia by Colonel Robertson were in fact the money and properties of the Peshwa. The judges also found no evidence to establish that Outia had in any way violated the terms of the capitulation at Rygheur and illegally carried sums of money to Poona. Moreover, they drew attention to the fact that after the conquest of Poona and adjacent territories, and after Elphinstone was made Commissioner, Elphinstone in this capacity had issued a proclamation signalling the end of the war. In this proclamation which was transmitted to Robertson, it was explicitly held that all property, 'real' or 'personal', would be secured by the British government. Robertson himself was made a Magistrate, and given civil and criminal powers.

In the light of the above facts, the judges held that it could not be said that a state of war continued to exist in July, at the time when Outia's money and property was seized. Citing several cases including *Campbell v. Hall*, the judges held that rights of conquest vested in the Crown, and Elphinstone's proclamation had to be interpreted as a convention that ended the war, enabling courts to function and thereby protect persons and property. The very existence and functioning of courts, the judges held – citing Coke and Hale – meant that war and martial law were at an end. This state of affairs also signified the fact that the native people were now subjects of the conquering force, and in such a context Prize money or the laws of war could no longer apply to them. The judges also alluded to the fact that they themselves had to adjudicate the case since no Admiralty Courts existed. And it could not be held that a municipal court did not have jurisdiction over the case at hand, for such an argument implied that people conquered and devastated by the Company would literally have no place to go to appeal for justice. In such a context, the King's Court, that is the Supreme Court of Bombay, certainly had standing and jurisdiction, always subject certainly to the King-in-Council. And this is precisely what happened once the defendants went on appeal.

On appeal, the case was heard by the King-in-Council (Privy Council), which overturned the decision of the Supreme Court (King's Court) in Bombay.[63] The lawyers for Elphinstone and Robertson contested the jurisdiction of the Supreme Court in Bombay by arguing that the seizure of Outia's properties took place in a time of war when martial law and military dominion were prevalent – a context in which no municipal court, including the Supreme Court, had any jurisdiction. Without any evidence on record, it was repeated that Outia violated the articles of capitulation at the fort of Rygheur and went to Poona carrying the 'public' property of the Peshwa, and he was therefore an alien enemy with no right to bring an action against the military officers of the East India Company in a civil court. The commanding officer Prother's assessment regarding Outia's violation of the terms of capitulation could only be corrected or judged by the government or his military superiors. It was not subject to any civil jurisdiction, such as that of the Supreme Court at Bombay. Pointing to evidence of continuing military conflicts and the existence of martial law in certain instances – such as the threat of courtmartial against any officer who entered Poona– the solicitor general tried to establish that no municipal court could exercise jurisdiction in the case at hand. Moreover, it was held that at the time of the seizure of Outia's property, no formal treaty or capitulation existed and therefore the territories of Poona had not yet been formally annexed to the Bombay government, once again signalling the inapplicability of civil laws or the jurisdiction of the Supreme Court. Only such a treaty could indicate the presence and applicability of laws and the claims of the conquered to British subjecthood as were held in *Campbell v. Hall.*

In response to this set of contentions, the lawyers for Outia argued that the Supreme Court by its charter was given jurisdiction over British subjects, and this in itself allowed them jurisdiction over Elphinstone and Robertson as British subjects. The fact that the seizure of Outia's property was made in July and the conquest was made in November of the previous year indicated that the state was one of civil law. Robertson himself was commissioned as a judge, and legal authorities from Coke to Hale had held that where the courts were open for hearing, martial law ceased. It was pointedly asked that if indeed Elphinstone's proclamation did not indicate the ceasing of war and the beginning of the operation of civil law, what legal act since could be pointed to as signalling the beginning of the civil state? No specific act had since formally signified the formal 'annexation' of the territories and no treaty of capitulation had been formulated even at the date of the hearing more than a decade after the fact. Was that to mean that even 1830, the time of the hearing, was a time of martial law in those regions? Could officers simply enter houses and seize property without being held accountable in the courts of law? If the Supreme Court did not have jurisdiction, to which courts or authorities could natives appeal when they sought justice against British (military) officers?

In response to the arguments that hostility and resistance remained in certain regions, the lawyers forcefully asked whether it would have been acceptable if William III did not adhere to his proclamation in Holland on the pretext that certain fortresses in Scotland remained to be conquered at the time of the 'glorious revolution'. Was it not the case that those who argued that the title of conquest allowed William to act as he pleased were dismissed *tout court* by the authorities of the time? Analogously, in this case, Elphinstone's proclamation, which promised the protection of personal and real property, had to be interpreted to mean the cessation of war and the inauguration of peace, and with it, (civil) laws. The Supreme Court at Bombay which examined the evidence for over twenty-one days did not find any evidence for the argument that Outia had violated any treaty when he went from the Rygheur fortress to Poona, and no such evidence was presently placed on record. Moreover, the fact that Prother claimed he did not know where Outia went put to rest the argument that Outia had violated the treaty and was sent to Poona as a prisoner of war, and was therefore to be treated as an alien enemy. In fact it was likely that Outia capitulated in response to Elphinstone's proclamation, and therefore it was necessary that he be treated as a British subject entitled to bring an action against Elphinstone and Robertson in a court of law. While the property seized was his own and no proof existed to prove that it was the Peshwa's, the same property that was brought from Rygheur to Poona, even if it was the Peshwa's property, was not something the military officer could seize in the manner that was done.

In a final response, the solicitor general reiterated the point that the seizure took place in a time and condition of war, a situation in which the actions and decisions of commanding officers could only be judged by government and not in a court of law. No response was given to the fundamental question of what legal action could be cited to indicate the coming of peace and the operation of civil laws since, if not Elphinstone's proclamation. Going by the solicitor general's argument, the regions conquered remained under martial law where a native's property could be confiscated by a military officer, and the native, not being a subject, had no right to appeal to a court of law.

In the final judgment Lord Tenterdon, the judge, agreed with the solicitor general. He stated that 'hostile seizure' was made, 'if not *flagrante*' then '*nondum cessanto bello*' with regard to time, place and person.[64] This meant that the municipal court had no jurisdiction and its decision was therefore overturned, and any appeal only lay with the government. While this was the decision of Lord Tenterdon, in the course of the arguments he made another fundamental point that is germane to the set of issues being discussed. The lawyers of Outia argued that the property entrusted to Outia was the private property of the Peshwa and therefore not subject to seizure as Prize, war having come to a close a while ago. In response, Tenterdon stated as a matter of fact that in the case of an 'absolute sovereign', one could not make a distinction between private and public property. While public property meant the property of the state, 'in the property of the absolute sovereign, who may dispose of everything at any time, and in any way he pleases'.[65] This implies that not only is the private property of the absolute sovereign 'public', but also that which is public or any individual's (private) property can also be termed as in fact his own (public) property. It would thus render all property that exists under the absolutist sovereign public property in fact and therefore Prize. On the other hand, accepting the 'fact' of war without providing any sign that might indicate its cessation or peace, the territories of India are once again defined as a state of war. And hence the question as to whether a (military) officer could at any time seize any one's property would have to be answered in the affirmative.

The *Deccan Prize Money* Case

The *Deccan Prize Money* case involved a contestation between Governor-General Hastings (and the Bengal army directly under his command) and Commander-in-Chief Hislop (who commanded the Deccan army) in respect of what were called the Anglo-Maratha wars, which included the conquest of Poona, as discussed above. The general issue to be decided pertained to the question as to who in fact was entitled to Prize money. Was it the divisions engaged in the 'actual capture', or was Prize money also due to divisions that played a more indirect role in capture and conquest? Governor-General Hastings claimed that as overall commander-in-chief of the armies which had captured and conquered the territories under Maratha control, he was entitled to a share. Moreover, the divisions directly under him, i.e. 'the Bengal army', was similarly entitled to Prize under the legal mechanism of 'constructive capture' because even if they did not actually capture territories, they played an important military role in preventing other armies from helping the enemy, cutting off their supplies and routes. Against this position, the lawyers of Hislop argued, first, that Governor-General Hastings was overall commander-in-chief, but the commander-in-chief of the Deccan army was Hislop, and the latter remained the commander-in-chief until and unless the Governor-General entered the territories where Hislop was in command. This entry did not take place in the case being adjudicated. And therefore Hastings could not claim Prize as commander-in-chief since the Deccan army was a distinct army with Hislop as commander-in-chief. Secondly, the lawyers argued that one had to adhere to the legal doctrine of 'actual capture', not 'constructive capture', where only those divisions which were directly involved in the battle and directly participated in the capture and conquest were entitled to Prize.

This celebrated case was seen as the most important one on matters of war and booty since Richard II in the fourteenth century.[66] It involved great sums of money and the conquest of great territories and rulers. These battles enabled an enormous expansion of British power, having subjugated the Scindias, the Holkars and the Peshwa. Outia, from the case discussed above, operates as a crucial figure in the interstices of the broader and grander *Deccan Prize Money* case, that also moves from the Lords of the Treasury (in charge of revenue) to the King's Council/Privy Council. While the Deccan case concerned the claims of Lord Hastings as commander-in-chief and the Bengal army, and Thomas Hislop as commander-in-chief of/and the Deccan army, it also involves and resolves Outia's case. In a final appeal to the Privy Council, Colonel Prother, who had captured Rygheur, claimed that the treasure recovered by Robertson from Outia was treasure and property that Outia had actually brought from Rygheur, and therefore as the actual captor of the fort he and his division were entitled to the recovered property as Prize money. However, the Privy Council agreed with the Lords of the Treasury that no proof existed to prove such a claim. Thus, in another sense, it seemed clear that the property recovered from Outia was not public treasure or the Peshwa's money that he had illegally brought from Rygheur to Poona in violation of the terms of capitulation. This confirms Justice Chambers's decision at the Supreme Court of Bombay that no evidence existed to establish that the money and property seized from Outia at Poona was the money/property of the Peshwa which had been entrusted to him, and which was brought from Rygheur. It is worth recalling that the case at Bombay involved a detailed examination of evidence and cross-questioning of witnesses, unlike the procedures followed in the Privy Council.

The Deccan Prize money decision at the Privy Council all the same validated the decision of *Ammerchand v. Bedderchund*, by allowing for the categorization of the properties/money recovered from Outia as Prize money and therefore legally acquired by British forces. The logic and mode of such an arrival is the long story of the *Deccan Prize Money* case, seen as the most detailed examination of Prize law in British history, involving the evaluation of the crucial distinction between 'actual capture' and 'constructive capture'.

The case moved from the Lords of the Treasury to finally the Privy Council, which accepted the decision of the former. But what was the case in fact?

The defeat of the Marathas involved distinct conquests, beginning with the conquest of the Pindaris, and then the defeat of the Holkars, Scindias and the Peshwa. After the initial defeat of the Pindaris, both Lord Hastings, the Governor-General, and the commander-in-chief Hislop had held that only the actual captors – the divisions directly involved – were entitled to the Prize and booty. However, after the defeat of the Holkars at the Battle of Mahindpur where the booty was of a much larger amount, the Prize Committees of the first and third divisions of the Deccan Army which had acquired much Prize money also claimed a share in the Prize realized by other divisions. When this was communicated to Lord Hastings through the commander-in-chief of the Deccan army, Thomas Hislop, Hastings determined that from that time onwards all armies, including the Bengal army under his direct command, would be entitled to Prize. The reasoning deployed was that if reserve troops, not actually fighting, did not pin down enemy armies such as those of Scindia and Amir Khan, battles would not have been won. Hastings argued that if not for the cooperation of the Bengal army under his direct command, the wars against the Maratha armies fought by the Deccan army under Commander-in-Chief Hislop would not have succeeded. Moreover, in certain instances, the divisions of the Bengal army actually participated in the conquests.

Hastings's contentions therein deployed the argument of 'constructive capture', where the entitlement to Prize and booty could not be limited to the actual captors but was due to those who aided in the battle. Those armies that were part of the larger object of war had a right by association. Thus Hastings's lawyers argued that the defeat of the Marathas was part of a larger plan formulated by Lord Hastings. In this context, the treaties with the Marathas, such as those entered into with the Peshwa and Amir Khan, which had been signed just prior to the conflict of 1818, were confirmed as but 'waste paper',[67] and not binding instruments in the carrying out of policy. The formal treaties were but deceptions and part of the larger strategy and plan formulated by Governor-General Hastings, that formed the larger frame of wars and conquests.

On the other hand, the lawyers representing Hislop argued that the principle to be followed for Prize was 'actual capture', and the doctrine of 'constructive capture' could not be widened to so large an extent as they accused Hastings's lawyers of doing. Sarcastically it was exclaimed, would the entire nation and all the British forces claim Prize, because there was some association and a common purpose between them and the Deccan army that fought and won on the battlefield? Using analogies from maritime warfare, which was the primary domain of Prize law, it was further insisted upon that 'constructive capture' could not be so widened as to weaken all incentive for those who actually hoped to gain Prize through exertion. This would be an injustice to them who so struggled and succeeded.[68]

Ultimately, the Lords of the Treasury accepted the principle of 'actual capture' and confirmed only Prize claims on such a basis, including the claims of the divisions of the Bengal army that had actually participated in the wars.[69] They did not recognize the Prize claims of the East India Company as a corporation, for reasons not clearly spelt out. To facilitate the division of Prize/booty, they appointed trustees in the persons of the Duke of Wellington and Mr Arbuthnot. However, in the course of attempting to draw out a schema for the division of the booty/plunder, the trustees came to the decision that most of the booty/plunder was that which was got from the 'general results of war' rather than that which was got in the course of 'actual capture'.[70] In the light of this new fact, the Lords of the Treasury reversed their earlier decision and now determined that the part of the booty which was derived from 'general results' was to be distributed to all the armies that participated, including the Bengal army, while the more limited money/property from actual capture, amounting to 150,000 pounds, was to be given to those divisions that were directly involved.

In more concrete terms, the Lords of the Treasury determined (1) 'that portion of the booty . . . which is described as having been "taken in the daily operation of the troops", the distribution should be made to the actual captors'; and (2) that

> with respect to that part of the booty which consists of the produce of *arrears of the tribute, rent or money due* to the Peshwa, it appears to my lords to have been acquired by the general result of the war, and not by the operations of any particular army or division . . . ought therefore to be distributed . . . amongst the forces of all the Presidencies engaged in the combined operations of the campaign.[71] (Emphasis added.)

With specific respect to the juridical case that was analysed above, i.e. Poona, the Lords held that,

> With respect to the booty recovered at Poona, alleged to have been removed thither from Rygheur, my Lords are of the opinion that this booty, cannot be

distributed on the principle of actual capture, to the force by which Rygheur was taken under the orders of the Government of Bombay, unless it can be proved, by the captors of Rygheur that the property in question was actually in that fort at the time when it was taken; in default of which proof, my lords are of the opinion, that this booty also ought to be distributed among the forces of all the Presidencies engaged in the combined operations of the campaign.[72]

And furthermore,

> with respect to the portion of booty which is stated to consist of money recovered on account of deposits made by the Peishwa, my lords are of the opinion that any part of the property which can be proved to have been at Poona at the time when that place was captured . . . ought to be distributed to the captors of Poona . . . upon the principle of actual capture; but that with respect to those parts of the above property as to which such proof cannot be established, such monies or effects must be considered as having been acquired by the general results of war, and as such ought to be distributed, amongst the forces of all the presidencies engaged in the combined operations of the campaign.[73]

In the final warrant, approximately 21 million rupees or 150,000 pounds were distributed to the actual capturers, and 41 million rupees or close to double were distributed as a 'general result of the war'.[74] Finally, T. Hislop was not treated as a commander-in-chief but as a lieutenant-general, and second in command to Marquis Hastings.

T. Hislop, Lionel Smith and Jopp (on behalf of Colonel Prother) appealed the decision of the Lords of the Treasury to the Privy Council. The issue was taken up in the House of Commons and discussed with sympathy shown towards Hislop's position. Hislop reiterated his claim that he be considered commander-in-chief and be given shares of the Prize commensurate with this position. Smith, who had commanded the division which conquered Poona, reiterated an earlier request that the amount of approximately 13.5 lakh rupees recovered as Prize in Poona ought to be given to his division, which had actually captured Poona. As part of the evidence Robertson, who was a civil magistrate at Poona, had stated that except for some money in the possession of bankers, none of what was recovered at Poona was there when it was (earlier) captured. Captain Jopp on behalf of Colonel Prother, who had commanded the division which captured Rygheur, stated that since this money was illegally removed from Rygheur to Poona in violation of the terms of the treaty, Prother, as actual captor, was entitled to the said money as lawful Prize. However, the

Lords had earlier determined – confirming the decision of the Supreme Court at Bombay – that no evidence was placed on record that the money recovered in Poona from Naroba Outia was indeed the same money that was recovered in Poona. In the light of this, once again the Lords had decided that the money recovered could not be claimed as 'actual capture', but had to be shared in common with the combined armies as the 'general results of the wars'.[75]

At the Privy Council it was confirmed that 'all booty and prize belongs to crown' except where statutory enactment gave specific classes of people particular rights. Since no such statute existed, it was argued that it rested with 'his majesty to deal with this property that has come to him by virtue of his prerogative and one of the rights of his crown and his judgment',[76] and those who constitutionally held the position to advise him, i.e. the Privy Council. The debate merely turned on the question as to the right to appeal to the Privy Council when the Lords of the Treasury had already given their opinion. In defence of the right to appeal to the Privy Council, the lawyers for Hislop and Smith argued that the Privy Council had original jurisdiction over matters of war and Prize, citing the texts of Hale on prerogative and the statutes from the time of Richard. Ultimately, the Privy Council chose to refer the question back to the Lords of the Treasury, who did not find reason to alter their decision.

It is recognition of that which was acquired by the 'general results' of war which allows us to loop back to Outia's case. The validity of 'general results' of war appears to confirm the worst fears of the lawyers of Outia, who had argued that this meant that the laws of war and Prize were infinitely and indefinitely elastic. Since even ten years after the actual conquest no formal treaty was signed or proclamation made beyond those made in 1819, it meant that seizures in the name of Prize could still be made. Not only was Prize indefinitely elastic in relation to time, it was also similarly elastic with reference to what it indicated, since it could include 'arrears of tribute, rent or money due to the Peshwa'. Nothing further was added that would fulfil the conditions of becoming 'British subjects' requiring protection, and therefore the laws of war would continue to prevail.

Epistemic Masking: John Austin and Henry Maine

John Austin: Legal Despotism, Habitual Obedience and Rude Liberty

Even though the above analysis on the subject pertains to the laws of war and conquest, it is not unrelated to the general ways in which the legal subject was construed in contemporaneous Britain. To gain some knowledge of this framing so as to better understand subjects of conquest and war, even when not directly treated or obliquely disavowed, the works of John Austin are analysed. It is seen how Austin's general legal schema both exposes and conceals the working of empire.

In fact, the narrative and analysis of the previous sections on the question of subjects and subjectification may appear more intelligible if one subtracts the idea of 'rights' from the very idea of the 'subject', or treat rights and the subject as always subtended by the more fundamental grounding of law. That is to say, one must not automatically assume that a subject has a right in itself, like the 'natural rights' perspective might have it. It is precisely such a view that is fully articulated in the roughly contemporaneous classic work on jurisprudence, *The Province of Jurisprudence Determined*, by Austin. Here, the argument is explicitly made that a sovereign can vest rights even in members (subjects) of a foreign independent political society, by virtue of 'imposing relative duties on members of its own community'.[77] Howsoever one interprets the status of the East India Company and the sovereigns and natives of India, such a perspective allows us to legitimately ask whether any such relative duties were imposed on the East India Company, even if the status of native subjects remained obscure. Were there any such implied rights that the natives of India had, and were they being honoured or enforced? It had long been established that Company officials as British subjects were indeed subject to the law of England, and therefore these questions remain pertinent particularly when their actions directly affected the lives of millions in the subcontinent. The trial of Hastings certainly gave this set of questions a renewed intensity, even if they did not provide any concrete guidelines.

Before addressing this specific question on the nature of the subject-status of natives, it ought to be stated at the outset that in his definition of a polity, Austin continues Fortescue's postulate that the continuity and unity of the kingdom-polity lay in its laws. Austin explicitly, like Fortescue before him, dismisses any necessary equivalence between a 'nation' – defined in terms of blood, lineage and common language – and an 'independent political society',[78] the phrase that Austin uses for what one might today conceptualize as a 'sovereign state'. No characteristic of a 'people' – whether blood or language – can constitute a political entity since the latter requires law and sovereignty, which, according to Austin, can only be conceptualized hierarchically as a command and (habitual) obedience. Nationality was itself a statutory affair when defined as subject-status, and might in its own way encompass many nationalities when the latter was defined in terms of blood or language. The sovereign state, or 'independent political society', is defined in terms of law and the 'habits of obedience' that a people observe towards a 'common and determinate' sovereign[79] which does not subordinate itself to any other entity. Yet Austin appears to allow for the fact that there might be cases where sovereign entities obey the commands of others, and these polities retain their sovereignty as long as such subservience is not habitual. Illustrations of such cases include France under Allied occupation after the Napoleonic wars where France was to have preserved its sovereignty, since its obedience was not 'habitual'.[80]

Such a description of an 'independent political society' had little to do with the old distinction between 'free' and 'despotic' governments. In Austin's work this was not an intelligible distinction because sovereigns and governments were not limited by law and therefore were, by their very nature, 'legally despotic'.[81] Since the distinction was not valid, the inference that 'free' government was in some sense superior to 'despotic' governments could not stand. Liberties and rights in themselves were not necessarily a good thing, Austin argued, since rights and liberties could be used both justifiably and unjustifiably, correctly or wrongly. Therefore, the mere presence of greater liberties or rights in one polity was no guarantee that it was superior to another which had fewer liberties or rights. While the legal powers of the sovereign could not be limited, every right or liberty had to be understood as a 'creature of positive law'.[82] A right could only be measured by justice, and justice necessarily had as its measure positive, existing, institutional law.[83]

Notwithstanding such broad pronouncements on sovereignty and positive law, Austin's specific interpretations of sovereignty and law are equally crucial to understanding his argument. Having defined sovereignty in terms of despotism, he makes it clear that it is a matter of 'fact', not 'law', as to whether a government is sovereign or not. And the fact to be discerned is whether the 'bulk' of society 'habitually obeys' the sovereign. All the same, Austin is more than aware that one cannot have a general rule or precise formulation to calculate the 'bulk' of society who 'habitually obey' the sovereign. In both historical terms as well as contemporary times, he recognizes that there are 'transitions' to 'independent political societies' where the precise point of transition is never easy to discern. The examples Austin gives in illuminating his argument is of seventeenth-century England, which transitioned from the state of civil war (where it was clearly split into two distinct societies at war) to become an independent political society.[84]

The contemporary example given is Mexico, which rebelled and then became an independent political society. Since no exact number (constituting the 'bulk') or precise heuristic (determining the nature of 'bulk') existed to determine habitual obedience or the point in time at which an independent society comes into being,[85] Austin makes the crucial manoeuvre of reframing the whole question of determining habitual obedience in historical-civilizational terms. This manoeuvre, as we will see, has a long after-life. Reiterating his undervaluing of liberties and rights, Austin states that a 'civilized' society is characterized by the fact that the bulk of society habitually obeys, whereas, on the other hand, in 'savage' societies there is no habitual obedience to a determinate and common superior-sovereign; here people might only unite for wars.[86] Such savage societies do not have *laws* in the proper sense and neither can they be said to have legal penalties. They only have 'customs' or general behaviour, which is that which governs and regulates behaviour. While no law but only the law of opinion exists in savage societies, in civilized societies one sees the characteristic of *habitual* obedience and therein law.

So civilization is defined in terms of a despotic sovereignty being the source of laws but which itself has no limits, while in 'savage' societies no such sovereignty or law exists; Hume and Rousseau no doubt form a vague backdrop.[87] How is one to understand England in such a schema? The exact nature of sovereignty needs to be established because only on this basis can one speak intelligibly of 'habits of obedience' and 'laws' as essential markers of 'civilization'. According to Austin, in the case of England, sovereignty lay in the King, peers and the commons (when in session), and the King, peers and the electoral body which elected the commons when parliament is dissolved. As sovereign, parliament cannot be limited and it has the power to legally enact any kind of provision, including the provision to make the King entirely sovereign or prolong the present House of Commons to a set of indefinite years. And yet, in what precise sense one is to understand the King, peers and parliament (when in session) as a sovereign that is common and determinate is not easily resolved by Austin, as we see below.

If civilization and laws require sovereign power, can one consistently speak of a separation of powers? Here Austin critiques his predecessor Blackstone who he accuses of making distinctions for which he finds no basis.[88] Thus the Blackstonian position that the King holds executive power and parliament legislative power is a distinction that is critiqued. Since both powers are conventionally distinguished in terms of institutional channels, Austin's critique points to the fact that the King too possessed 'legislative' powers (articles of war and the discipline of the army), while parliament also administered and executed laws in various ways.[89] Judicial procedure lay clearly within the King's domain, while judges carry out a 'legislative duty' in their judgments – an issue on which he departs from Bentham. Since members of parliament are 'trustees' of the people, sovereignty lay in the peers, King and members of parliament (as trustees and when in session).[90] There was all the same an 'ulterior legislature' formed by the King, peers and the electoral body, and it is only thereby that courts of justice could strike down as illegal the laws emerging from parliament, i.e. on the basis of the 'constitutionality' of the laws.[91] Yet, even while critiquing a 'separation of powers' doctrine, the precise nature of sovereignty in its unity and determinateness as the exemplary sign of civilization remains unclear. This difficulty takes on a particular edge when one considers his discussion on the precise legal status of the King, where Austin is not only imprecise but inconsistent.

In the first place, Austin makes it clear that the English King was not a monarch with absolute power. And yet he could not be characterized as a mere minister, in Hobbes's sense.[92] Hobbes had argued that when an individual's power was legally limited, he was but a minister of the sovereign power that limited his power. But in England, the King was also a constitutive part of the parliament that had the legal powers of limitation. In what sense, therefore, was one to characterize English kingship in such a context?

In more than one instance Austin defines the English King as a 'limb' of parliament,[93] and therefore subject to legal limitation, in theory, by King-in-Parliament. And yet, in practice and fact, Austin is clear that there can be no legal limitation to the King; and fact is after all sovereign.[94] Hence the continuing validity of the maxim of the King not being able to do or think wrong even if those who administer his decisions might be subject to law. Austin does not resolve this problem of the precise status of the King and his relationship to parliament, and in attempting to explain this situation he does not turn to the 'traditional' doctrines of the 'King's two bodies' that we have explored. In describing the status of the King and the nature of sovereignty in England, he does not account for the contemporaneous juridical fact and demand that allegiance be necessarily owed to a natural person, something that the earlier doctrines tried to ground and explain. Moreover, Austin does not confront the problem of the unity or continuity of the body-politic in terms of the heirs to the King.

The one place where he comes close to the difficulties in conceptualizing English kingship – and the need for doctrines like that of the 'King's two bodies' – is when he tries to account for a specific fact, i.e. the relationship between Hanover and the United Kingdom through the monarch.[95] How was one to understand kingship when the King was, as (1) King of England (and/as the limb of King-in-Parliament as well), (2) sole sovereign King of Hanover. The two could not be identified as one because if the former case was consistently followed through, it would mean that the sovereign of Hanover was King-in-Parliament (and not the King, who in Austinian terms was a mere 'limb' of King-in-Parliament). And if the latter was consistently followed through, England would be subject to the King as fully sovereign (and not King-in-Parliament). However, such inconsistency was legally the fact. The King was qualified in both ways – as sole sovereign in Hanover and as 'mixed' with parliament in England – even though this implied an irresolvable juridical inconsistency, even contradiction. Towards such an intractable and critical legal dilemma Austin merely says that the two statuses need to be conceived separately as 'practically distinct'.[96] But what is 'practically distinct', the natural person or the institution 'mixed' with the natural person? And is such a state of affair intelligible at all?

And yet, this particular 'fact' of the King as King of Hanover and King in England, expresses the fundamental problem of the body-politic and its constitution, the basis of the laws, the principles of subject, alien and enemy, that we have been tracing since *Postnati*, and the many bodies of the King, expanding from the Americas to the Indian subcontinent. To have reduced this vast and foundational issue to a seeming anomaly in the Hanover case appears to be a wanton epistemic repression – a repression that will only deepen with his successors, even if the Hanover case as a seeming anomaly will provide the pre-text for yet another foundational churn in citizenship with the *Stephen Election* case. Here, rather than shedding light on the nature of the King and its relationship to the body-politic, it is judicially affirmed that allegiance is owed *to the King* in his 'political capacity' and not 'personal capacity'. This distinction does little to sever the King's political capacity from his 'natural body' – *Postnati*'s term or the key term in the doctrine of the King's two bodies where 'politic' and 'natural' are inseparable. This inseparability is signified by the statutes with regard to crimes of high treason where it is the monarch's natural body, and those associated, which is involved. The abstraction of the state was thereby jurisprudentially avoided while the King survives unscathed and unchallenged in juridical and jurisprudential discourse. Until the passing of the Naturalization Act (1870), it was not possible to renounce allegiance. While this act made such renunciation possible, it still retained the oath of allegiance to the King/Queen.[97]

Henry Maine: Sovereignty and Property, Historical Trajectories and Contemporary Resonances

Austin's conceptual repression of the role of the King will be found to take historical form in Henry Maine. Maine has for long been recognized as a theorist of modernity, even though his conceptualization of modernity is not merely to be discerned in the supposed move from status to contract, collective forms of property to individual property rights. These 'developments' are themselves framed within the broader logic of territorialization, centralization and legislation as features of the 'modern', said to have been achieved in England most of all. In this sense, his characterization of the modern sovereign state is not admittedly different from the Austinian 'independent political society'. Yet his historical account of the development of such features curiously occludes both the role of the King and Crown and the amplification of empire from the seventeenth century onwards, the subject of the last two parts of this book. This is all the more curious, if not ironical, since Maine cannot but admit the contemporaneous importance of the Crown and its role in the British Empire in India, all the same failing to recognize this imperial form in its own *historical logic* of such territorialization, centralization and legislation[98] as expressed by the sword and conquest. This contradiction and its implications are analysed by beginning with a study of his broader historical studies before moving to his conceptualization of the British Empire.[99] Sticking close to this problematic is the close linkage between property and the state that Maine unravels, the specific relationship between the two often forming the unique signature of the particular political configuration at play.

One might say that there are three clues in Maine's complex work, *Ancient Law*, that exist in somewhat 'sinister isolation'. Detecting their kinship would go some way in shedding legal light on the schemes of historical transformation that he is best known for. The first two serve as crucial conceptual-historical moments and levers in what is considered Maine's singular scholarly contribution: the transformation from (patriarchal) joint property and custom to (legislative–modern–individual) contract. Only on the basis of this transformation is his foundational critique of natural law legible, which is integral to the broader historical narrative about status and contract that he wishes to establish. Both these moment-levers are related to war.

The first conceptual moment-lever is Maine drawing our attention to the fact that, in Roman law, Prize or booty as the right of acquisition through military combat and war becomes a *first* site of individual accumulation/acquisition, since it is protected *from* patriarchal claims.[100] The second conceptual moment-lever is Maine's argument that 'occupation' is a mode of acquisition of property from the conquered enemy, and emerges from an existing system of law clearly related to the above. This understanding of occupation is opposed to the natural right/law theorists of the seventeenth and eighteenth centuries for whom 'occupation' originally could be traced to a 'state of nature', where one occupied land which was not already under anyone's occupation.[101] And finally, the third conceptual moment-lever is one of obfuscation. Here, Maine – contrary to the explicit discussion of *Postnati* – compares the parson and the King, and treats the corporation sole as an 'office'. This is perhaps a first feeble attempt to detach the natural person of the King from his political capacity, anticipating Maitland and returning to the damnable proposition of the Spencers and the regicide of the seventeenth century that was denounced by the highest courts of even the late nineteenth century.[102] We know, as the discussion of the Elizabethan jurists onwards and never subsequently challenged legally or jurisprudentially, that kings had heirs, unlike corporations which had successors. In English kingship the purity of blood descends, lending a natural-bodily dimension to kingship that is the only basis for allegiance as much as high treason.

The three moments above can be used to effectively interpret the broader dual problematic that Maine confronts and articulates in his writings. This duality consisted in: (1) the relationship between law and territory; (2) the relationship between sovereignty and law. Maine agrees, as stated above, with Hobbes, Bentham and Austin, that in modern states in the west, sovereignty has a single source and legislation is the fount of law. However, he argues that this was itself a specific historical development that could not be found in other parts of the world. More interestingly he sees the influence of Roman law and feudalism *together* as leading to the modern condition defined by an absolutist sovereignty staged in a circumscribed territory; modern sovereignty is directly linked to a circumscribed territory. Central to his concerns is to explain this shift from forms of power that are not inherently (territorially) localized and differentially organized, to centralized, absolutist forms of territorialized laws. This entire theorization of both history and law has had a long shadow down to the contemporary, and is only enabled by the wilful obfuscation of the historical development of sovereignty and law that we have been involved in charting until now.

In explaining the peculiarities of modern law, Maine requires one to define law in specific ways that clearly differentiate it from other, older forms of rule and control. In substantiating this point he directly confronts the seeming contradictions that he saw, along with others before him, as characterizing eastern empires: the despotism of the sovereign and the customs of the village.[103] Maine argues that, contrary to contemporary forms of western absolutist sovereignty, the despot never made a law, even though he certainly organized an administration around the collection of revenue, and could punish and charge as he pleased. Laws, by which Maine meant the rules that govern societies in their everyday interactions, were in these despotic eastern empires to be understood as customs – practices derived by immemorial usage, and administered locally by families, village heads and village tribunals. The penal sanctions on which such customary practices in the east depended were 'superstition' or 'opinion', but 'to a far greater extent an instinct almost as blind and unconscious as that which produces some of the movement of our bodies'.[104] Similarly, the commands of the sovereign – in the administration of the revenues or the taxes – were implicitly obeyed, cruel and harsh though they might have been. Since instinct drove action, the sovereign's commands might be seen as laws instinctively obeyed.

This example from India was meant to be but a contemporary instantiation of the fact that sovereignty was neither absolute nor 'territorialized' in non-western/non-modern polities because the everyday rules and regulations that governed men were customs, not laws, expressed in the 'spasmodic' subjection to sovereigns for revenue and taxation.[105] Maine argues, in an account that echoes Smith's lectures on jurisprudence, that such was the case in England too prior to the seventeenth century, and it was only the King's law and the King's Courts in England that slowly but surely subsumed local laws. Parliament, through its statutes, built on these King's laws, and from thence emerged the sure road to a centralized sovereign legislation which was institutionalized in the seventeenth century, and most clearly expressed in Hobbes, Bentham and Austin.[106] These thinkers recognized the emerging institutionalized forms, and sought to render them more consistent and rational. Hobbes's suggestions in the seventeenth century regarding the registration of land titles, the fusion of law and equity, and a systematic penal code, were all measures that were on the 'eve of being carried out' in the nineteenth century in the making of a centralized, territorialized state that formed the locus of legislation.[107] No doubt, this was Maine's way of breaking apart Austin's 'despotic law', even as he took a cue from Austin in recognizing that there was no real or modern law to be found in the 'customs' of rude and savage societies.[108] Of course, there is a simultaneous admission that the Hobbesian idea recognized in the seventeenth century was yet to be fully accomplished.[109]

While these were arguments found in the *Lectures on the Early History of Institutions*, in *Ancient Law* Maine had given great importance to 'feudalism', in the coming into being of the sovereign-absolute territorialization of law.[110] In effect, he had argued that the monarchies which developed in the later middle ages had two models to emulate: there was the 'tribal-clan' form of kingship where the king/chief ruled as a 'first among equals' over an indeterminate territory, or there were the universal claims of the Roman emperors, which of course contrasted with their control over specified domains. The crucial step that 'feudalism' as a historical phenomenon took, according to Maine, was to link ownership of the soil with rights and duties. Benefices or land were given in return for military service. In this sense, the tenant's rights and duties to a particular patch of soil were related to his superior, which in turn were owed and linked to a superior, until it reached the King who was lord and not tenant. Blackstone's commentaries in the eighteenth century had already described as accurate this description of the feudal system where all ownership ultimately was 'held' of the King. Maine argues that this form of the territorialization of sovereignty, through monarchy, began in France and was subsequently emulated in many parts of the world including Norman England.[111] From here begins the slow territorialization of the sovereign and a sovereign territory. The form of property is thus a crucial feature of sovereignty.

This is seen specifically in the way the paradigmatic importance of the family and paternal power expresses itself in feudal land law through primogeniture. Maine finds this to be a genuinely unique development with no precedence in either Roman law or non-European legal systems, where land and property were ordinarily equally divided among the (male) progeny. He accounts for this through analogy – with the fact that in many legal systems while property devolved equally among progeny, political power and office devolved upon the eldest son. The feudal lord was analogous to the *pater familias* – and what the latter did through adoption, the feudal lord did though infeudation.[112] In this way the unity of the community land and its integrity were maintained, which gave it strength and durability against external forces. Originally the eldest, who succeeded in governance and thereby had rights over the entire property, could not be said to have 'ownership' of the specific land in an absolute sense, since such 'ownership' also involved correlative duties imposed on him. Moreover, such land was open to the claims of others, whether the agnatic group or the larger community under him. However, historically, Maine argues, the adoption of various aspects of Roman law required more absolute forms of ownership, and it was not long before the eldest as inheritor became the 'legal proprietor of inheritance'.[113] This process whereby the 'patrimony of the many' became 'the estate of the one' was also observable among the Scottish Highland clans and chieftainships.[114]

In the light of this detailed history of the historically contingent individuation of property and property rights, Maine's critique of Hobbes and Rousseau was that they projected to the primitive past what was in fact a late product of a refined and highly developed society and jurisprudence, i.e. the notion of exclusive individual possession and property right. Describing such 'social contract' theories as a speculative-historical transformation of Roman natural law theories, Maine further argues that one has to trace to these theories the idea that 'occupation' was the paradigmatic model for private property.[115] It was here assumed that originally the world was gifted by God, and existed as common inheritance. The individual who then occupied an unoccupied piece of land and worked on it thereby acquired a property right over it. In time, this possession became right. Therefore, property right emerged as an exclusive individual right because it was assumed that any object could become the exclusive property right of one person or the other. This was also said to be the basis of the legal term 'prescription' or 'adverse possession', where unchallenged and undisturbed possession for a specified time ripened into property right.

However, Maine argues that this understanding of property as exclusive and individual was something that took time to develop, and was a sign of modernity rather than being the original-historical condition for property. For the Romans, 'occupation' as a specific mode of legally acquiring property only existed within a well-entrenched legal-proprietorial system, and could not be abstracted from such a context into the sort of original condition speculated upon by Hobbes and Rousseau. Occupation referred to taking possession – with the *intention* of legal acquisition – of that which was possessed by no one (*res nullius*). This could include wild animals, deserted lands, jewels *and the property of the vanquished enemy.*[116] However, this legal development was the historical *result* of people possessing the idea of the inviolability of rights and the durability of property rights. As Maine asks, if one believed that possession was the original foundation of property right, there was no clear reason as to why anyone would respect such rights of possession. Why would the mere passage of time in itself imply a right?[117] Thus, occupation could only slowly emerge within a developed system of law which had notions of absolute property rights and could not be traced to an original 'state of nature'. What Montesquieu, along with the natural law tradition, had taken to be the origins of society, in the form of the pact or agreements, according to Maine, was but a late and peculiar development, not universal in nature, and yet to be found in many non-western societies in the nineteenth century.[118]

It is by investigating the origins of legal systems that Maine discusses the importance of patriarchal power and the powers of fiction. According to him, political power was originally exercised by patriarchal *potestas*, and a fiction allowed various members, including those incorporated by adoption, to collect together as a family.[119] The family was thus controlled by the clan head even while property was collective property and not individualized. Ancient law was analogous in a sense to modern international law, because it sought to mediate relations, not between individual proprietors, but between families (as corporations)[120]. Property as familial-collective ensured that the more dignified forms of property such as land were largely collectively owned, and less easy to transfer or be alienated. Maine's history of property law and jurisprudence tracks the story of the ways in which more and more forms of property become alienable with time. This alienability or transferability of property took place under the ambit of 'contract', whereas one's position in the patriarchal family denoted one's status. This power continued well into Roman law, and it is only within the interstices of the complex development of Roman law that one witnesses 'occupation' as one among several rights. Usucapio within Roman law could be granted even after very short periods of time precisely because there already existed a system of laws to recognize it.

Notwithstanding the distinction, Maine does not draw an easy or clear-cut contrast between 'status' and 'contract'. This is clearly illustrated if we take land law, and specifically, the development of feudal land law. While both Roman and feudal law appeared to countenance 'double proprietorship' – the superior ownership of the lord as well as the inferior ownership of the tenant – they were not necessarily the same. In Rome, patrician tenants of public land, though legally 'tenants at will', claimed that undisturbed possession had with time granted them some sort of ownership. This form of 'possessory ownership' was recognized by the praetor through equity and summary procedure, and was enforced by 'possessory interdicts'[121]. In England, equity and law, unlike in the Roman case, took the form of two distinct jurisdictions: the Chancery Court and the common law courts. Actual owners, finding the system of real actions in the common law courts to be too technical and cumbersome, resorted to the Chancery, thereby retaining their property as equitable property. Thus, the distinction between ownership and possession, law and equity became a complicated matter, nameable and discernable by the process chosen rather than denoting an *a priori* status or definition. Feudal land law also seemed to follow the specific Roman tenure of Emphyteusis, where the tenant was recognized to have some ownership rights by the praetor, such as the possibility to appeal an ejectment as long as a quit rent was regularly paid. These tenures were also heritable. Simultaneously, the author of the lease had the power of re-entry on non-payment, pre-emption in case of sale, and some control over the mode of cultivation. Veteran soldiers on the Austro–Turkish border also held land on the same tenure with the Roman state as public landlord, but paid in terms of their military service rather than a quit rent. The fact that these war veterans were often Germanic could be the reason, speculated Maine, as to why the Franks and the Lombards also granted tenures in return for military service, though specific 'incidents' were added, such as endowing the daughter, 'equipping the son' and being 'liable for guardianship during minority'. All these became sources of revenue for the King, and critical to the development of English kingship.[122]

In England, Equity and Chancellery jurisdiction was employed precisely to escape such feudal incidents through which the King demanded revenue. Lands and their legal titles were given to others so as to escape forms of taxes/revenue. And yet forms of 'ownership' and control of these properties – which were legally the property of others – were enforced though Chancery Courts. In this lies the origins of the notoriously complex English 'system' of uses and feoffees,[123] where the latter were 'trustees' holding legal title in the landholdings, for the use of the 'beneficial owner'. However, though the trustee had legal title in one sense, the beneficial owner could enforce a range of rights through Chancellery jurisdiction (Equity), and these kinds of property were thus called equitable estates. The fact that in the seventeenth century, in the great struggle between Coke and Ellensmore representing the Common Law and Chancery, the Chancery (Equity) proved its superiority, tells us of the nature and complexity of land law, possession and ownership.[124] While a common law decision could be appealed in the Chancery, the latter's decision could not be appealed in the common law courts. Possession as the physical holding and the intention to hold, as distinct from ownership as a legal title, were separated by a thin shifting line drawn by the relevant cases and jurisdictions at play, and could only be discerned therein and not through abstract definition.

None of the above are easily intelligible in terms of the binary, status and contract, and Maine's discussion of contract/conveyance shows that only the last form of the contract – 'mutual consent' – might signal what the moderns understand by contract, in terms of a mutual agreement recognized and enforceable by law. This once again reiterates that the Natural Law theorists could not begin with a 'state of nature', since all contracts required law and were results of the long development of law rather than their point of origin. And yet, in his scholarly description of the modernity of law – in terms of centralization, territorialization and legislation – Maine represses the history and changing functions of the British Empire, which he cannot avoid in his official capacity as the Law Member. This repression is clear in his equation of the King with the parson, as though the King only held an 'office', whereas the whole constitutional and jurisprudential argument from the Elizabethan jurists and *Postnati* onwards was that the King was *not* a parson. It was on this basis that the King could underpin and bind, conquer and acquire several jurisdictions and laws across the globe, an argument that became the effective motor of imperial expansion from the seventeenth century – all of which is wilfully forgotten in Maine's histories. And yet his own argument about 'Prize' being the mould of an alternative to both the patriarchal and the Natural law/right paradigms does indeed account for the expansive distension of the Crown and its territories from the seventeenth century onwards. Such distension does not respect any of the neat historical processes of centralization and territorialization otherwise described by Maine. Almost without knowing it, the isolated characterizations of Prize touched on above provide the clue to the intelligible transformations signalled by the great categories of patriarchal, Roman and feudal law – as opposed to the speculative theories of natural right.[125]

In his role as Law Member of the Governor-General's Council, however, the King and Crown cannot but surface. This is clearly illustrated in Maine's arguments on the Crown's relationship with the 'native princely states' in India. Let us see what precisely happens to centralization, territorialization and sovereignty, so prominent in his works discussed above. In the important minute on the native state of Kathiawar, he states very clearly that the 'proposition that territory that is British is not subject to British law does not appear to me to be tenable'.[126] This proposition leads him to his much-celebrated doctrine of 'divisible sovereignty', where sovereignty is defined as an 'assemblage of divisible and separate powers'.[127] Maine the legal historian, best known for his work on 'custom', in practice strategically scrambles Austin's conceptualization of sovereignty to occlude the legal manipulations and dissimulations of empire, as will be shown. While Austin had equated sovereignty with an 'independent political society', his definition of these terms as 'habitual obedience of the bulk of society to a common and determinate superior' led to certain consequences. For Austin, it could be the case that a sovereign or independent political society intermittently obeyed another political society, and thus intermittent obedience – since it was not habitual – meant that such a polity retained its sovereignty; as an illustration, France under Allied occupation is mentioned. On the other hand, Austin also recognized that political formations might exist, like in Germany, where rights of war and peace remained with the princes while they continued to recognize the appellate legal authority of the emperor. Even so, Maine distinguishes sovereignty from an independent political society by claiming that the former could be divided into greater and lesser portions. He uses this differentiation of sovereignty to theorize the relationship between the princely states and the British in the late nineteenth century, but he does so, all the same, for the purpose of asserting the overall control and authority of the latter (the British Empire) over the former (the native/princely states).

All this is done through obfuscating arguments, which can only be explained by the clarity of purpose in giving the British Empire unfettered power over native rulers. After defining sovereignty as an 'assemblage of separate rights and privileges', Maine asserts that the princely state of Kathiawar did possess certain of these 'sovereign' rights, such as the immunity from foreign laws. However, it is equally affirmed that, conceptually, the 'independent sovereign' is one who possesses the 'whole of the aggregate of [sovereign] rights'.[128] And in India, it is unequivocally affirmed, while 'many shades of sovereignty' might be found, the British were the only power who were an 'independent sovereign'[129] – the adoption of an Austinian phrase in its Austinian sense.[130] If the British as the independent had the *whole* of the aggregate rights, how could this not encompass the partial sovereign rights of Kathiawar which were to be found in the same locus? This 'encompassment', independent sovereignty over the divisible sovereign, the British Empire over the native state, is in fact directly affirmed by Maine.[131]

In one sense, this parallels the contradictions in Austin. Austin, as discussed above, allows for a sovereign to intermittently obey the commands of another sovereign. He also allows for a differentiation of sovereignty, illustrating this with reference to Germany. Maine too gives the same example to illustrate the same case, where German princes possessed some sovereign rights but at the same time recognized the German emperor as superior in others. By this is implied that Kathiawar, as a native state, is to be defined as sovereign while all the while submitting to the British. Maine clarifies that the British were *justified* in interfering in the matters of the native states, and this right to interfere is explicitly linked to their overall position as paramount and being the only 'independent sovereign'. Maine insisted on absolute powers – styled independent sovereignty – for the British in India as a whole, including Kathiawar. Thus, the staged 'division' of sovereignty was meant to merely characterize Kathiawar as partially sovereign, and was in turn meant to fulfil the purpose of actually affirming British sovereignty over Kathiawar as much as the other native states. Interference in 'partially sovereign' native polities, Maine argues, is to be done only on the grounds of intending the betterment of the princes and the people, and the interests of the British Empire; one discerns Metcalf's argument about the centrality of the intentionality of the superior as much as the general question of the King's equity and conscience. However, since he simultaneously states that the intentions of the British can never be doubted, it is virtually a *carte blanche* for British interference, reaffirming their absolute – styled independent – sovereignty that Maine now styles as 'suzerainty'; one is reminded of the East India Company's defence of its treatment of the Mughal ruler discussed in Part II, where the intentions of the powerful are all-determining. Maine's argument for the term suzerainty found its way into Statute 52 and 53 Vic. cap. lxiii, in 1889, to describe the status of 'her Majesty' Victoria in relation to the princes of India. Terminological word play thus attempts to mask the powers at operation, a ruse clearly derivable from the subterfuges of Lord Clive's 'double government'. Justification for interventions was sometimes worded as the subsumption of the 'legal' in the 'political', such as when the argument is made that notwithstanding the fact that legally the Travancore ruler had the right to try British individuals, this could be rendered impossible by the (political) superiority of the British government over Travancore. Law being trumped by Equity again?

Maine also justifies the right of the Crown to alienate and transfer dominions in India.[132] This raises the question once again of what kind of territory or right-less subjects exist in India who could be transferred as a piece of patrimonial property, as rewards for service rendered. The absence of such a right was that which was to have distinguished royal rule from despotic dominion; such rights are one more resurfacing sign of the despotic nature of British rule. The so-called modernity of centralization, territorialization and legislation, therefore, certainly had not succeeded even in the spatial contours of England, let alone the despotic practices of a planetary empire. Such practices could only be accounted for, not by the dreams and fantasies of such modernity, but rather by the ghostly archaic of the King's many bodies.

Marinating a Subcontinent: International Law and the International Order

Maine's wilful ignorance of the Crown and Prize jurisdiction affects his thesis on territorialization and centralization as the trajectory of modernity. For, the British conquest of India from the time of the East India Company onwards is perhaps best pictured as the protracted 'marinization' – the testing of products for a marine environment – of a subcontinent. While land was conquered in terms of the originally maritime patents of Prize, as shown in Part II, discrepancy found its formal end in the *Banda and Kirwee Booty* case; here, for the first time, booty distribution was officially adjudicated by the High Court of Admiralty. The *Deccan* case had clarified that it was the treasury which played the role of advisor to the Queen/King in matters of the distribution of booty acquired in land. In such a decision and in the arguments of the case, analogies with Prize cases were liberally employed, and many of the key terms of the decision and debate – such as actual captor and constructive captor – were only therein intelligible. There was a long history to this analogizing of Prize law with land, as was seen from the time of Plassey and Srirangapatnam, since no clearly juridical tribunal existed to adjudicate claims on booty acquired through land wars in the subcontinent.

The *Banda and Kirwee Booty* case, contemporaneous to Maine's meditations, was yet another one of adjudicating the rights of different divisions of the army to the booty captured in the course of repressing the great rebellion of 1857 in parts of Central India. The Admiralty Act of 1840 had established admiralty jurisdiction over Prize money, giving the High Court of Admiralty, should the Crown so wish, jurisdiction over booty in land, where the case law of Prize was used as precedent and analogy. The High Court exercised its jurisdiction for the first time in the *Banda and Kirwee Booty* case in relation to the wars of 1857–58.[133] In its final decision of 1867, the court referred to the principle of the *Deccan* decision, that Prize was not confined to the appropriation of property when a city or fort was 'stormed', but could be acquired at a time that bore an indefinite relation to the 'event' of capture and conquest.[134] These, as discussed above, were designated as the 'general results of the war', and the Privy Council had furthered cemented the infinite potential of such appropriation of property by the legally effective declaration that in India, absolutist conditions meant that no distinction was made between public and private property; all was subject to lawful Prize and no such act was justiciable in a (municipal) court. Moreover, no clarification was given as to when a war ended, in effect making the duration of the latter indefinite, and therein too the 'laws' of Prize and booty. The effect of such a marine mutation on terra-firma was fatal to any notion of law itself. The laws that allowed for capture at sea – which was, by its nature, of a limited duration and space – became in land through the employment of Prize laws and Privy Council decisions, a maelstrom radiating in time and place

International law as we know it historically emerged from maritime Prize Courts[135] that claimed to be adjudicating on the basis of international principles or the laws of nations, and not territorial local laws. There was no equivalent for the rules and regulations of land wars. From the late eighteenth century onwards, beginning with Vattel and Rousseau, continental thinkers argued that wars designated a relation between states and armies, not individuals, with the corollary that the property of private citizens ought to be respected even during a war, whether on land or sea.[136] This was a position that Britain strongly opposed in the nineteenth century, basing itself on older doctrines codified in British Prize Court decisions where enemy property – whether of private citizens or official navies – were liable to be captured as lawful Prize. This position was defended by English jurists of the late nineteenth century such as H. Phillimore, T. Twiss, J. Westlake and E. Hall, against their continental counterparts. It is in these discussions and debates that one finds the origins of 'modern' international law, and among the most respected English jurists were H. Phillimore and T. Twiss, who were also involved in the *Kirwee Banda Booty* case.

It is therefore not without irony when these lawyers make a case for the humanitarian practices of modern war. In his general discourse on such matters, Twiss argues that in cases where occupation by a foreign power is not met with resistance, the sovereign power of 'Christian nations' do not seize and confiscate the property of private individuals, but rest content with levying 'contributions' and 'requisitions' on the conquered populations.[137] These 'customs' mitigated but did not deny the right of the victor, sometimes called 'occupier', over the property of the vanquished.[138] Technically, the English maintained the old doctrine – as opposed to Vattel, Rousseau and their successors – that in a war, all subjects of the enemy state were to be lawfully treated as enemies and denied all rights. Britain also reiterated a more aggressive form of its Prize laws in what was called the 'rule of 1756', where even neutral ships and their (neutral) property could be captured as Prize if it engaged in commerce with an enemy country, which it did not do 'normally' in times of peace.[139] Such commerce took place in the form of colonial and costal trades, such as when the Dutch traded with French colonies in the Seven Years war, at a time when France was disabled from such trade by Britain's maritime supremacy. This 'rule of 1756' was at odds with principles that were applied later in the century, where a neutral ship's property could not be captured by a belligerent – a policy formally adopted by Russia. This policy was formally adopted by Russia, France and other countries in 1781.[140] The philosophical basis for such a principle – codified in the laws of these countries – was formulated by Rousseau in the maxim that 'war is a relationship between states'. That is to say, if war was a relationship between states, individuals of the respective states could be allowed to carry out commerce. Such a principle was also expressed in the French revolutionary principle of 'fraternity'. However, until the Declaration of Paris (1857)[141] the English followed the general principle, which could be modified by treaty, that enemies' goods in a neutral ship were liable to capture.[142]

English lawyers strongly insisted on the rights of maritime seizure and capture of private property in *both* theory and practice, once again against their continental and American[143] counterparts. The distinction was grounded in the principle that maritime commerce provided for the sinews of war, and therefore warring parties had a right to attack the enemy's commerce as a means to weaken.[144] Their sustained divergence from the continental position lay in their refusal to see the individual as detachable from the state, which reflected their very aggressive maritime policies of blockade and capture. One might say that the British concession to humanitarian practices in land war simply reflected the fact that they were not really involved in such wars in the eighteenth and nineteenth centuries. But in fact, they were involved in precisely such practices in the subcontinent – practices that never buoyed to visibility for the international lawyer's nautical telescope. The British, in their land wars in the subcontinent, captured private property in practice and theory to an indefinable extent, as evident in the catena of Prize cases. The rule of land war protecting private property from occupation and war was codified only by the Hague Peace Conference of 1899, but no such rule existed for maritime warfare, a rule that Britain was consistently opposed to. Articles 46 and 47, speaking of conditions of military occupation of a hostile state, had specifically prohibited 'pillage' and the 'confiscation of private property'.[145]

Notwithstanding the ravaging of the land by Prize law, it is the marine strategy of blockade and Prize that can be seen to give an overall structure and schema, a nautical thrust, to what has been called 'paramountcy'. Paramountcy involved the 'subsidiary alliance system' whereby the vanquished native states of India were isolated from each other and denied any independent commerce with any political entity. This can be understood in terms of the naval blockade, which was a 'legally' recognized and accepted procedure that, in addition to the appropriation of enemy property, allowed for the appropriation of 'neutrals' allegedly interfering with the blockade by trading with the enemy port – neutral property which was otherwise meant to be protected by the laws of war, except for the ever-elastic condition of military necessity. The blockade was a more extreme form of the customs that allowed warring navies to 'search' neutral vessels, including taking them for enemy goods. The laws of 'contraband', which could be seized even from neutral vessels, also meant that even provisions including items of food could be treated as 'contraband goods' and confiscated – as happened in the Napoleonic wars.[146] States could thus be 'blockaded' with very devastating effects at a time when so much 'national' trade, even of the most essential items, was maritime and at a scale that was scarcely imaginable in a siege. Importantly, it is not a coincidence that the first important royal patent for Prize granted to the Company in 1758 was in response to a request by the Company for Prize money made in 1757, when the famous 'rule of 1756' authorized aggressive campaigns against the French and its allies.

However, Prize law and its territorial application to vanquished and rebellious princely states in India posed interesting and unique questions. Maine was writing in the aftermath of 1857–58, and Prize laws were applied in the wars against 'rebel' leaders. Canning's proclamations regarding Prize money were cited by soldiers who fought for their Prize in long litigious cases that lasted decades, the most famous of these being the *Banda and Kirwee Booty* case. Such an employment of Prize law raises two distinct questions. (1) How was Prize law to be administered to 'subject-rebels' and not enemy states, since it was historically and conceptually traced to the 'laws of nations'? The application of Prize jurisdiction on 'subjects' effectively denoted the condition of 'martial law', since no municipal court could adjudicate or challenge Prize-taking as an 'act of state'. (2) The persistent question of in what sense were Prize laws – largely concerned with maritime jurisdiction – to be applied on land, and what was usually considered 'booty'?

In practice, the native princely state, as discussed above, was both a rebel-subject (judicially characterized as such and given royal amnesty under certain conditions) as well as an alien enemy (in being the subject of Prize laws). It was in such a context that international lawyers such as Twiss, Hall and Westlake conceptualized the British Empire in such a way as to keep India and its 'native states' outside the purview of international law. This was part of the more general argument that distinguished between the civilized and the uncivilized, state and not-state actors, evolving different standards and codes of conduct for each. A legal discourse emerged at the intersection between international law and the legal status of the British Empire in India, even while the moral, legal and historical grounds of the latter were not investigated.

The existence of several hundred princely states in conjunction with British territory in India as 'imperial' excluded these states from international law. Perhaps following the lead of Maine, the Queen was defined as the suzerain, and interestingly, legal discourse detected a strong continuity between the period prior to the direct assumption of sovereignty in India in 1858 and the post-1858 period. It was argued here that it was during the rule of the East India Company that this specific notion of the 'imperial' was in operation. Such an argument was two-fold, in that it at once recognized the status of the Company as but having a delegated sovereignty, and simultaneously stated that the Company's (imperial) relations with the native rulers was to be formulated, not in terms of 'international relations', but rather as subsumed within a 'feudal' and/or 'imperial'[147] system, with the Company – as trustee of the Crown – as the paramount power. The nexus, or interchangeability, between the 'feudal' and the 'imperial' is outlined further below.

In fact, English international law as a specific discourse and field developed as its first task, and had as one of its functions, the *exclusion* of princely states of the Indian subcontinents from its ambit. The very parameters of international law were seen to require sovereign independent states. Writers of international law – the phrase was 'invented' by Bentham, though he had used it far more expansively than was later the case – were firstly confronted with the problem of whether there was such a thing as 'international law'. Austin strongly argued that where there was no enforceable authority, there one could not speak of 'law'. In response, Travers Twiss, agreeing with F.D. Martens, wrote of law as a term that might refer to both unwritten and written law. And therefore law was an appropriate term to employ for the 'usage and customs' of nations, even though there was no specified law-giver or enforcer of the law.[148] However, this space of 'international law' specifically denoted the usage and customs of 'civilized' European states and nations; it was the 'consuetudinary law of Europe', not extending beyond.[149] The primary value of such an international law was that there would be a sanctity attributed to treaties, and states could not simply disregard them at will. However, in collapsing international law onto 'civilized' Europe, both the 'uncivilized' as well as the native states/princes of India, which were classified as 'protected dependent states',[150] were excluded. And this so-called sanctity attributed to treaties, the *raison d'être* of international law and civilized Europe, was in fact a means to disregard precisely such principles when it came to relations with the rulers of India.

In such a context it is not surprising that Twiss's classification of 'protected dependent states' was itself derived from the classification of 'native states' within India in relation to the East India Company by a military officer of the Company, J. Sutherland, writing in 1837. Sutherland defined as 'internal' all those princely states who had relinquished relations with one another and all other states in their treaties with the British government.[151] The differences between them only lay in their 'internal sovereignty', or in whether they allowed interference or the degree to which they allowed interference from the British government. However, this loss of an 'international' character was what enabled Twiss to argue that even in the post-1857 period, princely states could not be the subjects of 'international law'. For, as we will see below, it was true that even after 1858, the princely states indeed did not have the ability to communicate with one another, establish 'foreign' relations, or have an 'international character'.

This manner in which the existence of a state, civilization[152] and international law were combined so as to exclude different kinds of societies and states can also be seen in Edward Hall's *A Treatise on International Law* (1895). The features of a state included the following:

> a community in its collective capacity exercise undisputed and exclusive control over all persons and things within the territory occupied by it, that it regulates its external conduct independently of the will of any other community, and in conformity with the dictates of international law, and finally that it gives reason to expect that its existence will be permanent, are sufficient to render it a person in law.[153]

Many communities in Asia and Africa were seen as 'uncivilized', lacking these features of 'civilization' and therefore not accounted for in international law. Following Twiss, but in fact Sutherland, the native princely states of India as 'protected states' were explicitly denied any subject-status in international law. This was already signified in Alfred Lyall's definition, adopted by Tupper and others, that in relation to protectorates the influence of a rival power was excluded and a duty of defence imposed. While such states appeared to possess 'internal sovereignty', their relation to the British imperial government was defined by treaty, even though these treaties were themselves interpreted in the light of the ultimate principles of the imperial government and its interests.[154] Moreover, on aspects not covered by treaties a 'residuary jurisdiction' remained with the imperial government,[155] in addition to which the government could also intervene in native states in the name of the well-being of the people. Unlike Sutherland's 1837 classification where some native states allowed for interference and others did not, Tupper argued that in fact any and all interference could be made, ironically in the post-1858 period, when it came to the interests of the British Empire. And this principle is itself traced to the 'usage' and practice of the Company in the pre-1857 period. We thus see the implication of the use of 'usage', 'custom' and 'practice' that provided the source for an international law which had no law-giver, as recognized by Twiss.

That the Company was but delegated sovereignty was stated by Henry Phillimore in 1857, citing the *Deccan Prize* case as an example of and evidence for Crown sovereignty.[156] Charles Tupper, one of the foremost commentators on the subject, speaks of the trial of Zafar as a 'subject' as clear evidence of the 'feudal' nature of the relations between the Company (as a delegated sovereign) and the princes of India.[157] That Zafar, just as other rulers of India, could be 'tried' and 'punished' indicated that the relations that existed between the Company and native rulers – as embodied in treaties and agreements – were not relations between sovereign states but of feudatories (princes) and their supreme lord (the British government). The source of these relations between suzerain and feudatory was not the principles or practices of international law, but 'without doubt usage – the actual practice of the Indian Government itself in its dealings with its feudatories'.[158] As feudatories the princely states formed a 'protectorate', and this category may well find its origins in the argument, referred to above, of Wellesley when describing the relationship between the British government and the Mughal rulers from Shah Alam onwards. The argument was that the Mughal rulers had asked for 'protection' which was granted to them under stringent institutional conditions, which included full control of the ruler's 'foreign relations'. The stringent set of conditions, including such control, as well as control over native courts and their military apparatus, however can at least be traced to the Company's relations with the Nawab of Arcot in the eighteenth century. The point made by international lawyers at the turn of the century was that the policy of an imperial system evolved and took form in a 'subsidiary alliance system'. In fact this link between a subsidiary alliance and being a subsidiary to a suzerain can be seen in the wording of statutes in relation to Queen Victoria in the post-1857 period.

Westlake sees the legal challenge consisting in accounting for the acquisition of title by civilized sovereign states over uncivilized peoples and regions; Roman law doctrines of 'occupation' are found inadequate. In making the argument that international law was itself defined in terms of that recognition which is given to the appropriation of an 'uncivilized region' by a (civilized) sovereign state, he both extends and amplifies the arguments made by Twiss, Hall and Westlake. The rights of the uncivilized are left to the 'conscience' of the sovereign state, and international law which cannot take account of the 'uncivilized' is but that which regulates the conduct of (civilized) sovereign states.[159] This is because the 'uncivilized' do not have a notion of authority and therefore cannot be engaged with on legal civilized terms. For instance, the distinction between war and simple aggression would be unintelligible to these people, and hence international law is not concerned with them as much as civilized sovereign states, not as an enforceable rule but in terms of the *intentions* of regulating such possible conflicts in relationship to the uncivilized. The lack of the state was supposed to mean the lack of civilization. This no doubt reaches back to the King's conscience rather than law, but more specifically Metcalf's defence of the intentions of a superior force when interpreting any agreements or treaties entered into, which was analysed in Part II.

The history of the acquisition of territory in the Indian subcontinent is framed under this very same problem: of discussing the title of acquisition of territory over uncivilized regions by a sovereign state. This history is to include the history of the East India Company, since Westlake specifically argues that the Company was delegated powers by the Crown, and therefore the history of Company acquisition must 'belong not to international but to constitutional history'.[160] In his discussion on the Company he draws liberally from the work of officials who directly worked with India, Charles Tupper and Lee Warner. Charters are cited from the eighteenth century onwards to indicate the subordination of the Company to Crown and parliament.[161] The subsidiary alliance system was seen as slowly taking the form of a protectorate where native states that were part of such a system were denied any possibility of having external relations – princely states were increasingly in a state of 'subordinate isolation'.[162] From here, what might have been called internal relations turned into an 'imperial basis'. Contrary to Maine's argument, British jurisdiction entered into the 'foreign' territory of the native principalities in the context of cantonments and the railways, and here too one finds a direct continuation of the East India Company's policies in relationship to native states.[163] The Foreign Jurisdiction Act of 1890 clarified that the Queen had jurisdiction through her Courts over the peoples of protectorates.[164] While this was explained through the 'analogy' of conquered territories, in the case of Indian native states, it was difficult to discern one from the other.

Treaties signed during the rule of the Company were with time to be explicitly permitted by the British government in London, even though in the treaty itself the name of the Governor-General sufficed. International lawyers recognized that governors and viceroys in several cases, including the case of the Company, were empowered to initiate and received diplomatic relations.[165]

> [The] British government preferred to adopt on its own responsibility the principle that it was not only preponderant in India but paramount, not merely the strongest power, but the rightful superior, and that all treaties and grants of whatever date were to be construed as reserving the exercise of that superiority when needed for certain beneficent purposes.[166]

While this was not announced as a principle by proclamation or statute, it was regularly invoked and applied; the case of Delhi discussed above is but one instance specifically cited. The several treaties signed by the Company thus have to be seen in their totality, and interpreted only as guided by the principle of paramountcy and the 'usage' that enforced such rights.

The 'imperial', 'feudal' idea of paramount extended to the post-1858 period where the princes of India were similarly, ultimately, subject to the Queen who controlled their 'foreign' relations and exerted powers over them, much like the Company (for the Queen) did previously. In fact princes could neither communicate with one another nor with other states, and therefore were not subjects of international law, not having fulfilled the characteristics of independent states. This was one kind of state among the various kinds of states that Sutherland had classified. And yet this was taken to be characteristic of all princely states in the post-1857 period. The negative feature of not having any foreign relations was converted into the positive feature of being in explicit subordination to the British government as sovereign. This is only cemented by Tupper's argument that subjects of native princes owed a 'double allegiance': to their chiefs as well as, ultimately, to 'her Majesty the Queen

Empress'.[167] Statute and political decisions confirmed the subject-status of the subjects of native princes. These also took form in extradition treaties with foreign powers, and signified the powers that the British government had of intervening in the affairs of princely states. Hence we see that far from the post-1857 period promising princely autonomy, what happens is the cementing of an imperial ideal that requires and appropriates the history of the Company's policies and conquests. Finally, the East India Company's policy of having a say in, and control over, the succession of native rulers was continued in the post-1857 period. This idea of 'guardianship' no doubt recalled 'feudal' ideas, as did the 'sunads' that the Viceroy gave to princes, indicating a bestowing on them rights to adopt successors.[168] The guiding principle that all treaties were, and will be, subject to the ultimate interests of empire – from Company officials to Maine and Tupper post-1857 – paints a coat of irony on the founding defence of international law as that which enables a respect for treaty obligations. While statute bound the Crown to treaties entered into by the Company, what might such binding mean when all was permitted in the name of imperial interests, whether before or after 1858?

The Foreign Judicature Act of 1890 affirmed the right of the Queen to exercise jurisdiction independently of parliamentary statute, 'in the same and as ample a manner as if her majesty had acquired that jurisdiction by the cession or conquest of territory'.[169] Westlake openly affirms a 'peculiar mode of conquest' to operate on the nominally sovereign principalities of India: 'The imperial right over protected states appear to present a peculiar case of conquest, operating by assumption and acquiescence'.[170] The whole theorization of 'protectorates' allowed for precisely such conditions, and in the words of one of the authorities on the subject, 'in protectorates the exclusion of foreign European states is the primary object; external sovereignty is therefore appropriated together with so much of the internal sovereignty as is needed to be its complement'.[171] This was precisely the argument to be found in the despatches to England by Governor-General Wellesley in 1803, when speaking of taking the Mughal ruler into 'protection' so as to exclude the French. What was unabashedly defended in terms of the right of conquest – indexed by the distribution of Prize – in the construal of 'protectorates' took on the form of analogy to conceal the thing analogized. 'Protectorates' across the world were no less results of conquest than was the case in early nineteenth-century India, even though international lawyers saw in such cases of consent and cession, arguments not left unused earlier too. The prerogative of the Crown remained in foreign affairs what it was in the seventeenth and eighteenth centuries, and the foreign judicature Act defining the Crown's powers appeared little different from *Campbell v. Hall*, where the Crown is given powers to legislate independent of parliament in the immediate aftermath of conquest and before a treaty and proclamation.

And yet there was no general accounting for the specific theorization of the Crown, or the legal basis on which it had 'incorporated' the native states of India, or the in-mixing of legal instruments such as martial law and Prize money, as outlined earlier in this part. The Company's conquests were the ghostly moulds of 'sovereign' native states, which were always capable of being hollowed out. Once again – though missing in action as much as discourse – the only 'doctrines' that might account for the malignant metastasis of conquests and territorialization were the 'archaic' ones of the 'King's bodies' and 'the corporation sole'. As discussed in Part I, this fundamental attempt to guarantee unity in spatial differentiation and conquest as well as temporal continuity is what characterizes the doctrines of the King as corporation sole and the jurisprudential doctrine of the King's two bodies. Without this the imperial expansion eastwards and westwards could not be 'rationalized'. This constitutional doctrine of the importance of the King was deployed in court judgments as well as conquests, east and west.

Conclusion

To strip naked the Company's actions from the legal obfuscations of the nineteenth century, one might revisit the distinction between Hugo Grotius and John Locke. Grotius's well-known defence of the 'private' emerged at a juncture when the Dutch were in fact prosecuting two distinct kinds of private war. One was the 'civil war'/revolt against the King of Spain, and the other was the war against the Portuguese who were themselves subjects of the Spanish King.[172] Grotius had claimed that an equivalent status existed between the state and a private actor, since, according to his argument, the state was itself to be ultimately derived from the natural rights possessed by individuals who could use these rights to protect themselves.[173] Grotius derives this from an elaborate philosophical anthropology, where the individual is divinely endowed with the mandate and right to self-defence, which can progressively amplify itself into defending property.[174] In the act of protection and defence, *both*, the mortal blow to the enemy as well as the acquisition of his property was justified simultaneously and on the same basis. On the other hand, in Locke, while death-dealing was legitimized in war, there was far starker ambiguity when it came to rights to the property of the vanquished. Locke, in the light of imminent conquest by William III, argued that life might be taken but property could not.[175] This might be seen as an attempt to protect the over-riding right of property taken as a synecdoche for a social order from a change in political heads. Conquest thus had to be limited so as to legitimize the conquest as force taking the form of property right over the labour of others, Locke's 'turf'.

That the order of property is itself political in the sense of control over others, whether children, wives or servants, is an issue that Locke represses[176] – the traces of which is that one may 'punish' in the state of nature and one had control over one's servant's property in such a state.[177] But by attempting to limit conquest to the taking of life, and not real property, Locke appeared to be inverting the essential logic of Prize money that we have been tracing so far. For the laws of war as much as Prize – documented and detailed by Grotius – confirmed the right to the acquisition of property in war even while the taking of life may be incident to such a right. Defence of property or its rightful acquisition could legitimately involve the killing of the enemy. This was the rationale for the Prize charters of 1757–58 that became in many ways the basis of the Company's subsequent conquests,[178] whether through outright 'annexation' or cession in the context of victorious wars. This line of argumentation on defending rightful claims to property or acquiring it by war or treaty, institutionalized through the entire apparatus of Prize laws, is the thread by which one can account for the conquests of the subcontinent under the aegis of the sovereign – King and King-in-Parliament. It is only from such a perspective that the entire history of the Company and its sovereign actions is intelligible. The Lockean attempt at abstracting the political head from the propertied order, requiring nurturing and protection, cannot account for this dense and animated history of the Company where war repeatedly broke and appropriated existing 'societal' – tenurial-landed – orders in its various 'revenue settlements' and taxation apparatus. War as a mode of acquiring landed property necessarily loops back to the question of where the right of landed property in fact exists. If Locke had insisted on property rights in the form of legislation, this was institutionalized in representation in the House of Commons that served as such a guarantee. In his words,

> the Reason why men enter into society, is the preservation of their property; and the end why they chuse and authorize a legislative, is, that there may be laws

> made, and rules set as guards and fences to the properties of all the members of the society, to limit the powers, and moderate the dominion of every part and member of society.[179]

That no such consent or representation existed in the subcontinent and its experimental revenue settlements only served to reaffirm the lack of 'property' in conquered India, and the unfree and servile status of entire populations of natives at the receiving end of a perpetual war.

The Lockean line, denuded of its pressing military context, is picked up and reconfigured by later philosophers such as J. Stuart Mill. Such an intellectual orientation attempts to treat the social – the property-order – as a coherent plane, without analysing the formation of government, the question of sovereignty, the political powers involved in property, or the constitutive powers of war. Mill's argument for retaining the governing powers of the East India Company employs a rhetoric, the irony of which is unmistakable from the perspective of the history charted until now. In the name of the liberty of the 'nation', the argument is made that only by enabling the Company to retain its powers could the 'ominous' concentration of powers in the cabinet be avoided. Liberty of the metropolitan propertied nation could only be secured by 'double government' and 'divided responsibility',[180] with the Company retaining its autocratic government. Such specialized autocracy was indeed no different, it was said, from the individual specializations that took care of the management of lighthouses, the railways, urban administration, education and other such spheres of the empire. And only by such a divided responsibility could autonomy and efficiency be gained and the despotic concentration of power be put at bay. In no other way could the genius of the nation be preserved. 'Double government' and 'divided responsibility' were precisely how India was in any case being administered by the Company, subject as it was to King, parliament and the Board of Control. The Company was best suited to govern a 'dependency' and had demonstrated its accomplishments over the years because Indians were incapable of administering their own affairs. The corporation that had 'gained' India was no doubt the best qualified to administer it, experienced as it was in this specialized requirement.

In Mill's hand this becomes the mark of an efficient administration, a form of despotism justified when implemented over the barbarians, who needed to be civilized by rule and education and who could not be expected to govern themselves. However, it is not often noted that Mill's argument may be traced to Austin's distinction between the 'civilized' and the 'barbaric' peoples, which was itself embedded in a critique of the 'free'–'despotic' distinction used to characterize governments.[181] Since Mill does not directly analyse sovereignty or government, he does not take on board Austin's characterization of sovereignty as itself a 'legal despotism' in which the 'bulk of the subjects habitually obey'.[182] Mill thereby displaces the problem of investigating the nature of sovereignty and governance, the relationship between government and the governed, and turns it into one of elucidating the nature of *society*[183] as abstracted from the problem of government and its legal despotism. Of course, when it comes to a specific discussion, Mill reveals his colour. Must one be surprised that he strongly wrote against the abandonment of the right to capture private property, as 'the abandonment of our chief defensive weapon – the right to attack an enemy in his commerce'?[184]

While Austin had defined a 'political society' as one where the bulk of people *habitually* obeyed a sovereign, subtracting habitual legal obedience enabled Mill to disregard the institutional framework and legal circuitry of British government *as* empire– in essence, the set of issues that we have been tracking. Moreover, Mill reformulates Austin's 'habit' and 'custom' after displacing Austin's focus on the relationship between the governed and the government as the site of sovereignty and the laws. Through this displacement Mill inaugurates the (false) problem of the grand antithesis between custom and liberty, conformity and reason within the terrain of 'society', a social plane that has been depoliticized/delegalized in the process. In this abstracted hollow, Mill designs custom as the mechanical retention of existing practice. For him, all such unthought-of customs or habits ought to be tested on the touchstone of reason and debate. The relationship between custom and law, or reason and sovereignty, blacks out 'abstract right' or any normative principle of governance, and thereby ensures that no radical challenge can be mounted against the sovereign state. This is not surprising if we remember that Mill insists that the habit of obedience is itself the civilizational basis of principles of liberty. This basis undergirds and legitimizes the rule over barbaric and despotically customary societies such as India. Disavowing the legal aspects of sovereignty–despotism and the role of government and law in Britain's legal system allows Mill to rewrite conquest as education. Austin's primary habitual 'custom' – obedience to the laws – required the legal confirming of custom as law.

While Austin no longer linked the feature of 'despotism' with the Crown or King, the figure of despotism is silhouetted in nineteenth-century jurisprudence which followed Blackstone and his predecessors in holding that all land was ultimately held for and by the King.[185] It is therefore of no surprise that the fundamental importance of (landed) property right was recognized as closely linked to allegiance. The nexus between proprietorship and lordship was announced in the course of the Doomsday book, where all of the populace were to announce their allegiance to the Norman Conqueror, William. Legal doctrines had confirmed that conquest had to be ultimately the King's, and even when the English colonized so-called empty lands, they took their laws with them.[186] The fourteenth-century statute of Edward III had recognized children of the King's subjects born abroad as having the rights of inheritance to landed properties within the realm, because they inherited the allegiance to the King from their parents. *Postnati* circled around precisely the question of inheritance, and an alien was defined as one who could not initiate an action in law, such an initiation being the characteristic feature of a subject.

Only from such a context can one understand the King's Privy Council decision in *Lyons (Mayor) v. East India Company* (1836). The categories of subject and alien in the context of the Indian 'possessions' were at once clarified and obfuscated, even as the fact of the subjecthood of natives could no longer be denied. Much like *Posnati*, the Privy Council had to decide whether the specific English law regarding the incapacity of the alien to devise property extended to Calcutta and the mofussil. This however indexed a larger question of the nature and basis of laws operating in the East India Company territories. Like in *Postnati*, *Lyons (Mayor)* too made a distinction between (specific) laws and sovereignty. That is to say, in regions that have been conquered, it was held that it was not necessary that English laws were immediately applicable. The peoples of conquered regions might be 'subjects', but not subject to English law. Citing *Postnati* and *Campbell*, the Privy Council reiterated that the Crown had the right to introduce and alter law through its prerogative in cases of conquest such as the 'Indian possessions'.

However, it held that there was no evidence that the specific English statute regarding the incapacities of aliens was applied or had been transferred to these regions, and since there was no specific transfer, it could not be held that such a law was applicable. This however did not mean that the vanquished peoples in the subcontinent were not subjects, since conquest 'operates what they [the Court] term a virtual naturalization'.[187] Even while the Privy Council recognizes that specific rights of the conquered are only secured by concrete treaties, in the case of the 'East India possessions', since the transformation of the Company from subject to sovereign was so 'imperceptible', no specific act of such a sort was to be found. This essentially meant that there was no clear moment, or declaration, of when and in what sense the conquered subjects of the subcontinent became subjects. And therefore, no clear recognition or delineation of their rights as subjects. In the case of the conquests of India no such self-representative institutions were introduced, and hence the territory remained in some sense under the 'lawless' equity of the King, which had granted specific charters such as those on Prize law – particularly lawless in the context of the statutory immunities granted to the Company officials.

There is no other way to interpret the 'regulations' of the Company in their administration of the country. On the other hand, there were irresolvable differences on the precise rights of the Company to 'legislate' over newly conquered territories, with Cameron, member of the Law Commission, minuting that such powers were delegated by the Crown's prerogative, and Barnes Peacock, on the other hand, minuting that these powers were derived from statute, i.e. the Act of 1834;[188] this was in effect a moot point, since the channel of authority ascended to the King-in-Council and no such representative mode existed by way of which any parliament/assembly could represent the native. The Company at times claimed that its (despotic) actions were merely following local precedent, refusing to acknowledge the transformations that their own interventions had wrought.[189] And yet it is unclear why self-representative institutions were not introduced if *lex loci* had to be followed, within the perimeter and parameters of the King's sovereignty or the existing statutory framework. The legally indefinite expansion of war – and its rights in the name of Prize – as derived from royal charters starkly refuted any iota of a recognizable legal and propertied order in the subcontinent. On the other hand, in the name of following an inherited twinned custom/despotic local order, the Company ensured, through its varying revenue demands and unilateral determination of the same, that no such thing as 'property right' could be recognized under its rule. While the very concrete bearing such arguments had on land revenue have been much documented, this part has focused on the light it sheds on the granular violence of conquest. In a stunning embroidering of despotism and Prize, the Privy Council, as the highest court in the land, had held, as discussed above, that since local kingdoms were absolute in nature and all property vested in the ruler, all property of the kingdom was subject to acquisition as Prize in the course of war. That is to say, the alleged lack of distinction between private and public meant that nothing needed to be protected from the proceeds of plunder.

If Company rule can be characterized as despotic in the simple and certain sense that property was constituted by the ruler and a legal system without reference to the consent of the subject, the Company itself being subject to King and parliament implies that such a despotic feature must characterize Britain – or rather that in which 'Britain' takes shape, the British sovereign. From *Postnati* to *Campbell* it was well-settled that the King ruled in cases of conquest, but otherwise through assemblies which signified liberty and property at once. The differentiation between jurisdictions lay not in the fact that in Britain the King does not possess prerogative, for indeed he did, and even with respect to the British parliament, the King continued to call and dissolve it, and only through him could a Bill be enacted as law. However, while he had long stopped using his powers of 'veto' over British parliament, this was not the case with other jurisdictions such as Canada and New Zealand. And such power over these jurisdictions was executed with the advice of Britain. Historically, therefore, differences in jurisdiction and the precise legal relationship between self-representative institutions in conquered (Ireland) and colonized (America, Australia and New Zealand) territories are measurable by the relationship between the King and representative assemblies, and the concentration of power in the cabinet of the imperial (British) King-in-Parliament. While in America, initially, self-representative institutions in the colonies critiqued the interference of the British parliament while accepting the superordination of the King, in New Zealand such institutions critiqued the King's power transmitted to the figure of the governor.

In the subcontinent, on the other hand, even a modicum of self-representative institutions was denied until the protracted negotiations for 'responsible government' in the twentieth century. In so far as the various 'land settlements' were concerned, which unilaterally decided on the nature of property and tenure with no reference to constituted representative bodies, such actions can only be characterized as 'despotic' or a terrorizing equity, not law. In fact it is perhaps a delicious irony that Mill's 'liberal' advocacy of divided responsibility and 'double government' for the retention of the governing powers of the East India Company may well be traced to Lord Clive, but rather than a division of power, the 'arrangement' was explicitly designed as a masking, a concealing of power, so as to escape the accountability that the formal assumption of such power would invite; a doubling duplicity of power.

This form or strategy would have been familiar to every Englishman, since it pervaded the notoriously complex history and system of English land law. Real property in English law was characterized not by 'absolute ownership', but the contest over 'possession'. It is in such a context that historians have richly described the contests over customary and common right, the enclosures and the increasing intervention of the legislature in forms of dispossession.[190] Legal ownership did not mean absolute ownership, since in England, the system of uses and trusts ensured that one could be a legal owner and still obligated to the grantor – an obligation that was enforced by the Chancery Court and the law of persons. The strategy to privately transfer/grant forms of proprietorship to others was a way to initially avoid the feudal charges of lords and Kings; no real property was absolute since all land was 'held' of a lord, which ultimately was held of the King.[191] Thus, a process of masking ownership in grants and transference gave rise to a 'legal ownership' which was not absolute, but obligated in turn. It is this form of 'masking' to avoid forms of accountability that we can find in the structure and purpose of Clive's 'double government'. The same form pervades the (legal) rights to property that cannot be understood as absolute, but always as something involving obligations, fusing the legal distinctions between proprietorship (rights to a thing against the world at large) and obligations (rights to/of persons), law and equity. In England equitable jurisdiction was rendered superior when it came to a contest between the two, and law was therefore subject to equity, mirroring the supreme authority of the King as that which allows for 'complete justice', a justice that completes any defects of law that arise precisely from their universality.

The historiographical tendency to read the Company's demand for clear title as an indication of the existence of such clear title in England – with its paraphernalia of liberal government and individual rights – betrays a lack of knowledge of the state of affairs in England, and a stark misconstrual of state power and its intentions. The mammoth appropriation of lands on the pretext of a lack of clear and legitimate title[192] was but the other face of the continuous unilateral 'settlements', 'permanent' or otherwise, which were nothing less than indices of war and conquest, recalling the crowning settlements of bloodied conquests such as the Doomsday book and the Down Survey. Even basic common law principles enunciated in *Postnati* and before on property title being grounded in the nexus between (local) taxation and representation are brazenly and consistently violated with land settlements being made without any consent or consultation of the title holders involved – the ultimate irony being the history and historiography which see in this process the introduction of the rules and laws of property in the subcontinent.[193] Rammohan Roy once again is helpful as an early indication of native recognition of the hollowed-out promises of property right for the proprietary class as much as the labouring classes.[194] Even after the promise of a full subject-status with the Queen's proclamation, self-representative assemblies took a long time to see the light of day. While, on the one hand, this can be contrasted with colonization and conquest in Ireland and other colonies, on the other hand, it must be noted that in each of these cases peoples like the Africans and Native Americans were denied the same subject-status and representation in matters of law. Their subjugation and exploitation – and expulsion from the political community of representation – is the violent dark penumbra that surrounds and defines the fact of colonization. Communities within Britain like the Catholics, and Jews too, were given rights of representation only with time.

It is a wonder that the hegemonic post-history of Locke confines its attention to property emerging from labour without questioning the sovereign-proprietary right over labour, whether in the forms of slavery or servitude. The history of the Company warns us against the liberatory halo put around the contract, since only those lacking property were forced to contract, in ways that always benefited the powerfully propertied. It might be recalled that slavery too was interpreted and justified by figures like Grotius and several thereafter well into the nineteenth century as a 'contract',[195] as did the most oppressive forms of servitude. This manifests at the level of sovereignty when it comes to treaty-making, where the treaty is the dictation of the rules of subordination and recognized as a fruit of victory rather than an engagement brimming with freedom and free of power. Moreover, as analysed above, Prize jurisdiction led to the legal construal of the subcontinent as being veritably under martial law, supplemented by the immunities granted to government officials. The matching of demanding revenue without any representation while conquering and policing without law ground any notion of right or property into a dust so fine as to be without measure.

If the founding moment of entering the contract is re-examined one might ask with Maine: How did sheer abstract time create a right? Prescription already assumed a legal system, and could not be assumed to be the foundation of one. Or, for its survival, it had to continuously make use of force for its sustenance, where military might merely have perfected the law. Both Austin and Maine provide a clue to the history and practices of sovereignty by defining sovereignty in terms of 'fact'. This recoups an Aristotelian interpretation of 'executive' power, where sovereignty is not to be understood in terms of a neo-

Kantian self-identical system of logic-law with 'application' and 'execution' serving as subordinating functions, but rather where the executive/action determines the law-case ('fact') at hand, shedding colour on Hobbes's 'person' as much as Locke's and Blackstone's 'executive'. This is where the historical site of Prize rather than the mythical site of a state of nature might provide for the emergence of the irrepressible antagonistic violence concealed in property as much as the constitution of international law through empire, before the mid-twentieth-century normative generation of the grammar of nation-states and self-determination began their own dissimulating script. Grotius theorized Prize in the context of a private corporation of a rebelling state, thereby grounding it in the principles of natural as much as Roman law. Here appropriation – rather than a *state* of nature – was of the enemy's property, ostensibly in self-defence. Prize indicated the individual labour of this acquisition as much as the right of the political entity of which the individual was a part. While it has been shown that the logic of nationality or the nation-state did not operate in the nineteenth century, the amplification of empire in its conquests staged an arena of 'international law' in which only 'civilized' states were allowed entry.[196]

The terra-firma of land – as the primordial template of logic – is thereby seen to be the *chaur*-formation that has as its basis the maritime cross-currents of war perfecting trade regulations. In fact the legal armature and practices of maritime law and maritime warfare, from the Navigation Acts to Prize laws, morphed and coalesced into the territorial domination of the Indian subcontinent – nothing less than the history of 'free trade' and the military engineering of the economy. And so the lawyers of international law saw in the development of the British Empire in India and subsequently in its relations with princely states, an arena immune to international law but fittingly described as an English constitutional design of protection – seeds sown as far back as the earliest Company conquests emerging from the surf of marine sovereignty.[197] All of this was to be accomplished through a reiterated and renewed theorization of the sovereign King/Queen towards the end of the nineteenth century. Without it the entire legal order of the late nineteenth and early twentieth centuries would have been impossible; that this has not been theoretically accounted for speaks to the utter failure of contemporary 'theories' of nationalism, that tend to assume the 'state' or 'nation' as a theoretical and historical point of departure rather than what one might call a marine sovereignty which enacts the logic of the construction of lines of administration and war, seamlessly moving from the 'economy' to the 'political'. No historiographic divides between 'mercantilism' and 'free trade', 'nation-state' and 'empire', can dissimulate the strict continuity between the royal charters of Prize enabling the appropriation of property, the revenue settlements which were unilaterally determined and extorted having King-in-Parliament statutory sanction, and the royal prerogative dictating the subordination of 'protected' 'princely states'. Such an immensely blood-letting and extractive empire no doubt finds its lasting granular measure in the never-ending battles of resistance, which can only be alluded to here.[198] It is from these entrails that the hoary conventions between empires on the treatment of soldiers as they take shape in the Hague conventions may be measured, with no such guarantees for the 'protected states' within.

Notes

[1] See *Nawab of Carnatic v. East India Company* (1789 and 1793). This did not prevent natives, including successive Mughal rulers, appealing to the authorities in London against the perceived oppressions of the East India Company, as is discussed below.

[2] See the discussion in Elizabeth Kolsky's *Colonial Justice in British India* (2010). Kolsky makes out an argument for linking the codification of law to the demand for immunities as British subjects by non-East India Company-related British individuals in India, in the context of their violence towards natives. The very documentation of this violence is an important contribution of her work.

[3] In 1708 an Act was passed whose intent was the naturalization of all Protestants, but the Act also stated that denizens suffered certain limitations such that they could not become members of the Privy Council and the Houses of Parliament. See the discussion in Francis Piggot, *Nationality Including Naturalization* (1907): 48–49. The complexity of the issue was signalled in the late seventeenth century by *Craw v. Ramsey* (1670), which articulated the distinction between dominions of the Crown of England (like Ireland) and dominions of the King (like Scotland), thus disallowing any equation of the rights of inheritability in England between the Irish and the Scots.

[4] F. Pollock, *Land Laws* (1883): 7. Referring to an example of a park and manor house, Pollock writes, 'The lord of all this is himself a tenant, though not in the popular sense or much practical effect. His lands are held of the Crown, or perhaps of some other superior who himself holds of the Crown.' See also, F.W. Maitland, *Township and Burrough* (1898): 92; 'We know that according to law every landholder is connected with the King by some longer or shorter thread of tenure. C holds of B and B holds of A and A of the King.'

[5] As Pollock explains, 'The notion of ownership, as the maximum of claim or right in a specific thing allowed by law (a), is not primary, but developed out of conflicting claims to possession and disposal'; F. Pollock, *The Expansion of the Common Law* (1904): 11–12.

[6] Pollock argues that despite the legislative interventions of the nineteenth century, 'Very few land owners are in a position to make out their title if strict proof is required at every step which it may be in the absence of special conditions'; ibid.: 169. See the discussion in the last part, ibid., 'Modern Reforms and Prospects': 161–93.

[7] Recently, Thomas Piketty has made important interventions by underlining the various forms and trajectories of inequalities on a global scale that involves the centrality of empires. In the case of inequality within Britain, drawing on the work of David Cannadine, he states that it has been estimated that in 1880s, 80 per cent of the land in the United Kingdom was in the hands of 7,000 noble families or less than 0.1 per cent of the population. Analogously, in the 1860s, three-quarters of the seats in the House of Commons were still occupied largely by the aristocracy, which was seen to be less than 0.5 per cent of the British population of that time. See Thomas Piketty, *Capital and Ideology* (2020): 165–66.

[8] Piggot, *Nationality Including Naturalization* (1907): 106.

[9] See the Acts which are reproduced in the appendices of Piggot (1907): 283–302.

[10] *Stepney Election Petition*, https://groups.google.com/g/alt.lawyers/c/jbvWkJ26UB0?pli=1

[11] Ibid.

[12] *Mayor (of Lyons) v. East India Company* (1836).

[13] See T. Macaulay's *A Penal Code Prepared by the Indian Law Commissioners* (1837) and Justice Grey's comments in *Appendix to the Report on the Affairs of the East India Company*, Vol. V (1831). This entire problematic eludes the studies of those like Bernard Cohn on the significance of 1857–58.

[14] https://www.indiacode.nic.in/repealed-act/repealed_act_documents/A1852-30.pdf

[15] See Victoria's Proclamation, https://www.bl.uk/collection-items/proclamation-by-the-queen-in-council-to-the-princes-chiefs-and-people-of-india

[16] See Pramod Nayar, ed., *The Trial of Bahadur Shah Zafar* (2007).

[17] There was no clarification, as took place in the case with Ireland in *Craw v. Ramsey* (1670).

[18] This issue is analysed below in the sections on Maine and International Law. On the Queen transferring dominions, see M.E. Grant Duff and Whitley Stokes, eds, *Sir Henry Maine: A Brief Memoir of his Life; with some of his Indian Speeches and Minute* (1892): 396. See W. Lee-Warner's detailed studies in this respect in *Protected Princes of India* (1894): 305–26.

[19] I wish to register my gratitude to the Cambridge-Hamied Trust which enabled me to visit Cambridge and London on a Cambridge Hamied fellowship to conduct the archival work that has been critical to the writing of this section.

[20] See A.B.M. Habibullah, 'Shah Alam's letter to George III' (1940): 97–98; Kalikinker Dutta, *Shah Allam II and the East India Company* (1965): 49–52; Michael Fisher, *Counterflows to Colonialism* (2005): 86–88. East India Company officials prevented Shah Alam's letter and money from reaching I'stam-Al-Din and Captain Archibald Swinton who were designated by Shah Alam as his envoys to George III. Such delays forced I'stam-Al-Din and Swinton to board a French ship to London, where they were unable to meet the King. However, while Fisher shows evidence of the letter having reached the King, it appeared that Clive presented Shah Alam's presents as though they were his own.

[21] Ibid.: Habibullah (1940); Kalikinker Dutta (1965); Fisher (2005).

[22] See Roy's address to the King-in-Council in K. Nag and K. Burman, eds, *The English Works of Raja Rammohan Roy* (1951): 11–24.

[23] See the petitions to the Supreme Court and the King-in-Council, in J.C. Ghose, *The English Works of Rammohan Roy*, Vol. II (1906): 435–69.

[24] P/A/6 553. See the wording of the 'treaty of Allahabad' in Herbert Cowell, *History and Constitution of the Courts and Legislative Authorities in India* (1936): 30.

[25] See *The Defence of Warren Hastings Esq. at the Bar of the House of Commons* (1786). See Hastings's citation of letters from the Court of Directors to approve of his actions in stopping the tribute; ibid.: 76–77.

[26] Ibid.: 82.

[27] See the correspondence between the Governor-General, Lord Lake, and Shah Alam regarding this issue, J.K. Majumdar, *Raja Rammohun Roy and the Last Moguls: A Selection from the Official Records* (1939): 6–10.

[28] Ibid.

[29] Ibid.: 1–3.

[30] Ibid.: 11–44.

[31] Ibid.: 33, Letter from Governor-General in Council to the Secret Committee of the Court of Directors, 2nd June 1805.

[32] *Treaty with the King of Delhi* (1831).

[33] Ibid., Article 1: 6.

[34] Ibid., Article 11: 6.

[35] Ibid., Article 2: 3.

[36] Ibid., Article 7: 4.

[37] Ibid., Article 8: 5.

[38] Majumdar (1939): 31–32, Letter from the Governor-General in Council to the Secret Committee of the Court of Directors, 2nd June 1805.

[39] Ibid.: 30, Letter from Chief Secretary to Government to the Military Secretary to the Commander in Chief transmitting copy of letter containing orders of the Government on the subject of the provision for H.M. Shah Alam and his family, 23rd May 1805.

[40] Ibid.: 35–58, 61–85.

[41] Ibid.: 154, Letter from the Governor-General in Council to the Court of Directors, 13th June 1823.

[42] Ibid.: 161, Letter from the Resident of Delhi to the Political Secretary to Government, 30th June 1827.

[43] Ibid.

[44] Ibid.

[45] Ibid.: 162–63.

[46] *Treaty with the King of Delhi* (1831): 1.

[47] In the letter to the heir apparent; ibid.: 117–18, 120–21. It is important to note that the title 'Raja' was given to Roy by the Mughal ruler when he was made an envoy to represent the Mughal ruler's case to the King of England and authorities there, and that Roy wrote to the Governor-General asking for his permission to be able to accept that title. Roy also says that the title could be accepted because the English had, according to specific regulations, given the Mughal ruler the authority to bestow titles. See ibid.: 115–16. There is some confusion with regard to his status as an envoy because while, on the one hand, Roy writes to the Governor-General in Calcutta that he would be in England only as a private individual representing the Mughal ruler and have no official status (ibid.: 117), on the other hand, he later requests the Chairman and Deputy Chairman of the East India Company that his status as an envoy be recognized and argues that this in no way could be construed as a violation of English laws on the matter (ibid.: 121). For a detailed account of Roy's trip to England, see Brajendranath Banerji, *Raja Rammohun Roy's Mission to England: Based on Unpublished Sources* (1926); this text

also contains ample primary source documentation. See also Fisher (2005) and Lyn Zastoupil, *Rammohan Roy and the Making of Victorian Britain* (2010).

[48] See J.C. Ghose, *The English Works of Rammohan Roy*, Vol. II (1906): 445–69.

[49] H 708/P2, Court of Directors to Board of Commissioners, 24th August 1832, APAC, London.

[50] Ibid.

[51] Ibid.

[52] Majumdar (1939): 20–27.

[53] Ibid.

[54] H 708/P2, Letter from Board of Commissioners to Court of Directors, 29th August 1832, AAC, London.

[55] Ibid.

[56] Banerji (1926).

[57] One sees this in the renewed attention to the theories of F.W. Buckler by scholars such as Bernard Cohn. Ironically, while Cohn emphasizes Mughal ritual and British 'contract', a detailed study of their relations reveals the Mughal ruler as emphasizing the violation by the Company of their contracts and treaties, as well as the conscious manipulation of symbols and rituals – manipulations which are recognized and combated by the British in their relations. Emphasis on cultural differences occludes the nature of power and law in operation, and therein the question of violence and violation. It would also be clear by now that the approach adopted in the present work is critical of the 'invention of tradition' argument in general, but also the specific arguments in relation to the British monarch made by David Cannadine and Bernard Cohn in E. Hobsbawm and T. Ranger, eds, *The Invention of Tradition* (1983). Cohn does not recognize the question of subjecthood and allegiance in his study of the East India Company and 1857–58.

[58] See the entire correspondence around the 'mission' of Shah Haujee (1809–1812) in Majumdar (1939): 85–139. Haujee was seen as an agent/representative of Akbar Shah, tasked with the attempt to assert Mughal authority through the use of symbols such as the *khillat*/robes/honorary dresses over the British as well as native rulers. There is a deep recognition of symbols and their meanings, and hence the refusal of the Governor-General to accept the gifts and presents, including 'honorary dresses', from the Mughal ruler. In a letter to the Court of Directors, the Governor-General wrote on 1st August 1809 (ibid.: 122): 'Your Honourable Court will observe that the first act of the Haujee was to violate the condition under which the British Government consented to his mission, by avowing that he was charged with an Honorary Dress for the Governor General notwithstanding His Majesty's solemn and repeated declarations to the Resident at Delhi that he had abandoned all intention of sending any Honorary Dress; and by proposing to invest His Lordship with it, accompanied by every mark of exterior ceremony and submission which was calculated to represent the exercise of imperial authority on the part of His Majesty, and to manifest to all the States of Asia a public acknowledgment of vassalage and submission on the part of the British Government to the Throne of Delhi.' The letter alludes to the attempts of the Mughal ruler to assert his authority over other native rulers. Similarly, there are very detailed discussions on language and styles of address that the British were well aware of, in calibrating their relationship with the Mughal ruler. See the discussion on this issue by the Persian Secretary, in ibid.: 171–73.

[59] See Pramod Nayar, ed., *The Trial of Bahadur Shah Zafar* (2007). It was not a regular court

but a military tribunal that proceeded to judge Bahadur Shah Zafar. The developments of military law and martial law have been cursorily discussed in the previous part. It would not be incongruous to mention here that in the twentieth century, Bhagat Singh too was tried by a tribunal established by a special ordinance. Much less work has been done on the functioning of military tribunals in the conquest of the Indian subcontinent; an exception in this regard is Bhavani Raman, 'Law in Times of Counterinsurgency', in A. Balachandran, R. Pant and B. Raman, eds, *Iterations of Law* (2018).

[60] The co-relative dimension of Prize money in the context of the wars of subjugation around 1857–58 will not be investigated here, as it has been done elsewhere. Rosie Llewellyn-Jones is that rare scholar who has documented the enormous amounts of Prize money claimed by the British in their wars around 1857–58 while plundering Delhi and Lucknow; see *The Great Uprising in India, 1857–58: Untold Stories, Indian and British* (2007): 129–54.

[61] For historical accounts of Anglo-Maratha relations in the late eighteenth and nineteenth centuries, see Stewart Gordon, *The Marathas 1600–1818* (2007) and Randolf Cooper, *The Anglo-Maratha Campaigns and the Contest for India* (2003).

[62] *The Oriental Herald*, Vol. XIV, London, 19 November 1827: 1140. The facts of the case, described below, are based on the narrative emerging from the judgment.

[63] Jerome Wm. Knapp, ed., *Reports of cases argued and determined before the committees of His Majesty's most honourable Privy Council, appointed to hear appeals and petitions, 1829–31* (1831–36); *Elphinstone v. Bedreechand*: 316–61.

[64] Ibid.: 360–61.

[65] Ibid.

[66] Alfred Kinloch, *Abridgement of the Report of the Proceedings in the Case of the Deccan Prize Money, with supplementary papers collected from various authentic sources* (1864): ii.

[67] Ibid.: 68.

[68] Apart from the dispute on capture, the lawyers argued that there were in fact two distinct armies with two distinct commanders-in-chief, and so an argument for a common purpose could not be so easily made. The Governor-General was commander-in-chief of the army only when he entered the territories of the commander-in-chief of one of the regional armies, something that did not happen during the case at hand. Therefore, Hislop remained commander-in-chief, and he was subordinate to Lord Hastings only in the latter's capacity as Governor-General. Any and all communications between the two were between Hislop as commander-in-chief and Hastings as Governor-General. This was to counter the argument of Hastings's lawyers that communication between the two showed concert, and the unity of the two armies, with the actual superiority of Hastings as commander-in-chief of the unified army.

[69] Jerome Wm. Knapp, ed., *Reports of cases argued and determined before the committees of His Majesty's most honourable Privy Council, appointed to hear appeals and petitions 1831–34* (1831–36): 104–07.

[70] Ibid.: 112–16.

[71] Ibid.: 114–15.

[72] Ibid.

[73] Ibid.: 115.

[74] Ibid.: 116.

[75] Ibid.: 116–22.

[76] Ibid.: 141.

[77] J. Austin, *Province of Jurisprudence Determined* (2012): 283.

[78] 'An independent political society is often styled a "nation"; or a "sovereign and independent nation". But the term "nation" or the term "gens" is used more properly with the following meaning. It denotes an aggregate of persons, exceeding a single family which are connected through blood or lineage and perhaps through a common language. And, thus understood, a "nation" or "gens" is not necessarily an independent political society.' Ibid.: 224–27 note 19. The implications of not accounting for this specific argument may well lead to questionable interpretations of both Austin and allied figures like Maine. As notes 130 and 131 below show, this is an argument against Lauren Benton's argument in *A Search for Sovereignty* (2009).

[79] Austin (2012): 193–94.

[80] Ibid.: 196–97. Austin also gives examples like that of Germany where political societies may be independent in their foreign relations – as much as war and peace – but still subject themselves to an appellate jurisdiction; such was the relationship between the princes and the emperor.

[81] Ibid.: 271; 'Every supreme government is free from legal restraints; or (what is the same proposition dressed in a different phrase) every supreme government is legally despotic.' One might compare this concept with that of Quesnay's 'legal despotism'.

[82] Ibid.: 278.

[83] Ibid.: 189–90; 'For when by just we mean anything but to express our own approbation, we mean something which accords with some given law.' See also Austin's subsequent criticism of both Mansfield (in whom he sees confusion between morality and legality) and Bentham (affirming 'judge-made law' and its importance).

[84] Ibid.: 204.

[85] Ibid.: 206.

[86] Ibid.: 202–10. 'Inasmuch as the given society lives in the savage condition, or in the extremely barbarous condition which closely approaches the savage, the generality or bulk of its members is not in the habit of obedience to one and the same superior. For the purposes of attacking an external enemy, or for the purposes of repelling an attack made by an external enemy, the generality or bulk of its members, who are capable of bearing arms, submits to one leader, or to one body of leaders. . . . And as the bulk of the given society is not in a habit of obedience to one and the same superior, there is no law (simply or strictly so styled) which can be called the law of that given society or community. The so-called laws which are common to the bulk of the community are purely and properly customary laws, that is to say which are set or imposed by the general opinion of the community but which are not enforced by legal or political sanctions'; ibid.: 208–09.

[87] This is another way in which the present thesis links with my previous one in *Infinite Double* (2015).

[88] Austin (2012): 233–34, 236.

[89] On the King, Austin specifically says, 'The political powers exercised by the king which surely may be deemed legislative are of vast extent and importance. As captain general for examples he makes articles of war; that is to say, laws which regard especially the discipline or government of the soldiery. As administering the law, through subordinate courts of justice he is the author of the rules of procedure which they have established avowedly or in the properly legislative mode: and (what is of greater importance) he

is the author of that measureless system judge-made law, or rules of law made in the judicial manner, which has been established covertly by those subordinate tribunals as directly exercising their judicial functions'; ibid.: 236–37.

[90] Ibid.: 230–31.

[91] Ibid.: 232–33. 'Constitutional law – in the sense of moral expectations from the government by subjects – was no different from international law, since rather than enforceable they could only be understood in terms of moral sanction. Constitutional law as such was merely positive morality, since unless called so by the courts, there could be no legal limitation of parliamentary laws'; ibid.: 231.

[92] Ibid.: 222 note 18.

[93] Ibid.: 264, 293.

[94] Ibid.: 264–66. 'But in some mixed monarchies which are styled limited monarchies, the so called limited monarch is exempted or absolved from legal or political duty. For example: According to a maximum of English law, the king is incapable of committing wrong; that is to say he is not responsible legally for aught that he may please to do, or for any forbearance or omission'; ibid.: 266. See the various twists and turns in the following arguments that are not wholly resolved, leaving the King in a position following from the cited maxim. Later on, Austin reaffirms this position: 'our own King, though not properly sovereign, is completely free in fact from legal or political duties. Since he is free in fact from every legal obligation, no one has a legal right (in the proper acceptation of the term) against the King'; ibid.: 293.

[95] Ibid.: 243–44.

[96] Ibid.: 244.

[97] Piggot, *Nationality Including Naturalization* (1907): 136, 289–98. Piggot begins his work by speaking of 'statutory allegiance', but does not explain the form, history or implications of the figure of the King/Queen.

[98] As Maine argues on the fundamental history of centralization, legislation and territorialization, in *Lectures on the Early History of Institutions* (1974), https://oll.libertyfund.org/title/maine-lectures-on-the-early-history-of-institutions. 'Two causes have done most to obscure the oldest institutions of the portion of the human race to which we belong: one has been the formation throughout the West of *strong centralized governments, concentrating in themselves the public force of the community*, and enabled to give to *that force upon occasion the special form of legislative power*; the other has been the influence, direct and indirect, of the Roman Empire, drawing with it an *activity in legislation* unknown to the parts of the world which were never subjected to it' (emphasis added); ibid.: 10–11. 'There is abundant proof that legislative and judicial power are not distinguished in primitive thought; nor, again, is legislation associated with innovation'; ibid.: 17. 'The States of modern Europe must be conceived as having been formed in a manner different from the great empires of antiquity (save one), and from the modern empires and kingdoms of the East, and a new order of ideas on the subject of *legislation* must be conceived as having been introduced into the world through the empire of the Romans. *Unless these changes had taken place, I do not believe that the system would ever have been engendered in the brain of its authors* [analytical jurists including Austin]. Wherever these changes have not taken place, I do not believe the application of the system to be of value'; ibid.: 154. 'The capital fact in the mechanism of modern states is the energy of legislatures. Until the fact existed, I do not, as I have said, believe that the system of Hobbes, Bentham and

Austin, could have been conceived'; ibid.: 159. 'Sovereignty and Law, regarded as facts, had only gradually assumed a shape, in which they answered to the conception formed of them by Hobbes, Bentham and Austin, but the correspondence really did exist at their time, and was tending constantly to become more perfect. They were thus able to frame a juridical terminology which had for one virtue that it was rightly consistent with itself, and for another that, if it did not completely express facts, the qualification of its accuracy was never serious enough to deprive it of its value and tended moreover to become less and less important as time went on'; ibid.: 158–59. In *Ancient Law* (1908), Maine had written, 'Many contemporary writers on International Law tacitly assume that the doctrines "Sovereignty is territorial" territory and of their system, founded on principles of equity and common sense, were capable of being readily reasoned out in every stage of modern civilization. But this assumption, while it conceals some real defects of the international theory, is altogether untenable, so far as regards a large part of modern history. It is not true that the authority of the *Jus Gentium* in the concerns of nations was always uncontradicted; on the contrary, it had to struggle long against the claims of several competing systems. It is again not true that the territorial character of sovereignty was always recognized, for long after the dissolution of the Roman dominion the minds of men were under the empire of ideas irreconcilable with such a conception. An old order of things, and of views founded on it, had to decay – a new Europe, and an apparatus of new notions congenial to it, had to spring up before two of the chiefest postulates of International Law could be universally conceded'; ibid.: 28.

99 Maine's telescoping of large swathes of history from Roman law onwards to the feudal monarchies serves precisely such a purpose in the wilful forgetting of the Crown, even if traces of recent history remain stubbornly recalcitrant.

100 H. Maine, *Ancient Law* (1908). 'The true enigma of Patria Potestas does not reside here, but in the slowness with which these proprietary privileges of the parent were curtailed, and in the circumstance that, before they were seriously diminished, the whole civilized world was brought within their sphere. No innovation of any kind was attempted till the first year of Empire, when the acquisitions of soldiers in service were withdrawn from the operation of Patria Potestas, doubtless as part of the reward of the armies which had overthrown the free Commonwealth.' This was the broader context of '*Castrense Peculium*', given to Roman soldiers and included booty/property acquired in war; ibid.: 38. This argument ought to be combined with Maine's elaboration of the doctrine of 'occupancy' in Roman law, where the property of the enemy was treated as *res nullius*; ibid.: 65.

101 As Maine argues in *Ancient Law*, 'The law of Warlike capture derives its rules from the assumption that communities are remitted to a state of nature by an outbreak of hostilities, and that, in the artificial natural condition this produced, the institution of private property falls into abeyance, so far as concerns the belligerents. As the later writers on the law of nature have always been anxious to maintain that private property was in some sense sanctioned by the system which they were expounding, the hypothesis that the enemy's property was res nullius has seemed to them perverse and shocking, and they are careful to stigmatize it as a mere fiction of jurisprudence.' Maine continues to offer a more detailed critique of Blackstone in this regard on the next page; see ibid.: 66–67. This is a continuation of Maine's critique of the idea of the 'state of nature', as found among writers of modern natural law, such as Rousseau; ibid.: 24.

[102] The casual tone adopted in *Ancient Law* for such a fraught jurisprudential issue is well worth recording: 'A Corporation aggregate is a true corporation, but a corporation sole is an individual, being a member of a series of individuals, who is invested by a fiction, with the qualities of a Corporation. I need hardly cite the King or the Parson of Paris as instances of the Corporation Sole'; ibid.: 50. Maitland continues with the very same obfuscation, as discussed in the introduction of this book.

[103] Maine, *Lectures on the Early History of Institutions* (1874): 152.

[104] Ibid.: 157.

[105] Ibid.: 154.

[106] Ibid.: 158.

[107] Ibid.: 159.

[108] Maine writes that all of Austin's remarks on customary law were 'comparatively unfruitful' (ibid.: 157), and extends this critique by giving examples of 'Oriental' and other kinds of societies. However, his argument really works within Austin's distinction between modern civilized societies (where legislation is said to exist) and savage and barbaric societies (where 'custom' operates). See above.

[109] Ibid.: 159.

[110] Maine, *Ancient Law* (1908): 28–29; 'Territorial sovereignty – the view which connects sovereignty with the possession of a limited portion of the earth's surface – was distinctly an offshoot, though a tardy one, of feudalism.'

[111] Ibid.

[112] Ibid.: 60–65.

[113] Ibid.: 64.

[114] Ibid.: 64.

[115] Ibid.: 24, 82–83.

[116] Ibid.: 66.

[117] Ibid.: 68.

[118] Ibid.: 83.

[119] 'We must look on the family as constantly enlarged by the absorption of strangers within its circle, and we must try to regard the fiction of adoption so closely simulating the reality of kinship that neither law nor opinion makes the slightest difference between a real and an adoptive connection'; ibid.: 36, 49. Fictions are theorized as 'agents of legal change'; ibid.: 45. Of course this may well be traced to Socrates and his 'noble lie'.

[120] Ibid.: 45.

[121] Ibid.: 77–79.

[122] Ibid.: 80–81.

[123] Enfeoffment was a kind of contract enforced by the Chancellor. Equity signified obligations towards persons, which was not the same thing as the ownership of a thing, where rights to the thing were rights against the world at large. The feoffee was the trustee, and he had legal rights to transmission and alienation, and was therefore from an 'internal' perspective a form of proprietary right (a right against the world). However, the trustee had an obligation, and this could be enforced against the inheritor or the original trustee.

[124] This dispute has been traced by, amongst others, Maine, Maitland, Pollock and, more recently, Milsom.

[125] It is this larger context and the specific logic of 'repression' traced here in Maine – and its expressions in the Indian site – that make it difficult to accept Karuna Mantena's

argument about 'indirect rule', Maine and the mid-nineteenth century break. See Mantena (2010).

126 Duff and Stokes, eds (1892): 320.

127 Ibid.: 322.

128 Ibid.: 323.

129 'Accordingly there may be found in India every shade and variety of sovereignty, but there is only one independent sovereign that is the British government.' Ibid.: 323.

130 The opposition between Maine and Austin is not as clear-cut as Benton makes it out to be in *A Search for Sovereignty* (2009): 246, where she curiously describes Austin's concept of sovereignty as one that is applicable to 'nation-states'. Where Maine is later cited using the phrase 'independent' sovereign, Benton does not note the Austinian reference, and thereby misconstrues the import of Maine's argument. The interpretation provided here of Maine as well as its implications for a broader understanding of empire is at critical variance with that of Benton.

131 'Their chiefs have also been allowed to exercise (within limits) civil and criminal jurisdiction, and several of them have been in the exercise of a very marked (though minor) right – the right to coin money. By far the largest part of the sovereignty has obviously resided in practice with the British Government, and among the rights which it has appeared to exercise, appears to me to be an almost unlimited right of interference for the better order of the States.' And later, '[But] the motives of the Government of India in effecting an arrangement of affairs of Kathiawar are above suspicion, and the course that it is proposed we should take has its justification not only in the indefinite obligations contracted by us in the capacity of Paramount Power, but in the fact adverted to by Colonel Durand, that our Government of India has in a sense been a cause of this anarchy in Kathiawar.' That the motives of the British are 'above' suspicion reiterates a familiar argument from earlier on, the 'intentions' of the East India Company being the determinant of the meaning of a treaty. Failure to take this into account leads Benton to see this as 'a theoretical limit' to intervention (see Benton 2009: 249); this accepted role of the intention was also formalized in the discourse of international law, as will be analysed in the next section. Moreover, Benton's exposition has no place for the Queen as central to the broader legal architecture. And, in the context of Travancore, 'I do not think that Mr. J.D. Mayne, of Madras, has over-stated the truth in laying down that Parliament has not the power to legislate away the jurisdiction of Travancore. What Parliament can do, if it chooses, is to compel the executive to annex foreign territory to the Queen's dominions or to put pressure on the foreign state and force it to abstain from trying British subjects – *and, of course, in the case of a Native state, this pressure would be irresistible*' (emphasis added); ibid.: 234–35, 400.

132 'In my humble judgment, the power of the Crown to alienate portions of Indian territory cannot be questioned. Even as regards dominions of her majesty, which are not in the peculiar position of British India, it is now too late to deny that the Crown may cede parts of them, subject to the risk of Parliamentary impeachment incurred by those who have advised the improper cession. But in respect of her Indian dominions, I venture to think, that the Queen has Parliamentary sanction for any alienation of territory she may think proper to make'; ibid: 396. The extension of British laws into native territory is detailed by Lee-Warner, *Protected Princes in India* (1894): 326–67. The powers of the King/Queen over 'confiscations' of the property of 'rebels' was well recognized, and

Maitland alludes to an Act of 1715 in this regard referring to such properties as 'vested in the King' and 'for the use of the Public'; see Runciman and Ryan, eds (2003): 38–39. In the Indian context, E. Stokes has detailed 'confiscations' in the context of 1857–58, in *The Peasant Armed* (1986). For a more recent work, see Vishal Singh Deo, 'Empire in the Doab: Interrogating the Political Economy of Western Uttar Pradesh circa 1803–1950' (2023): 145–48; Deo's is an important study of the determining and long-lasting effects of colonial law and political economy on community, ecology and caste with little amounting to anything like 'property' as conventionally understood.

[133] In arguing the case, Twiss cited Lord Stowell's dicta in a previous case, where it was held that while no act existed for military booty, it was to be distributed under the 'same principles of law' as naval Prize; *Banda and Kirwee Booty, Proceedings and Judgment* (1866): 711.

[134] Ibid.: 16.

[135] Twiss, *The Law of Nations Considered as Independent Political Communities* (1863), Vol. 2: 115–16.

[136] The attribution of such a position to Vattel and Rousseau was commonplace among nineteenth-century international jurists; ibid.: 270, 461–62. Hall, in *A Treatise on International Law* (1895): 68–70, cites Portalis, the commissioner of the Prize Council, repeating Rousseau's dictum, thus establishing that the idea of war being a relation between states was more than a mere philosophical idea. The continental writers advocating this position include Bluntchelli, Fiore and De Laveleye.

[137] Twiss (1863), Vol. 2: 124.

[138] Ibid., Vol. 2: 123. The distinction between 'right' (of confiscation of all including individual/private property) and more humane 'practices' (where private property is spared) is repeated by Maine (see *International Law*, 1890: 131) through a discussion of 'manuals'.

[139] R.P. Phillimore, *Commentaries Upon International Law* (1885), Vol. 3: 370–86; Hall (1895): 639–42; Maine (1890): 111–12.

[140] Ibid.: Phillimore (1885), Hall (1895), Maine (1890).

[141] Ibid.

[142] There were differences in the positions of international lawyers on the question of whether Britain's interests were served in adhering to the Declaration of Paris and giving up on certain belligerent rights that she had possessed. While Phillimore was critical of this concession, Twiss and Hall were not.

[143] Norman Bentwich, *The Law of Private Property in War* (1907).

[144] Twiss (1863): 135.

[145] Bentwich (1907): 141 (appendix on the Hague resolutions).

[146] Maine (1890): 107.

[147] Charles Tupper, *Our Indian Protectorate* (1893). Tupper's history of the East India Company's conquests of native kingdoms applies the ideas of the imperial (British Crown) and the feudatories (native) as part of one seamless argument and narrative; see ibid.: 48–128.

[148] Twiss (1863): xl–xli.

[149] Ibid.: xxxix.

[150] Ibid.: 27–28; Hall (1895): 29, 127.

[151] See *Sketches of Relations subsisting between British Government in India and different States*

(1837). The historical works of Michael Fisher, including *Indirect Rule in India* (1998) and *The Politics of British Annexation in India* (1997), are critical to the issues being investigated here.

152 The exclusionary criterion of 'civilization' as a function of imperialism has been insightfully examined in Anghie (2005) and Keene (2002).

153 Hall (1895): 21.

154 Hall (1895): 29; Westlake, *Chapters on the Principles of International Law* (1894): 190–232; Lee-Warner, *Protected Princes of India* (1894). Also see the case of the Mughal ruler represented by Rammohan Roy, analysed above.

155 Tupper (1893): 17; Hall (1895): 205–06.

156 H. Wheaten, in *Elements of International Law* (1836): 295, speaks of 'delegated sovereignty'; Sir Robert Phillimore uses the same characterization in *Commentaries Upon International Law* (1885), Vol. 3: 140. This was the characteristic used in court cases up to the Privy Council already referred to, from *Nawab of Arcot v. East India Company* to *The East India Company v. Kamachee Boye Sahaba.*

157 Tupper (1893): 5.

158 Ibid.: 10.

159 Westlake (1894): 136. Interestingly, Koskenniemi speaks of Westlake's scepticism towards a notion of 'conscience' in the 1860s. A rich discussion on 'the double meaning of conscience [is] exploited to merge a romantic sensibility with Enlightenment rationalism' through Rolin, Westlake and Bluntschli and the discourse of international law follows. However, one possible genealogy through (coercive) monarchical equity, as suggested through a study of the British empire in India and the East India Company, is not considered. See Koskenniemi (2001): 11–51

160 Ibid.: 193.

161 Ibid.

162 Ibid.: 212–13; Lee-Warner (1894): 90–122.

163 Westlake (1894): 222–23, 224–27; Lee-Warner (1894): 326–67.

164 Westlake (1894): 185–87.

165 Phillimore (1885), Vol. 1: 138. Phillimore writes that the sovereignty that the East India Company exercised in entering into treaties and conducting war was one which was delegated to it by Crown and Parliament; 'therefore the responsibility of the international acts of the Company rests upon Great Britain as much as the acts of any other of her accredited public agents'.

166 Westlake (1894): 205.

167 Tupper (1893): 354; W.E. Hall, *A Treatise on the Foreign Powers and Jurisdiction of the British Crown* (1894): 127–29.

168 Tupper (1893): 83–114; Lee-Warner (1894): 37–40, 153–59.

169 Hall, *A Treatise on the Foreign Powers and Jurisdiction of the British Crown* (1894): 287.

170 Westlake (1894): 209.

171 Hall, *A Treatise on the Foreign Powers and Jurisdiction of the British Crown* (1894): 224.

172 The importance of Grotius for thinking through the question of imperialism has been insightfully analysed by Edward Keene, *Beyond the Anarchical Society* (2002).

173 See H. Grotius, *Commentary on the Law of Prize and Booty* ([1603] 2006).

174 Ibid.

175 Locke, *Two Treatises on Government* ([1689] 1988); see the discussion in Part I.

[176] Ibid.; see Part I.

[177] Ibid.: 323; 'That the master of the family has a very distinct and differently limited Power, both as to time and extent over the several persons that are in it; for excepting the Slave (and the family is as much a family and his power as paterfamilias as great whether they be any slaves in his family or not he has no legislative power of life and death over them).'

[178] See the discussion in Part II.

[179] Locke ([1689] 1998): 412–3.

[180] See J.S. Mill, 'A Constitutional View of the India Question' (1990): 175.

[181] 'Liberalism', as has well been documented, was only applicable in so-called civilized societies, while 'despotism' was justified in ruling barbarians, 'provided the ends are improvement and the means justified by actually effecting that end'. There was no contradiction seen between a 'civilized society' conquering and lording over a 'barbaric' people. The world consisted of more advanced and less advanced peoples, and the former could well be ruled by the latter.

[182] Austin (2012): 262.

[183] This builds and captures some of the detailed discussion in *The Infinite Double* (Govind 2015).

[184] See P.Q. Wright, *Prize Money* (1913): 118. This was in a letter that Mill wrote to *The Times* on 11 March 1871 where he seemed to be reversing an earlier position on the matter. Wright's short text is a useful exposition of Prize law.

[185] See note 5 above.

[186] *Campbell v. Hall* and *Lyons (Mayor) v. East India Company.*

[187] *Lyons (Mayor) v. East India Company.*

[188] See, *Minutes by Sir Barnes Peacock* (1901), 4–12. There is the characteristic discussion of *Campbell v. Hall*, and notwithstanding his interpretation of the derivation of the Company's authority from 2 & 4 William IV c. 85, Peacock does recognize the 'right of the Crown' in cases of conquest.

[189] These arguments about the respect for local precedence should not be confused with ways of claiming authority and right, which were always rooted in London. However, these arguments combined in the most surprising ways with contemporaneous so-called scientific arguments, such as James Mill combining the argument of the government as landlord following oriental precedent with Ricardian arguments. See my discussion in 'Revenue, Rent . . . Profit?' (Govind 2011a) and *The Infinite Double* (Govind 2015).

[190] The importance of enclosures and the legislative interventions in this regard are recognized from Karl Marx to Henry Maine. J.M. Neeson, in *Commoners: Common Right, Enclosure and Social Change in England, 1700–1820* (1996), has more recently demonstrated the resilience of these issues and the importance of the peasant agriculture in England well into the nineteenth century. This can also be gauged by colonial land legislation where, for instance, the notorious rights of 'distrait' granted to zamindars in Bengal had well-established precedent in English agrarian history.

[191] See notes 4 to 6 above.

[192] The entire literature around 'resumptions' from Bengal in the late eighteenth century to every conquered territory involved the Company appropriating land revenue on the basis of arguments that native titles were unclear, thus dispossessing a range of native landholders of various kinds, once again voiding any claim to protecting and ensuring

'property right' through law. For instance, see the work of Ranajit Guha and Despina Iliopoulou for Bengal and Burton Stein for the southern regions. One ought to compare this situation with the one Pollock describes in nineteenth-century England, where title was anything but clear. Yet representative institutions for the properties helped protect such property, even while no such protections were possible in the subcontinent.

193 I am here building on my own earlier work on revenue settlements as well as drawing on the established historiography on colonial property, from N.K. Sinha, Ranajit Guha and Amiya Bagchi to Despina Iliopoulou, whose works have been cited above. However, a more recent corpus of work – Robert Travers, *Ideology and Empire* (2007); Jon Wilson, *Domination of Strangers* (2010); Andrew Sartori, *Liberalism in Empire* (2014) – does not take into cognizance the precise ideological, institutional and legal forms of property (and the 'state'–'empire') as they take shape in England and the Company settlements, which have been traced and analysed here, and therefore the relationship between modernity, political economy and conquest as articulated in their work is misconstrued. Analogously, the fact that one cannot speak of 'private property' in any meaningful sense in the colonial setting is what mars Partha Chatterjee's structuring assumption about the 'formal establishment of private property in land' in *Bengal 1920–1947: The Land Question* (1984: 8), with lasting implications for the theorization of 'organized'–'unorganized', 'political society'–'civil society'. For a recent valuable entry-point into the specific form of (non)property introduced by the Company in relationship to Islamic jurisprudence and colonial practice, see Faisal Chaudhry, 'Property and its Rule (in Late Indo-Islamic and Early Colonial) in South Asia: What's in a Name?' (2018).

194 See Rammohan Roy's arguments in 'Essay on the Rights of Hindus over Ancestral Property', his comments on the Permanent Settlement and critique of Company policies in relationship to 'land resumption'. This issue is examined in detail in my paper, 'The Spiritual, the Religious and the Secular in Rammohan Roy's Hermeneutic Praxis' (forthcoming).

195 For a rich discussion and critique of the contract that moves from seventeenth-century 'natural law' writers to nineteenth-century defences of American slavery, see Pateman (1988): 39–177.

196 The subtle ways in which religious exclusion operated from the strictures of *Postnati* to the initial royal charters, including the mid-eighteenth-century Prize charters that granted special rights to the Company in their relations with non-Christian polities, remain to be investigated. The importance of *Postnati* and the role of religion in war have often been ignored in standard accounts such as J.T. Johnson, *The Holy War Idea* (2001): 59, which assumes that Grotius and Victoria inaugurated the rejection of religious justifications for war leading to a form of moral reasoning in the 'West' laying the basis for the 'state as a political entity'. On the other hand, for the continuing centrality of religion and Christianity in thinking about war, see Philip Buc, *Holy War, Martyrdom, and Terror: Christianity, Violence, and the West, ca. 70 C.E. to the Iraq War* (2015).

197 It is revealing that the contemporary – and celebrated – British historiography continues in this form of British constitutional protectionism but never granting the status of British conflicts in India as 'wars', reserving such an appellation for conflicts within 'civilized' Euro-America. See, for instance, Linda Colley's *Britons: Forging the Nation* (1992), which is particularly ironical considering its thesis about nationalism and imperialism.

[198] Writing a history of resistance and rebellion, one has to take seriously Marx's contention that it might well be the case that the Silesian weavers in their protests perfected the achievements of the French Revolution; see 'Critical Notes on the Article: "The King of Prussia and Social Reform by a Prussian"', in Livingstone and Benton, trans., *Karl Marx: Early Writings* (1992). It is in this context that one may view the studies of peasant insurgency in Ranajit Guha's, *Elementary Aspects of Peasant Insurgency* (1983), which I have interpreted along such lines in 'Amplitude of the Will and the Ruin of Culture' (2017b). Sanghamitra Misra's *The Long Conquest: Community, Sovereignty and Cotton in the Garo Hills, Circa 1760 to 1900* (forthcoming) establishes definitively the protracted way in which colonial conquest structured community through the brutality of law and political economy even while such a state was consistently recognized and combated in what can only be described as a decades-long war-cum-insurgency.

Conclusion: Revolution *contra* Empire

The Problematic and Its Iterations

As is difficult to avoid in any conclusion, here too the penumbra of this work may well shade off into nebulae of more general concern, ungainly lurching from the all-too speculative to the not-sufficiently concrete.

Dominant paradigms of political philosophy and law with its debates around the 'veil of ignorance', the 'night-watchman state' and 'imagined communities' have been untouched and untrammelled by events or structures, particularly those that would be projected as 'international', whether the singular nuclear genocide of a defeated enemy or the channels of transnational corporate unaccountability that could leave unjudged the rampant blepharospasm of the Bhopal Gas Tragedy.[1] In this sense, twentieth- and twenty-first-century academic discourse of the human sciences in its dominant forms is indeed a worthy successor to the nineteenth century: the century which had provided a new social epistemology in the form of a hallucinogen, which, much like classical mechanics, treated the political state as self-constitutive without inquiring into the ways in which it was constituted by its mobile ratio with its media or other objects. Not just this, but the simultaneous and paradoxical attribution of such an immaculate conception to the more specifically historical nation-states of Europe in their respective identities, from which the contemporary ideals of democracy, law and individual freedom and right are seen to have laboured into being. Beached on the shores of abstraction, these 'Robinsonades'[2] tilt at distinctions between night-watchmen states and veils of ignorance.[3] Perhaps more than a political or legal philosophy, it is a morphology that is required.

In combating such a perception, this work has argued for the centrality of conquest and empire in the twining forms of doctrinal kingship and imperial law, in the constitution and construction of the regions comprising (the British) empire from the seventeenth to the nineteenth century. It has thereby been established that well into the nineteenth century there existed no such things as nation-states or representative democracies, and in no sense can one see either of these phenomena transiting into their true natures. Any attempt to encrust a philosophical theory of a democratic state with the history of empires such as England is therefore not merely untenable, but in fact consistent with the ideological fictions of empire. Attention to such a history would therefore graft the conceptualization of sovereignty at the juncture of the problem of real and fictive jurisdictions. That is to say, this would involve a scrutinizing examination of the concrete claims and channels of sovereignty and law in their explicit manifestation as much as their strategic staging, the paradigmatic form of which has been charted. However, such a conceptual schema cum historical account does not intend to deny, let alone annul, the revolutionary accomplishments, ideas and ideals bursting in modernity regarding universal rights and political self-constitution, whether in the 1640s Putney, the 1790s France and Haiti, or elsewhere across the globe. These moments are not reducible to their temporal or spatial enclave, having a historic force that confounds any such *a priori* sequestering. A clue to this understanding, as much as understanding this 'fact', may be gleaned in Kant, who saw in the French Revolution and its reception – in the risks and intentions of secular self-constitution and world peace as much as their 'enthusiastic' response – something deeply antagonistic to the imperial political formations of the day. Kant saw these concrete intentions and responses as carrying a power that was inexhaustible, and therefore the very sign and measure of progress as much as its possibility.[4]

In such twilight, this conclusion articulates a two-fold aim. First, the argument over the last three parts is used to diagnose and critique a paradigm where the ideals of the French Revolution – of universal natural rights and the self-constituting (national) community – are mischievously incorporated into the facts and forces of European history. Only thereby is achieved the erasure of kingship and empire as engines of historical motion from the seventeenth to the nineteenth centuries, as traced in this work, to complete a picture of an ascending Euro-American political modernity during these times.[5] This incorporation of revolutionary aims as much as the erasure of empire is particularly ironic since, in fact, much of the locomotive logic of these centuries lay in the determined and largely successful crushing of such aims by the latter. Empire in its legal, institutional and ideological manifestations functioned as nothing less than the most vicious adversary of the potential nation-state norm in its various revolutionary articulations, which had conjoined a theory of universal human rights to political self-constitution.[6]

One can speak coherently of the nation-state *norm* only as the coincidence of a universally recognized right to political constitution by a people, and this does not gain any global currency until the twentieth century. As an ideological paradigm, while discernable in the logic of the revolutionary moments in France, Haiti, Russia, India, as in numerous other places, it never existed as an acceptable politico-institutional norm until the wholesale rejection of empire. For, rather than the myths of the Westphalian origins of the nation-state norm in the seventeenth century,[7] it is only in the moment of the dismembering of the British Empire and nationalist decolonization, in roughly the middle of the twentieth century, that one can see its global emergence.[8] For instance, combating the British Empire and inspired by the revolutionary ideas of rights and self-determination, the Indian National Congress can be seen to aim at precisely such a revolutionary paradigm by insisting on a Constituent Assembly and emphasizing fundamental rights.[9] This broader critique of the picture of an ascending European political modernity is argued for through critical engagement with Hobsbawm's influential thesis on nations, democratization and nationalism – along with Richard Tuck's recent account of the 'invention of modern democracy' – which distils the essential logic of the conventional account.

The second argument undertaken in this conclusion is aimed at establishing the fact that the very distinctive grammar of the Indian constitutional order is indelibly marked by the shadow-rules of precisely what it repudiates, i.e. imperial conquest. Notwithstanding the enunciation of the revolutionary ideals of fundamental natural rights and self-determination, any scrutiny of the experience of independent India reveals the undeniable undermining of such rights by novel uses of the inherited weight of, what is named here and will be distilled as, the legal paradigm of imperial-English military-martial law. A paradigm which, it is argued, best captures the asymmetrical punitive powers of the state in the everyday laws and everyday lives of the Indian democratic order. This invocation of military law is justified with reference to the argument that just as in martial-military law, public 'servants' acting in public capacity are shielded from the channels of accountability that are attached to ordinary citizens in the name of the state or national interest even in a constitutional order (otherwise) enshrining equality and liberty to all. Thereby emerges a primal fault-line, the double standards that poison and imprison the heart of the democratic order. Just as the military man is ruled by a different order and is therein, and thereby, rendered unaccountable to instituted and 'ordinary' laws, such a status analogously embeds the workings of public servants at large against citizen-subjects. This is the power wielded by the political class, which may well render all constitutional promises to the people weak and nugatory. The initial polarity, between the laws of empire and the revolutionary calls for self-determination, on the one hand, and its reiteration in the constitutional order, are articulated and analysed in sequential order, forming the substance of this conclusion.

The Global: Revolutionary Universality *contra* Imperial Conquest

At the threshold of the twentieth century, if one were to join the study of (the 'British') empire undertaken so far with the fact that the other major political entities were also empires, it would not be controversial to claim, as is borne out by much extant scholarship, that imperialism constituted the grammar generating the rules of the world order. There can be no confusion between, or conflation of, the establishment of such a politico-legal territorialization and the constellation of normative principles that one identifies with universal natural-human rights, and the self-constitution of political communities in identifiable territorial loci, the constituents of the nation-state norm. Just as the argument has been made at a theoretical level that empire has to be conceived of as a force coordinating and forming the territorial-temporal order, the mentioned constellation of principles, as a force unique to itself, cannot be reduced to the histories of particular ethnic or national identities. There is nothing particularly French about the French Revolution whose ideals repudiated – and were repudiated in – absolutist and imperial-republican France,[10] just as they could take inspiring form in Ambedkar's Mahad Satyagraha in colonial India.

The above thesis of the unique features of the French revolutionary self-constituting state of popular sovereignty would not be controversial. For instance, Hobsbawm clearly distinguishes this conception, where individuals freely constitute themselves into a nation-state, from the other conception of the nation where it is assumed to exist *a priori*.[11] However, from outlining such a conception of a revolutionary nation-state, Hobsbawm makes what can only be described as an inexplicable presumption. He assumes that the post-French revolutionary state norm was clearly manifested in actual fact as a nation-state, and moreover that in the nineteenth century, nobody could deny that Britain, France and Spain were 'the oldest and most unquestioned nation-states'.[12] In the analytical discussion of the forms of nations and nation-states, not only is there no mention of empire and imperial politics by Hobsbawm, but rather, the 'liberal' position of the category of the nation as embodying a particular stage embedded in a larger historical social evolution is uncritically accepted.

This assumption by Hobsbawm of a global social evolution is particularly ironic because John Stuart Mill,[13] who is cited by him most frequently as a proponent of such an ideology of the nation-state forming as a stage in an evolutionary progress, is discussed without engaging with the fact that such a formulation of the nation was a well-honed ideological strategy that was used to explicitly justify and defend British imperialism and conquest. At the end of the twentieth century, Hobsbawm, as one of the most celebrated Marxist historians, is thus unwittingly stage-managed by the puppet-strings of Maine and Mill, whose epistemic paradigm is outlined in the previous part. It is only by disavowing empire and its logic that Hobsbawm can curate an abstracted history of European 'democratization' and state-led nationalism that is held to have ultimately led to the First World War in his explanatory schema. This disavowal of empire as the motor of the European state form – from Britain to France to Germany – does not stand historical scrutiny. If the norms of the French Revolution are taken as forming the idea of the nation-state, neither was (universal) franchise established nor fundamental rights recognized in any of the major European empire-states[14] prior to their imperial conquest(s); in fact, increasing franchise in metropolitan areas moved *pari passu* with exponential imperial territorialization. Rather than being established, the ideals of the self-forming community were largely crushed. Once again, in emphasizing 'democratization' and 'mass politics' by bracketing out the imperial question, Hobsbawm's thesis fits well into the nineteenth century's intellectual programme of imperial subterfuge. The deeper roots of such forms of democratization can be traced to notions of a 'transition' to capitalism that was to have been achieved by England, where historians such as Robert Brenner do not account for the kind of capitalism which involved not merely feudal royal grants of colonization, whether in the Americas or the subcontinent, as has been discussed, but also slavery on a planetary scale.[15]

On the other hand, while Richard Tuck in his recent book, *The Sleeping Sovereign*, fleetingly recognizes the problem of the relationship between democracy and territoriality, he too, like Hobsbawm, sees the nineteenth century as the time of 'democratic revolutions'.[16] Tuck argues that a democracy would mean that the sovereign people can assert itself through majority voting in plebiscitary forms to ensure that there is no monopolization of political power by representative or other such bodies. While making this argument, however, he does note a possible critique in the form of the argument that such 'majoritarianism' might work through the exclusion of sections of the people, such as foreigners and children. He sees in this critique an 'aspect of a very general problem for theories of democracy, namely the territoriality of the modern state'.[17] Acknowledged therefore is the fact that it would be 'hard on any view of democratic politics to explain the significance of boundaries and the rights that the state possesses over anyone who steps across them'.[18]

While this is posed as a more general normative problem, the deeper problem is that Tuck's intellectual-genealogical account of 'democracy', through a reading of figures from Bodin to Jefferson, works to conceal rather than illuminate the 'hard' difficulties of the relationship between sovereignty, jurisdiction and property that lie at the very heart of the 'democratic' problematic. For instance, the book subtly makes an argument that the distinction between sovereignty and government (or administration) lay in the fact that the sovereign was defined by two essential features. It was the seat of 'ultimate legislation' as well as chose the officials of government. This idea was traced to Bodin, for whom the sovereign could be either a monarch or the 'people', but such a distinction between sovereignty and government enabled, in other hands, the radical argument that in democratic states, the people as sovereign remained politically active even in contexts of elected representative governments.[19] It is in such a context, that Tuck makes his argument about plebiscitary ratification that is found in the seventeenth-century interregnum, Hobbes, the American colonies, as well as Rousseau and the Girondins.[20] On the other hand, Tuck had traced to Bodin and this eminently democratic possibility the idea that sovereignty needed to be characterized as 'perpetual', and this is to have entailed an implicit critique of monarchies, particularly elected ones.[21] This entire discussion of the distinction between the sovereign and the government, which is meant to enable the sovereign people to have the capacity to direct governance and administration through and beyond representation, tends to assume a specified homogenous self-evident locus of a sovereign people. It is this fact that is eminently questionable from the perspective of the facts of imperialism, making it impossible to characterize the nineteenth century as involving 'democratic revolutions'. Tuck's argument about the 'invention of democracy' does not account for the fact that in each case the state included in its governance people who were excluded from any form of political power, in the form of slaves, unpropertied labourers, dissident sectarians, imperial-colonial subjects and certainly women. Neither is the question of 'perpetuity', 'sovereignty' and 'territoriality' – as conceptualized and practised – by the King's bodies in the (British) imperial empire engaged with.[22]

While the normative problem in today's democracies with universal franchise and demarcated territories might well involve the problem of the status of foreigners, the historical period that Tuck traverses to make his argument can in no sense be seen to have witnessed 'democracies'. This is because of the qualifying exclusions at work during the period between the seventeenth and the nineteenth centuries, problems that have been at the centre of this present investigation. This also entails more specific interpretative occlusions such as Tuck's reading of the Locke, the American colonists as much as the Girondins, as enunciating the democratic politics of a 'sovereign people' (or Lockean 'community') meant to exert control over representative bodies, without considering the excluded depoliticized status of slaves, religious dissidents and non-propertied 'servants' that was integral to such 'sovereignty'. Tuck is therefore at one with Hobsbawm and the nineteenth-century ideologues who attempt to epistemically screen out the majority subject populations being directly affected by imperial ventures in sustaining a myth of an increasingly democratic and civilized 'west'.

Such an ideological programme works strenuously against the arguments of Marxist revolutionaries from Lenin to Luxemburg, who discerned in the European states an imperialist-capitalist logic, leading, inevitably, to the First World War. It appears irrefutable that the articulation-effectuation of the revolutionary idea of a self-constituting community grounded in natural and universal rights was viciously and systematically combated by empires, and could never therefore form part of their ratio, whether French or English. The ideas and norms of natural rights and self-government ineluctably flow into one another, because both are grounded in the natural and universal individual capacity to reason and reason into the self-constitution of a just community. One must take seriously the logical conjunction between the demands for the (universal) rights and freedoms of humans which enables the self-constitution of a community. The community as 'a work of reason' found its ratio in self-government (liberty and equality) as much as (universal) fraternity, thereby decisively rejecting the inequalities and expansionist logic of empire.[23] These ideas, far from manifesting into reality, were in fact subject, even in their articulation, to a most forceful critique by (the British) empire at ideological and institutional levels, from Burke to Bentham to Mill, notwithstanding differences that are well-recognized.

This rejection was so fundamental that it could not be based on a differentiation between the natural rights of the colonizer and the colonized, since the idea of fundamental natural rights described above was not acceptable by British thinkers or their constitution. Not only would they by their very nature militate against dynastic monarchy or (imperial) parliamentary sovereignty, such rights could not be attributed (even) to those in the metropolis who were governed by the rules and laws of those in authority.[24] Thus, if the First World War has been attributed to nationalism, it was a nationalism of an imperializing core, having little to do with the revolutionary paradigm of the nation as a self-constituting community where self-constitution was a perpetual 'right' and peace the paradigmatic aim. Enunciated principles of self-determination for select races too took shape after the war, resulting in a 'mandate system'.[25] None except revolutionary Marxists like Luxemburg and Lenin consistently recognized self-determination as a universal right during the early twentieth century, notwithstanding differences, and radically critiqued the imperial-capitalist war as representing itself as one of national interest.[26]

Not until after the world wars, when the last and greatest empires were on the brink of collapsing and movements for self-determination were growing in strength, did there emerge some consensus on the universal applicability of ideas regarding natural human rights and the self-constitution of states or the self-determination of peoples. No doubt, the evolution of such a norm, perhaps most dramatically in the United Nations' Declaration of Human Rights, should not be taken to imply that global history since then has not consistently undermined such principles in various ways, from outright military invasion to the setting up of fictitious sovereignties and puppet regimes to further national-state interests. Yet, the distinctive novelty of the norms of human autonomy and the self-determination of peoples, in distinction to their active imperial repulsion previously, cannot be denied. European states can then claim no priority of being nation-states or modern states of any sort

– defined in terms of delimited territory and natural-universal rights – before they were forced to give up their imperial form in the wake of war, nationalist movements and decolonization. The disintegration of empire was what led to the formation of nation-states for *both* the metropolitan-imperial as well as the conquered-subject populations.[27]

A conceptual account and critique of empire as a force of world history thereby enables an interpretation of popular movements for national freedom and self-determination in early twentieth-century colonial India bereft of ideologically motivated standards which one assumes to be characteristic of 'western modernity'. The antagonistic distinction between the imperial and the revolutionary paradigm is crucial in this regard. In the light of the above, the recognition and acceptance of the King-Emperor as legitimate sovereign by those considered nationalist heroes such as Naoroji, Gandhi and Tilak do not represent an 'incomplete' or mimetic nationalism, by the standards of Europe. They merely register and index the political norms and facts of the day: a world of dynastic monarchies and empires which had no place for the nation-democratic norm or popular sovereignty. At the level of organized mass mobilization that slowly began claiming a national status, leaving revolutionaries aside, Gandhi inaugurated something incontestably novel, in his success if nothing else, by openly rejecting the essential English political doctrine of allegiance and law in his sedition case in 1921.[28]

Yet such forms of mass mobilization built upon the theoretical critique of the irredeemably exploitative structure of empire that was undertaken by the so-called 'moderates'.[29] Parallel to this economic critique of imperialism was articulated a discourse that took inspiration from moments in French and Russian history, by mandating armed insurrection and/or a more total social transformation not limited to political rule but involving questions of social-proprietorial structure.[30] This more radical conception often coloured organized peasant movements from the 1920s onwards, which at times intersected with, but at other times diverged from, the Gandhian mobilizations.[31] In terms of organizations, the extent of the challenge to colonial-imperial rule can be measured by British policies towards Communist organizations, the Congress, as much as organizations such as the Muslim League, the Hindu Mahasabha and the Rashtriya Swayamsevak Sangh (RSS).[32] While Communist organizations were persecuted and banned, the Congress was punitively dealt with particularly during its powerful anti-colonial mass struggles which challenged empire, and organizations which spoke most stridently of Hindu religious-nationalist regeneration or an Islamic state, and did not undertake anti-colonial mass movements, were left unperturbed.[33] The earlier banning of the Communist Party of India meant that many Communists entered the Congress to radicalize its mass movements, leading to internal frictions and tensions within the Congress party[34] – frictions so deep that they were seen to manifest in fundamental issues in the Constituent Assembly debates. Moreover, all such mobilizations intertwined with and built upon existing popular discontent and the deep well of popular protests and peasant rebellions that had characterized the entire history of the British rule; no doubt more research is required to be done on unearthing the ideological contours and concrete trajectories of the several forms of popular mobilization that characterized this centuries-old arc.

Much scholarship has noted such discrepancies between and within Gandhian mass movements on fundamental questions such as whether the protests and demands were geared merely against the colonial state (revenue), or simultaneously took aim at forms of proprietorship held by local Indians (such as zamindari property) as well as their instituted and socialized forms of domination, whether on the register of religion or of caste.[35] This, along with failed constitutional negotiations on religion and nationality, large-scale 'riots', and partition provided the specific and undeniable context which shaped the founding tensions of the Constituent Assembly debates of the 1940s, all of which enunciate an idiom and normative grammar far removed from the Gandhian emphasis on the village. The role of Ambedkar in expressing this grammar of rights and representation in more general terms as well as in articulating the caste question and forcing Gandhi and the Congress leadership to confront its horrors is foundational. The centrality of justiciable fundamental rights and direct parliamentary representation, as opposed to the Gandhian valorization of the 'village', has simultaneously to be seen, drawing from anti-colonial peasant and labour movements and forming the basis of such movements in independent India. Illustrative of the distance from the Gandhian vision of 'village India' is the importance for the Constituent Assembly, and later the Parliament and Supreme Court, of two intertwined questions regarding the relationship between the legislature and fundamental rights, as well as, subsequently, questions pertaining to zamindari abolition and land ceiling among other 'land reforms' and preventive detention.[36] The discussions and resolutions in the Constituent Assembly cannot be understood without an awareness of the prior history of peoples' struggles on these matters.[37] The warning of the sole Communist in the Constituent Assembly, that the fundamental rights were being framed from the point of view of a police constable, cannot be so easily dismissed out of hand.[38] Therefore, the final document of the Constitution of India as much as its after-life including amendments and (changing) judicial interpretation, in all its charged polarities, bear the signs and marks of this past history of struggle as much as a specific 'revolutionary' normative grammar or rights, representation and law that cannot be derived from national pasts. Nothing is gained by making abstract comparisons with false models of European history or grounding such praxis in claims of an unarticulated, repressed 'aboriginal' epistemology whether in a religious grammar or not, which has survived intact throughout Indian history unaffected by empire and the struggles against it. This position often takes the claim of requiring the unearthing of such an epistemology as the only means to comprehend and engage with the history as well as contemporaneity of the present conjuncture in India. Such an approach is not merely assailed by the problematic quasi idealist notion that one can recover wholesale an epistemological apparatus and apply it to understand the phenomena at hand, but also the fact that while this approach is constantly reiterated, it has scarce succeeded in exhibiting any concept that succeeds in accomplishing such a task anywhere, whether in the legal, economic, scientific or social domain.[39]

To better place – and therefore understand – the significance of constitution-making and its future in India one would have to be better attuned to the grain of its voice. For once again, contrary to both the epistemic 'aborigines' (in the sense of claiming an immaculate origin and not in the taxonomical sense of referring to peoples dispossessed) and modernity theorists, the nationalist demand for fundamental rights was itself at complete odds with the 'British' constitutional principles and the imperial architectures of all major political powers. The adoption of the French-revolutionary constituent assembly model, even approved by Gandhi, was to directly contradict British 'liberal' thought and practice, whether at home or in the colonies. That the British constitution was imperialist to the core is succinctly revealed in the words of one of its ablest late nineteenth-century spokesmen, when he says that the Crown and Acts of the imperial (British) parliament form the unalterable 'constitution' on the basis of which the Legislative Council of India could act. In explanation Dicey remarks that the Legislative Council's power of law-making in India was no different from the powers of a railway company in making by-laws, both being subject in the same way to the imperial parliament.[40] This gives some indication of the politically servile status and the 'rule of law' when it came to subject populations – not even the hint of a recognition of the irony of such a comparison. This understanding of the 'constitution' as (King in) parliamentary sovereignty directing forms of conquest and subject populations is as far removed as imaginable from the written Constitution enshrining fundamental rights formulated by a Constituent Assembly determined on universal franchise[41] in India.

The misunderstanding of this fundamental difference takes the form of epistemic obstacles. As an illustration of this hindrance to reading the significance of the Constituent Assembly one might refer to the fact that contemporary discussions of the citizenship question in India are often framed by the distinction between 'jus soli' and 'jus sanguine', with the former being defined by birth in a particular place or territory and the latter indicating descent by blood. 'Jus soli' is often traced to the common law tradition and *Postnati*, while 'jus sanguine' is often associated with the French post-revolutionary situation. This categorical framework then becomes a lens by which to examine the question of Indian citizenship. However, as this work has shown, such an understanding is deeply flawed and misleading, and not simply in its interpretation of common law; from *Postnati* onwards descent by 'blood' was recognized as much.[42] More fundamentally, the theory of 'jus soli' as attributed to a particular place rather than seeing in the matter the modality of allegiance and conquest only succeeds in obscuring the central facts and forces of the modern world in the imperial territorialization described in this work.[43] This categorical framework is in fact based on a fictitious screening of European history that essentially consists in little more than the denial of empire.

Such a misleading characterization of 'jus soli' and the concomitant misrecognition of territory is but an offshoot of a more fundamental misconstrual in political thought, where (British) liberalism is treated as a general doctrine of fundamental individual rights. On the contrary, when the Congress party adopted a language of fundamental rights in the late 1920s and ultimately enshrined these ideas in the Indian Constitution, they were explicitly departing from the British and French empires in trying to retrieve the revolutionary grammars from historical moments which had often been repudiated in their own countries, whether in institutional or ideological forms; the British and French empires could hardly be seen subscribing to ideas of universal franchise or fundamental rights. The embedding of the question of citizenship within a constitutional regime and order of fundamental rights and universal franchise means that it is impossible to make any comparison between the Indian case and the English-imperial one.

In other words, the different national and imperial contexts have transformed the meaning and import of 'jus soli', and it would do well not to derive the Indian constitutional debates on this question from the British-imperial structure as common law. Such an enunciation of fundamental rights clogged by questions on the relationship between legislative acts and fundamental rights – on the registers of property and liberty – while completely different from anything in the British-imperial constitutional experience, continue to form and haunt us today in markedly distinctive ways of their own.[44]

The Indian Nation: Revolutionary Natural Right *contra* Imperial Inheritance

The second fold in the two-fold objective of this conclusion has been reached in the following polarity: independent India is moulded by the revolutionary enunciation of fundamental rights on the one hand, and the grinding weight of the imperial-military paradigm on the other. A.V. Dicey, in his classic work, attempts strenuously to contrast English common law to what he calls the French 'administrative right', which lies essentially in the fact that in the former case no immunities against the common law courts are given to administrative, government and military personnel. While recognizing the potential for such a situation in the time of the Stuarts, such a tendency was supposed to have been defeated by subsequent constitutional and legal developments post 1689–90.[45] Such a history, as indicated earlier, is possible only by falsely abstracting from King and empire and therein the legible forms of royal jurisdictions, whether in the colonies or in the subcontinent; that the Parliamentary Acts of 1781 and 1784 provided such immunities to Company officials as did other regulations is not taken cognizance of.[46] As is shown below, independent India too is haunted by such an imperial inheritance.

But first, one might indicate the 'revolutionary enunciation' by referring to *Justice K.S. Puttaswamy (Retd) v. Union of India* (2018) in a nine-judge constitutional bench, which in its judgment specifically employed a 'natural rights' rather than 'liberal' framework in its recognition of privacy as a fundamental right.[47] In articulating such a position the judgment clearly and explicitly negated the reasoning and judgment of the majority of the five-judge bench case *ADM Jabalpur v. Shivkant Shukla* (1976), which held that fundamental rights and their justiciability by the courts could be rescinded by legislation.[48] *K.S. Puttaswamy*, on the other hand, held that the specified fundamental rights guaranteed in the Constitution were meant to guarantee what were in fact 'natural', 'primordial' rights and values that were inherent to the human personality. In this sense such 'rights' were not created by either the state or the Constitution. Rather, the Constitution was meant to act as a 'firewall' in protecting such rights from the state, including legislative violation. In this sense the judgment drew from the dissenting judgment of Justice Khanna in *ADM Jabalpur*, who held that the sanctity of life and liberty were not exhausted by specific articles of the Constitution and were the basis on which the very notion of 'rule of law' operated. Citing a chilling example, Justice Khanna wrote that if one were to identify legislation or 'enacted law' with law as such, it would mean that there was no scope to critique the 'organized mass murders of the Nazi regime'.[49] *K.S. Puttaswamy* repeated this dire warning in the name of fundamental rights.

Apart from holding that fundamental rights were framed to guarantee certain 'natural' and 'inherent' rights and qualities such as privacy, which might not find explicit mention in the Constitution, *K.S. Puttaswamy* also reaffirmed the position taken in *Maneka Gandhi v. Union of India* (1978), which, in overriding *A.K. Gopalan v. State of Madras* (1950), held that fundamental rights could not treated in isolation from one another. In their 'holistic' treatment it had to be recognized that 'natural law rights were meant to be converted into our constitutionally recognized fundamental rights'.[50] *K.S. Puttaswamy* also specifically reiterated *Maneka Gandhi* in holding that the standard for reviewing or evaluating state legislation was not merely confined to asking whether the legislation was formulated by the competent authority or had achieved its intended objective.[51] Rather, enacted legislation had to be tested on the touchstone of reasonableness, justice and fairness, and could not be fanciful, oppressive or arbitrary.[52] One can read this over-riding of legislative enactment as a contest between the British doctrine of (imperial) parliamentary sovereignty and the Indian constitutional order of popular sovereignty as signified by the complex of 'natural rights'. This opposition becomes starker when it is remembered that fundamental rights operated with universal franchise, unlike the imperial parliament as the centre of descending graded constitutional orders that included self-governing colonies and jurisdictions such as India, with no commitment to fundamental rights of the individual non-propertied right to franchise.

The Supreme Court in 2018 therefore emphasized that legislation required to be evaluated according to the effects it had on the fundamental rights of the citizen-individual, rights that were in fact inherent to her/him as a human being. It is this natural and universal conception of the human being as such that enables the argument about the state, law and the Constitution being attempts to preserve and guarantee such pre-existing qualities and features. In the inherent back-and-forth of judicial pronouncement, *K.S. Puttaswamy* returned to the dissenting judgment not only of Justice Khanna, but also of Justice Fazal Ali in *A.K. Gopalan*, who had dissented against the narrow interpretation of 'liberty' which had enabled the judiciary to uphold preventive detention law in the year of the promulgation of the Constitution.[53] The present judicial basis of protection against democratically enacted law in *K.S. Puttaswamy* amplifies the position of *Kesavananda Bharati v. State of Kerala* (1973) that one cannot speak of 'parliamentary sovereignty' in India, since parliamentary legislation has to adhere to the 'basic structure' of the Constitution.[54] If the basis is indeed a natural and universal conception of human reasonableness, justice and right, one has entered into the core paradox of the revolutionary idea of right, self-determination and nationalism, which sees the multiplication and division of states as essentially the work of human reason. The self-determination and inherent rights of nation-making would strictly imply the complete 'artifice' of the nation-state, as but an instrument towards the ends of peace, freedom and justice. It is only in a world bereft of irony – and humour – that self-determination today in many places is considered nothing less than treasonous for the nationalist.

Needless to say, such a conception of natural rights as subtending citizen and state cannot be found in the imperial European formations of the early twentieth century and before. When Indians however chose the revolutionary route of affirming themselves in a Constituent Assembly, they encountered fast-metastasizing aporias, such as the ones between zamindari and property right, liberty and preventive detention.[55] Notwithstanding the complex constitutional issues regarding parliamentary legislation and judicial interpretation discussed in much of the extant scholarship, and touched on above, the debate itself assumes a particular grammar of fundamental rights and popular sovereignty and therefore cannot be directly derived from earlier British-imperial institutional debates around the relationship between statute and common law. Moreover, this latter problematic was framed in terms of kingship, parliament, assemblies as the King's bodies, and such could not be the figures employed in independent India. Though a radically different situation spawning the novelty of a written Constitution guaranteeing fundamental rights in a non-monarchical democratic order, the question remains as to whether such rules and regulations escape unscathed by the weight of an imperial legacy.

More concretely, an obvious place to start an investigation of the King or his possible surrogates is with the institution of the President and the Governors, possessing the uncannily familiar royal powers of mercy and non-culpability – in part, to manage the problem of jurisdiction which takes a federal form. These features, particularly in recent times, have received much commentary, in so far as they present a tussle between elected and non-elected representatives, thereby going to the heart of a democratic order where ancient English dicta on the King being bound by the advice of his Council is replicated and contested.[56] Of course, there is no constitutional doctrine equivalent to the King's bodies, since the offices of President and Governor are not biological-natural attributes, and neither is meant to possess several bodies in natural and political capacities. And yet, in a very real sense, the King's bodies might indeed be seen to exist and flourish in the time of independence. There is no doubt that the spectre of the King haunts and preys on the democratic order by instituting a clear division between public servants including the armed forces, and individual citizens. For public servants are indeed encrusted with royal immunities not enjoyed by ordinary subjects.

The fear is that fundamental rights may well be ground into the nugatory by a series of interlocking statutory measures and judicial pronouncements. This is seen particularly in the overlapping cases of armed forces and public servants, where the powers given to this class of individuals is meaningful only in terms of the different standards that are instituted between them as state actors and those who do not belong to this class, i.e. ordinary subjects. It is not powers but differential standards of justice that are instituted at the heart of legislation. An elucidation of this differentiation between state actors (as a class) and non-state subjects can be traced to the intersection between English military and martial law which provides its clearest theoretical paradigm, and has been analysed in Part II. Military law, in the British historical context, is the royal government of military personnel. And the existence of this law as concurrent with civil law implies that in specific cases which involve military and non-military personnel, there is no uniform legal procedure or standard through which these classes can be treated equally.

In the case of India, military forces are governed not by any King but by parliamentary legislation in the form of the Army Act or other legislative acts such as the Armed Forces Special Powers Act (AFSPA),[57] and here too, the possibility of concurrent jurisdiction with non-military courts is very real. In such cases, it is not the extinction of law but rather the inability of the aggrieved civilian to appeal to a law which she knows and to which she has committed herself, that is the root of inequality. It is either the military court or the central government, not a judicial tribunal that will have the last word in certain classes of cases between civilians and the armed forces, through a procedure that is neither public nor transparent – in a sense, not 'judicial'.[58] This asymmetry lies at the basis of lack of accountability. Therefore it is nothing less than parliament which legislates a difference, in this case by the Army Act and AFSPA, on as radical a ground as fundamental rights. This is indicated in a looping sense by Article 33 and the 50th Amendment, where the armed forces and other specified public servants may have their fundamental rights abridged, which can however take the form, in turn, of the grant of specific immunities not enjoyed by common citizens. Yet this reiterated difference between certain classes of the armed forces, and public servants and civilian citizens, on the other hand, has not been seen to constitute a challenge to the constitutionally guaranteed fundamental right to equality. This was affirmed by the constitutional bench in *Ram Swarup v. Union of India* (1957), where the court held that the (recognized) distinction between the procedures of military and civil courts did not violate the fundamental right to equality as embodied in Article 14. The question nonetheless remains as to how one is to understand such a pronouncement.

Something may yet be gained by tracing the concertina wires of law as principle and law as legislation to the mechanisms and subterfuges of British sovereignty that is the subject of the present work at its core. Notwithstanding 'fundamental rights', the question remains as to whether British imperial history has seeped into the contemporary democratic order through a deeply instituted normative differentiation. While it was a constitutional principle in Britain that the King could not be legally proceeded against, analogous protections were mimetically endowed to his ministers and servants by law. In such a context, it comes as no surprise that the Pitt India Act of 1784, in the wake of disputes between the Governor-General and the Supreme Court at Calcutta, armed the former as well as other East India Company officials with immunities against judicial review, for actions carried out in their 'public capacity'. This parliamentary statute, as discussed in Part II, enabled the detention of individuals without judicial oversight, and was reiterated in several subsequent regulations, the most notorious of which was the Bengal Regulation of 1818. It is worth emphasizing that one of the most dreaded of regulations emerged from British parliamentary statute named after the 'Whig-Liberal' William Pitt.

From the seventeenth century, as has been noted, there was always in

England a controversy over the relationship between military, martial and common law. The subjugation to military law and the resultant immunities from common law had long been protested. The problem was exacerbated by statutory provisions which allowed the use of armed forces during 'riots' and other 'civil' disturbances. While civil authorities could always be held responsible since it was they who called for the aid of armed forces, problems surfaced as to the judicial principles and standards to be used in the adjudication of such cases where civilians were killed by the armed forces in the situations of riot. The military/armed man appeared to be under two laws that could pull in two directions, caught in the proverbial horns of a dilemma. According to the mutiny acts and articles of war, he had to obey his military superiors, and any indiscipline could count as capital. On the other hand, in riot conditions, were his actions to result in the death of a civilian, any judgment on the basis of common law could also be capital.

In the words of Charles Napier, the military man engaged by civilian authorities during a riot had the choice of disobeying his superior and being shot by a military court, and/or obeying his superior and being (possibly) hung for murder by a common law court. While the legal position cemented a common law court's jurisdiction over his actions, his peculiar condition was recognized by the fact that the standards of judgement in such actions differed from those of ordinary trials. In the words of Justice Holt, the judgment in such cases had to be made on basis of the judge's impression of where the accused man's 'heart' lay. The principle to be followed was that since he was assumed to be following orders and doing his duty as a public servant, his intentions were presumed to be good, and he could not therefore be punished except if there was evidence to prove the contrary. Only proven malice could lead to culpability and punishment. Clearly, his actions therefore were being judged differently from those of 'ordinary' civilians, as they were being held up to different standards. Such formalized and institutionalized differences of founding judicial principles that spread beyond the military forces form the heart of the distinction between 'public servants' and 'subject citizens' in independent India.[59]

This fact is discernable in the various overlaps between the Code of Criminal Procedure (CrPC), on the one hand, and legislative acts such as AFSPA and Unlawful Activities Prevention Act (UAPA), on the other. Section 129 to 131 of the CrPC empowers the civil magistrate to call on the police as well as the armed forces to disperse what is construed as unlawful assembly, by lethal force if necessary. Section 132 protects the police and armed forces from prosecution if they acted 'in good faith'.[60] This clearly replicates the logic of Judge Holt on the question of using the standard of the 'heart' in such situations. While UAPA is construed as an anti-terror legislation, it also involves sections that protect prosecution against the armed forces when the latter act in 'good faith' while involved in operations directed against terroristic activity.[61] Section 4 of AFSPA analogously protects the armed forces and their operations from civil jurisdiction.[62] This is in line with the fact that while civil and military courts may hold concurrent jurisdiction, though the latter is conventionally given precedence, in certain contexts, if contested by the former, the ultimate course of appeal lies with the central government.[63] Thus, in situations of conflicts between public servants and citizen-subjects, it is the executive and not the judiciary that is the ultimate tribunal. This is apart from the fact that even the prosecution of public servants requires special permission from the government according to Section 197 of the Code of Criminal Procedure. Rather than the fundamental right of equality, everyday law is pockmarked with what one can only call quasi-feudal immunities.

In such a context, it is not surprising that the highest courts cite 'the old English authorities' to argue that the expression 'war' in Section 121 of the Indian Penal Code (IPC), on 'waging, attempting to wage or abetting waging of war against the government of India', is not to be understood merely as 'war' in the sense of two nations or states in conflict.[64] Rather, the true criterion is that of an *intent* which is not private but public, and aimed at challenging law or the government. War is therefore not to be derived from factual features such as the numbers involved or the kind of weaponry used.[65] This entails the possibility of an indefinite distension of the category 'war', and is a correlate of the semantic plasticity in the legal construal of terrorism. This semantic inflation enables the use of legislation that in many ways places the burden of proof on the accused rather than the prosecution, thereby upending conventional jurisprudence and the judicially enshrined doctrine of fundamental rights. An extreme possibility thus mitigates the rigours of legal procedures with regard to a range of activity, including, most recently, the crime of money-laundering.[66] The postulated possibility of terroristic violence may thus become a mould for activities that many would not directly link with violence, such as the possession of certain kinds of literature or association.[67] And while investigative agencies thus are enabled to deprive the freedoms and rights otherwise available to citizen-subjects, the legally enshrined immunities of the former ensure that there is little by way of legal accountability for their actions. Empirical studies have shown not merely very low conviction rates and several cases where individuals have been acquitted after being broken and irretrievably damaged, psychologically and materially, by long years of incarceration, but simultaneously few measures or examples of accountability for the prosecutors in such cases appear to exist.

To pose this series of dilemmas as a clash between the values of security against liberty and translate it into a merely philosophical question does little to illuminate the concrete shape-shifting of the problem at hand. More importantly, the philosophical idiom is spectatorial in seeing as its value the neutralizing of praxis. And yet there is scarce any other justification for knowledge in a world undeniably in the throes of deep-seated injustice. Human suffering, even in the form of physical pain, has an irreducibly normative dimension, in which may lie the core of experiencing injustice. It is only when so grounded that the knowledge of the human sciences can find orientation and measure. If the revolutionary idea of community as a work of reason is taken seriously as the core of both fundamental rights and popular sovereignty, this would imply the generation of a community whose ultimate goals cannot be measured in quanta of technical or material progress, but in the extent of experienced justice. What forms of accountability and legibility are required in relation to power, whether in the forms of the prosecution or the police and the armed forces? Can assumptions of 'in good faith' in the carrying out of public duty be immune to even inquiry? And is inquiry worth its salt if the final decisions remain opaque and lacking in transparency? After all, as has been noticed even by judgments, no state can be so impenetrably dark, when even the possibility of an inquiry, the deeply human quest for knowledge even in the face of an aggrieved loss, is legally barred. And yet, one of the most dismal signs of recent trends is when individuals in public interest activate Article 32 on fundamental rights, the very demand praying to be attended to, they are judged culpable even before an investigation or before being given a hearing.[68] Who will be held accountable for the death of 84-year-old, Parkinson's-afflicted Stan Swamy, denied a sipper, straw and adequate medical attention while imprisoned cannot but be asked by anyone who reads a former Supreme Court judge's account of this deeply tragic and disturbing turn of events?[69] Or for the many suffering years of incarceration prior to conviction, having been denied bail because of stringent legislation?[70] It is examples of the courage of individuals and mobilizations as much as their vicious suppression that take the characteristic shape of the conundrums of the day, stretched between 'fundamental rights' and their consistent denial. Appeals to an 'aborigine' epistemology as blanket panacea not merely reveals the strange idealist discrepancy between theory and practice that lies at its root, but also exposes the complicity between intellectual and political posturing.

For, this study of empire is an investigation of justice and jurisdiction, its staging as much as its masking. In this narrative, an economic history of trade is exposed as a determined militarized-legal practice of war and subjugation, which several historians have seen as an age of sociable commerce and roaring liberty keeping at bay a 'night watchman state'. In contrast, this work has described the political ecology in terms of a fierce maritime regulation ineluctably leading to military domination, from Prize laws to monopolization and military conquest: a veritable *matsya-nyaya*. This is the ecosystem of 'trade' that birthed the empire in India, wielded chains of command and accountability in the form of a shadow-play that can hardly be disaggregated into the block-prints of space or culture. It is in this institutional denial of participation in that through which one's condition is in fact deeply determined that lies the essence of injustice, and to which arguments about rights and democracy respond. If the imperial period exhibits this epistemically decoyed circuitry, the subsequent era of nation-states is hardly invulnerable to the same charge. For, within as much as across nation-states, modes of determination are not reflected in channels of accountability. The chains of causality that directly affect life provide no mechanism to inspect or resist such binds, and none of this is achievable by the fictitious idea of nation-states as discrete sovereignties. The latter are manoeuvred and manipulated to form specific networks that govern and occlude their effects. The challenges for the human sciences lie in exposing the historical and current subterfuges in channelizing accountability, across time and space.

The nature of the problem being global – in its inheritance as much as its reach – the measure of an adequate praxis for its detonation can only be solidarities across, epistemic as much as political. For it is undeniable that the deepest divides in the world order, in terms of territory, technology and wealth, have no doubt been generated by the matrices of European, and then American, imperialism. Howsoever one evaluates the emergence of revolutionary moments in Russia and China, there can be no doubt that the conditions to which they responded were the unspeakably immiserating conditions generated by a profoundly violent imperial world order – the same global context which produced an independent India weighed down by its own distinctive features. Whether land laws or criminal legislation, the imperial precedent is overbearing, even if in a radically different context of 'fundamental rights' and democratic freedoms.

The present work tries to catch the hem of the Marxist inheritance by therefore insisting on a universalist horizon dictated by an epistemology in the image of justice. Praxis in the image of justice requires a clear and definitive conception that is not amenable to formulated laws. It is in this sense that Marx could see through the fictions of state sovereignty and their attempts to conceal the common causal nexus through which the dominant expropriate the dominated in the manipulation of national boundaries. This is testified to by the fact that he, unlike the nineteenth-century figures analysed including those named 'liberals', scrutinized the close linkage between exploitation in the metropolis and exploitation in the colonies – not merely in his journalistic writings, but also in his theoretical categorization of the 'conjugation' between primitive and capitalist accumulation, slavery, servitude and wage-labour, unlike conventional mechanistic evolutionary schemas.[71] Praxis had to be undertaken in the image of a future that was inherently global. Fundamental right is not the Robinsonade protective enclosure of a contingent historical condition as timeless, but the accomplishable norm of a common humanity.[72] Only such an epistemology will be saved from nugatory trivia in the name of discovering the new, the strident self-exoticization in the name of a radical cultural alternative, and ideological servitude in the name of positivistic science. The human sciences have to see in their method a purposive activity towards the consensual norm of justice if they do not wish to be blindly supportive of the most violent of political tendencies of the times, in claiming to recover an indigenous epistemology that will work as a magic wand or proudly proclaim a civilizational inheritance that is unamenable to a common politics and accepted canons of right and freedom. This would be nothing less than a flight from the most precious and difficult struggles that are voiced today in the normative grammars that we have traced in individuals as well as movements. This fight for justice is eminently practical and normative at once, and unlike representation, does not deny its nature as an act so as to falsely claim the exposure of an immaculate essence. In the transformation of knowledge into information, causality multiplies into the indefinite, receding into its spectating spell. Dazed, it lacks the dexterity of accomplishing praxis or meaning in the world. Towards such an aim, this work hopes to articulate in imperial conquest a perfection of the law so as to expose a political form and resilient history by which some of the most violent excesses have been committed. And in whose denial some of the most fabulous myths have been nurtured.

Notes

[1] While the dissenting judgment of Justice Radhabinod Pal at the International Military Tribunal for the Far East provided reasoning for its dissent including referencing the use of atomic weapons, this has had as little effect on the judgment as on the dominant frameworks of academic discourse on the nature of polities and law as imperial effects. Literature sensitive to these questions no doubt exists, and some of it is mentioned in note 6 below.

[2] See Marx's critique of the figure of the isolated individual as the point of departure in classical political economy in the *Grundrisse* (1993): 83–108. Such an abstracted conception of the individual is duplicated in the conceptualization of the nation-state.

[3] See Carol Pateman's devastating critique of the false abstractions involved in Rawls and other twentieth-century contractarian ideology in *The Sexual Contract* (1988). As indicative, one may cite the following: 'Rawls' parties merely reason and make their choice – or the one party does this as the representative of them all – and so their bodies can be dispensed with. . . . He merely takes it for granted that he can, at one and the same time, postulate disembodied parties devoid of all substantive characteristics, and assume that sexual differences exist, sexual intercourse takes place, children are born and families raised'; ibid.: 43. While Pateman is critical of Marxist thought, she explicitly shares with it the critique of the ideologically driven abstractions of 'liberal' thinking.

[4] See Kant, 'An Old Question Raised Again', in *Conflict of the Faculties in Religion and Rational Theology* (1996). There is a rich commentary on this text from Hannah Arendt to J.F. Lyotard and Michel Foucault, although little attention is given to the risk involved in spectating, which makes it action-like. On the other hand, there is an important discussion around the place of race in Kant's thinking – critical and defensive – that cannot be entered into here. Only a very specific Kantian argument is being used, and no claim is made to exhaustive interpretation.

[5] This applies as much to figures sensitive to the question of 'conquest' such as Michel Foucault. The present work builds on *The Infinite Double* (2015): 35–40, where I had argued that notwithstanding Foucault's 'bracketing' of empire, his theorization of governmentality had to be linked with questions of conquest.

[6] This imperial institutional assault on the revolutionary ideals of self-representation and fundamental rights is reiterated in contemporary historiography's critique of revolutions. For instance, Orlando Figes's *A People's Tragedy: The Russian Revolution, 1891–1924* (1998) continuously and consistently interprets Russian history – Czarist Russia and the Bolshevik Revolution – from the perspective of what he sees as 'Western liberalism', which he takes to be an accurate description of the British constitution. Not only is the nature of (the British) empire erased, but its role in supporting the larger imperial ecosystem that supported Czarist Russia, as well as its support of those forces antithetical to the revolutionary aims articulated in Russia, are strategically left out of the analysis.

[7] Several works in recent decades have questioned the 'Westphalian' model of the history of nation-states and their emergence as the basis of empire. Among other works, see Peter Fitzpatrick's *The Mythology of Modern Law* (1992), Edward Keene's *Beyond the Anarchical Society* (2002), Nasser Hussain's *The Jurisprudence of Emergency* (2005), Antony Anghie's *Imperialism, Sovereignty and the Making of International Law* (2005). In this sense, the present work builds on such a historiography.

[8] See Anghie (2005) and the discussion of the 'mandate system' which all the same encoded forms of imperialism even if there was a claim to be moving away from the more explicit (imperial) positivism of the earlier period.

[9] See G. Austin's discussion of the Nehru Report amongst other discussions and demands for 'fundamental rights' from the 1920s onwards; Austin (1966): 67–73. Studies on anti-colonialism and nationalism in early twentieth-century India rarely take sufficient cognizance of the complexity of the (imperial) state-form in this period, tacitly assuming an already formed theoretical and institutional template of a territorial nation-state. The exception to taking such a template as an irresistible historical given is Faisal Devji's *Muslim Zion* (2013).

[10] A particularly egregious imperial instance of post-French revolutionary monarchical and 'republican' France was its exactions from Haiti – based on military threats of conquest – in the name of compensation for slave-holders. Piketty has a discussion of extraction by Charles X of a promise to pay one hundred and fifty million gold francs, which is calculated to be the equivalent of forty billion euros today. See Piketty, *Capital and Ideology* (2020): 217.

[11] Hobsbawm (1992): 19–24.

[12] Ibid.: 33. It is revealing that in Hobsbawm's discussion of the economy from the sixteenth to the twentieth century, he moves from 'mercantilism' (sixteenth to eighteenth centuries) to calling it 'free trade liberalism' and 'international' (nineteenth and twentieth centuries); ibid.: 25. There is no place for either King or empire, and it no wonder that in speaking of Adam Smith and John Stuart Mill as liberals, no cognizance is taken of their justifications of imperial conquests.

[13] Ibid.: 33.

[14] I am not referring to smaller political units like the Swiss cantons, which were certainly more representative. On the other hand, even while speaking of increasing franchise within the artificially abstracted 'domestic' regions of Britain or Germany in the nineteenth century, the (legislative) roles and importance of the non-popularly elected Bundesrat and the House of Lords, apart from, and in conjunction with monarchs, make any kind of equation with 'democracy' difficult to accept. Piketty's two crucial arguments about increasing inequalities and imperialism in Piketty (2020), in fact need to be combined, since real inequality can only be measured if one takes as the unit as the empire and not the artificially extracted (domestic) state, as is usually done.

[15] Needless to say, slavery in the Americas was part of the (British) imperial formation until 1776 and therefore has to be accounted for in terms of capitalism, if that is the term to be used for this period.

[16] Tuck (2015): 262.

[17] Ibid.

[18] Ibid.

[19] Ibid.: 18–27. In elucidating 'perpetuity' as a central feature of Bodinian sovereignty, Tuck points to the fact that Bodin greatly made use of Roman dictatorship. The Roman dictator was for a limited time given complete power – his actions could not be appealed – and yet he was not considered sovereign. Tuck reads this argument to enable a critique of the sovereignty of monarchs, particularly elective monarchs. Interestingly there is little discussion of Carl Schmitt's differing interpretation of Bodin's conception of

dictatorship, as well as the distinction between Bodin and Grotius on the question of law and perpetuity. See Schmitt (2014): 20–32.

[20] The examples and their analysis constitute the main building blocks of the work.

[21] On Tuck's reading of perpetuity in Bodin, see Tuck (2015): 18–27. On Grotius's handling of the problem through the ideas of 'common' and 'proper' subjects, see ibid.: 74–83. Tuck's entire thesis frames thinkers and practices along the axis of the clear presence or absence of this distinction between sovereignty and government.

[22] *The Sleeping Sovereign* only touches on the English case at various points. Even while there is the extensive discussion of America, the constitutional issues raised from the McIlwain are not addressed, except for a fleeting mention of Nelson's *Royal Patriotism*. See Tuck (2015): 198.

[23] See Kant (1996).

[24] So while, on the one hand, the British constitution did not have a conception of 'fundamental rights' – even if it did have a vague notion of fundamental law – the exclusionary dimensions of American 'rights', including slavery, in their historical importance have been much commented upon. See J. Whitman's *Hitler's American Model* (2017), for a fascinating and powerful exploration of the continuing legislative legibility of race in American law in the early twentieth century, as well as the argument that in certain contexts it was studied by and imitated by the Nazis.

[25] See Carl Schmitt's *Nomos of the Earth* (2003) and Antony Anghie's *Imperialism, Sovereignty and the Making of International Law* (2005) for the imperial politics at the heart of the 'mandate' system.

[26] For a study of this position as it differed from Wilson's arguments for 'self-determination', see Radha D'Souza (2013). For an argument about the resilience of a Marxist critique of what is conventionally termed nationalism, see Rahul Govind (2013b).

[27] It is another matter that Britain remains a (constitutional) monarchy with significant implications for characterizing its political order on other grounds such as that of secularism, having for instance established churches, but that does not concern us here at this moment.

[28] While there is much scholarship on the fundamental importance and novelty of Gandhian mass mobilization for a history of nationalism, two perspectives on the issue can be kept in mind. One, the fact that such mobilization itself depended on existing popular movements and rebellions; for the making of such a case, see Ranajit Guha (1983). And secondly, Mithi Mukherjee's argument that Gandhian nationalism was novel, not in the sense of simply extending the involvement of the people, but in the sense of breaking the existing Congress ideology and practice that was caught in the specifically judicial paradigm of 'petitioning'; see Mithi Mukherjee (2010).

[29] For a forceful development of this nationalist literature for an understanding of empire and its legacy, see Utsa Patnaik and Prabhat Patnaik (2021). For a detailed discussion of the nationalist literature itself, see Bipan Chandra (1966).

[30] For the global importance of the October Revolution, see Vijay Prashad (2020). On the tensions within mass peasant movements, the more radically communist and socialistically inspired tendencies, and those more interested in retaining aspects of the proprietorial structure, see, among other works, Adrienna Cooper, *Sharecropping and Sharecropping Struggles in Bengal* (1988), D.N. Dhanagare, *Peasant Movements in India*

(1991), F. Frankel, *India's Political-Economy* (2005), C. Jaffrelot, *India's Silent Revolution* (2003).

[31] Ibid.: Cooper (1988); Dhanagare (1991); Frankel (2005); Jaffrelot (2003).

[32] Needless to mention, what is merely indicated here is the subject of a rich and contentious historiography on the relationship between religious and national identity, as well as the role of the colonial state in community formation.

[33] The British-colonial state launched a series of conspiracy cases against the Communists in the 1920s and 1930s, incarcerating several leaders and banning their organization in 1934. This ban was lifted in 1942 and Communist leaders released from jail, when they decided to support the British war effort, aligned with the Soviet Union against the global threat of Nazism and Fascism, and opposed the Quit India resolution of the Congress. Congress leaders were now jailed, and released in 1945, after which negotiations for independence were begun. As Sumit Sarkar has argued in an important essay, during this period of 1945–47, while the Congress was involved in negotiations, the Communists continued to organize forms of mass resistance in urban and rural areas on fundamental socio-economic issues considered to be integral to any form of political independence. See Sarkar, 'Popular Movements and National Leadership', in *Essays of a Lifetime* (2018).

[34] See for instance Dhanagare (1991). That the divisions within the Congress regarding the Communists were strong is indicated by Rajagopalachari's intention to continue with the ban of the Communist Party after the victory of the elections of 1937, despite the contrary view of Gandhi as expressed in a letter to Rajagopalachari in 1938. See R.K. Misra and N. Shukla, eds, *The Selected Works of C. Rajagopalachari*, Vol. VI: 1936–1939 (2021): 254–55. Nehru and the Congress Socialist Party represented another side. The relations with the 'communists' was complicated, but clear divisions emerged during the Congress-led Quit India movement, which was supported by the 'Socialists'.

[35] See note 23 above.

[36] An entry-point into this discussion would be G. Austin, *The Indian Constitution* (1966): 106–45.

[37] This approach has been sanctified in the Supreme Court's judicial interpretation of the Constitution. See Sudhir Krishnaswamy, *Democracy and Constitutionalism in India* (2009), and its analysis of *Kesavananda Bharati v. State of Kerala* (1973) and the use of history in this critical judgment (ibid.: 33–37).

[38] Constituent Assembly Debates on 29 April, 1947, https://indiankanoon.org/doc/747690/

[39] In political terms one knows that at the time of the emergence of the Constitution there were many arguments, from Gandhians to elements within the Rashtriya Swayamsevak Sangh, which claimed that the Constitution was too dependent on foreign traditions and a Constitution better suited to local conditions needed to be made. As Austin had argued in the 1960s, the fact that peoples' struggles had consistently drawn on the ideals of the Constitution was proof enough of how misleading such claims could be. Moreover, the role of Ambedkar and the complex ways in which Constitution-making both drew on colonial history as well as articulated a new idiom have been studied in C. Jaffrelot, *Dr Ambedkar and Untouchability: Analysing and Fighting Caste* (2005) and Rochana Bajpai, *Debating Differences* (2011). There has also been much literature showing the variance between the Gandhian argument for trusteeship and a preservation of his aversion to any radical change in the proprietorial order and the demands emanating from peasant

and labour movements, some of whose ideals found voice in the Constitution. See F. Frankel, *India's Political-Economy* (2005): 3–71; D.N. Dhanagare, *Peasant Movements in India* (1991); and C. Jaffrelot, *India's Silent Revolution* (2003), Part I. On the other hand, attempts to derive the modern principles of secularism, tolerance or rights from what is taken to be a purely indigenous history have not succeeded because the norms of universal (political) rights to representation and principles of equality, including gender, in political self-representation, within which contemporary secularism is to be found embedded, have not been proved in such efforts. Analogously, claims for indigenist knowledge have rarely been able to contribute, on such a basis, to burning contemporary conundrums from problems of the economy and employment to preventive detention to assessing institutions such as courts and parliament in relationship to each other.

40 A.V. Dicey, *Introduction to the Study of the Law of the Constitution* ([1889] 1982): 94. This insensitivity to the situation of unrepresented subject populations in the name of efficient rule is reminiscent of J.S. Mill's defence of the East India Company discussed in Part III.

41 Notwithstanding the commitment to universal franchise, in actual fact sections of the population in so-called 'tribal areas' were left out initially. See Ornit Shani, *How India Became Democratic: Citizenship and the Making of the Universal Franchise* (2017).

42 See, for instance, Ayelet Shachar, *The Birthright Lottery: Citizenship and Global Inequality* (2009) and its discussion of 'jus soli', which does not take into account either empire or the importance of blood in the common law tradition. This exclusion of empire gives a misleading framing of the problem of citizenship as divided into the two kinds of 'jus soli' and 'jus sanguine'.

43 Niraja Gopal Jayal, in *Citizenship and its Discontents* (2013), has an important discussion on the differential aspects of citizenship for Indian subjects of empire: something that is divided into the site of imperial citizenship (Indians in relation to British subjects of other regions, such as the self-governing colonies) and the inter-related site of 'colonial citizenship' (indicating the differences within Indian subjects on registers such as [limited] franchise, where property restrictions were crucial); ibid.: 29–48. However, Jayal does not explore either the normative grammar from which these differences in citizenship emerged, nor does she see in imperial citizenship a means to challenge the narrative of a history of Britain and its claims to democratization. The latter seems evident when she argues that, 'Unlike the struggle of the working classes and of women for the franchise in Britain, or the civil rights movement in the United States, sections of the Indian people did not have to struggle specifically to achieve citizenship. They won it when they won independence; to be free from colonial rule was also to have exchanged the oppressive status of an imperial subject for the liberating one of citizen of a sovereign state'; ibid.: 12.

44 In fact the imperial institutional weight is evident from very early on, as has been shown by Sabujkoli Mukherjee's important argument in her MPhil dissertation, according to which Crown sovereignty and British nationality legislation were still applicable in the subcontinent during partition, thereby creating very specific and concrete problems in the context of migration, violence, as well as legal identities and protections. See Sabujkoli Mukherjee, *Citizenship and the Making of Postcolonial India* (2022).

45 Dicey, *Introduction to the Study of the Law of the Constitution* ([1889] 1982): 213–68.

46 See Parts I–III. As indicated in the introduction, Dicey in his discussion of martial law, for instance, explicitly makes clear that he is speaking only of England and not the

empire; in what sense this can be a coherent argument is the question. On the other hand, the *Marias* (1902) ruling seemed to have almost indefinitely extended the scope of emergency and martial law (in the sense of non-justiciability by common law courts), appearing to both draw from nineteenth-century practices in the colony as well as foreshadow events like the Amritsar massacre, as Nasser Hussain argues in his insightful discussion. See Hussain (2003): 99–133. For a similarly rich account of the use of emergency in the trial of Bhagat Singh, Shivaram Rajguru and Sukhdev Thapar, see A.G. Noorani, *Trial of Bhagat Singh* (1996).

[47] *Justice K.S. Puttaswamy (Retd) v. Union of India*, https://indiankanoon.org/doc/127517806/. The language of 'natural rights' was employed by Justice D.Y. Chandrachud, Chief Justice J.S. Khehar, Justice R. Nariman, Justice Abdul Nazeer, Justice S.K. Kaul, Justice S.A. Bobde and Justice A. Sapre.

[48] *ADM Jabalpur v. Shivkant Shukla*, https://indiankanoon.org/doc/1735815/

[49] Ibid.

[50] *Maneka Gandhi v. Union of India*, https://indiankanoon.org/doc/1766147/

[51] *Justice K.S. Puttaswamy (Retd) v. Union of India*, https://indiankanoon.org/doc/127517806/

[52] *Maneka Gandhi v. Union of India*, https://indiankanoon.org/doc/1766147/

[53] *A.K. Gopalan v. State of Madras*, https://indiankanoon.org/doc/1857950/

[54] This argument that the assumption of parliamentary sovereignty in the context of India is a mistaken one can be seen in Upendra Baxi's interpretation of Supreme Court jurisprudence. See his insightful discussion in 'Some Reflections on the Nature of Constituent Power', which outlines the theoretical and juristic challenges posed by *Kesavananda*. For a book-length treatment of *Kesavananda* and the 'basic structure' doctrine, see Sudhir Krishnaswamy, *Democracy and Constitutionalism* (2009): 206–18, which is also a carefully argued defence of the same. However, unlike the present approach, Krishnaswamy does not give much value to 'natural rights' either as a conceptual underpinning of the Constitution (ibid.: 20), or in the judicial reasoning of constitutional interpretation by the courts of 'popular' and 'shared' sovereignty (ibid.: 220), as against parliamentary sovereignty. Krishnaswamy's book was written well before *K.S. Puttaswamy (Retd)*.

[55] The best starting point for these constitutional issues remains Austin's *The Indian Constitution* (1966), as well as Upendra Baxi's long critical review, 'The Little Done, The Vast Undone' (1967) – particularly the detailed and illuminating analysis of *Golaknath*, a nexus of concepts relating fundamental right to the order of questions concerning property and markets, something that continues well into Baxi's later work. For a forceful reading of preventive detention, from its constitutional origins to its contemporary deployment, see Arvind Narrain, *India's Undeclared Emergency* (2021); the threads of reasoning from *A.K. Gopalan* to *K.S. Puttaswamy (Retd)* are therein critically analysed.

[56] This has recently been documented in cases regarding the respective powers of the Lieutenant Governor and the elected Government of Delhi. Several judgments use the phrase 'the binding nature of the council' in relationship to the Governor, which goes back to the late medieval period, as discussed by E. Kantorowicz in his analysis of the relationship between King and Council in *The King's Two Bodies* (1957).

[57] The following analysis of AFSPA is much dependent on and indebted to *The Report of the Committee to Review the Armed Forces (Special Powers) Act, 1958*, which was submitted in

2005; the Committee was mandated by the Government of India to examine the issue.

58 See the Supreme Court judgment in *Extra Judicial Execution Victim ... v. Union of India and Ors* (2017), https://indiankanoon.org/doc/51378140/

59 See Part II above.

60 https://indiankanoon.org/doc/295559/#:~:text=132.,acts%20done%20under%20preceding%20sections.&text=(a)%20with%20the%20sanction%20of,Government%20in%20any%20other%20case.

61 See the discussion in *The Report of the Committee to Review the Armed Forces (Special Powers) Act, 1958* (2005).

62 Ibid.

63 *Extra Judicial Execution Victim ... v. Union of India and Ors* (2017), https://indiankanoon.org/doc/51378140/

64 *State (N.C.T. of Delhi) v. Navjot Sandhu @ Afsan Guru* (2005), https://indiankanoon.org/doc/1769219/

65 Ibid. It is not surprising that the judgment cites eighteenth- and nineteenth-century jurists such as Fitzjames Stephen and Michel Foster. As argued previously, that these English authorities did not have a conceptualization of the state outside of the person of the King is not noted, even though the question of the bearing of these 'old authorities' is raised. Fitzjames Stephen has perhaps most commonly been invoked in India with regard to sedition, and recently, Sunny Kumar, in his analysis of Stephen and critique of the extant historiography on the subject, raises the important question about the extent to which these sedition laws were indeed 'colonial', grounded as they were in many ways in English law and jurisprudence; see Kumar, 'Is Indian Sedition Law Colonial? J.F. Stephen and the Jurisprudence on Free Speech' (2021). Adding to this, one may underline the fact that Stephen laid great importance on the nineteenth-century statutory codification of 'constructive treason', and the widening of 'conspiracy' that coloured both treason as well as sedition. It is this widening of 'conspiracy' to an indefinite extent that contemporary jurisprudence and case law in India also feed upon.

66 This is has been upheld in the recent case of *Vijay Madanlal Choudhary & Ors. v. Union of India & Ors.*, upholding provisions of the PMLA (Prevention of Money Laundering) Act.

67 https://www.thehindu.com/news/national/Anti-terror-laws-being-misused-says-rights-activist/article12557787.ece

68 This has been the case recently where human rights defenders, while taking up cases of others, have themselves been punitively dealt with. On Teesta Setalvad and Himanshu Kumar, see https://scroll.in/article/1028510/courts-penalising-petitioners-will-discourage-indians-from-approaching-them-for-justice

69 See the former Supreme Judge Madan Lokur's article, https://thewire.in/law/killing-him-softly-with-his-song-a-requiem-for-father-stan-swamy

70 It must be kept in mind that there are several studies that have documented the fact that individuals have been found not guilty and have yet had to spend years in jail. See https://www.outlookindia.com/website/story/framed-damned-acquitted/282369

71 This builds on my work on Marx, most recently in my essays, 'Capital and Imperialism: A Vanishing Point?' (2022b), 'Imperialism, The Organization of Knowledge and Marx' (2021b) and 'Method Object Praxis: Marx and the Historians of Science' (2022). In this broad context, Marxist historians of Britain, by confining themselves to questions of

the transformation of feudalism to capitalism, have not sufficiently interrogated central dimensions to such capitalism, whether it be imperialism, the slave economy (which operated as part of the 'English' political economy until American independence) or their interconnections, unlike Marx's own writings. It is on the register of such questions that one might see the significant differences among Marxists, such as the debate between David Harvey on the one hand and Utsa Patnaik and Prabhat Patnaik on the other, documented in Utsa Patnaik and Prabhat Patnaik, *A Theory of Imperialism* (2016).

[72] To protect a fundamental right cannot then be the ahistorical preservation of a status quo that is itself historically conditioned whether at the level of nation or class, but has to be attentive to such conditioning in its articulation of a transformative politics that is common and universal. In 'On the Jewish Question' and other earlier works, in his analysis of the 'natural rights' of the French Revolution, Marx cautions one against treating the 'natural', egotistic individual abstracted from society as the goal of the political constitution, just as he critiqued what he saw as the Jacobin method to directly attempt to erase social difference through the force of the state. See R. Livingstone and G. Benton, trans., *Karl Marx: Early Writings* (1992) and *The Holy Family*, https://www.marxists.org/archive/marx/works/1845/holy-family/index.htm

Bibliography

Archival Sources

Asia, Pacific and African Collections, British Library, London.
Home (Miscellaneous), 1750–1850.
Home (Public), 1750–1850.
Board's Collection, 1750–1850.
Western Manuscripts, British Library, London.

Cases Cited

Calvin's Case (1608).
East India Company v. Sandys (1684).
Campbell v. Hall (1774).
Rafael v. Verelst (1775).
The Trial of Maha Rajah Nundocomar, Bahader, for Forgery. At Calcutta, in the Province of Bengal (1775).
The Trial of Joseph Fowek, Francis Fowke, Maha Rajah Nandacomar, and Roy Radachurn, for a Conspiracy against Warren Hastings, Esq. Governor-General of the Presidency of Fort William in Bengal. At Calcutta or Fort William in Bengal aforesaid (1775).
Le Caux v. Aden (1781).
Nubob v. East India Company (1793).
Elphinstone v. Bedreechand (1830).
Case of the Army of Deccan (1833).
Lyons (Mayor of) v. East India Company (1836).
The Secretary of State in Council of India v. Kamachee Boye Sahaba (1859).
Lachmi Narain v. Raja Partap Singh (1878).
Stepney Election Petition (1893).
A.K. Gopalan v. State of Madras (1950).

Ram Swarup v. Union of India (1957).
Kesavananda Bharati v. State of Kerala (1973).
ADM Jabalpur v. Shivkant Shukla (1976).
Maneka Gandhi v. Union of India (1978).
State (N.C.T. of Delhi) v. Navjot Sandhu @ Afsan Guru (2005).
Extra Judicial Execution Victim... v. Union of India and Ors. (2017).
Justice K.S. Puttaswamy (Retd) v. Union of India (2018).
Vijay Madanlal Choudhary & Ors. v. Union of India & Ors. (2022).

Works Cited

A Collection of Statutes and Charters with Reference to the East India Company (1817), George Eyre and Andrew Strahan.

Agamben, G. (2005), *State of Exception*, Chicago: University of Chicago Press.

Alexandrowicz, C.H. (1967), *An Introduction to the History of the Law of Nations in the East Indies*, Oxford: Clarendon Press.

An account of some transactions in the honourable House of Commons, and before the right honourable Lords of the King's most honourable Privy Council, relating to the late East India Company together with the said companies new charter (1693), https://ota.bodleian.ox.ac.uk/repository/xmlui/bitstream/handle/20.500.12024/A38195/A38195.html?sequence=5&isAllowed=y.

Anghie, A. (2012), *Imperialism, Sovereignty and the Making of International Law*, Cambridge: Cambridge University Press.

Apostle, H.G. (1966), *Aristotle's Metaphysics*, Grinnell, Iowa: The Peripatetic Press.

Appendix to the Report on the Affairs of the East India Company (1831), Vol. V, House of Commons.

Ariew, R., ed. (2000), *G.W. Leibniz and S. Clarke Correspondence*, Indianapolis: Hackett.

Aristotle: De Anima (1985), translated by Lawson-Tancred, London: Penguin.

Armitage, D. (2000), *Ideological Origins of the British Empire*, Cambridge: Cambridge University Press.

—— (2013), *Foundations of Modern International Thought*, Cambridge: Cambridge University Press.

Austin, G. (1966), *The Indian Constitution*, Delhi: Oxford University Press.

Austin, J. (2012), *Province of Jurisprudence Determined*, Delhi: Universal Law Publishing House.

Bagchi, A.K. (1992), 'Land Tax, Property Rights and Peasant Insecurity in Colonial India', *Journal of Peasant Studies*, 20 (1), October: 1–49.

Bagehot, W. (1867), *The English Constitution*, London: Chapman and Hall.

Bajpai, R. (2011), *Debating Differences*, Oxford: Oxford University Press.

Baker, J. (1971), *Introduction to English Legal History*, Oxford: Oxford University Press.

Balachandran, A., R. Pant and B. Raman, eds (2018), *Iterations of Law*, Delhi: Oxford University Press.

Banda and Kirwee Booty, Proceedings and Judgment (1866), London: G.E. Eyre and W. Spottiswoode.

Banerji, B. (1926), *Raja Rammohun Roy's Mission to England: Based on Unpublished Sources*, Calcutta: N.M. Raychowdhury.

Baxi, U. (1967), 'The Little Done, The Vast Undone', *Journal of the Indian Law Institute*, Vol. 9, No. 3, July–September: 323–430.

—— (1978), 'Some Reflections on the Nature of Constituent Power', in R. Dhavan and A. Jacob, eds, *Indian Constitution: Trends and Issues*, Bombay: N.M. Tripathi Pvt. Ltd.

Bayly, C.A. (1989), *Imperial Meridian*, London: Routledge.

—— (2004), *Making of the Modern World*, London: Wiley-Blackwell.

Beaufort, F.L. (1875), *A Digest of the Criminal Law of the Presidency of Fort William*, Calcutta.

Bentham, J. (1830), *Emancipate Your Colonies!* London: C. and W. Reymell.

—— (1843), *Essay on the Influence of Time and Place on Legislation*, https://www.laits.utexas.edu/poltheory/bentham/timeplace/index.html

—— (2018), *Writings on Australia, VI. A Plea for the Constitution*, edited by T. Causer and P. Schofield, pre-publication version, The Bentham Project, https://discovery.ucl.ac.uk/id/eprint/10055304/1/6.%20Plea.pdf

Benton, L. (2004), *Law and Colonial Cultures*, Cambridge: Cambridge University Press.

—— (2009), *Search for Sovereignty*, Cambridge: Cambridge University Press.

Benton, L. and Benjamin Strauman (2010), 'Acquiring Empire by Law: From Roman Doctrine to Early Modern European Practice', *Law and History Review*, Vol. 28, No.1.

Bentwich, N. (1907), *The Law of Private Property in War*, London: The Law Publishers.

Bergson, H. (1912), *Matter and Memory*, Kansas: Digireads.

Bhattacharya-Panda, N. (2008), *Appropriation and Invention of Tradition*, Delhi: Oxford University Press.

Black, B.A. (1976), 'The Constitution of Empire: The Case for the Colonists', *University of Pennsylvania Law Review*, Vol. 124, No. 5.

Blackstone, W. (1765), *Commentaries on the Laws of England*, https://avalon.law.yale.edu/subject_menus/blackstone.asp

—— (1828), *Reports of Cases Determined in Several Courts of Westminster-Hall* London.

Bourguignon, H.J. (2004), *Sir William Scott, Lord Stowell*, Cambridge: Cambridge University Press.

Bowen, H.V. (1991), *Revenue and Reform*, Cambridge: Cambridge University Press.

Brenner, R. (1993), *Merchants and Revolution*, London: Verso.

Bruce, J. (1810), *The Annals of the Honourable East India Company*, 3 vols, London.

Buc, P. (2015), *Holy War, Martyrdom, and Terror: Christianity, Violence, and the West*, Pennsylvania: University of Pennsylvania Press.

Burns, R. (1900), 'The Idea of Absolutism', in J. Miller, ed., *Absolutism in the 17th Century*, London: Macmillan.

Brewer, J. (1989), *The Sinews of Power*, London: Unwin Hyman.

Broglie, Louis de (1953), *The Revolution in Physics*, New York: The Noonday Press.

Castoriadis (2002), *On Plato's Statesman*, Stanford: Stanford University Press.

Chandra, B. (1966), *Rise and Growth of Economic Nationalism in India*, Delhi: People's Publishing House.

Charters Granted to the East India Company from 1601 (1774), https://indianculture.gov.in/reports-proceedings/charters-granted-east-india-company-1601-also-treaties-and-grants-made-or

Chatterjee, P. (1984), *Bengal 1920–1947: The Land Question*, Calcutta: K.P. Bagchi and Co.
—— (1986), *Nationalist Thought and the Colonial World*, London: Zed Books.
—— (1993), *The Nation and Its Fragments: Colonial and Postcolonial Histories*, Delhi: Oxford University Press.
—— (2004), *Politics of the Governed*, New York: Columbia University Press.
—— (2008), 'Democracy and Economic Transformation', *Economic and Political Weekly*, Vol. 43, Issue No. 16, 19 April.
—— (2012a), *Lineages of Political Society*, New York: Columbia University Press.
—— (2012b), *Blackhole of Empire*, Princeton: Princeton University Press.
Chaudhry, F. (2018), 'Property and Its Rule (in Late Indo-Islamic and Early Colonial) in South Asia: What's in a Name?' *Journal of the Economic and Social History of the Orient*, 61: 920–75.
Chaudhury, S. (1995), *From Prosperity to Decline*, Delhi: Manohar.
—— (2000), *Prelude to Empire*, Delhi: Manohar.
Clode, C.M. (1869), *The Military Forces of the Crown*, London: John Murray.
—— (1874), *The Administration of Justice under Military and Martial Law*, London: John Murray.
Collection of Statutes Concerning the Incorporation, Trade and Commerce of the East India Company (1794), London: printed by Charles Eyre and Andrew Strahan, Printers to the King's Most Excellent Majesty.
Colley, L. (1992), *Britons: Forging the Nation*, New Haven: Yale University Press.
Commentaries or Reports of Edmund Plowden (1816), London.
Cooper, A. (1988), *Sharecropping and Sharecropping Struggles in Bengal*, Calcutta: K.P. Bagchi and Co.
Cooper, R. (2003), *The Anglo-Maratha Campaigns and the Contest for India*, Cambridge: Cambridge University Press.
Cowell, H. (1936), *History and Constitution of the Courts and Legislative Authorities in India*, Calcutta: Thacker Spink.
Davis, R. (1997), *The Lives of Indian Images*, Princeton: Princeton University Press.
Deo, Vishal Singh (2023), 'Empire in the Doab: Interrogating the Political Economy of Western Uttar Pradesh circa 1803–1950', unpublished Doctoral dissertation, Department of History, University of Delhi.
Deshpande, A. (1992), 'Limitations of Military Technology: Naval Warfare on the West Coast, 1650–1800', *Economic and Political Weekly*, Vol. 27, No. 17: 900–04.
Derrett, J.D.M. (1976), 'Nandakumar's Forgery', in *Essays in Classical and Modern Hindu Law*, Leiden: Brill.
—— (1999), *Religion, Law and State in India*, Delhi: Oxford University Press.
Devji, F. (2013), *Muslim Zion*, Cambridge, Mass.: Harvard University Press.
Dhanagare, D.N. (1991), *Peasant Movements in India*, Delhi: Oxford University Press.
Dicey, A.V. ([1889] 1982), *Introduction to the Study of the Law of the Constitution*, Indianapolis: Liberty Fund.
Dirks, N. (2001), *Castes of Mind*, Princeton: Princeton University Press.
Douglas, Sylvester and W. Free (1813), *Cases Argued and Determined in the Court of the King's Bench*, London: Reed and Hunter, Law Book Sellers.
D'Souza, Radha (2013), 'Imperialism and Self-determination: Revisiting the [illegible] in Lenin', *Economic and Political Weekly*, Vol. XLVIII, No. 15.

Duff, M.E. Grant and Whitley Stokes, eds (1892), *Sir Henry Maine: A Brief Memoir of His Life; with some of his Indian Speeches and Minutes*, London: John Murray.

Dutta, K. (1965), *Shah Allam II and the East India Company*, Calcutta: World Press Pvt. Ltd.

Figes, O. (1998), *A People's Tragedy: The Russian Revolution, 1891–1924*, London: Penguin.

Figgis, J.N. (1896), *Divine Right of Kings*, Cambridge: Cambridge University Press.

Finch, H. (1759), *A Description of the Common Laws of England*, London: printed for A. Millar.

Fisher, M. (1997), *The Politics of British Annexation in India*, Delhi: Oxford University Press.

—— (1998), *Indirect Rule in India*, Delhi: Oxford University Press.

—— (2005), *Counterflows to Colonialism*, Ranikhet: Permanent Black.

Fitzpatrick, P. (1992), *The Mythology of Modern Law*, New York: Routledge.

Forrest, G.W. (1985), *Historical Documents of British India*, 2 vols, Delhi: Anmol Publications.

Frankel, F. (2005), *India's Political-Economy*, Delhi: Oxford University Press.

Ghose, J.C. (1906), *The English Works of Rammohan Roy*, Delhi: Cosmo Publications.

Gleig, G.R. (1841), *Memoirs of the Life of the Right Hon. Warren Hastings, First Governor-General of Bengal*, Vol. I, London: Richard Bentley

Goldie, M. (1977), 'Edmund Bohun and Jus Gentium in the Revolution Debate, 1689–1693', *The Historical Journal*, Vol. 20, No. 3, September: 569–86.

—— (1983), 'John Locke and Anglican Royalism', *Political Studies*, XXXI: 61–85.

Goldsworthy, J. (1999), *The Sovereignty of Parliament*, Oxford: Clarendon Press.

Gordan, S. (2007), *The Marathas 1600–1818*, Cambridge: Cambridge University Press.

Govind, R. (2008), 'Antinomies of Political-Economy', unpublished Doctoral dissertation, History Department, Columbia University.

—— (2011a), 'Revenue, Rent . . . Profit? Early British imperialism, political economy and the search for a *differentia specifica* (*inter se*)', *Indian Economic and Social History Review*, Vol. 48, Issue 2.

—— (2011b), 'Equality, Right and Identity: Rethinking the Contract through Hobbes and Marx', *Telos*, 154.

—— (2013a), 'The Fade-Out of the Political Subject: From Locke to Mill', *Telos*, 162.

—— (2013b), 'Nation-State in the Age of Imperialism', *Economic and Political Weekly*, Vol. 48, No. 14: 48–58.

—— (2015), *The Infinite Double*, Shimla: Indian Institute of Advanced Study.

—— (2017a), 'The King's Plunder, The King's Justice: Sovereignty in British India', *Studies in History*, 33 (2).

—— (2017b), 'Amplitude of the Will and the Ruin of Culture', *Jesus and Mary College Review*, Vol. 1.

—— (2021a), 'Criminalizing unto Death', *Law Culture and the Humanities*, 1 October; published online first.

—— (2021b), 'Imperialism, the Organization of Knowledge and Marx', *Social Scientist*, Vol. 49, Nos. 7–8, July–August.

—— (2022a), 'Method Object Praxis: Marx and the Historians of Science', in Renny Thomas and Gita Chadha, eds, *Mapping Scientific Method: Disciplinary Narrations*, New York: Routledge.

—— (2022b) 'Capitalism and Imperialism: A Vanishing Point?' *Social Scientist*, 50, May–June: 29–46.

—— (forthcoming 2023), 'The Haunting Image of the Frozen Jew (in Christian Self-

Understanding), the Self-Determining Universality of Human Reason and Anticipating the Secular Nation-State: From Hobbes to Kant and Beyond', *Cultural Critique*, 122.

Grotius, H. ([1625] 2005), *The Rights of War and Peace: Political Thought and the International Order from Grotius to Kant*, edited by R. Tuck, Indianapolis: Liberty Fund.

—— ([1603] 2006), *Commentary on the Law of Prize and Booty*, edited by M. Julia van Ittersum, Indianapolis: Liberty Fund.

—— (1657), *De rebus belgicis, or, The annals and history of the Low-Countrey-warrs*, translated by T. Manley, https://quod.lib.umich.edu/cgi/t/text/text-idx?c=eebo;idno=A42214.0001.001

Guha, R. (1963), *Rule of Property for Bengal*, Paris: Mouton.

—— (1983), *Elementary Aspects of Peasant Insurgency*, Delhi: Oxford University Press.

Habibullah, A.B.M. (1940), 'Shah Alam's Letter to George III', in *Indian Historical Records Commission*, Vol. XVI, Shimla.

Hale, M. (1976), *The Prerogatives of the King*, London: Selden Society.

Hall, W.E. (1894), *A Treatise on the Foreign Powers and Jurisdiction of the British Crown*, Oxford: Clarendon.

—— (1895), *A Treatise on International Law*, Oxford: Clarendon.

Hallham, H. (1884), *The Constitutional History of England*, London: John Murray.

Halliday, P. (1998), *Dismembering the Body Politic*, Cambridge: Cambridge University Press.

—— (2010), *Habeas Corpus*, Cambridge, Mass: Harvard University Press.

—— (2014), 'Blackstone's King', in Wilfred Prest, ed., *Re-Interpreting Blackstone's Commentaries*, Oxford: Hart Publishing.

Halliday, P. and E. White (2008), 'The Suspension Clause: English Text, Imperial Contexts, and American Implications', *Virginia Law Review*, Vol. 94, No. 3: 51–61.

Halper, E. (1989), *One and the Many in Aristotle's Metaphysics: The Central Books*, Columbus: Ohio State University Press.

Harris, T. (2006), *Revolution: The Great Crisis of the British Monarchy 1685–1720*, London: Penguin.

Hobsbawm, E. (1992), *Nations and Nationalism since 1780*, Cambridge: Cambridge University Press.

Hobsbawm, E. and T. Ranger (1983), *The Invention of Tradition*, Cambridge: Cambridge University Press.

Hobbes, T. ([1651] 1994), *Leviathan*, edited by E.M. Curley, New York: Hackett.

—— (1681), *Dialogue Between a Philosopher and a Student of the Common Laws of England*, https://oll.libertyfund.org/title/hobbes-the-english-works-vol-vi-dialogue-behemoth-rhetoric#lf0051-06_head_001

Holdsworth, W.H. (1902), 'Martial Law Historically Considered', *Law Quarterly Review*, XVIII.

Hooker, R. ([1597] 1989), *Laws of the Ecclesiastical Polity*, edited by A.S. McGrade, Cambridge: Cambridge University Press.

Hoppit, J. (2000), *A Land of Liberty: England 1689–1727*, London: Oxford University Press.

Horne, T.H. (1803), *A Compendium of the State Laws*, London: W. Clarke and Sons.

Howell, T.B., ed. (1816), *Complete Collection of State Trials from the Earliest Period to the Year 1783*, 21 vols, London: T.C. Hansard.

Hulsebosch, D.J. (2003), 'The Ancient Constitution and the Expanding Empire: Sir Edward Coke's British Jurisprudence', *Law and History Review*, Vol. 21, No. 3.

Hunt, B.C. (1936), *Development of the Business Corporation*, Cambridge, Mass: Harvard University Press.

Hussain, N. (2003), *The Jurisprudence of Emergency*, Ann Arbor: University of Michigan Press.

Ilbert, C. (1898), *Government of India Being a Digest of the Statute Law Relating Thereto,* Oxford: Clarendon Press.

Iliopoulou, D. (2001), 'The Uncertainty of Private Property: Indigenous versus Colonial Law in the Restructuring of Social Relations in British India', *Dialectical Anthropology*, Vol. 26, No. 1.

Islam, S. (1979), *The Permanent Settlement in Bengal: A Study of Its Operation, 1790–1819,* Dacca: Bangla Academy.

Jaffrelot, C. (2003), *India's Silent Revolution*, Ranikhet: Permanent Black.

—— (2005), *Dr Ambedkar and Untouchability: Analysing and Fighting Caste,* London: Hurst & Co.

Jain, M.P. (1966), *Outlines of Indian Legal History*, Bombay: N.M. Tripathi.

Jayal, N.G. (2013), *Citizenship and its Discontents*, Cambridge, Mass.: Harvard University Press.

Johnson, J.T. (2001), *The Holy War Idea,* Pennsylvania: Pennsylvania State University.

Kant, I. (1996), 'An Old Question Raised Again', in *Conflict of the Faculties in Religion and Rational Theology*, edited by A. Wood, Cambridge: Cambridge University Press.

Kantorowicz, E. (1957), *The King's Two Bodies*, Princeton: Princeton University Press.

Keene, E. (2002), *Beyond the Anarchical Society*, Cambridge: Cambridge University Press.

Keith, A.B. (1922), *Speeches and Documents on Indian Policy*, London: Oxford University Press.

—— (1936), *A Constitutional History of India*, London: Methuen & Company.

Kinloch, A. (1864), *Abridgement of the Report of the Proceedings in the Case of the Deccan Prize Money, with supplementary papers collected from various authentic sources*, London: Harisson and Sons.

Knapp, Jerome Wm., ed. (1831–36), *Reports of cases argued and determined before the committees of His Majesty's most honourable Privy Council, appointed to hear appeals and petitions*, London: J. & W.T. Clarke.

Koenigsberger, H.G. (1978), 'Monarchies and Parliaments in Early Modern Europe', *Theory and Society*, Vol. 5, No. 2.

Kolsky, E. (2010), *Colonial Justice in British India*, Cambridge: Cambridge University Press.

Korman, S. (1996), *Right of Conquest*, Oxford: Clarendon Press.

Koskenniemi, M. (2001), *The Gentle Civilizer of Nations: The Rise and Fall of International Law, 1870–1960*, Cambridge: Cambridge University Press.

Krishnaswamy, S. (2009), *Democracy and Constitutionalism in India*, Delhi: Oxford University Press.

Kumar, S. (2021), 'Is Indian Sedition Law Colonial? J.F. Stephen and the Jurisprudence on Free Speech', *Indian Economic and Social History Review*, 58 (4): 477–504.

Lambert, S., ed. (1975), *The House of Commons Sessional Papers in the 18th Century*, Wilmington, Delaware: Scholarly Resources.

Lee-Warner, W. (1894), *Protected Princes of India*, London: Macmillan.

Lenman, B. (1987), 'The East India Company and Emperor Aurangzeb', *History Today*, Vol. 37, Issue 2.

—— (2016), *The Machiavellian Moment*, Princeton: Princeton University Press.
Pollock, F. (1883), *Land Laws*, London: Macmillan and Co.
—— (1904), *The Expansion of the Common Law*, London: Stevens and Sons.
Prashad, V. (2020), *Red Star over the Third World*, Delhi: Leftword Books.
Prendergast, H. (1855), *The Law Relating to Officers in the Army*, London: Furnivall Parker and Parker.
Reports of Cases Argued and Determined in the Court of the King's Bench (1813), Vol. I, London: Reed and Hunter, Law Book Sellers.
Richards, E.H. (1902), 'Martial Law', *Law Quarterly Review*, XVIII.
Riley, P., ed. (1988), *Leibniz: Political Writings*, Cambridge: Cambridge University Press.
Risso, P. (2001), 'Cross-Cultural Perceptions of Piracy: Maritime Violence in the Western Indian Ocean and Persian Gulf Region during a Long Eighteenth Century', *Journal of World History*, Vol. 12, No. 2, Fall: 293–319.
Robson, J.M., M. Moir and Z. Moir, eds (1990), *John Stuart Mill: Writings on India*, Toronto: University of Toronto Press and Routledge.
Runciman, D. and M. Ryan, eds (2003), *Maitland: State, Trust and Corporation*, Cambridge: Cambridge University Press.
Sargent, S.D., ed. and trans. (1982), *On the Threshold of the Exact Sciences: Selected Writings of Annerliese Maier on Late Medieval Natural Philosophy*, Philadelphia: University of Pennsylvania Press.
Sarkar, S. (2018), *Essays of a Lifetime*, Ranikhet: Permanent Black.
Sartori, A. (2014), *Liberalism in Empire: An Alternative History*, Berkeley: University of California Press.
Schmitt, C. (1985), *Political Theology*, Cambridge, Mass.: The MIT Press.
—— (2003), *Nomos of the Earth*, translated by G.L. Ulmen, New York: Telos.
—— (2014), *Dictatorship*, Cambridge: Polity Press.
Schuyler, R.L. (1929), *Parliament and the British Empire*, New York: Columbia University Press.
Seeley, J. (1902), *Expansion of England*, London: Macmillan and Co.
Sehgal, M. (2021), *Creating an Early Colonial Order*, Delhi: Oxford University Press.
Sen, S. (2002), *Distant Sovereignty*, New York: Routledge.
Shachar, A. (2009), *The Birthright Lottery: Citizenship and Global Inequality*, Cambridge, Mass.: Harvard University Press.
Shani, O. (2017), *How India Became Democratic*, Cambridge: Cambridge University Press.
Sherlock, W. (1691), *The Case of the Allegiance Due to Sovereign Powers*, Dublin: reprinted for A. Chalmers and J. Vallange.
Sinha, N.K. (1962), *Economic History of Bengal*, 2 vols, Calcutta: P.K. Ghosh at Eastend Printers.
Sketches of Relations subsisting between British Government in India and different States (1837),Calcutta: Bengal Military Orphan Press.
Smith, Adam (1999 [1776]), *Wealth of Nations*, London and New York: Penguin Books.
Smith, J.H. (1950), *Appeals to the Privy Council from the American Plantations*, New York: Columbia University Press.
Sommerville, J.P., ed. (1991), *Robert Filmer: Patriachia and Other Writings*, Cambridge: Cambridge University Press.

Stephen, James Fitzjames (1883), *A History of the Criminal Law in England*, 3 vols, London: Macmillan and Co.
—— (1885), *The Story of Nuncomar*, 2 vols, London: Macmillan and Co.
Stern, P. (2011), *The Company State*, New York: Oxford University Press.
Stokes, E. (1959), *The English Utilitarians and India*, Oxford: Oxford University Press.
—— (1986), *The Peasant Armed*, Oxford: Clarendon Press.
Stoner Jr., J.R. (1992), *Common Law and Liberal Theory*, Kansas: University Press of Kansas.
The Defence of Warren Hastings Esq. at the Bar of the House of Commons (1786), London: J Stockdale.
The History of the Trial of Warren Hastings, Esq. Late Governor-General of Bengal (1796), London: J. Derett.
The Oriental Herald (1827), Vol. XIV, London, 19 November.
The Parliamentary history of England from the earliest period to the year 1903 (1753–65), Vol. XV.
The Report of the Committee to Review the Armed Forces (Special Powers) Act, 1958 (2005), Ministry of Home Affairs, Government of India.
Travers, R. (2007), *Ideology and Empire in Eighteenth Century India*, Cambridge: Cambridge University Press.
Treaty with the King of Delhi (1831), London: John Nicholas.
Tuck, R. (2015), *The Sleeping Sovereign*, Cambridge: Cambridge University Press.
Tupper, C. (1893), *Our Indian Protectorate*, London: Longman, Green and Co.
Twiss, T. (1863), *The Law of Nations Considered as Independent Political Communities*, 2 vols, Oxford: Clarendon Press.
Upton, F. (1861), *Law of Nations Affecting Commerce During War*, New York.
Washbrook, D. (1981), 'Law, State and Agrarian Society', *Modern Asian Studies*, Vol. 15, no. 3.
Waterfield, R., trans. (1999), *Aristotle's Physics*, London: Oxford University Press.
Watson, B. (1980), 'Fortifications and the "Idea" of Force in Early English East India Company Relations with India', *Past and Present*, No. 88: 70–87.
Westlake, J. (1894), *Chapters on the Principles of International Law*, Cambridge: Cambridge University Press.
Weyl, H. (2009), *Philosophy of Mathematics and Natural Science*, Princeton: Princeton University Press.
Wheaten, H. (1836), *Elements of International Law*, London: Sampson, Low, Son and Co.
Wheeler, H. (1956), 'Calvin's Case (1608) and the McIlwain–Schuyler Debate', *The American Historical Review*, Vol. 61, No. 3, April: 587–97.
Whitman, J.Q. (2012), *The Verdict of Battle*, Cambridge, Mass.: Harvard University Press.
—— (2017), *Hitler's American Model*, Princeton: Princeton University Press.
Wilson, J. (2010), *Domination of Strangers*, London: Palgrave Macmillan.
—— (2016), *India Conquered*, London: Simon and Schuster.
Wilson, K. (2003), *The Island Race*, New York: Routledge.
Wood, E.M. (1992), 'Locke against Democracy: Consent, Representation and Suffrage in the "Two Treatises"', *History of Political Thought*, Vol. 13, No. 4, Winter: 657–89.
Wood, N. (2021), *John Locke and Agrarian Capitalism*, Berkeley: University of California Press.

Wright, P.Q. (1913), *Prize Money*, Chicago: Project Gutenberg.

Yelle, R. (2019), *Sovereignty and the Sacred*, Chicago and London: The University of Chicago Press.

Zastoupil, L. (2010), *Rammohan Roy and the Making of Victorian Britain*, New York: Palgrave Macmillan.